D0897614

Episodic Behavioral Disorders
A Psychodynamic and Neurophysiologic Analysis

This volume is published as part of a long-standing cooperative program between Harvard University Press and the Commonwealth Fund, a philanthropic foundation, to encourage the publication of significant scholarly books in medicine and health.

Episodic Behavioral Disorders

A Psychodynamic and Neurophysiologic
Analysis

by Russell R. Monroe, M.D.

A Commonwealth Fund Book
Harvard University Press
Cambridge, Massachusetts 1970

Preface

It is hard to say when I first became interested in impulsivity and "epileptoid" behavior but as a clinical clerk in 1943 I saw two patients within a week manifesting the triad of schizophrenia, epilepsy, and diabetes. Assuming that such an occurrence by chance alone was highly unlikely and finding that none of my professors were aware of such a triad, I reviewed the literature and found no mention of it. Unfortunately fame was to be denied me; over the next twenty-four years I have seen only one other such patient. However, this was the start of my interest in behavioral disorders associated with seizures.

My next experience with impulsivity and acting out occurred with my first psychoanalytic control patient, who is briefly described in this volume (Patient 102). Acting out is terrifying to the neophyte and disturbing even to the experienced psychoanalyst. Yet acting out within the psychoanalytic therapy is the rule rather than the exception, and it is one of the most difficult problems with which the psychoanalyst has to cope. The symbolic meaning of acting out, and the substitute gratifications obtained are usually obvious to the therapist, and in time, even obvious to the actor-outer. But a certain driven quality to the behavior that makes it appear beyond any form of inhibitory control remains unexplained. Acting out, then, became a preoccupation of mine, as it is for all psychoanalysts in active practice.

In 1951, during the depth electrode studies of the Tulane Schizophrenic Project, hypersynchronous electrographic activity was recorded from subcortical structures in schizophrenic patients, and this hypersynchronous activity was similar to that seen in epileptic patients (Heath, 1954). This sustained my interest in the relationship between schizophrenia and epilepsy. A review of the literature at that time revealed no definite answers to such a relationship, nor is a definite answer forthcoming in this volume, fifteen years later. During the interim, however, much data have been added that need reinterpretation, and this I have attempted to do. One cannot help but be struck by the similarities between the actions of patients suffering from complex psychic seizures and those demonstrating acting out and impulsivity during psychoanalytic therapy. Despite the divergent source of data there was a convergence in the clinical phenomena. A clarification of the motivational and epileptoid elements in such behavior has such obvious therapeutic implications that it is surprising more effort has not been devoted to the subject in the past. Equally surprising is that the phenomena which I call episodic behavior disorders are so neglected. The problem of predicting whether an aggressive act directed toward the self or others is likely to occur or to be repeated in the future is one of the most frequent and difficult tasks facing the psychiatrist today. Its social importance, however, is reflected in the recent episodes involving Oswald, Ruby, Speck, Whitman, Ray, and Sirhan.*

* I did not have the opportunity to see these individuals personally, nor review the psychiatric evaluations, but it is obvious from the published accounts that in each instance, the homicide involved was a break in the life style of the individual. This is particularly true of Richard Speck (who killed the Chicago nurses) and Charles Whitman (who terrorized the University of Texas campus with the senseless and devastating sharpshooting). In the case of the political assassins, such as Lee Harvey Oswald (John F. Kennedy), Jack Ruby (Oswald), James Earl Ray (Martin Luther King, Jr.) and Sirhan Sirhan (Robert Kennedy), the published evidence at least gives little credence to theories of political conspiracy, but does provide much evidence that the person assassinated was a symbolic representation of an earlier conflictual situation. Thus the assassination must have been an example of acting out, or impulse dyscontrol as we have defined them.

The fact that many patients showing impulsive or acting-out behavior often manifest typical epileptic seizures—a high incidence of paroxysmal electroencephalographic abnormalities, and a clouded sensorium during the impulsive behavior with a subsequent amnesia for their behavior—suggests the importance of neurophysiologic considerations in approaching this area. At the same time, psychiatric data suggest that even in the presence of these neurological abnormalities disordered behavior does not occur without a psychologically traumatic past. It is obvious, then, that an evaluation of these patients requires a determination of the balance between "faulty equipment" and "faulty learning" and that to the clinician this has important therapeutic implications. In making such an evaluation we must rely on introspective data even though strictly speaking such a technique would limit us to an experimental group of one because only in ourselves can we make direct introspective observation. However, we are assuming that if a proper doctor-patient or experimenter-subject relationship has been established we can obtain reliably reported introspection and in this way extend our series beyond ourselves. For this reason, the present volume has been limited to a study of human subjects; only in the humans is this introspective data available.

The purpose of writing this book can then be described as follows:

1. To establish a systematic nosology of patients manifesting impulsivity, acting out, or other intermittent behavioral disorders. This group we have chosen to designate as those showing episodic behavioral disorders.
2. To examine the possible motivated and epileptoid mechanisms behind such behavioral deviations.
3. To establish criteria at a descriptive, neurophysiologic, and psychodynamic level that will distinguish between those patients whose episodic disorder is predominantly motivated and those whose disorder is predominantly epileptoid.
4. To clarify specific pharmacologic and psychotherapeutic techniques for treating the episodic behavioral disorders.

Fifteen years of clinical and research observations have been devoted to these subjects, and the conclusions expressed in this book are based on the study of 700 subjects. I have published 18 articles on the subject with 14 different collaborators (Heath, 1954, Monroe, 1955b; Lesse, 1955; Heath, 1955b; Monroe, 1956a,b,c; Monroe, 1957; Monroe, 1959; Monroe, 1961; Monroe, 1961; Monroe, 1963a,b; Balis, 1964; Monroe, 1965a,b; Monroe, 1967a,b). Though the present monograph is written by me alone, most of the data were collected in cooperation with other investigators; hence the use of the editorial "we" in the text. The present volume includes also a critical analysis of the literature, with a bibliography of over 500 items. In referring to these reports only the first author's name has been used, even though this slights many investigators who made significant contributions to this area. Furthermore, in the discussion of this literature the singular person was used; again this erroneously implies that the data are those of only the mentioned author.

When the manuscript was written, it was mentioned that the literature was difficult to evaluate because so few authors made the distinction between episodic disorders and the more chronic persisting psychopathologic reactions. In section 6.2 it was originally suggested that the Japanese psychiatrist, Hisatoshi Mitsuda, apparently did, but I based this assumption on a few articles, written in English by his students, which referred to Mitsuda's concept of the "peripheral" or "atypical" psychoses. I lamented the fact that Mitsuda's writings were not available in English. Shortly before this book went to the printer, I discovered that Mitsuda and many of his students' writings had been recently translated. His concepts and data, both clinical and electroencephalographical, are remarkably similar to those presented here. If this work had been available earlier, it would have been discussed in detail at many points in my review of the literature. However, as his findings support rather than modify my hypothesis, I did not further delay publication by making these additions. Where appropriate, reference has been made to this work. Mitsuda's book reviews extensively both the Japanese and the German literature, and therefore supplements my bibliography, which is primarily limited to the English literature. The reader who is interested in pursuing the subject of the episodic behavioral disorders in depth is referred to this book by Mitsuda (1967).

During the past seven years, 70 adults and 15 children have been studied intensively, with follow-ups now ranging from two to five years after hospital discharge or therapy discontinuance. Most of the illustrative clinical material utilized in this book comes from the group of 70 adults. Twelve of the 70 were private patients of mine in psychoanalysis or psychoanalytically oriented therapy two to five times a week over a period of three to five years. However, all patients who were treated by cooperating psychiatrists were seen several times by me and were evaluated in my electroencephalographic laboratory. The adult patients in this study are denoted by the 200 series and were further designated by O, S, or F, in front of the number. An O means that the resting baseline electroencephalogram as well as the activation record was normal. The S signifies that the activation response was diffuse, bilaterally synchronous, paroxysmal, high amplitude slow waves with or without occasional hypersynchronous forms. The F means that either the resting baseline or the activated record (usually both) showed focal or more precisely "specific" abnormalities, generally associated with temporal lobe or centrencephalic epilepsy. Detailed case histories, selected from this group, are presented in Appendices 1 through 9 as illustrative examples of the diagnostic categories proposed in the book.

Clinical vignettes of 82 other subjects were used as illustrative examples to clarify a point being made in the text. As these patients may have been used several times, a patient index has been included in Appendix 10. The 0–99 series were patients with chronically implanted subcortical electrodes; the 100–199 series, early activation studies; the 200–299 series was mentioned above; the 300–399 series, normal controls or contrast subjects; the 400–499 series, children (preadolescent); and the 500–599 series, chronically hospitalized patients who were the subjects of specific drug studies.

The electroencephalograms were not only read by the author,

but also by experienced electroencephalographers. Patients numbered from 0–199 were read by Walter A. Mickle, M.D., now at the Electroencephalographic Laboratories, Touro Infirmary, New Orleans, Louisiana. The electroencephalographic technician in this study was Charles Fontana in Dr. Robert Heath's laboratory, Department of Psychiatry, Tulane University School of Medicine. The electroencephalograms of patients numbered 200–599 were read by Morton D. Kramer, M.D., Assistant Professor of Neurology, Department of Neurology, University of Maryland School of Medicine. The electroencephalographic technician was Edward Terry, trained by Dr. Curtis Marshall, Johns Hopkins University School of Medicine.

The studies completed thus far and summarized in this volume are mainly of the hypothesis-exploring rather than hypothesis-testing type. The natural course of the disorder was preserved, and with rare exceptions, no specific therapeutic interventions were planned; rather each of the cooperating physicians treated the patient as he saw fit. It must be remembered that in the medical sciences a clinical hunch developed on the basis of carefully collected empirical data leads to a preliminary hypothesis. This hypothesis may become what the clinician would consider a "clinical truth" long before the precise etiology and underlying mechanisms of the disorder are understood. What is truth to the clinician is determined by the heuristic value of his hypothesis in establishing a diagnosis that in turn suggests a specific and effective therapeutic regime. The effective therapy is the proof of the hypothesis. It may be some years before it is realized that the hypothesis, however helpful in developing an effective therapy, must be considerably modified or even completely discarded; thus we are often right but for the wrong reasons, and it is suspected that this historical sequence will occur many times in the area of mind-brain correlations such as we are attempting in this volume. The author believes, however, that the present volume will clarify the clinical phenomena sufficiently so that now rigorous hypothesis-testing can take place.

Analyzing such diffuse clinical data is an arduous and time-consuming task which would have been impossible without freedom from one's usual routine administrative, teaching, and clinical responsibilities. Such freedom was provided by a special research fellowship under the National Institutes of Health (MH31727), with both the Commonwealth Foundation and the Rall Foundation providing additional funds. However crucial such support was, it would have been in vain without the whole-hearted support of Eugene B. Brody, M.D., Director of the Psychiatric Institute, and Professor and Chairman of the Department of Psychiatry, University of Maryland School of Medicine, not to mention the University itself which provided the sabbatical year for this endeavor. Physical facilities and the intellectual climate necessary to complete the task were provided by the Medical School of the American University of Beirut. Despite the many tempting distractions in this beautiful and historical part of the world the setting was a true inspiration for work on the manuscript.

Finally, appreciation must be expressed to the readers, editors, and typists of the manuscript. Alfreda Honigfeld edited the rough manuscript. Her editorial help and technical knowledge of both the psychological and electroencephalographic fields were particularly helpful. Arthur Epstein, M.D., Professor of Psychiatry at Tulane University, read the manuscript and made a number of important suggestions. Particular thanks should be given to Barbara Hulfish, M.D., Assistant Professor of Neurology, Department of Psychiatry, University of Maryland School of Medicine, who not only meticulously edited the final copy, but because of her vast experience in dealing with similar patients to those investigated by the author was particularly helpful in eliminating many of the obscurities that had crept into the manuscript. Mrs. Evelyn Pfannkuche worked a year with the author in assembling raw data, while Sylvia Envers and Frances Knott patiently typed and retyped the manuscript.

Russell R. Monroe, M.D.

Baltimore, Maryland
April 1969

Contents

Part Two   Neuropsychiatric and Neurophysiologic Data

    4.1   Studies Utilizing Chronic Electrode
          Implantations   67
    4.2   Studies Utilizing Acute and Subacute Electrode
          Implantations   84
    4.3   Behavior Changes with Ablations and Cortical
          Stimulation   87
    4.4   Summary   93

5   EPILEPSY AND BEHAVIORAL DISORDERS   96

    5.1   Definitions   96
    5.2   Discriminating Between Ictal and Interictal
          Behavior   97
    5.3   Discriminating Between Ictal and Nonictal
          Behavior   99
    5.4   Chronic Behavioral Deviations: The Epileptic
          Personality   103
    5.5   Epilepsy and Episodic Behavioral
          Deviations   111
    5.6   Epilepsy as a Precursor of "Schizophrenia"   143
    5.7   Summary   146

6   ELECTROENCEPHALOGRAMS AND EPISODIC BEHAVIOR   149

    6.1   Correlations with Antisocial Behavior   150
    6.2   Correlations with Psychotic Behavior   166
    6.3   Correlations with Affective Disorders   171
    6.4   Correlations with Other Personality
          Disorders   173
    6.5   Summary   174

7   ELECTROENCEPHALOGRAPHIC ACTIVATION OF THE
     EPISODIC BEHAVIORAL DISORDERS   176

    7.1   Sleep Activation   178
    7.2   Analeptic Activation   179

Part Four Therapy

Tables

Figures

Episodic Behavioral Disorders

Introduction: Definition of Episodic
Behavioral Disorders

The term *episodic behavioral disorder* refers to two types of
disordered behavior: disordered acts that have been referred to
in the literature as "acting on impulse," "impulse neurosis,"
"irresistible impulse," or "acting out"; and episodic psychotic,
sociopathic, neurotic, and even physiologic reactions usually not
identified by a specific label, although the episodic psychotic
reactions are often called *intermittent, reactive, atypical,* or *recurrent* schizophrenia. The psychopathology vaguely covered by
these poorly defined terms is almost universally recognized, but
not rigorously defined or officially labeled.* In Chapters 2 and 3

* DSM–I, the American Diagnostic Classification in effect from 1952 until
1968 provided for no systematic classification of the episodic behavioral
disorders. To be officially classified, such disorders would have to be forced
into one of the following categories: acute brain syndrome associated with
convulsive disorders; schizophrenic reaction of the acute undifferentiated
type; disassociative reaction; conversion reaction; or emotionally unstable
personality. The new classification, DSM–II, takes more cognizance of episodic disorders and allows for a somewhat more precise classification in such
categories as psychosis with epilepsy; nonpsychotic organic brain syndrome
with epilepsy; acute schizophrenic episode; depersonalization neuroses; explosive personality; hysterical personality; episodic drinking; an unsocialized
aggressive reactions of childhood or adolescence. The current International
Classification (ICD–8) provides even further diagnostic categories for the
episodic behavioral disorders as reactive excitation; reactive confusion; acute
paranoid reactions; and reactive psychosis–unspecified. It is still apparent,
however, that there is no systematic and coherent official classification for
these disorders.

we hope to describe rigorously this group of behavioral disorders at the phenomenological level, while in Chapter 9 we will further define them at the etiologic and psychodynamic levels.

Definitions can be quite arbitrary and the reader may sometimes feel that these concepts have been limited unnecessarily. The value of defining terms at the onset is that, if we remain consistent, communication will be enhanced and abbreviated. However, if the definitions are to have heuristic value for the clinician, they should show an internal consistency between the phenomenologic, etiologic, and dynamic levels that will facilitate our prognostic acumen and therapeutic planning.

Definitions require labels and here we face a dilemma. The value of this book depends in part on the uniqueness of the definitions and, by all rules of logic, if the definitions are unique so should be the labels. However, we are creatures of habit. The introduction of new labels is slowly accepted, in fact even vigorously resisted. Therefore, at times we have used old labels in new or at least more limited ways. Fig. 1 gives a broad outline of the behavioral categories we will identify. Under the broadest category of disordered behavior (which at this point we will not define except to designate it as maladaptive behavior) we identify two large subgroups. One is categorized but not labeled as *nonepisodic behavioral disorders.* These behavior disorders are usually covered in the standard psychiatric diagnostic manual, but in contrast to the episodic behavioral disorders they are either persistent, established maladaptive patterns (character disorders), or insidiously developing neurotic, psychotic, and psychophysiologic reactions. Some of these disorders, as we will see later, have a waxing and waning quality, such as the cyclic manic-depressive reactions, but such disorders we will not consider as examples of episodic behavioral disorder.

As a generic term episodic behavioral disorder will refer to any precipitiously appearing maladaptive behavior which is usually intermittent and recurrent, and which interrupts the "life style" or "life flow" of the individual. The disordered behavior then is a discontinuity in terms of space-time relationships, particularly time. Usually the present "stands as reality between the

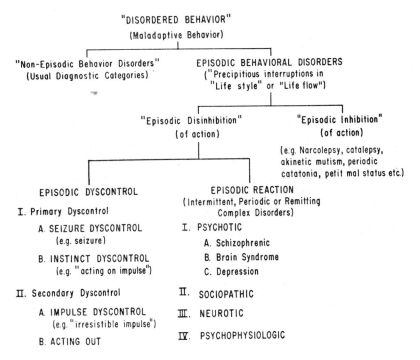

Fig. 1. Classification of disordered behavior

past as memory and the future as planned" (Jasper, 1963). But in the episodic behavioral disorders this present has seemingly become disconnected from the past and the future. It has lost the reality of directed time. There is a sudden change in personality or "life style" as compared with the "before" and the "after" patterns of behavior.

The episodic behavioral disorders can either be inhibitory or disinhibitory interruptions of the life flow. In this monograph most of our attention will be focused on the episodic disinhibitions. In turn, there are two distinct ways that the episodic disinhibitions can interrupt the life style of an individual. In the first instance the interruption is an abrupt single act or a short series of acts with a common intention carried through to completion, that is, with either relief of tension or gratification of a specific need. Such disordered acts are of relatively short duration, and although they may be repeated often, the break in the life style occurs at the time of the specific act. The disordered acts, if they interrupt the life style, or if they appear both out of character for the individual and out of context for the situation, are labeled *episodic dyscontrol*. If on the other hand, the interruption is more sustained, although still intermittent and recurrent and still characterized by a precipitous onset and an equally abrupt termination, the behavior is designated *episodic reaction*. Despite the abrupt onset and remission, such periods of disordered behavior may last anywhere from hours to years and is characterized by typical psychotic, sociopathic, neurotic, or physiologic symptoms. During the episodic reaction, there are frequently manifest dyscontrol acts, but such acts occur in clusters and reflect multiple intentions. In this way, the episodic reactions can be differentiated from episodic dyscontrol characterized by a single act, or a short series of acts with a single intention.

In Chapter 2 we will subdivide the episodic dyscontrols into hierarchial levels of dyscontrol at the seizure, instinct, impulse, and acting-out levels. Patients with episodic dyscontrol in particular, but sometimes even patients with episodic reactions, show some characteristics similar to an ictal phenomenon which we associate with epilepsy (or, as we later define epilepsy, with "excessive neuronal discharges" within the central nervous system). At other times even such short-lived precipitous changes in behavior are obviously provoked by the environment, representing motivated eruptions of inner drives and urges, or failure of inhibitory controls, or combinations of both. The evaluation of the relative importance of ictal and motivational factors in the episodic behavioral disorders has obvious prognostic and therapeutic import. Hence, it is a primary focus of this book.

The episodic inhibitions are, as indicated in Fig. 1, a second possible division of the episodic behavioral disorders. These episodic inhibitions are characterized not by maladaptive precipitous action, but, on the contrary, by precipitous inhibition of action, illustrated by such syndromes as narcolepsy, cateplexy, hypnoidal states, petit mal attacks, periodic catatonia, and akinetic mutism. Although this group of disorders properly belongs to the episodic behavioral disorders, full consideration of them would involve another volume. When they are considered here it will be to contrast them with the episodic disinhibitions. We will see that these episodic inhibitions can also represent mixtures of epileptoid and motivational mechanisms.

Part One   Psychiatric and Psychoanalytic Concepts

1 Acting Out and Impulsivity: Episodic Dyscontrol

The concepts of acting out and impulsivity must be considered in detail in order to understand how these terms have been used in the past. This will allow us to reach some consensus regarding a more precise definition for the present monograph.* This chapter will focus primarily on the phenomenology of these two concepts, while the etiology and psychodynamics of acting out and impulsivity will be considered in Chapter 9.

1.1 ACTING OUT

1.1.1 *Freud's concept of acting out.* Freud first used the term *acting out* in 1905, to describe the precipitous termination of therapy by "Dora." He interpreted this acting out as a resistance to therapy, saying, "she [Dora] took her revenge on me as she wanted to take her revenge on him [Herr K.], and deserted me as she believed herself to have been deceived and deserted by him. Thus she *acted out* an essential part of her recollections and fantasies instead of reproducing it in the treatment" (Freud, vol. VII). He further elaborated on this resistance to therapy in his paper on technique, published in 1914, entitled "Further

* For the terms *acting out, impulse disorders,* and *instinctual drives* as defined by the American Psychoanalytic Association, see Moore, 1967.

9

Recommendations in the Techniques of Psychoanalysis, Remembering, Repeating, and Working Through" (Freud, vol. XII). In discussing the influence of the transference neurosis he pointed out that the infantile conflicts were remobilized with the patient developing a "compulsion" to repeat past experiences as if they were present reality. He added, "the greater the resistance, the more extensively will acting out [repetition] replace remembering," later stating that if the transference becomes unduly intense, therefore in need of repression, "remembering at once gives way to acting out." Thus Freud equated acting out with what he also called "repetitions" or "repeating" and suggested that it facilitated repression. What does the person repeat? Freud says, "everything that has already made its way from the sources of the repressed into his manifest personality—his inhibitions and unserviceable attitudes and his pathological character traits." From this statement one might assume that acting out would refer to any and all neurotic action. As will be seen later, we try to discriminate between acting-out behavior and neurotic action.

1.1.2 *Post-Freudian elaboration of acting out.* The next significant elaboration of the concept of acting out was made in 1930, when Alexander pointed out that this type of behavior was not limited to psychoanalytic therapy, but was a persistent pattern in some people whose behavior was not adaptive in the light of current reality, but was rather aimed at relieving unconscious tensions. He designated this as a character neurosis and said, "there are individuals whose whole lives can be interpreted as clearly as an isolated neurotic symptom," adding that these neurotic characters show (1) irrationality, (2) stereotyped repetitions of behavior patterns, and (3) self-destructiveness. For these people, actions in life were not adjusted to reality, but were repetitions of childhood situations in attempts to end infantile conflicts. This disorder has subsequently been referred to by others as "acting-out character," "fate neurosis," and "neurosis of destiny." Fenichel (1945a) considered these to be related in some respects to the "impulse neurosis." Supposedly, what all these disorders had in common was an "alloplastic readiness to act," meaning that the conflicts were carried out in the external world rather than as in the neurotic where the conflicts are "autoplastic," occurring within the individual. In terms of psychoanalytic structural theory, the conflict was between the ego and the external reality, whereas in the neurotic it was between the id and the superego. The important contribution of Alexander was to indicate that acting out occurred in situations other than psychoanalytic therapy. However, the way he and later psychoanalysts broadened the connotation of acting out, the differences between a neurosis of action (acting out) and a neurosis of intention (neurotic behavior) are unclear.

In 1945 Fenichel provided the most systematic description of acting out and proposed a definition that is largely accepted today: "An acting which unconsciously relieves inner tension and brings partial discharge to ward off impulses (no matter whether these impulses expressed directly instinctual demands or reactions to original instinctual demands, e.g., guilt feelings); the present situation somehow associatedly connected with the repressed content is used as an occasion for the discharge of repressed energies; the cathexis is displaced from the repressed memory to the present derivatives and the displacement makes the discharge possible." Thus Fenichel restated the definition in "economic" terms (energy displacement and discharge). A significant elaboration on this definition was made by Sacks (1957) who pointed out the failure in anticipatory planning in those who act out. "Acting out behavior represents an aberrant or incomplete development of the ego: tension is not contained by the process of thought; motor discharge cannot be delayed; action is aimed at immediate gratification of desires; and ability to differentiate the true from the untrue is impaired. Since acting out individuals do not have the capacity for adequate fantasy in the service of the ego, they possess little ability to project into the future. Thus, there is no means available to them for judging the consequences of their behavior."

The importance of acting out as a nosological entity and a need to understand this behavior in dynamic terms in order to handle it in a therapeutic setting is reflected by a series of symposia on the subject since 1945. These have dealt with such issues as the relationship of acting out to other psychopathology and restated the problem from various metapsychological points of view, not only the dynamic but also the structural and economic (Abt, 1965; Kanzer, 1957; Study Group on "Acting Out," 1965; Symposium on "Acting Out," 1963, 1968). Unfortunately, inadequate attention has been paid to the phenomenology of acting out, so that while most reports make a contribution in terms of understanding the illustrative clinical material, they have tended to obscure rather than to clarify the general characteristics of acting out. In fact, the term is now used so loosely as to become almost meaningless, being applied to any behavior that is inappropriate or unacceptable either to the participant or to society or both. Too little attention has been placed on understanding the "act" itself; acting out has not been clearly distinguished from other neurotic behavior; nor has it been clearly differentiated from the underlying but only peripherally related psychopathology. Also, too little attention has been paid to the altered levels of awareness or consciousness associated with these acts. A more detailed discussion of all these points will be taken up in this and the following two chapters. Our goal should be, as Beres points out, to identify what set of factors establishes a predisposition to act out as a means of coping with difficult situations, distinguishing between this and that which gives shape and content to the individual patterns of acting out, the latter representing at least in disguised form, the individual's own past life and conflicts (Study Group on "Acting Out," 1965).

1.1.3 *The act itself.* "In the beginning was the deed" (Goethe, *Faust* I.3), said Freud in "Totem and Tabu," published in 1913. He wrote: "It is no doubt true that the sharp contrast that *we* make between thinking and doing is absent in both of them [primitive man and children]. But neurotics are above all *inhibited* in their actions: with them the thought is a complete substitute for the deed. Primitive men, on the other hand, are *uninhibited:* thought passes directly into action. With them it is rather the deed that is the substitute for the thought" (Freud, vol. XIII). In an even earlier publication, "The Interpretation of Dreams," Freud stated that "actions and consciously expressed opinions are, as a rule, enough for practical purposes in judging man's character. Action deserves to be considered first and foremost" (Freud, vol. IV). Intuitively it seems obvious that the ultimate expression of psychic function is the act.

The appropriateness of the act in adaptive terms, that is whether it is a pathological or a normal operational function is not always easy to judge, because the act itself implies an "intention" (Jaspers, 1963), which can be clear to the observer from the nature of the act, but may be clear only after an explanation by the actor. It was the important contribution of psychoanalysis to point out that sometimes this intention was not even clear to the person performing the act. It would seem that the effectiveness of the act itself depends upon two factors: first, the skill with which the act is performed, that is how efficient are the means to the end; and second, how appropriate are the intentions for the reality situation, that is the adaptive quality of the end itself.

Few analysts have focused on the act as a normal function. Levy (1962) considered the "act as a unit" and points out that this represents an ongoing process so structured as to resolve in or tend towards completion. As the act goes on, the energy directed towards its completion increases. It is easier to stop the act when the impulse to act arises; it is more difficult to stop after the act has begun; and most difficult when the end point, or goal, is near. He adds that procrastination in certain people is due to the feeling that once they have started an act, they are caught up in a process and will not be able to let go until the act is completed. He implies that in evaluating the adaptive value of the "act as a unit," the overall all-encompassing goals of the individual should be viewed in the larger sense; that is, the act maintains a continuity over space and time, regardless of such normal interruptions as sleep. There seems to be a biologic need to complete this act, even though interrupted by states of altered awareness. In fact, one of the essential elements in the training of children is to teach them to be able to interrupt or discontinue an act once started, if the act subsequently becomes inappropriate. Generally an act is initiated by mounting tension or urges, and completion of the act results in a discharge or lessening of this tension (satiation). Interruption of the act before completion results in continuing tensions (there are special situations where tension keeps rising, even after an act has been completed, and may continue for some time). As we will see, these characteristics of actions in general, such as mounting tension, difficulties in interrupting the act, and alleviation of tension on completion of the act have sometimes been described as characteristic of the pathological act. It would seem, however, that these are characteristics of most acts not in themselves pathological and should not be used to differentiate what is morbid from what is normal.

In general, psychoanalysts have tended to see the act as pathological if there is little or no delay between the impulse to act and the act itself; that is, no interposition of the "experimental kind of acting" represented by realistic thinking. In Freud's paper, "Formulations on Two Principles of Mental Functioning," published in 1911, he wrote: "Restraint upon motor discharge (upon action) which then became necessary, was provided by means of the process of *thinking* . . . Thinking was endowed with characteristics which made it possible for the mental apparatus to tolerate an increased tension of stimulus while the process of discharge was postponed. It is essentially an experimental kind of acting, accompanied by displacement of relatively small quantities of cathexis together with less expenditure (discharge) of them" (Freud, vol. XII). Wiedeman (1965) explains the pathological aspect of this lack of delay by noting that "acting out is the shortcut from immature magic type of thought (primary process) to action, omitting reality syntonic secondary process thinking." What is overlooked in all these formulations is the fact that there are situations in life when this very shortcut from impulse to action must have critical adaptive value, so that the "short circuit" in itself cannot be considered as psychopathological. In such situations a delayed or considered act might be detrimental to the ultimate well being of the actor. The pathology of the act should be determined only by the inefficiency of the act itself and the inappropriateness of the intention or goal for the situation, and not by any other single factor.

It is generally agreed that thought and fantasy not only delay action, but in some sense are substitutes for action, an experimental kind of acting, or practice for later action. Childhood play or play acting seems to be something in between this unpremeditated action and the volitional act. It can be viewed as a practice for later "sincere" action (Eckstein, 1965). It is a common psychoanalytic observation that during the therapeutic process there seems to be a reciprocal relationship between thought and action. Usually the more reflective the individual is, the more cautious and considered his actions. That there is less need for action might also be said for those with a vivid and gratifying fantasy life (Kanzer, 1957). There are other clinical observations which seem to support the idea of a reciprocal relationship between thought and action. Gardner (1963) points out that acting out and autism are seldom seen in the same child, and clinical experience with adults suggests that during periods when the patient's behavior is dominated by acting out, there is less thought, reflection, and fantasy, whereas during periods when the fantasy life is predominant there is less tendency to act out. A similar reciprocal relationship between action and speech has been suggested. Both action and language are ways of orienting oneself to reality (Carroll, 1954), and it has been noted that when acting out dominates therapy, there may be associated language disturbances such as slips of the tongue, malapropisms, spoonerisms, or pseudoaphasias (Greenacre, 1950). Whether the verbal skills are impaired in the "normal" man of action has not been demonstrated, but in pathological acting out it has been shown that verbal skills as measured by psychological tests do seem to be impaired (Abt, 1965).

In summarizing our considerations of the normal act, it becomes obvious that one must be careful not to underestimate the value of the act, even the value of the impulsive act. Because of the emphasis on thought and fantasy in psychoanalytic therapy, there is a tendency to devalue the impulsive act. The ultimate expression of the psychic mechanisms and the individual's ability to cope with reality depends upon his ability to act. Therapeutic success depends not on insight alone, but on being able to carry insight into action. Since action requires coordination and motor skills, and these can be obtained only through practice, the adaptive value of the act must be evaluated not only in terms of its immediate utility value, but in terms of its long-term practice effect as well. Finally, it is clear that the morbidity of an act depends solely on the inefficiency of the act itself and the inappropriateness of the goals or intentions of the act for the current reality.

1.1.4 *The pathological act.* A review of the "act as a unit" would suggest that Fenichel's definition (1.1.2) might just as well apply to many normal adaptive acts, as all action brings about a certain discharge of tension, may ward off impulses, and may in the long run express instinctual demands. Except for the first act, all subsequent action must be associatedly connected with previous experience. Most of these experiences will have been forgotten, even though not necessarily pathologically repressed, and certainly there is a connection between the present reality and these past experiences. To repeat, the morbidity of the act should be determined solely by the inefficiency of the motor behavior and the inappropriateness of the intention. Some acts are pathological because they are incomplete, such as tics or mannerisms. The symbolic act (a partial act associatively connected with some past experience of a non-conflictual nature) is in the same category, as is the symptomatic act (again a partial act associatively connected with past *conflictual* experiences). In these instances the pathology is in the incompleteness of the act, representing only a fragment of an intention, hence of no adaptive value (Levy, 1962). The fact that these are incomplete acts means, according to our later definition, that they would not be labeled episodic dyscontrol, and hence will not be subject to our present consideration.

The classical neurotic patient, despite the inhibitions in his action is forced to act in his everyday living, and many of his acts are maladaptive, being motivated by conscious or unconscious neurotic intentions. It is also a mistake to broaden the concept of acting out to apply to such behavior, which is essentially what Alexander (1930) did in describing his "neurotic character."

Fenichel also agreed that his definition of acting out did not clearly differentiate such actions from ordinary neurotic behavior. He tried in a descriptive way to clarify this point by saying that in acting out, the act itself is particularly important; that is, a complex, organized activity rather than a single movement or gesture. The act was rationalized in order to become egosyntonic, and there was a certain "alloplastic readiness," perhaps constitutional, to act. These qualities were all in contradistinction to the neurotic's tendency to inhibit action. Fenichel went on to say that those who acted out failed to differentiate between past and present, showed an unwillingness to learn, and substituted rigid reactive patterns for flexible adaptive responses (Fenichel, 1945b). Greenacre (1950) tried to distinguish between the actor-outers and those with neurotic action by saying that the former failed to understand current reality because of their inability to perceive the uniqueness of the current situation, their persistent memories of earlier experiences, and their inadequate sense of reality. None of these statements clarify the difference between the neurosis of action and the neurosis of intention. We are left with the rather vague suggestion that an "alloplastic readiness to act," or the need to act rather than to reflect, distinguishes between acting out and neurosis.

Others object to this vagueness in differentiating acting out and neurotic action. In fact, Angel's solution (1965b) to the dilemma would be to restrict the concept of neurosis to the "classical" formulation where "inversion occurs, then fantasy formation, then repression, then symptom formation" with a clear-cut infantile neurosis. This is in contrast to those he would label actor-outers, in whom the conflicts are either not internalized or else "re-externalized." That is, in acting out the conflict is between one individual and another, and not within the individual himself. This is a mere restatement of the problem rather than an explanation and, even as an explanation, is not too accurate. In both the actor-outer and the neurotic there are varying degrees of self-awareness and introspective capacity. It would seem that many people adequately characterized as actor-outers or for that matter as impulsive, in retrospect do see their behavior as a response to inner conflict. This seems to be borne out by psychological studies done on the actor-outers who show varying degrees of anxiety and guilt concerning their behavior (Symposium on Acting Out, 1963).

The complications in finding a satisfactory definition for acting out have been reviewed by Moore (1965). We propose to distinguish between acting out and neurotic action by the fact that the former is an *abrupt* interruption of the life style or the life flow of the individual. The act then comes as a surprise sometimes even to the actor, but always to the observer. It is an abrupt change in the life style, both out of character for the individual and out of context for the situation. If it is superimposed on a neurosis or even psychosis, it is also out of style for the underlying neurosis or psychosis.

There are other problems in trying to clarify the concept of acting out. One problem stems from confusing the dynamics of acting out itself with the dynamics of acting out as utilized secondarily in the service of the underlying psychopathology. To merely list them, acting out has been associated with psychopathy, borderline states, psychoses, hysteria, obsessional behavior, addictions, alcoholism, phobias, accident proneness, and depression. As an example of how acting out can be used in the service of this underlying pathology, one has only to think of the phobic or obsessional patient who may occasionally act out, either within the therapeutic setting or in his everyday life. But this action is an expression of forbidden desires and/or at the same time, because of its self-defeating consequences, a seeking of punishment to placate an overly severe conscience. In essence this is a periodic rebellion against the tyrannical and sadistic superego. The important dynamic consideration in acting out, however, is to understand the disinhibitory mechanism at the moment of the act itself.

It has also been noted that in borderline conditions acting out may be utilized to establish or prevent loss of identity (Angel, 1965a). This has been interpreted on the basis that action has a crucial place in identity formation, which it undoubtedly has. But one must not overlook the fact that in borderline states loss of identity is a central problem and, if one looks closer, most of the behavior of these individuals, acting out or otherwise, will be found to be an attempt to prevent this loss of identity. It would be pertinent in this situation to identify whether the patient places a special value on action in establishing reality and in differentiating himself from objects.

Acting out has often been associated with sociopathic behavior, in part because the term is now applied to any socially unacceptable act. However, even discounting this unnecessarily broad elaboration, there are other reasons for the association of acting out with psychopathy. Acting on impulses, often aggressive, either toward others or toward oneself, means that the intention of the act is frequently antisocial. However, the term should not for this reason be applied to all individuals who are antisocial. To apply it to those individuals whose ego ideal is antisocial or to those whose calculated antisocial acts result from material or emotional deprivation seems to be another confusing elaboration. As we will see later, on the basis of our definition, acting out would not even apply to those groups of individuals, often adolescents, described by Johnson (1952), where "the antisocial acting out is unconsciously initiated, fostered and sanctioned by the parents who, through their children's acting-out, unconsciously receive gratification of their own poorly integrated forbidden impulses." Superficially, this appears to be acting out because the communication between the authoritative figures and the dependent one is at the unconscious level, but no matter how deviant the behavior is from the overtly expressed expectation, it is really an egosyntonic conflict-free act on the basis of this unconscious communication. Bird (1957) suggests in these instances that instead of open verbalized communication, there is a symbiosis between the parent and child, where the parent's id covertly influences the child's ego, and the child's id in turn covertly influences the parent's ego.

1.1.5 *Definition of acting out.* Inasmuch as none of the previous attempts at defining acting out have been entirely satisfactory, we will propose the following, which will circumvent many of the objections discussed. This definition will be considerably elaborated upon in Chapter 2 on nosology and in Chaper 9 where the psychodynamics of acting out will be discussed. *Acting out is a circumscribed, yet complex and significant act (or short series of acts) with a common intention carried through to completion and resulting in at least partial or substitute gratification of a need. The act is so patently inappropriate to the situation, so out of character for the actor and so inadequately explained by the person committing the act that one can only conclude the act is determined by unconscious motives and is an attempt to resolve repressed conflicts.*

Although at times this behavior may appear as if there is little or no delay between the stimulus and the act, psychodynamic considerations reveal that unlike true impulsive behavior there is considerable premeditation at the unconscious level. During the act itself the behavior is relatively nonconflictual, hence ego-syntonic. However, in retrospect even the actor often recognizes the inappropriateness of the act. The essential difference between acting out and neurotic action is that the former interrupts the life style of the individual actor. We will clarify the difference between acting out and impulsive behavior in the following section.

1.2 IMPULSIVE BEHAVIOR

Impulse is a common, nontechnical term. Its standard dictionary definition is "the act of driving onward with sudden force . . . a sudden spontaneous inclination or excitement to some usually unpremeditated action." This has the connotation of an irrational act, but irrational in our general language does not have the same implications of pathology that it does in our technical language. Nevertheless, when the word impulse or impulsiveness is used by the psychiatrist or psychoanalyst it implies pathology or morbidity, which is not necessarily true when the layman uses the term. For instance, *spontaneous* or *instinctive* are synonyms for *impulse*. The word *spontaneous*, both to the layman and to the professional, has the connotation of a normal or natural act, no matter what other similarities there are between this and the impulsive act. On the other hand, the connotation of *instinctive* is less clear. To Jaspers (1963) it connotes a normal impulsiveness or spontaneity, yet *instinctive* in the general psychoanalytic sense implies an act of primitive, usually maladaptive quality (Michaels, 1957).

1.2.1 *Phenomenology of impulsivity.* Jaspers (1963) has suggested that there is a progressive series of acts from the primary, contentless, nondirectional action on an urge at one extreme, to the rational act with a consciously conceived goal accompanied by an awareness of the necessary means and consequences, at the other extreme. As he describes it, any action is a result of urges, instinctual activity, and purposeful ideas providing the motivations or stimulus for an act, balanced by conflict, choice, and decision. The more the act is dominated by urges without choice and decision, the nearer it approaches what he labels the instinctual act. The more purposive the motivation and conscious the choice, the more it approaches the volitional act. He distinguishes between the instinctual and the impulsive act in the following manner: an act primarily dominated by urges and instincts, but still under the "hidden control" of the personality in an instinctual act, a frequent occurrence in normal behavior; the more the act is uninhibited and totally without control, the more it becomes the "impulsive act." Pointing out that there is an adaptive form of precipitous, impulsive, or spontaneous behavior, whatever one chooses to label it, is an important contribution. But the distinction between this and the morbid impulsive act needs considerable elaboration, and, according to our common professional use of the word *instinctual* this is probably not the best label for normal impulsivity. Instead we will choose to refer to this normal impulsivity as a *spontaneous act* and use the words *instinctual* and *impulsive* to refer to specified pathological acts.

A detailed phenomenological description of impulsivity is undertaken by Shapiro (1965) in his book entitled *Neurotic Styles*. To Shapiro the impulsive act is characterized by the statement, "I just did it; I don't know why." This he says, is an experience of "having executed a significant action . . . without a clear and complete sense of motivation, decision, or sustained wish, so that it does not feel completely deliberate or fully intended." He goes on to characterize the subjective phenomena of the impulsive act as something usually referred to by the actor as a whim, impulse or urge. To the outsider the act is something speedy, abrupt, and discontinuous with the previous and subsequent behavior. The act appears unplanned, but further investigation usually reveals that it is not entirely unanticipated by the actor. Judgment seems arbitrary or reckless and the act more concerned with gratification of the actor's needs than with the characteristics of the objects acted upon. As the impulsive act evolves into the volitional act, the impulse to act becomes integrated with the stable long-term aims of the personality and is enriched by a variety of associative and affective connections. The object then takes on an added dimension other than merely a means for simple, personal gratification. The acts become future oriented with a more stable time sense. This last observation seems to be confirmed by a number of psychometric studies (Barndt, 1955; Levine, 1959; Davids, 1962; and Siegman, 1962).

1.2.2 *Morbid impulses*. The morbid impulse is discussed in some detail by Frosch (1954) who defines it as a "sudden, unpremeditated welling up of a drive toward some action which usually has the quality of hastiness and lack of deliberation." He further characterizes the morbid impulse by the fact that the act is often explosive and violent with a disregard for others; the setting for the action generally inappropriate; the act egosyntonic and characterized by an understandable quality in terms of the normal instinctual urges; it is in harmony with the momentary aims of the psyche; there is a pleasurable component at the moment of completion, hence the actor wants to carry out the act (e.g., in contradistinction to the compulsive act); there is minimal distortion of the original impulse (e.g., in contradistinction to the symbolic act or symptomatic act); and finally there is an irresistible quality to the act which, he believes, is the particular quality which gives the act its morbid nature. We will see in the next chapter that these qualities of impulsivity proposed by Frosch can be used to distinguish hierarchial levels of impulsivity, or what we have called *episodic dyscontrol*.

In the psychonanalytic literature the word *impulse* has been used to label a group of disorders (the impulse neuroses) closely related to the perversions and distinguished from the classical neuroses, particularly compulsions. Thus Fenichel (1945a) says, "in the former (impulse neuroses) the morbid impulses are pleasurable or at least are given in to in the hope of achieving pleasure, whereas compulsive acts are painful and performed in the hope of getting rid of the pain." He adds that there are exceptions to this, and that the statement itself does not adequately distinguish between compulsions and impulsive acts. He sees the compulsive neurotic as one who feels forced to do something that he does not like to do, while the pervert feels forced to like something even against his will. He adds that the impulsive neurotics feel the impulses as they are felt by normal people and that what makes them abnormal is the irresistible quality. Fenichel (1945b) maintains that Freud's simple formula that persons who react to sexual frustrations with regression to infantile sexuality are perverts, while persons who react with other defenses or who employ other defenses after regression are neurotic. Most psychoanalysts now view this as an oversimplification, pointing out that the acts of the pervert are not typical of polymorphously perverse infantile sexuality, except perhaps in those instances where the perversion is a symptom of the underlying disorganization of the personality such as seen in the psychoses. Apparently, by arbitrary convention, if the impulse was sexual, it was labeled a perversion; while if the impulse was not sexual (usually aggressive), it was labeled an "impulse neurosis." If it is important to distinguish between the perversions and impulsivity on one hand, and neurotic behavior on the other, then labeling one group of the former as "impulse neuroses" can only lead to confusion.

A further characteristic distinction between neurotic behavior and impulsive behavior was the supposed egosyntonic quality of the latter. However, this egosyntonicity has a peculiar quality to it, largely overlooked in the literature. It is seldom explicitly stated that although during the act itself the behavior may be egosyntonic, from a more distant and objective perspective even the actor may view the behavior as ego-alien. This is related to another peculiar aspect of the impulsive act, that is the sense of responsibility for the act itself. It is an oversimplification to conclude as Shapiro (1965) does that when the patient says, "I didn't really mean to do it," he is making the plea for "guilty without premeditation." The perpetrator of an impulsive act may sometimes deny moral responsibility for the act, as for example those individuals with complete amnesia for the act, yet they seldom question the idea that they were the initiator or actually committed the act in question. In fact, they not infrequently assume moral responsibility for this behavior with such statements as "if I did it, I deserve to be punished." One might say that if the act needs to be defensively denied or repressed, it implies, at least at the unconscious level, a recognition of the individual's responsibility, as well as a recognition of the ego-alien quality of the act. The egosyntonic character of the behavior then is only true if one examines the attitude during the act itself. Furthermore, the fact that impulsivity is often described as having an irresistible quality implies that the act is ego-alien. If the act were completely egosyntonic, it would be a contradiction to raise the issue of "irresistibility."

Nosological confusion was compounded when Alexander (1930) applied the term *neurotic character* to those individuals whose persistent life pattern was the impulsive acting out of behavior not adaptive in terms of current reality but aimed at relieving unconscious tensions. The term utilized by Shapiro (1965) as *impulsive style* might be best applied to those patients whose dominant manner of coping with conflictual situations is through the impulsive act. This has the advantage of avoiding the confusing connotations of the word *neurosis* as applied to this group of patients who show not an inhibition of action, but an alloplastic readiness to act.

Moore (1965) has discussed the confusion that arises in lumping together those patients whose acting out is an occasional event and those in whom it has become a life style. Shapiro (1965) points out that those individuals with an impulsive style seem to have an initial impulse, hunch or guess which then becomes their final conclusion. To these individuals the world appears discontinuous

and inconstant, "a series of opportunities, temptations, frustrations, sensuous experiences and fragmented impressions." Their
behavior is affected by the immediately concrete and the personally relevant with a failure to perceive the objective, abstract,
and independent. It is not surprising that the behavior is often
amoral, as moral values, to have meaning, depend on a stability
and continuity that is lacking in these individuals' view of the
world. As we will see in the next chapter, individuals whose
life style is impulsive will not be considered as examples of
those persons with episodic behavioral disorders; thus they would
not be examples either of the actor-outer or impulse dyscontrol,
as we define it.

Psychoanalysts are acutely aware of the confusion and overlap
in what they discern as the impulse disorders and acting out. A
symposium on this subject took place at the 1956 American Psychoanalytic Association meeting (Kanzer, 1957) and again at the
meeting of the International Psychoanalytic Association in 1967
(Symposium 1968). One point of general agreement seems to
have been that acting out may or may not be further characterized as impulsive. Michaels (1957) would differentiate acting out
from "acting on impulses." The latter is characterized by primary
thought processes and appears to be more malignant and closer
to the psychosomatic patterns. Others emphasize that this impulsivity reflects primary process thinking as well as primary
narcissism; therefore, it is closely related to psychosis. Michaels
also points out the similarities between "acting on impulse" and
the traumatic neuroses, as well as epilepsy. He described the impulsive person on various levels: at the biological level there is a
reduced capacity for enduring pain and a heightened instinctual
life; at the neurological level a short-circuiting of stimuli to channels of motor discharge; at the psychological level an intolerance
of tension with little reaction formation, a distorted sense of time
which contributes to a sense of urgency and a poorly differentiated ego unable to neutralize aggression. On the other hand,
acting out was felt to be a higher level disorder, requiring a more
mature ego which gave the acting out a defensive quality. It is
described as a secondary elaboration of the primary impulses of

"more advanced and organized, if still deficient, delay patterns." In summary, Kanzer says, what is common to both acting out and impulse disorders is a fixation at the pregenital and preverbal phase of development marked by the inadequacy of secondary process thinking and a poor tolerance to the frustration of drives. However, Robbins (1957) pointed out in the same seminar that the concepts of impulsivity and acting out were either incomplete or connotatively erroneous and suggested that we merely speak in more general terms of "disorders of control over impulses," feeling that what is needed is a more precise phenomenology of these precipitous behavioral patterns before one undertakes a dynamic and genetic description. If a precise description of impulsivity and acting out can be made, dynamic and genetic factors will have truly explanatory value and in turn will lead to further refinement in the phenomenological descriptions. An attempt at such refinement is made in Chapters 2, 3 and 9.

1.2.3 *Definition.* In place of the word *impulsivity* in the broad sense as it has been used in the psychiatric and psychoanalytic literature, we will substitute the label *episodic dyscontrol.* As we define episodic dyscontrol it will include what has been called in the literature "impulse neurosis," "acting on impulse," "impulsivity," "morbid impulse," "irresistible impulse" or "disorders of control over impulse" as well as "acting out." We will reserve the terms impulse and acting out as labels for subcategories under episodic dyscontrol.

As a definition for episodic dyscontrol we propose the following: *An abrupt single act or short series of acts with a common intention carried through to completion with at least a partial relief of tension or gratification of a specific need. As a subclass of the episodic behavioral disorders it also has the characteristic of a maladaptive, precipitous interruption in the life style or life flow of the individual.* The broadest generalization one can make at the dynamic level is that episodic dyscontrol is an imbalance between drives and controls, wherein the drives overwhelm inhibitory control mechanisms. All of these points will be elaborated on in the next chapter as well as in Chapter 9.

2 Nosology I: Episodic Dyscontrol

This chapter and next are devoted to nosology, the classification of disease. The disease, or as we prefer in psychiatry, the disorder under consideration, we have labeled *episodic behavioral disorder,* defined as "precipitiously appearing maladaptive behavior, usually intermittent and recurrent, which interrupts the life style and the life flow of the individual." Sometimes this maladaptive interruption is a single act or a short series of acts with a single intention. Such episodic disorders are placed in a subclass termed *episodic dyscontrol* rather than labeled *impulsivity* and *acting out* and are to be discussed in this chapter. In other instances, although the interruption might be precipitous, the disordered behavior is not limited to a single act but is a sustained deviation in behavior lasting days, weeks, months, even years, yet clearly episodic because the deviation in behavior remits equally precipitously with a return to the earlier more persistent or stable behavioral pattern. These disorders likewise have a tendency to recur and are included in a subclass called *episodic reactions.* These will be discussed in the following chapter.

2.1 Previous Nosological Schemes

Although impulsiveness and acting out are important clinical symptoms and present rather specific therapeutic and prognostic problems, there is no way to categorize such behavior utilizing the official APA nomenclature (see Introduction). Because of this, the concepts have been misused or broadened so as to have little operational value. They are often used interchangeably and seem to be applied to almost any activity that is inappropriate from the point of view of the individual committing the act or the value orientation of society.

There have been several attempts to remedy this situation, but none has been highly successful or widely accepted. The most complex one was proposed by Frosch (1954), who used a mixture of phenomenological, dynamic, and developmental considerations to divide the impulse disorders into two large groups: those characterized by more or less discrete symptoms, therefore resembling the classical neuroses which he designated as symptomatic impulse disorders; and those where the expression of impulsivity is characterized by a "diffuseness of the impulse disturbance which permeates the personality without specifically attaching itself to any one kind of impulse," which he labeled impulsive characters. His diagnostic system with subcategories follows:

A. Symptomatic impulse disorders
    1. The perversions and impulsive sexual deviations
    2. Impulsion neuroses, such as kleptomania, pyromania, addictions
    3. Catathymic crises
B. Impulsive characters
    1. Psychopathic personality
    2. The organic syndromes
    3. The impulsive actor-outers
    4. Neurotic character disorders

Although dividing the impulse disorders into two large groups, the symptomatic and characterologic, is important, the subclassifications under each are not clearly defined, nor do they seem to be necessarily subgroups of the generic category.

Another classification proposed by Karl Menninger (1954) described these disorders as "regulatory devices of the third order" or "episodic dyscontrol," but was merely a list of a number of possibilities such as assaultive violence, convulsions, panic attacks, catastrophic demoralizations, and acute remitting schizoid attacks. A third classification was devised by Michaels (1957), who proposed two large categories: those showing primary acting out or what he called "acting on impulse," and another group of secondary acting out representing a distorted or deflected impulsivity on the basis of an operating, if deficient ego control mechanism which is designated "acting-out." From what we have already discussed, it should be apparent that these attempts fail either because they are too general, lack specific phenomenological clarity, or are perhaps too conventional, thus maintaining some of the confusion they hope to circumvent.

2.2 EPISODIC DYSCONTROL: EGO-ALIEN AND EGO-SYNTONIC

Fig. 2 is a schematic attempt to categorize systematically the behavior defined as episodic dyscontrol, which in turn is one of the subgroups of episodic disinhibition under the broad category of episodic behavioral disorders (see Fig. 1). Under the category of

Phenomenological Differentiation				Retrospective Self Evaluation			Dynamic Differentiation	Etiologic Probabilities
				Ego Syntonic	Defensively Ego Syntonic	Ego Alien		
No Delay S-R ↑↓	Uninhibited action ↑↓	Uncoordinated action ↑ Transition ↓	Primary Dyscontrol	SEIZURE DYSCONTROL			Tension Relief ↕ ↑ Direct Need Gratification	"Faulty" Equipment
				Seizure Disorder	Seizure Neurosis	Seizures	Inhibited Reflection ↑ Inhibited Intention ↑ Inhibited Reflection ↓ CS Intention	
				INSTINCT DYSCONTROL				
				Instinct Disorders	Instinct Neurosis	Instinctual Acts		
Delay S-R ↑↓	Inhibited action ↑ Transition ↓	Coordinated Act ↑↓	Secondary Dyscontrol	IMPULSE DYSCONTROL			Transition ↕ ↑ Indirect Gratification	"Faulty" Learning
				Impulse Disorders	Impulse Neurosis	Impulsive Acts	Transition ↓ Excessive Reflection ↑ Uncs Intention	
				ACTING-OUT DYSCONTROL				
				Acting-out Disorders	Acting-out Neurosis	Acting-out		

Fig. 2. Hierarchical levels of episodic dyscontrol

episodic dyscontrol we have established four hierarchial levels of organization, proceeding from the lowest or most primitive to the highest as seizure, instinct, impulse, and acting-out dyscontrol. Each of the four hierarchial levels has been subdivided into three categories: dyscontrol acts, dyscontrol neurosis, and dyscontrol disorder, depending upon how the act is retrospectively viewed by the actor himself. This is not just an arbitrary complication of the scheme but has considerable diagnostic, prognostic, and therapeutic import.

2.2.1 *Dyscontrol acts.* The literature on impulse disorders and acting out repeatedly emphasizes the ego-syntonic quality of the act. We agree with this to the extent that once the act is initiated it seems to be carried out without hesitation, doubt or conflict. This is implicit in our statement that these acts are abrupt, quick, complete acts carried through until either relief of tension or gratification of a need. What has not been emphasized is that many times the act is either quickly or ultimately evaluated retrospectively as a surprise to the actor himself, who recognizes that either the quality of the act was inappropriate for the situation, or the consequences unexpected. The actor (as well as society) sees the act as out of character for the individual, and out of context for the situation. If the actor quickly realizes this, it is because of his evaluation of his own behavior. Delayed recognition usually comes because the actor is surprised or unprepared for the environment's response to his behavior, but blames himself rather than the objects acted upon for this unexpected response, because he did not properly anticipate the consequences. In either case we can say that the action is retrospectively ego-alien and in our scheme is represented at the four hierarchial levels as seizures, instinctual acts, impulsive acts and acting out. An example of ego-alien episodic dyscontrol follows:

S228 is a fourteen-year-old boy with a history of typical grand mal seizures since age four, usually occurring at night. However, one year before admission he became preoccupied with "terrible thoughts," which during the course of therapy were revealed as incestuous fantasies regarding his mother. For some months his guilt was relieved by confessing to his priest. The incestuous feelings had a reality basis in the extreme stimulation by his mother who (because of his "seizures") had been sleeping with her son. Also, she would dress and undress in front of him and act in otherwise provocative, seductive ways. The act which precipitated hospitalization was a sudden jumping up and for unexplained reasons charging at his father, throwing him against the wall of the house. His rage was of such intensity that the family became frightened enough to seek psychiatric consultation. In the hospital he also had sudden explosive outbursts of rage without any particular warning, the personnel becoming frightened enough to insist on transferring him to a maximum security ward in a state hospital. His own evaluation of his behavior was "I become so destructive and my behavior so bad that I can't understand it myself. I don't know what gets into me." As a child he had been seen in therapy by a psychiatrist and, when asked what three wishes he would like, the last wish was "to be a good boy and not lose control." It is obvious then that for a number of years this adolescent has seen his sudden aggressive outbursts as ego-alien, feeling a certain "drivenness" to his behavior. He recognized the act as something alien to his personality, and inappropriate for the situation.

2.2.2 *Dyscontrol neuroses.* Perhaps even more frequently in episodic dyscontrol the actor denies the inappropriateness of his actions, viewing the consequences of the act, no matter how destructive, as just what he expected ("it's a harsh world," "that's fate," "all men are beasts"), or as failures of the objects acted upon to understand and therefore act appropriately ("he doesn't understand me," "my wife has to coerce all people"). Nevertheless, in these individuals there is considerable covert and sometimes even overt anxiety regarding the act. Defensive maneuvers are necessary to justify the act, which means that at some level, usually unconscious, there is recognition that the act is inappropriate and unacceptable. In these situations the act may be completely repressed (covered by an amnesia), defensively rationalized, or projected onto the environment. In Fig. 2 we have represented this as defensively ego-syntonic; thus, the act is made acceptable to save face, alleviate guilt, or maintain self-esteem. Because of these very elements of guilt, anxiety, and often repression, as well as other neurotic defenses that accompany the act, this type of dyscontrol has been labeled neurosis; at the various hierarchial levels, it appears as the seizure neurosis, instinct neurosis, impulse neurosis, or neurotic acting out. The act in these instances then is still basically ego-alien but, as we will see later, it becomes important from the dynamic, etiologic, and therapeutic points of view to distinguish between those subjects in whom the ego-alien quality of the act is consciously recognized and accepted and those in whom it is consciously denied while unconsciously accepted. Of course, in establishing these subcategories we are setting arbitrary boundaries between classes which in clinical practice seldom exist, most patients manifesting transitional characteristics. However, for expository purposes we feel this is justified. An example of such a patient follows:

Patient S219, because of her own resentment at being female, particularly a wife and mother, would pick a fight with her husband almost every evening. This was, as ultimately became apparent, an attempt to denigrate or castrate him. To excuse her explosive rage she would raise a rapid succession of "double binds" wherein he could not win. First she would complain of how tired she was, saying "nobody cares enough to help me," and then when he tried to prepare the meal, would claim that he was only cooking because he had no confidence in her ability. She would insist that is was her responsibility to wash the dishes and then after he was settled to watch his favorite television program, would break some dishes ("purely by accident") and demand he clean it up. She would begin putting the children to bed, but get in such an uproar that he would have to intervene. She would seductively ask him to come to bed, but by the time he got there be "too tired." When he tried to go to sleep, she insisted on watching a television show. When he finally did fall asleep, she would wake him up and ask him to get her pills. After such a series of provocations he would become angry, then she would suddenly explode, verbally berating him or physically attacking him. When in self-defense he left, she panicked because of her "burglar" phobia. She was quite willing to admit that the total pattern of behavior was neurotic, that is the tiredness, headache, panic, etc., but that the acting out and impulse dyscontrol were justified, "because my husband is inconsiderate and doesn't realize how sick I am— you know, he is not too smart."

2.2.3 *Dyscontrol disorders.* Finally there is the group of patients whom we have designated at the various hierarchial levels as characterized by seizure, instinct, impulse, and acting-out disorders. In these individuals the act is so ego-syntonic that, despite the often disastrous characteristics of the act and the tension induced among others in the immediate environment, there is no acceptance by the actor of true responsibility for this state of affairs. Sometimes psychometric or physiologic studies fail to indicate even covert anxiety. An example follows:

Patient S282 indulged in antisocial acting out which consisted of stealing automobiles, credit cards, and money. He insisted that he did this just for the "kicks" and liked to think of himself as the tough, rebellious adolescent. He showed no anxiety concerning his behavior, nor remorse for the acts. He was not aware of the fact that he was fighting his passive dependent wishes and trying to establish an identity with a father he did not know, but whom in his fantasy he had built up as a hard-drinking, tough, antisocial male. He was hospitalized not because he felt any need for such but because the courts insisted on psychiatric treatment.

At first glance one might assume that the dyscontrol "acts" are ego-alien precisely because they occur relatively rarely, hence are more dramatic interruptions in the "life style" of the individual. While at the other extreme, the dyscontrol disorders are ego-syntonic because of their frequent occurrence. Although this is often the case, as we will see later, it is not necessarily so. The frequency of the act does not in any way determine the subcategory. However, in making an evaluation of a patient, it will be useful to characterize the episodic dyscontrol as to frequency (isolated, rare, frequent) and further characterizes it as to the pattern, such as periodic (e.g., regular with menstruation), unpredictable, or phasic (alternating with episodic inhibitions). Such observations can give us further clues to diagnosis, prognosis, and treatment.

2.3 HIERARCHIAL LEVELS OF EPISODIC DYSCONTROL: PRIMARY DYSCONTROL

For expository purposes we will describe the hierarchial levels of episodic dyscontrol in terms of (1) the intensity, quality, and discrimination of the instinctual drives behind the act; (2) the coordination and complexity of the motor patterns expressed during the act; and (3) the specificity of the motivations or goals of the act for the situation. To put it in other terms, we will be looking at the quality and quantity of the drives, the efficiency of the means, and the appropriateness of the ends. This is similar to the idea proposed by Fenichel (1945) when he suggested evaluating the impulsive acts in terms of (1) the external stimulus; (2) the instinctive physiologic state; (3) the conceptual goals; and (4) the derivatives of the warded off impulses. Those elements of Fenichel's fourth category which are not included under our "motivation or goals of the act" would be secondarily derived defensive elaborations of the act in the service of the more chronic and persistent disordered behavior.

Again we have to set rather arbitrary boundaries for our four-level hierarchial organization of episodic dyscontrol, but of course this is a continuum, with any given individual likely to fall somewhere between one level and another, or to manifest acts of episodic dyscontrol characteristic of several hierarchial levels. A patient may at times demonstrate seizure dyscontrol and at other times instinct dyscontrol or impulse dyscontrol, although, in general, patients tend to show a dominant pattern.

2.3.1 *Seizure dyscontrol.* The pattern of the act of seizure dyscontrol is characterized by explosive affect and chaotic motor behavior, so diffuse and uncoordinated that the act may have no object or the object is the nearest thing at hand. The affect seems undifferentiated, with mixtures of rage, fear, and sexuality expressed simultaneously or in rapid sequence. The motor behavior is chaotic with a flailing, thrashing quality and accompanied by primitive reflexes. The intention of the act, as already mentioned, is diffuse, multidirectional, and so lacking in specificity that it may be impossible to identify the object. One immediately thinks of the infant's reaction to unfulfilled urges, or what Mahler (1952) referred to as "organismic distress" or what Freud referred to in "Inhibitions, Symptoms, and Anxiety" (1926) as an affecto-motor-storm-rage reaction (Freud, vol. XX). In fact, Freud pointed out that the infant, as long as he acts according to the pleasure principle, discharges tensions immediately, experiencing any excitement as a trauma which, before he has developed the physiological capacity for mastering motility, results in completely uncoordinated discharge of motor movements (Freud's "Formulations Regarding the Two Principles of Mental Functioning," vol. XII). As Fenichel pointed out, the aim in this type of act seems less a positive one, such as achieving a goal or relieving a specific need, than a negative one of merely relieving tension (1945a). Thiele, as reported by Jaspers (1963), described this behavior as resulting from "primitive urges which are elementary, aimless, undirected tendencies to discharge which arise out of unpleasant restlessness and tension." In these instances any object seems to be sufficient, whereas in the higher levels of organization only specific objects will do. Epilepsy and, particularly, atypical major motor seizures are examples of seizure dyscontrol.

Referring to Fig. 2, we have designated the subgroups as seizures, seizural neuroses, and seizural disorders. We have selected the word *seizure* because at this level of episodic dyscontrol the affective and motor characteristics of the act are typical of an ictal phenomenon, and in many instances an ictal concomitant, that is associated with widespread, often centrencephalic "excessive neuronal discharges." To indicate that this is not invariably true, we have chosen the more noncommittal word *seizure* rather than *ictal* to refer to these acts. In this group we usually find little or no delay between the stimulus and the motor response, which is dramatic and uninhibited, as well as uncoordinated and ineffective. In fact, the act is usually so maladaptive as to be incapacitating. As we will see when we discuss dynamic considerations, such seizural acts can often have defensive value in avoiding the effective consummation of an impulsive act that characterize the dyscontrol acts at higher hierarchial levels of organization. At the same time, the seizural act, while avoiding disastrous consequence, allows tension discharge. This is in contrast to the group of episodic inhibitions (such as momentary motor paralyses, catalepsy, or transitory altered consciousness such as petit mal or hypnoidal states) which, although they may have a similar defensive quality in avoiding the effective consummation of an impulsive act, do not result in a discharge of tension (Barker, 1948; Dickes, 1965).

2.3.2 *Instinct dyscontrol.* The dyscontrol act at this hierarchial level is also represented by an abrupt, uninhibited motor response with little or no delay between the impulse and action. At this level, however, the affects are differentiated, specific needs are gratified, and a specific object is acted upon. The acts are primitive and relatively undisguised, either as a withdrawal response (fight or flight), or as a reaching out response (bodily contact, closeness, sexual gratification). The act itself is coordinated and efficient, although primitive, direct and lacking subtlety. For example, if the aggressive act is turned outward, it may result in strangulation or brutal beating; if turned inward, a bizarre mutilation; if the affect is predominantly fear, it is a frantic escape mechanism. Sexual affects are accompanied by abruptly occurring orgastic experiences and lack the sophistication of seductive behavior. As we will see later, the acts are often not as explosive as those of impulse dyscontrol. There are simple associative connections between the affect and the object that determine whether the object is animate or inanimate, male or female, old or young. To the outsider the act is so primitive and direct and the intention so inappropriate that the act is often labeled "motivationless." Examples are some of the bizarre brutal murders such as those described by Guttmacher (1960) and MacDonald (1961). We will see however that such homicidal actions are even more likely a consequence of impulse dyscontrol. The associational links, are vague and diffuse, the victim for example being a young child because of intense sibling rivalry, an older woman because of ambivalent relationships to mother, or self-mutilation because of primitive castration fears. The instinctual dyscontrols are what the analysts usually refer to as "acting upon impulse" or "primary" acting out. What clearly differentiates this level from seizure dyscontrol is a rather specific need-gratification rather than just relief of tension which accompanies the seizural act.

The act, while it often does not appear explosive, is seen as erratic, reckless, or unmindful of consequences. The act is highly complex, but the affect and intention are barely disguised, if at all. The following is an example of instinct dyscontrol:

Patient 0258 discusses his long period of mounting tension as caused by a desire to "kill my family." These impulsive acts are largely controlled, even though at times he has to go to desperate extremes to enforce his control. At the time of hospitalization, for example, he had gone to the police and asked them to lock him up because he was fearful he would harm his family, saying "I know how Lee Oswald felt." On the other hand, and this may have dynamic significance, instinctual acts do occur. At such a time he will suddenly, without explanation, and without being aware of any particular mounting tension or appropriate stimulus, jump up, attack people, and break up furniture in a coordinated but indiscriminate manner. One can see little symbolic significance in this behavior, except for the fact that the instinctual act expresses his rage, which otherwise would be manifest in a more serious impulsive act directed against his parents.

2.4 HIERARCHIAL LEVELS OF EPISODE DYSCONTROL: SECONDARY DYSCONTROL

2.4.1 *Impulse dyscontrol.* Acts of impulse dyscontrol are characterized by abrupt explosive expressions of primitive affects, usually rage and aggression, characterized by overt homicidal, suicidal, or sexually aggressive behavior. At the purely phenomenological level there is little difference between the act of impulse dyscontrol and the act of instinct dyscontrol, except for the likelihood that the former is more explosive. What does differentiate impulsive acts from acts of instinct dyscontrol is that the impulsive act is preceded by a period of varying duration in which there is mounting tension with debate and indecisiveness about whether the urge should be obeyed or whether controls should be maintained. Finally this tension becomes unbearable and overpowering. At this point the explosive act occurs, but the act has been preceded by much wavering doubt and concern about the direct expression of the urge and often rather elaborate attempts, even bizarre ones, to control the impulse. During the act itself there may be little expression of affect and following the act there is a tremendous sense of relief, not only because of the gratification of the basic need or urge, but also because the tension of brooding doubt accompanying the indecisiveness has ceased.

The sequence of events surrounding the act of impulse dyscontrol can be repeated throughout one's life, but often is a unique or isolated event. An example of this kind of behavior is Hamlet's murder of his uncle. A detailed case history of an individual exhibiting impulse dyscontrol is included in Werthem's book, *Dark Legend* (1941). This type of act is referred to legally as the "irresistible impulse" and Werthem has called it a "catathymic crisis" (1949). Examples of such acts are included in the report by Segal (1963) in which the impulsive act was a perverse or partial sexual response, resulting in orgasm, the mounting tension seemingly precipitated by a repudiation by a significant love object that sets into motion a desperate, frantic search for a substitute to overcome the sense of helplessness and loneliness. Segal labeled this behavior "impulsive sexuality." Greenson (1957) identified a somewhat similar group of acts characterized by what he called "impulsive depression." Despite the explosive quality of the act, the fact that it is often efficiently executed, sometimes with superb competence, and has rich associative links between the object of the act and significant individuals in the patient's past suggests the long period of premeditation that precedes the act. However, the intention and the object are far less disguised than in the case of acting out that will be discussed later (see 2.4.2). For example, if the murderous impulses are toward the father, the act is often an explosive murderous act on the father himself rather than a deflection of this intention, such as rebellion against authoritative figures. A disguised or deflected act would be more characteristic of acting out.

Kleptomania, pyromania, exhibitionism, scoptophilia, and some fetishes would often fall at this level of hierarchial organization of episodic dyscontrol because of the subjective awareness of the mounting urge and attempts to control these urges. In the above examples, however, there is usually considerable deflection of the true intention based on repressed unconscious needs, so that these represent a transitional state between what we would consider impulse dyscontrol and acting out. If the conscious premeditation is limited, and the unconscious mechanisms or deflection marked, it would be better to classify these disorders as acting out rather than impulse dyscontrol. A brief example of impulse dyscontrol follows:

Patient S204 is a sixteen-year-old girl who was hospitalized because of "falling spells," which in themselves would have been classed as seizure dyscontrol. She also demonstrated blind rage and flight episodes that were characteristic of instinct dyscontrol, but the most typical reaction and the one most troublesome during the course of her therapy was what we would describe as impulse dyscontrol. This usually occurred following a real or an imagined rejection. Others noted that she was becoming increasingly irritable and restless, hyperactive, and she herself reported mounting tension with "waves" of hopelessness. This was soon followed by conscious urges to be aggressive, which she would attempt to control in one way or another until they reached explosive proportions; even during the act itself she would sometimes deflect her behavior. Preceding the actual explosion she would have bodily sensations of warm feelings, or flushings, traveling up over her body and over her face and head with a "sense that everything is closing in on me." The culmination of these episodes was varied. For instance, (this episode precipitated hospitalization) she ruminated about choking her baby sister. She resisted the temptation, locked herself in a room to keep away from the baby, but suddenly went in and began furiously choking the infant. Fortunately, in the middle of this act she became distraught, dropped the child, and ran downstairs confessing her behavior to her mother. Other times the aggressive acts would be deflected by one of the "falling spells." Frequently, however, they were carried through to completion. She would drown, torture, or otherwise harm animals, destroy furniture, and occasionally indulge in self-mutilation during these impulsive acts.

2.4.2 *Acting out.* We defined acting out as a circumscribed, complex, and significant act, or short series of acts, so patently inappropriate for the situation, so out of character for the actor, and so inadequately explained by the actor that we can only conclude that the act was primarily determined by unconscious motives attempting to solve repressed neurotic conflicts. Although the act itself might at times have all the qualities of a seizural, instinctual, or impulsive act, because there is evidence for considerable unconscious premeditation and planning, it would be labeled acting out. This definition would in no way contradict Freud's application of the term acting out. It was obvious that Dora had been considering termination at an unconscious level for two days, as was reflected in the dream she reported in the previous session.

Behavior in acting out may be subtle enough so that to the casual observer the behavior would not appear deviant, but it is seen as such as such by the actor himself or someone who knows the actor well. It is apparent then that acting out cannot be differentiated from the other hierarchial levels of episodic dyscontrol or even normal behavior, or for that matter other neurotic actions except at the dynamic level that reveals the act as both out of character for the actor and out of context for the situation. What makes the act out of character and out of context, as we will discuss in more detail later, is the excessive and inappropriate associations with past experiences, the deflected or disguised intention of the act, and the indirect gratification of the needs. In both acting out and impulse dyscontrol there may be manipulation of the environment which invites the triggering stimulus and considerable delay between the stimulus and the response. We will see later that what further characterizes the actor-outer is not an "alloplastic readiness to act," but, in general, an inhibition of decisive action, even though at the time of the dyscontrol act the conflict is being expressed in action.

Thus far we have not made explicit the difference between acting out and ordinary disordered actions, whether antisocial acts, compulsive acts, or other deviant behavior. The maladaptive behavior seen in the nonepisodic disorders requires motor action, and usually the severity of the psychopathology is measured by the maladaptive quality of the action. But such disordered or neurotic action should be distinguished from episodic dyscontrol. What then specifically differentiates acting out from neurotic action or, in the broader sense, disordered action from episodic dyscontrol? In episodic dyscontrol there is a precipitous interruption in the life style or the life flow of the individual, so that it is seen both out of character for the individual and out of context for the situation. The neurotic disordered action of the compulsive is certainly out of context for the situation, in fact that is precisely why it is maladaptive. But it is not out of character for the individual who has developed the obsessive character and obsessive pattern of reaction as part of his life style, no matter how ego-alien this may be. The interruptions of life style are quite obvious in the primary dyscontrols and also in impulsive dyscontrol, but, as we have already indicated, may not be so obvious for acting out. The motor act itself may be highly coordinated and efficient and the intention may superficially appear appropriate. Again, however, careful evaluation of the behavioral pattern reveals that the act is a surprise either to the individual actor or to the informed outside observer. The following patients demonstrate what we would define as acting out:

Patient F246 acted out by running away from her family, flying to Puerto Rico, and marrying a policeman she met at the airport. Running away had occurred on several other occasions, and because there was mounting tension, doubt, and indecisiveness her plans had all the characteristics of impulsive acts. In fact, the episode required that she quite conspicuously pawn her belongings, with the obvious hope that her parents or friends would intervene and detain her. What gives the dyscontrol act its acting out quality is the symbolic nature of the precipitating event. Her father, obviously jealous of her adolescent boyfriend, had been harshly punishing and restrictive, and her obviously ambivalent feelings in this "family romance" were induced by her tolerance of, yet resentment toward him. However, when he broke the lock on her bedroom door, the plan was initiated. Running away from the threatened incestual encounter, she found her own boyfriend (an older policeman) and had her first sexual experience with this father substitute.

In Fig. 2 there is no representation for those situations where the dyscontrol actions become so frequent as to become the way of life that Shapiro (1965) called an impulsive style. As he said, "these individuals seem to have an initial urge, hunch, or guess which then becomes their final conclusion. To these individuals the world appears discontinuous and inconstant, a series of opportunities, temptations, frustrations, sensuous experiences, and fragmented impressions." However, such behavior has become a way of life; hence, would not be considered acting out or any other form of episodic dyscontrol according to our definition. The erratic unstable life patterns have only a pseudo-episodic quality, merely reflecting an alternation between mounting needs and periods of satiation. It is particularly this group that shows the "alloplastic readiness to act," but there are usually other readily acceptable labels that would apply to their behavior, such as hysterical personality, emotionally unstable personality, or sociopathic personality. Acting out has often been applied to the behavior of these individuals, and there are certainly both dynamic and phenomenological similarities between the two. However, labeling such behavior as acting out or even as an impulse disorder so broadens the applicability of the label it loses operational value.

The term *acting out* has also been applied to the behavior of psychotics who carry their delusions into actions, something that all psychotics do with varying degrees of frequency and completeness. The extent to which the psychotic does this again reflects an alloplastic readiness to act, but we have repeatedly emphasized that this characteristic is not a criterion for what we have defined as either acting out or the other episodic dyscontrols. There is another group of patients whose capacity for self-reflection or self-awareness is limited. This means we can only observe such patients through their actions. They may or may not have an alloplastic readiness to act, but because they lack introspective capacity and can be evaluated only through action does not mean it is useful to designate them as actor-outers.

In summary, then, we would limit the concept of acting out by not applying it to (1) neurotic action in general; (2) acting on psychotic fantasy; (3) where an alloplastic readiness to act makes dyscontrolled action a way of life; and (4) where the capacity for introspection is so limited that the only data we have regarding maladaptive behavior is through acts. Furthermore, we limit the term acting out to a subgroup of maladaptive precipitous acts that interrupt the patient's life style, and where the precipitous acts are preceded by varying periods of predominantly unconscious premeditation regarding the decision to act. Even if there is premeditation, when it is largely conscious we do not consider it acting out but label it a lower form of episodic dyscontrol which we have designated as impulse dyscontrol. If there is a true "short circuit" between impulse and action (what we later call a lack of reflective delay) the behavior will be designated as even more primitive forms of episodic dyscontrol; that is primary dyscontrol (instinct or seizure dyscontrol).

2.4.3 *The spontaneous and the volitional act.* As our focus is on disordered behavior, we will only briefly mention normal acts. The spontaneous act has many of the attributes of the acts of episodic dyscontrol; namely it is a precipitous, abrupt, quick, direct action carried through to completion with little or no delay between the stimulus or urge to act and the act itself. There is no period of reflection. The act, too, may have all the quality of surprise to the actor, but in terms of its motor expression the act is efficient and the intention appropriate .The adaptive quality of the act suggests that either the individual's instinctual urges are so well integrated and controlled through his identification and sublimation that the expression of the basic urge finds outlet only in appropriate situations; or, that in similar situations in the past there has been considerable premeditation regarding the response to the stimulus, which has now become appropriately automatic. The appropriateness of the behavior depends upon the situation requiring snap judgment and immediate action. Such spontaneous acts are often referred to as creative or inspired acts.

The volitional act is one which has conscious goals and is accompanied by an awareness of the necessary means of obtaining these goals, as well as by an understanding of the long-term consequences of the act. In the volitional act there is a decision which, as Jaspers says, "comes after weighing up, wavering, and conflict." In volitional awareness there is the phenomenon of "I will" or "I will not," thus some experience of choice and decision (Jaspers, 1963). There is a conscious or preconscious selection or rejection of objects on the basis of cognitive discrimination. The act itself becomes evaluated in terms of the truthfulness or reality of the observation, the appropriateness of the situation, and the moral rightness of the range of alternatives selected, as well as a balancing of the need for gratification and the need for postponement. There is also a balancing of personal needs in contrast with the social usefulness or value of the act. Such aspects of the volitional act are discussed in detail in a monograph edited by Parsons entitled "Toward a General Theory of Action" (1951).

2.5 Episodic Inhibition of Action

Referring again to Fig. 1, we know that there are abrupt changes in behavior which rather than being characterized by abrupt actions are at the other extreme, abrupt interference with action when action is necessary. These interferences with action fall into two large categories, that is abrupt alteration in awareness, such as seen in petit mal attacks or hypnoidal states (Barker, 1948; Dickes, 1965) or abrupt interferences with motor responsivity, such as cataplexy (Levin, 1953). Other episodic inhibitions can be combinations of the two (e.g., narcolepsy). Rather arbitrarily these and related disorders such as the periodic catatonias are not discussed in detail because this would require another volume; however, they rightfully constitute another subclass of the episodic behavioral disorders (Smith, 1959; Cravioto, 1960). Since they are often defenses against episodic dyscontrol, we will discuss them to some extent in Chapter 9 and 10 where psychodynamic (motivational) and neurophysiologic integration is attempted. The following patient provides an example of episodic inhibition:

> Patient S243 is a thirty-year-old housewife with repeated, acute psychotic episodes of excitement accompanied by persecutory ideas, religious delusions (e.g., she is the Virgin Mary), visual hallucinations (hearing God's voice). During these episodes she becomes acutely assaultive towards her family and is confused and totally disorganized in her thinking. These episodes appear abruptly, usually last only a few hours, but occasionally persist for several days and then clear equally precipitously. At times, instead of these excitatory episodes, she has an inhibitory reaction, similar to a catatonic attack. She calls these "trances," during which her eyes roll back into her head, her body stiffens, and she falls to the floor remaining motionless for several hours to several days. Again these episodes appear precipitously, without obvious stress, and clear up equally abruptly. Sometimes the inhibitory episode will last only a few minutes and then be followed by acute excitement. She was once observed on the ward to go through these alternations in behavior, four times within an hour. When unresponsive, she appears to want to respond but makes only unintelligible noises.

The reader may question the necessity for such a complicated subclassification of the episodic dyscontrol as has been presented in this chapter and summarized in Fig. 2. Is it really necessary to establish four hierarchial levels of episodic dyscontrol and then further to divide each of these into three groups on the basis of the retrospective self-evaluation of the patient regarding his dyscontrol acts? Certainly if one is undertaking an epidemiologic or statistical analysis of these behavior disorders such complexity would be unnecessary; it would probably be sufficient to classify episodic dyscontrol as primary or secondary. The heuristic value in our more detailed classification will only become apparent after we consider the psychodynamic and neurophysiologic mechanisms of episodic dyscontrol (Chapter 9) and the therapeutic regimens, whether drug therapy (Chapter 11) or psychotherapy (Chapter 12). Fig. 2 does illustrate that both phenomenologic and dynamic considerations differentiate clearly the four hierarchial levels of episodic dyscontrol designated as seizure dyscontrol, instinct dyscontrol, impulse dyscontrol, and acting-out dyscontrol.

3 Nosology II: Episodic Reactions

3.1 DEFINITIONS AND GENERAL DESCRIPTION

Many similarities between episodic dyscontrol and episodic reactions are illustrated in the detailed clinical histories. (See Appendixes). For example, episodic reactions are often accompanied by intense affects or urges for which the patient seeks relief through a dyscontrol act, frequently with homicidal, suicidal, or sexual intent. In both episodic dyscontrols and episodic reactions control mechanisms seem to be overwhelmed by the drives or urges, and in both, although this is often overlooked, there is usually an altered state of consciousness or level of awareness, that may in part explain the failure of control mechanisms. Furthermore in both there is an association more often than would be expected in the general population with convulsive disorders or at least epileptoid phenomena (Monroe, 1959). Frequent seizures, however, may reduce the number or severity of other types of episodic behavioral disorders. The essential difference between these two subclasses of episodic behavioral disorders is the more sustained morbidity in the episodic reaction, while the morbidity in episodic dyscontrol is represented by a single act or short series of acts. This difference, while it may not reflect a basic difference in the underlying mechanisms, certainly has the utmost practical importance.*

* Temkin (1965) quotes Hughlings Jackson as pointing out the necessity for both a scientific and an empirical classification to exist side by side. Medicine as a science needs a classification that advances knowledge, whereas medicine as an art needs a clinical classification that has practical significance, even if in other ways it is arbitrary.

Episodic reactions, aside from being characterized by series or clusters of dyscontrol acts, usually have associated manifestations of other marked behavioral deviations that could be classified as psychotic, neurotic, sociopathic, or physiologic. During the periods between episodes the patient's behavior is not necessarily normal; in fact, episodic behavior, whether dyscontrol or reaction, is often superimposed on more persisting pathology. Therefore, in studying episodic reactions it is necessary to note carefully signs of morbidity during the intervals between episodic reactions was well as the pattern of response during episodic reactions. If the patient's morbidity simply waxes and wanes but the morbid characteristics during periods of exacerbation are merely a quantitative increase in the persisting psychopathology, the disorder would not be considered an episodic reaction by our definition. To be classified as such there would have to be something qualitatively new added to the morbid behavior (e.g., such as disinhibition in action in contrast to inhibited action). Of course, this would be necessary if the disorder were to fit our definition of episodic behavioral disorders; that is, a true interruption in the life style and life flow of the individual. As we have already noted in discussing episodic dyscontrol, sometimes this interruption in life style or life flow is not characterized by the appearance of disordered acts or actions, but quite the contrary, is characterized by an episodic inhibition in action. An example of an episodic inhibitory reaction would be periodic catatonia, although episodic catatonia would seem to be a more appropriate label (see Appendix, Patient S243).

3.2 REVIEW OF PREVIOUS LITERATURE

In view of the frequency of episodic reactions and the many articles in the literature describing these disorders, it is surprising that there is no official recognition of them in the American Psychiatric Association nomenclature.* Kraepelin, as reported by

* The German literature contains a number of articles on episodic disorders, most during the pre-EEG era, so they have not been systematically reviewed for this monograph. However, mention should be made of Kleist

Gjessing (1961), surmised that 2 to 3 percent of the hospital population fell into a group which he labeled "periodic catatonia."
Meduna (1950) and Reardon (1964) believe that there is a significant group of intermittent psychotic reactions which they would
designate oneirophrenias. The usual association of some clouding of sensorium and at least partial amnesia for the behavior
during these episodes suggests that they are an ictal phenomenon
borderline between schizophrenia and epilepsy (Monroe, 1959).
A discussion of the possible epileptoid nature of these disorders
will be taken up in Chapters 4 through 8. Some studies indicate
that these episodic reactions might occur in as many as 30 to 40
percent of the young, acutely psychotic, hospitalized patients
(Monroe, 1967).

Karl Menninger (1954) has given adequate nosological consideration to the episodic reactions. He proposed a drastic revision of our psychiatric nomenclature in terms of the hierarchial
levels of the regulatory functions of the ego. If the "normal"
devices of the ego fail to cope with the vicissitudes of life, the
first level of disorganization would occur in the form of persistent
"stress awareness." The defenses utilized in these "regulatory
devices of the first order" are essentially exaggerations of normal
functions that have an uncomfortable quality. These are suppression, repression, excessive alertness or emotionalism, restlessness, mild obsessional thinking, over-compensation, and minor
somatic disturbances. In turn, if these fail, "second order regulatory devices" are called into play, these being characterized by a
partial detachment from reality. By this Menninger means what
we usually call neurotic disturbances, minor character disorders,
and milder psychosomatic disturbances. In turn, if these fail,
there occurs a massive "rupture," but not a complete disorganiza-

_____

(1926), who published a monograph on the subject, and a review by Seige
(1955) who followed up a group of such patients twelve to fourteen years
after the original diagnoses were made. The episodic quality was emphasized
in these patients, some exhibiting inhibitions (narcolepsy or sleep) while
others displayed disinhibitions (aggressive acts and antisocial behavior); still
others displayed episodic alcoholism and depressions, and others, epileptoid
twilight states. Mitsuda (1967) has an extensive bibliography of the German
literature on this subject.

tion of the ego, and this could be either episodic or persistent. If these are episodic, he would consider them regulatory devices of the "third order" and designate this group of patients as suffering from "episodic dyscontrol." He dramatically characterizes this rupture as follows. "The ego seems to give way; some of the dangerous primitive impulses whose pressure is largely responsible for the tension, which all of the previously described device were designated to control, elude its restraints, they escape; they are enacted; they go toward targets and they wreak their destructive purposes." As he says, the internal tension has been relieved but the external pressures mount. These are relatively brief episodic discontinuous phenomena from which there is a prompt recovery, but with a tendency to recur. He would group these "episodic dyscontrols" under five headings: (1) assaultive violence (homicidal and suicidal); (2) convulsions; (3) panic reactions; (4) catastrophic demoralizations; and (5) schizo attacks (e.g., ten-day schizophrenia).

His proposal for a drastic revision of the nomenclature based on dynamic rather than phenomenological considerations has not met with popular approval. In part this is because we are not yet ready to classify disordered behavior in purely dynamic terms and in part because, by grouping such diverse clinical phenomena together, he is obscuring both etiologic and dynamic principles. The one aspect of this classification that has obtained some recognition is the "third order of regulatory devices," that is the "episodic dyscontrol." We have chosen to divide his "regulatory devices of the third order" (what we have called episodic behavioral disorders) into two subgroups: episodic dyscontrol and episodic reactions.

3.3 SUBCLASSES OF EPISODIC REACTIONS

3.3.1 *Episodic psychotic reactions: schizophrenic and acute brain syndrome.* Accompanying the enactment of primitive urges in the episodic reactions there are usually other pathological deviations characteristic of psychoses, neuroses, etc. One large group of patients with episodic reactions have associated schizophrenic symptoms. Such reactions are usually referred to in the literature as remitting, intermittent, atypical, or reactive schizophrenia and are characterized not only by acts of dyscontrol, representing action based on the patients' autistic preoccupations, but also by primary process thinking and other fundamental symptoms such as disturbances of affect and ambivalence. Also there may be perceptual or conceptual distortions in the forms of hallucination or delusion; hypochondriacal preoccupations or somatic delusions; disturbed associations and bizarre concrete thinking. Most often the patients suffer from dreamlike states, altered awareness, and at least a partial memory loss for the episode itself. The patient will refer to these episodes as "attacks." During remissions the individual may make a relatively normal adjustment or may, as we have emphasized before, demonstrate chronic, severe, insidious psychopathology. The precipitous onset of an altered state of consciousness or level of awareness and abrupt remission suggests an ictal phenomenon, particularly if the disturbed intervals are short. Therefore, this behavior has sometimes been designated as a complex psychic seizure. Since schizophrenia is defined as a disturbance of the total personality without clouding of sensorium, such behavior could be, but usually is not, identified as an acute brain syndrome, probably because the disturbed behavior so far overshadows any clouding of sensorium that the latter fact is overlooked. If it is noted, the assumption would be that the etiologic agent behind the acute disturbance is an exogeneous toxin. Such a toxin can seldom be discovered, so this may be a reason that the clouding of sensorium is neglected as an important clinical symptom. As we will discuss in more detail in later chapters, this disturbance in sensorium may be the result of "an excessive neuronal discharge" in the central nervous system.

Patient 0262 (described in detail in Appendix 5) provides an example of a true episodic schizophrenic reaction, where marked delusional and hallucinatory material appeared precipitously and remitted equally abruptly after a relatively short period, but in this example there was no significant clouding of sensorium.

Patient 0262 showed a "change" in personality two weeks before her admission to the hospital. Previously a devoted mother, she now wanted to give her children for adoption and on the day of admission became so physically abusive toward them that she was hospitalized for the children's safety. At that time she showed press of speech, incoherency, and poorly organized delusions that she was under some mysterious control from the outside and that unidentified enemies were going to destroy her family. Although she would not describe them, she also admitted to auditory hallucinations (apparently of a sexually accusatory nature). These disappeared four days after hospitalization. During the periods between her occasional, rageful, aggressive behavior she showed a silly, bland indifference toward her situation, despite the threatening nature of her delusions. One week after admission or three weeks from the onset of her acute symptoms she was already gaining insight into the fact that her behavior was bizarre and her ideas illogical.

This patient in the past would have been described as exhibiting "hysterical" psychosis or "ten-day schizophrenia," but it is proposed here that the symptoms be designated as episodic schizophrenic reactions with a strong motivational component and a secondary exploitation of the psychosis in the service of the underlying personality conflicts. What distinguishes this patient from the one described below is the lack of clouding of sensorium. Patients manifesting schizophrenia with the clouded sensorium have been referred to as oneirophrenia but we would designate their symptoms as the "episodic brain syndromes." As we will see later, we propose that the explanation for these episodic "organic" symptoms is the fact that these reactions are basically epileptoid. A clinical example follows:

Patient S229 (described in more detail in Appendix 5) had shown some changes in her behavior for the year preceding hospitalization, the most significant being "thoughts racing through my mind," and mild referential ideas. However, two weeks before admission her symptoms became florid: she believed that she was being influenced by mental telepathy, changed into a mulatto, and that her husband was "Eichmann." At times she felt that the hospital personnel were her persecutors and the hospital was a concentration camp; at the same time she was disoriented as to date and time, place and situation, and otherwise gave evidence of an acute brain syndrome that was not just a delusional misinterpretation of her environment. There was some glimmering insight into this change, leading to considerable perplexity. The patient asked "why the whole world seemed so different." At times she recognized that something must be wrong with her, while at other times she interpreted these changes in a delusional way, that some outside force was responsible. Two weeks after she had been hospitalized sensorium was clear and she spontaneously said, "I haven't imagined anything for the past four days."

Patient S243, described briefly in section 2.5, is another example of a patient with confusional states, exhibiting symptoms similar to what Meduna (1950) has labeled oneirophrenia. Both of these patients, although having normal baseline EEG recordings, showed abnormalities after activation, which, as we will discuss in Chapter 7, indicate possible epileptoid mechanisms.

Reports in both the American and European literature identify these syndromes of episodic schizophrenia or brain syndromes (Kleist, 1926; Seige, 1955; Mitsuda 1967). The authors reporting on such patients (Meduna, 1950; Monroe, 1959, 1967a; Reardon, 1964) feel that this group can be distinguished not only by specific phenomenological but also by etiologic differences. Rodin (1957b) suggested that this syndrome is phenomenologically related to schizophrenia but etiologically to epilepsy, and he proposed the term *symptomatic schizophrenia*. Gjessing (1961), in studying a group of patients that would fit this category, which he labeled periodic catatonia, reported that the patients, whether showing catatonic excitement or inhibition, demonstrated metabolic changes, preceding the behavioral changes, that suggested para-sympathetic dominance. Vaillant (1963), in an eighty-five-year old retrospective study to discover the natural history of what he called the "remitting schizophrenias" emphasized the recurrent quality of the disturbance and the frequent shift in diagnosis from schizophrenia to manic-depressive psychoses. In his study, 50 percent of the patients ultimately became chronic and either died or will probably die in a mental hospital. On the other hand, there were, even in these patients, long periods of relatively successful independent existence outside the hospital. To him the recurrent course of the illness suggested that the term *reactive schizophrenia* was inappropriate, and that remitting schizophrenia would be best classified in the official nomenclature as acute, schizo-affective disorders (as defined by Kasanin, 1933).

Garmezy (1965) has reviewed the literature on "reactive schizophrenia, comparing it with the so-called "process" schizophrenia. One of the primary differences between the two, although this is often only implicitedly stated, is the prognosis, which is more favorable for reactive schizophrenia. Analyzing the schizophrenics in terms of those who recover and those who do not reveals that the recovered patients had an acute onset with considerable affect, including anxiety, depression, and hostility, which is frequently environmentally precipitated. These patients had made a good social and sexual adjustment before the onset of their symptoms and the length of the psychosis was relatively short. The recurring characteristics of the disorder are probably not emphasized because of the relatively short follow-up in most of these studies.

In a number of the episodic schizophrenic reactions one can see such regularity that the episodes acquire periodicity. This has been noted particularly in women where the episodes are associated with premenstrual or menstrual tension. Altschule (1963) reported such patients in an early adolescent group. During menstruation these patients had auditory hallucinations, confusion, fright, over-talkativeness, and restlessness. Williams (1952) reported a series of 16 such patients with an age range of twelve to thirty-five years. The symptoms generally appear premenstrually, beginning with minor somatic complaints followed by hallucinatory experiences, insomnia, increase in weight, and symptoms typical either of manic-depressive manic reaction or catatonic reaction. In both studies the authors noted confusion and memory impairment; thus these symptoms fit what we describe as an episodic brain syndrome.

3.3.2 *Episodic sociopathic reaction.* Other patients with episodic reactions show behavior more typical of sociopathic behavior; their symptoms would be designated as episodic sociopathic reactions. However, as all patients characterized by episodic reactions tend also to manifest dyscontrol acts, and since these acts are responses to primitive affects, so often antisocial, the diagnosis of an episodic sociopathic reaction must be made carefully. For example, evidence of central integrative defect would indicate that the proper diagnosis should be an episodic psychotic reaction. Antisocial acts that reflect a rebellion against excessive but inappropriate conscience mechanisms usually associated with over-inhibitions would suggest that the episodic reaction was neurotic despite the antisocial characteristics of the acts themselves. Nevertheless, there are patients whose predominant symptomatology is characterized by clusters of antisocial acts, with no evidence for an integrative defect nor for an overly severe or childish conscience. It is this group for whom the diagnosis would be termed episodic sociopathic reactions. Many of these patients give a history suggesting diffuse organic involvement of the nervous system and have been noted for their hyperkinesis, clumsiness, short attention span, distractibility, difficulty in maintaining quiet attitudes, and explosiveness even in normal motor movements. Patient 413 and Patient 403 are two children representing this syndrome. A detailed phenomenological study, such as those done on reactive and process schizophrenia, to see whether similar reactive and process sociopathy could be identified, remains to be done. We will review some of these episodic sociopathic reactions where there is some evidence of diffuse organic involvement or epilepsy in Chapter 6. A brief clinical example follows:

Patient S212 (Appendix 9) presented a picture of pseudo-impulsivity and what was probably basically an episodic sociopathic reaction. Although for long periods she could be a dutiful and faithful wife, in fact had been such for a number of months at the time of follow-up, in the past she had repeatedly become sexually promiscuous and perverse. Again this was not an isolated act, but a sustained period of promiscuity lasting for several days to several months. There was also evidence of seizure dyscontrol, as well as impulse dyscontrol, and a definite history of mounting irritability and excitement before these episodes. However, again the irritability and excitement was not relieved by any particular act and persisted for the total period of her sociopathic promiscuous behavior.

3.3.3 *Episodic neurotic and episodic physiologic reactions.* We will see in the subsequent chapters that a number of episodic reactions have been identified as concomitants of epileptoid phenomenon. For example, some acute episodic depressions occur with precipitous, unexplained onset and with equally abrupt and unexplained remissions (Weil, 1959; Yamada 1967). Although these depressions at times may last for days, they may only last for an hour or two. They can be differentiated from the usual psychotic depression in that they are accompanied by intense anxiety, but less motor retardation and less expression of guilt and inferiority feelings (see 6.3). There are other common episodic neurotic reactions, such as periods of acute hypochondriasis, which may be a reflection of a diencephalic epileptoid phenomenon (Van Buren, 1963; Shimoda, 1961, discussed in more detail in 6.4, and 7.5). There is also increasing evidence that other episodic neurotic reactions are ictal or subictal responses (Jonas, 1965). Detailed discussion of these epileptoid disorders will be reserved for Chapters 4 and 5.

In our experience, episodic neurotic reactions occur in many diverse forms but the most common forms are diffuse anxiety reactions, phobic symptoms, depressions often accompanied by hypochondriasis, clusters of conversion symptoms, and finally, dissociative states. It is important to emphasize that these reactions sometimes last for only a few minutes, often no more than a few hours and at the most several days, although they may often recur with only short symptom-free intervals. Several clinical vignettes to illustrate the episodic neurotic reactions follow:

Patient F250 (Appendix 6) would describe depressions as if they were auras, that is, a wave of depression would overwhelm him. This would be so intense that he would almost have a visual sensation of being engulfed by flames or a kinesthetic sensation of being swallowed by the sea. During these periods he would develop somatic preoccupations, the idea that he had a brain tumor, liver disease, memory loss, heart trouble, or arthritis, all complaints which had some slight basis in reality. The sensations were so overwhelming that they occasionally led to contemplation of suicide and quite often to dramatic appeals for hospitalization.

Patient S248 was a young boy with nonepisodic schizophrenia. Without any particular change in his delusional content, he would suddenly be overwhelmed by phobias, particularly by fear of the dark, fear of being alone, and, what placed him in a dilemma, a fear of being on the streets or among people. At these times he would hang around the hospital begging for help until either his physician or another would admit him.

Patient S278 was admitted to the neurology service in status epilepticus. She was transferred to the psychiatry service when, upon recovering from her epilepsy, she developed blindness, hemianesthesia, hemiparesis, and aphonia. These symptoms cleared rapidly under minimal reassurance, but would recur again in clusters (as would the seizures), under psychological stress.

Patient F284 (Appendix 6) had had a series of head and spine injuries which required hospitalization and neurological work-up. Whenever diagnostic studies were performed he developed hemiparesis, hemianesthesia, and aphasias, as well as mild torticollis.

Patient o289 (Appendix 7) manifested dramatic dissociative reactions. She repeatedly changed personality during which time she adopted a new name and the identity of a wild, promiscuous, single girl, when in fact she was a very conscientious, prudish mother and respected member of her community.

The episodic dysphoria that accompanies these reactions often leads to a frantic attempt on the part of the patients to abort the "attacks" through the use of alcohol (F250, F227, F283, and O260) or drugs (F206, F227, F287, O255, O265, S239, and S290).

3.4 EPISODIC DYSCONTROL OR EPISODIC REACTION AS A SYMPTOM OF OTHER DISORDERED BEHAVIOR

The intermittent quality of episodic dyscontrol does not imply that the behavior between episodes is necessarily normal. In fact, more often than not there is a severe underlying "nonepisodic" behavioral disorder. Although the episodic dyscontrol may be the presenting symptom, and is often serious enough to precipitate hospitalization, careful scrutiny reveals that it may be but a minor aspect of the psychopathology, the dyscontrol acts secondarily exploited in the service of this underlying psychopathology. For example, the dyscontrol act might be a cry for help, such as an impulsive suicidal attempt (Glaser, 1965), or rebellion against phobic or obsessive inhibitions, or an attempt to prevent loss of identity (Angel, 1965), or an attempt to differentiate self from others (Carroll, 1954; Kanzer, 1957). It has already been noted how important it is to distinguish between the dynamics and the etiologic mechanisms of this underlying persistent nonepisodic psychopathology and the superimposed episodic dyscontrol. A comparative evaluation between the level of regression of dyscontrol behavior and the basic psychopathology often gives us significant diagnostic and prognostic clues. The more regressive the basic psychopathology, the more regressive should be the episodic dyscontrol. Should there be a marked disparity between the two organizational levels, the more complicated will be the dynamic and etiologic interpretation. That is, if the patient under consideration has a well-organized defense neurosis and yet manifests episodic dyscontrol at the level of the seizure or instinctual act, one would have to investigate several alternatives to explain this disparity. These alternatives would be (1) the current reality has an overwhelming traumatic implication; (2) the structured neurosis was really covering a more regressive psychotic potential; (3) the seizure or instinctual act was epileptoid, toxic, or metabolic. This issue will be considered in detail in Chapters 9 and 10. The clinical examples that follow are of dyscontrol acts in patients with persisting psychopathology in which the episodic disorders were relegated to a secondary, rather than a primary, position.

Patient 0281 is a twenty-four-year-old white male, single, a student, and an identical twin, who apparently made a more than adequate social adjustment in a reasonably healthy family until his junior year in college. It might be significant that at this time his twin brother elected to leave the school both were attending; thus a dependent yet competitive relationship between the identical twins was broken for the first time. The only abnormalities before this had been some obsessional concern about "coincidences" during high school and a paradoxical orgasm under tension. The onset of his present illness began with compulsive repetitive behavior, such as setting and unsetting alarm clocks, turning water faucets off and on, turning light switches off and on. He became so concerned with these rituals that his school work gradually deteriorated until he had to drop out of school in midsemester. While under psychiatric care for the obsessions, he rather precipitously became destructive, tearing off his clothes, biting his own feces, tearing holes in the curtains —behavior that obviously required hospitalization. The patient remained in the hospital five months, having a spontaneous remission without specific therapy. Within several days after discharge, however, he again became destructive, threatening homicide, suicide, and again tearing off his clothes. He was returned to the hospital where he now was given 30 electro-shock treatments. After several months he left the hospital against advice, but again within several days went "berserk," this time threatening to kill his brother. In the hospital his behavior vacillated between contrite, obsequious, relatively "sane" periods and rageful, destructive episodes of exposing himself, or physically attacking other patients. No definite evidence for hallucinations could be elicited, nor were there any well-developed delusions, although he sometimes referred to himself as an animal in a cage, and would ask for restraint of his "forelegs."

Psychological evaluation also revealed his ritualistic doing and undoing, as well as his attempts to control his impulsivity through stereotyped conforming responses; but delusional tendencies were noted, as well as strong underlying paranoid trends. Basically the patient expressed a passive-dependent attitude. Underneath his conformity and compulsive self-defeating behavior there was seething anger that threatened to break through into violence and uncontrolled acts.

At the time of the follow-up study the patient was still hospitalized. It had become obvious during this period that the acute dyscontrol acts were usually precipitated by desertions. At the same time the patient invited or sought these desertions through his bizarre, intolerable behavior. In talking about these acute episodes in retrospect he described them as dreamlike states. Even after fourteen months of hospitalization, it was obvious that this man had extreme tension that was just barely contained and that his mood was distinctly depressed. The diagnosis was chronic undifferentiated schizophrenia with secondary impulse dyscontrol.

Patient S205 is a thirty-two-year-old married white housewife who has had three hospitalizations for acute episodic panic reactions, but has basically manifested a chronic, paranoid schizophrenic reaction for the past seven years. Paranoid delusions and hallucinations include accusatory voices, usually the neighbor's, coming through the radiators. For long periods she can handle these experiences by covering the radiators with sheets or talking back to the voices. Her first hospitalization occurred some months after the symptoms had developed when she manifested an acute panic reaction and was found sitting on the floor, crying and talking to herself while clutching a crucifix and a picture of her son. At the same time she was expressing a feeling of impending doom and inability to breathe. After several weeks the acute symptoms remitted and the patient was taken out of the hospital by her husband. However, she was rehospitalized a month later with similar symptoms, being discharged the second time five weeks later. She adjusted by talking back to her voices, and her environment tolerated this behavior for the next four years. Hospitalization was again necessary when she became so agitated that taking care of her house or maintaining her employment (which she had done despite her psychotic symptomatology) was no longer possible. Her early history is replete with dyscontrol acts of an impulsive nature, including a suicidal act at 18 by an overdose of sleeping pills, and another two years later by ingestion of rat poison.

Psychological evaluation revealed a woman with definite evidence of central nervous system impairment. There was also evidence of a hysterical personality structure now overshadowed by the schizophrenic thinking and paranoid ideas. There was also considerable depression, free-floating anxiety, and a surprising ability to critically evaluate her own bizarre ideation. The diagnosis in this patient was schizophrenic reaction, paranoid type, with superimposed episodic anxiety reactions and occasional impulse dyscontrol.

In both of the above patients, episodic behavioral disorder is overshadowed by the persisting psychopathology. Even though this persisting psychopathology might have a waxing and waning quality, it does not truly represent an interruption in the life style or life flow of the individual and so does not meet our definition of an episodic behavioral disorder.

Part Two   Neuropsychiatric and Neurophysiologic Data

4 Subcortical Electrograms and Behavior

In the next five chapters on neuropsychiatric and neurophysiologic data we will report on studies of mind-brain correlations. As already suggested, etiologic, dynamic, and developmental mechanisms behind the episodic behavioral disorders may be significantly influenced by "faulty equipment," that is, disorders of the central nervous system. On an a priori basis of the way we have defined acting out, we would surmise that is is more likely a manifestation of "faulty learning," while the lower hierarchical levels of dyscontrol acts would be more significantly influenced by impaired functioning of the central nervous system. We have also pointed out that the episodic behavioral disorders are similar to ictal phenomena in that they have a precipitous onset and an equally sudden remission, and the patients themselves often refer to the episodes as "spells" or "attacks." We have also noted the frequent occurrence of typical epileptic seizures in patients who manifest other episodic behavioral disorders.

In establishing mind-brain correlations we will be relying heavily on introspective data in the study of the mind and must make such correlations in humans because only the human can provide us with this data. In studying the brain we will rely heavily on electrical recordings, usually the electroencephalograph, from the central nervous system. However, Goldesohne (1963) concluded his discussion on the relationship between epilepsy and the EEG as follows: "Are there predictable scalp

EEG correlates for consciousness? It appears not. For interference with memory? It appears not. What are the scalp EEG correlates for ictal hallucinatory and other psychic and mood experiences? Practically none. Is there a characteristic type of scalp EEG discharge during psychomotor attacks? No, not always. When does a seizure start? When does it end? The scalp EEG frequently does not tell us. The answers to all these questions are generally negative, because the attenuated potentials that are found at the cortex are only approximate and incomplete indications of the underlying cerebral dysfunction which is responsible for ictal and post-ictal behavior." For this reason we will emphasize the subcortical electrographic studies reported in this chapter despite the limited numbers of individuals that have been studied with this technique. A symposium on this subject, "Electrical Studies on the Unanesthetized Brain," took place in 1960 (Ramey). These studies reveal that more precise data are obtainable from electrodes in direct contact with brain tissues. It has been repeatedly demonstrated that high amplitude paroxysmal activity can occur in subcortical structures without being reflected on the cortex. It is also reported that hypersynchronous activity can be recorded from cortical electrodes but not from scalp electrodes directly over the same cortical area (Abraham, 1958). In fact, precise implantation of subcortical electrodes with x-ray clarification of position reveals that hypersynchronous activity is recorded from one pair of electrodes while a similar pair five millimeters away will show no such activity (Heath, 1960). Recording directly from brain tissue, despite the increased sensitivity in precision of the recording, has its drawbacks also. The justification for such a drastic procedure, even with such refined techniques as stereotaxic placements, allowing the introduction of electrodes with closed surgical techniques, and effective antibiotic therapy to protect against post-operative infection, must still be limited to patients with severe pathology where operating intervention usually is the treatment of choice only as a last resort. Sem-Jacobsen (1968) discusses these problems in considerable detail.

Data collected by recording directly from the brain come from three sources. The first are those epileptic patients where temporal lobectomy is planned and where recording and stimulation take place during the operation itself in an attempt to identify the pathological focus. In a few instances schizophrenic patients undergoing frontal lobotomies have been studied in a similar manner. One advantage of this technique is that localization of the stimulating or recording electrodes can be verified, either by direct observations or from histological examination of the removed tissue. The limitations of such data are obvious because of the circumscribed behavioral possibilities in an operating room. A second group of patients could be considered subjects for subacute investigation in that implanted electrodes are left in place for a few days to a week before final surgical intervention, usually again temporal lobectomy. However, the traumatic effects of the operation on the immediate postoperative behavior (not to mention the trauma to brain tissue from electrode placement) limit the value of these studies. A third group of patients are those with chronically implanted electrodes left in place over a period of some months and even years. Techniques have been developed so that this can be done with a low morbidity rate. The same electrodes are used both for stimulation and recording. In fact, techniques have been developed so that minute amounts of drugs or metabolites can be introduced through a micropipette system. More recently patients have been wired for self-stimulation, with the frequency and location of stimulation determined by their subjective preference (Heath, 1960; Sem-Jacobsen, 1968). In this last group there is an unlimited opportunity to study for sustained periods the cortical and subcortical electric activity of the brain. A wide range of behavioral patterns and extensive introspection make this group a particularly important one for establishing mind-brain correlations.

4.1 STUDIES UTILIZING CHRONIC ELECTRODE IMPLANTATIONS

The only extended series of patients with chronically implanted electrodes have been those reported by Heath and his associates (1954), and Sem-Jacobsen (1968). Their studies began in 1950.

The rationale for utilizing such drastic procedure was discussed in the original monographs on the subject. By 1961 Heath (1962b) reported that 48 such patients had been studied, 36 subjects with schizophrenia, six with intractable pain, and six with psychomotor epilepsy (two had seizures only and four had seizures plus behavioral disorders). These studies included correlations between subcortical electrograms and behavior, the effects of drugs on subcortical electrograms and behavior, direct instillation of drugs and metabolites in the brain tissue through micropipettes, and finally intracranial self-stimulation. A summary of this work has been presented by Heath (1960, 1966) and will not be repeated here. However, considerable data, both published and unpublished, that pertain to our present discussion will be reviewed.*

4.1.1 *Stimulation studies.* Animal studies suggest that the rhinencephalon (limbic system or olfactory brain) is intimately associated with the expression of emotion. This pointed the way for a particular study of these structures in psychotic humans, inasmuch as it is precisely this group that show outstanding defects in the emotional sphere. A dramatic example of the importance of the rhinencephalon in emotional expression was given by Heath (1955b) in reporting on the stimulation of the amygdaloid area in schizophrenic patients. A precise threshold for stimulation could be established which would elicit either a rage or fear reaction. The patient would be well aware of the affect expressed during the stimulation and would recall it completely afterwards. The affect was well integrated with the patient's thinking and basic emotional state; that is, directed

* From 1950 to 1960 I was associated with the Tulane Project, primarily as the psychiatrist evaluating behavioral changes and correlating these changes with subcortical electrograms. The unique and intricate technical procedures, including stereotaxic equipment, electronic recording of data, manipulative skill in implanting and maintaining the chronic electrodes, and the subsequent development of intracranial stimulation and cerebral instillation of drugs was beyond my skill. The techniques evolved from a multidisciplinary team including neurologists, neurophysiologists, neurosurgeons, psychiatrists, biochemists, and electronic engineers under the leadership of Robert G Heath, M.D., Professor and Chairman, Department of Neurology and Psychiatry, Tulane University School of Medicine.

towards appropriate objects in the immediate environment, such as the ward physician or nurse, and was a reflection of either fear or rage, depending upon the basic mood at the time of stimulation. The response, however, was a surprise to both the patients and the observers in that the intensity was unusual for this individual who was usually a rather meek, passive, and emotionally flat person. Similar affective responses to stimulation have been reported for epileptic patients (Bickford, 1953; Braizer, 1954; Chapman, 1954; Sem-Jacobsen, 1968) but Heath did not report the confusion, unresponsiveness, and automatisms with amygdala stimulation that was noted in acute studies on epileptics reported by these authors. Chapmen states that "electrical stimulation of the amygdala was found to provoke practically all of the somato-motor sensory, autonomic and behavioral phenomenon which characterizes temporal lobe seizures." Heath (1955b) also reported that stimulation of the tegmentum of the mesencephalon induced a rage reaction, but this was qualitatively quite different from that elicited by amygdala stimulation, being characterized by a diffuse, uncoordinated, primitive striking out, directed towards whoever or whatever was closest at hand; a reaction which phenomenologically is what we have designated a seizural act. A third type of fear-rage response was elicited from hypothalamic stimulation, one where the visceral-motor components suggesting fear and rage were predominant. The patient would show shallow, rapid breathing, pilomotor reactions, tachycardia, and elevation in blood pressure. (Sem-Jacobsen, 1968, presents a detailed analysis of those parts of the brain where stimulation elicits an autonomic response.)

Van Buren (1963), stimulating deep in the temporal lobe of epileptics, induced subjective abdominal sensations that were reported by the patient in such a way that a psychiatrist might well have diagnosed hypochondriasis, somatic delusions, or just somatic symptoms of anxiety. These findings suggest that episodic physical symptoms as well as episodic emotions are possibly associated with subcortical ictal phenomenon. The evidence that in humans stimulation in the amygdala area elicits fear-rage responses is supported by the study of Delgado (1954), who found that subcortical amygdaloid stimulation increased social aggressiveness in a group of six monkeys.

This response is in marked contrast to the behavior elicited by stimulation in the septal region, which not only has an alerting or normalizing effect on the level of consciousness, but is subjectively perceived by the patient as a pleasant experience, increasing his sense of well being (Heath, 1954). This was also found by Sem-Jacobsen (1968).

4.1.2 *Electrographic correlations with spontaneous behavioral changes.* A more naturalistic investigative method is a repeated monitoring of subcortical electrograms whenever there have been spontaneous changes in the patient's behavior. The following patient, who has been reported in the literature on several occasions in different contexts (Monroe, 1956c; Heath, 1957, 1960), is an outstanding example:

> Patient 021, a twenty-seven-year-old housewife and mother of two mentally retarded children, was admitted to the hospital for evaluation and treatment of episodic psychotic reactions, lasting from a few hours to a few weeks, and severe enough on six occasions to require hospitalization or incarceration in jail. These episodes, described as "spells" by her husband, were preceded by mounting irritability, hypochondriasis, and severe occipital headaches. As the attack progressed, there would be withdrawal and lack of emotional response, accompanied by a staring, vacant look in the eyes; this would be followed by outbursts of rage and destructiveness, at which time the patient would be physically abusive toward her husband and children, or self-mutilative, and, on two occasions, suicidal. These "spells" would be accompanied by visual hallucinations, particularly of her children cringing in fear, or at other times of her mother, husband, and children calling her names and admonishing her. She would also break up furniture, tear off her clothes, and tear at her hair "to get the snakes out of it." These attacks would be accompanied by varying degrees of confusion and disorientation. Although she claimed complete amnesia for the episodes, detailed questioning revealed that there was some hazy recollection of the event. Following

the attack, these would be a period of depression and re-morse. Amobarbital (Amytal) sodium intravenously would often control the behavior and sometimes abort the attacks. At other times hospitalization was required for as long as two months, the patient receiving electroshock treatment (EST) and subcoma insulin therapy. During the intervals between attacks, the patient was hostile and irritable, constantly taunting her husband about past mistakes and suspiciously accusing him of extramarital affairs, whereas she herself was occasionally promiscuous. She had constant hypochondriacal complaints which led to frequent visits to her doctor and several hospitalizations with two laparotomies.

The patient is the oldest of five children, the others being boys, born into a family of low economic and social status. The emotional climate of the home was unstable. The father, who apparently was affectionate toward the patient and gave her some emotional security, was described, never-theless, as an alcoholic who was irresponsible and frequently away from home philandering. On the other hand, the mother, who was reliable and supported the family, was described as having a personality much like the patient's, being particularly hostile and restrictive toward the patient, while favoring the boys. The mother never allowed the pa-tient to socialize freely, and during adolescence restricted her social activities, while accusing her unjustly of sexual promiscuity. She conveyed to the patient her own suspicious-ness and sense that the world was a hostile place.

The patient says of herself, "I was always different and confused." She was shy and isolated, while quick-tempered and belligerent, rebelling against authority and fearful of school. She had numerous phobias, particularly concerning darkness and fire. The latter had a realistic basis, because at the age of three years, she sustained severe third-degree burns over her body and face, requiring repeated plastic surgery, which left her face considerably scarred and dis-torted. She was attached to her father but furious about his philandering, with her anger directed toward his girl friends more than toward father himself. However, after the father's divorce and subsequent remarriage, she accepted both her father and his wife, often expressing a desire to live with them. Her childhood and adolescence were characterized by isolation and only superficial emotional relationships with peers or family. She married after a short courtship and had difficulties in adjusting to marriage from the start. Sexual adjustment was always poor, with the patient failing to attain orgasm until the last year or so. Attempts at coitus, as well as her pregnancy and delivery, were accompanied by much of the aggressive behavior described above.

Aside from the scarring on the face, hands, and trunk, physical and neurological examinations were noncontributory. Laboratory findings were all negative except for the routine EEG, which showed some short runs of 6, 7, and 7½ per second activity and a small build-up with hyperventilation, with immediate return to normal. The record was read as a generalized slightly slow record, consistent with, but not indicative of, epilepsy.

At the time of admission to the hospital, the patient was somewhat irritable and suspicious but otherwise cooperative, showing no evidence of the episodic behavior described above. Intellectual testing and a routine mental status examination revealed no abnormality. However, during the course of her hospital stay, she would show the typical "spells," which would generally last for 24 hours, but might persist for weeks.

This patient represents a typical example of what we have labeled episodic psychotic reaction because of the rather prolonged psychotic episodes with precipitous onset and remission, characterized by complex symptoms including hallucinations, delusions, hypochondriasis, some confusion and disorientation, and intense rage reactions resulting in aggressive and destructive acts. At times her behavior is characteristic of what we have described as impulse dyscontrol in that she was aware of mounting tension which was relieved only by some explosive motor act. Even during periods of remission she would have been judged an incipient paranoid schizophrenic because of her pathological jealously, delusions of infidelity, and poorly developed but quite obvious paranoid ideation. Characteristic of chronic schizophrenics in general, her electrograms showed subcortical abnor-

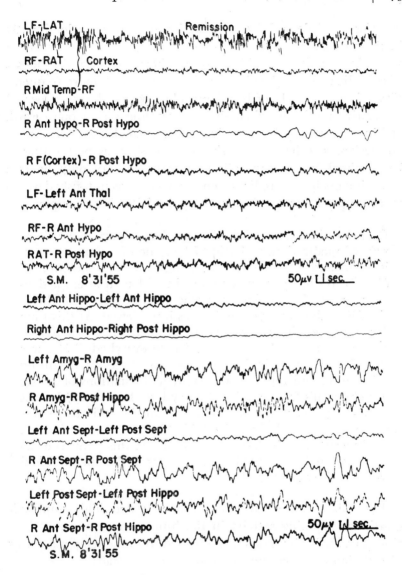

Fig. 3. Subcortical recording during remission

Source: R. B. Heath and W. A. Mickle, "Evaluation of seven years' experience with depth electrode studies in human patients," in Estelle R. Ramey and D. S. O'Doherty, eds., *Electrical Studies on the Unanesthetized Brain* (New York: Paul B. Hoeber, 1960), p. 229.

malities as evidenced by spike and slow waves predominantly in the septal region (Heath, 1960). During periods of remission such abnormalities would be rare, whereas during the height of episodic reaction the abnormalities were much more frequent. Fig. 3 is an example of her depth electrogram during a period of relative remission when she was residing on an open ward, visiting her family four to five hours each day and overnight on weekends. When out of the hospital she was performing at her optimal level. Hospitalization was necessary only because it was impossible to predict when she would precipitously develop an acute psychotic reaction, such as the following example:

> One morning she awakened early, began pacing the floor, refused medication, and said "I feel one of my moods coming on," and again later, "I'm going to tear up something." She put on her clothes without aid and then attempted to escape from the hospital. Apprehended, she was brought to the EEG laboratory where she was interviewed. At this time she expressed intense anger, resentment, and negativism, saying repeatedly, "I hate you, I hate everybody." She was slow but accurate in her response to questions regarding orientation and reported recurrent hallucinations of seeing her children's faces, adding, "They look frightened, I must have done something to them." Following this there was a long pause and then she said, "I see my boy, I don't really want him, in fact I hate him." At this point she became agitated, attempted to tear up the bedclothes and had to be forcibly restrained.

The subcortical electrograms now revealed high amplitude multiphasic spiking activity in the hippocampus and septal region (Fig. 4). At times this was recorded from the temporal cortex directly but not from the corresponding scalp leads.

> Later in the morning she was given 0.5 grams sodium amobarbital which had ameliorated her behavior in the past. The anger almost immediately disappeared, followed by depression. She said contritely, "I'm not really bad, am I?"

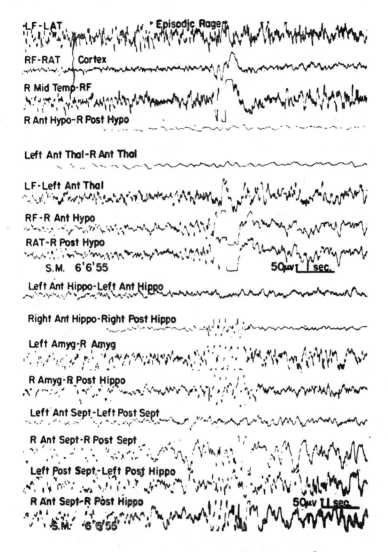

Fig. 4. Subcortical recording during episodic dyscontrol

Source: R. B. Heath and W. A. Mickle, "Evaluation of seven years' experience with depth electrode studies in human patients," in Estelle R. Ramey and D. S. O'Doherty, etc., *Electrical Studies on the Unanesthetized Brain* (New York: Paul B. Hoeber, 1960), p. 230.

Although for a while she still hallucinated of her children, their faces were now reported as smiling. She seemed to have an amnesia for the events immediately preceding the amytal injection, but not for most of the period of disturbed behavior. With the injection of amytal, high amplitude spindling activity replaced the paroxysmal hypersynchronous abnormalities in the limbic structures. Before she returned to the ward three hours later, the barbiturate response was on the wane and the paroxysmal hypersynchronous activity was returning. Simultaneously there was a return of her uncontrolled hostility. She threw objects throughout the ward and again tried to run away. Restraint was necessary and again she became depressed and tearful. The next morning her behavior was unchanged and a repeat electrographic recording showed abnormalities similar to those of the day before.

This is an example then of the episodic reaction correlating quite directly with increased abnormalities in the septal and hippocampal areas with minimal or no reflection on the scalp recordings, even though at times in the past there had been abnormalities seen in scalp recordings. There was some confusion and mild clouding of sensorium. Another example follows:

Patient 019 was a quiet, withdrawn, autistic, paranoid girl, very suspicious and reluctant to give significant introspective material. She was described by family and friends as cold, aloof, withdrawn, even in childhood, having been nicknamed "Queenie" by her peers because of her aloof, haughty attitude. Hospitalization had become necessary because she was so withdrawn and idle that she could no longer look after her own personal needs. This patient showed a chronic paranoid schizophrenic reaction with little evidence for episodic behavioral disturbances like that reported above. However, after a series of stimulations to subcortical structures the spike-wave patterns in the hippocampal-septal region gradually built up over a period of several weeks. During the same time her mother reported mounting irritability, culminating in explosive verbal outbursts directed towards either the mother or hospital personnel, and she indulged in numerous aggressive fantasies involving the same people. There was some confusion and mild disorientation with memory defects inasmuch as she had trouble recalling whether she had taken her medication. As the hypersynchrony continued to build up it finally spread to the cortex with the appearance of diffuse slow activity. Concurrent with this the patient became frightened, saying "I'm going to pass out."

This is an example of artificially induced impulse dyscontrol, manifest by gradually increasing tension, culminating in explosive verbal outbursts during a period when seizural activity was recorded directly from the hippocampal region but not from the cortex.

In Heath's series of schizophrenic patients hypersynchronous activity was always recorded from the septum, usually from the amygdala and hippocampus, but not from the hypothalamus, caudate, tegmentum of the mesencephalon, or from the cortex. This hypersynchrony was not recorded from the septal, amygdala, and hippocampal areas in the six control subjects operated on for the treatment of intractable pain or other nonpsychotic disorders (Heath, 1960). Similar abnormalities were seen in epileptics with subcortical chronically implanted electrodes, but the variability in waveform and location was much greater than in the psychotic patients. In the epileptics with episodic behavioral disorders the hypersynchronous paroxysmal activity was even greater than in the typical schizophrenic, but the abnormalities were more pronounced in the amygdala-hippocampal areas. Heath thought that, although there were similarities in the areas involved and the wave forms in both the schizophrenic and epileptic patients, there was a basic metabolic difference between the two groups of patients. This is indicated in the differential response to drug instillation in epileptic and schizophrenic patients (discussed 4.1.4). Heath also reported one epileptic patient who, although showing definite seizural discharges in the hippocampal-amygdala area, had no concomitant behavioral changes (1963a). It is important to note that scalp recordings "never appropriately reflect the storm of abnormal activity present in specific subcortical structures" (Heath, 1962b), and that at times this storm of abnormal subcortical activity is dramatically correlated with acute behavioral changes which would appropriately fit our classification of either episodic dyscontrol or episodic reactions.

One of the most precise correlations between behavior and changes in subcortical recording was discovered by the Tulane Group (Heath, 1954) and reported in more detail by Lesse (1955). The original observation was made during testing to see whether one could elicit electrical changes within the "olfactory" brain by having the patient sniff various distinctive odors (e.g. turpentine, perfume, beer). Somewhat surprisingly these odors consistently elicited bursts of 14 to 17 cycle per second waves in the hippocampus and 20 to 30 per second waves from the amygdala area. However, the extent of this spindling activity did not seem to depend upon the intensity of the odor but on the individual's associations with the odor. Thus, one subject showed a prolonged electrographic response while smelling a bottle of beer, which stirred up associations of a homosexual encounter in a bar room.

It was only a short step from this to the discovery that any remote memory associated with strong affect, whether pleasant or unpleasant, could elicit this response. Performing abstract mental functions, such as simple arithmetic problems, would immediately terminate the fast activity, as would recalling recent emotional events. For example, memories of finding an electric train under the Christmas tree during early childhood, stress during World War II, remembering pleasant summers spent on a grandmother's farm all elicited the response. However, the recollection of an acutely disturbing television program the night before or the false accusation of a nurse two days before, both associated with intense affect but of relatively recent origin, would not elicit the response. This observation was repeated hundreds of times in a number of patients. This suggests that this area of the brain is somehow connected with what Kubie (1953) has called "gut" memory, that is a memory that has meaningful and intense emotional connections. However, these electrographic changes apparently only occur in association with a recollection if these memories have become "consolidated," that is fixed over a significant period of time. This is one example of how it is possible, even with present techniques, to make precise correlations between the mind and the brain.

4.1.3 *Subcortical electrographic correlations with behavior altered by drugs.* Another method for making mind-brain correlations is through inducing behavioral changes by the use of psychoactive drugs, particularly psychedelic and tranquilizing drugs. I have reported studies of patients receiving d-LSD 25, mescaline, and chloralose, both with and without concurrent tranquilizing medication such as chlorpromazine and reserpine (Monroe, 1956b, 1957). Changes in electrical recordings for the psychedelic drugs were described in terms of a generalized response associated with anxiety, and a specific response correlated with psychotic behavior. The generalized response recorded from the cortex included a disappearance of alpha activity and an increase in fast activity in the beta range. If there was rhythmic theta or underlying delta, this would also decrease in the cortical leads and be replaced by fast beta activity. Subcortical electrograms, particularly from the caudate, amygdala, hippocampal and septal areas would often show similar changes; that is, a decrease in amplitude and an increase in fast activity. Frequency analysis indicated that when fast activity appeared in the subcortical areas there was often a shift in the background slow activity to even slower frequencies. These findings were similar to those of Schwartz (1956a, b).

The most significant finding was that d-LSD and mescaline induced in the septal, amygdala and hippocampal regions paroxysmal activity easily distinguished from the background. This paroxysmal activity was described as any one of the following patterns: high amplitude waves in the range of 6 to 10 cycles per second, occasional short bursts of high amplitude delta, and sharp waves; high amplitude sharp waves followed by a slow component, a low amplitude diphasic spike alone, or followed by low amplitude slow waves; and monophasic spikes. All of the patients receiving psychedelic drugs were in fact schizophrenic, and had electrographic abnormalities in their baseline records. However, under the influence of drugs, the difference was striking in terms of frequency, amplitude and paroxysmal quality of the abnormalities. These abnormalities occurred only if the drugs were effective in changing behavior. The depth electrographic changes could be blocked by pretreatment with chlorpromazine, and when this occurred there was also a failure to develop clinical symptoms. Alpha-chloralose was also associated with subcortical paroxysmal activity, but unlike the psychedelic drugs this usually spread to the cortex. Other studies have indicated that in patients particularly prone to show episodic behavioral disorders alpha-chloralose would not only activate EEG abnormalities but also precipitate acute behavioral disturbances that simulate very closely their spontaneous episodic attacks (Monroe, 1956a, c; *also see* 7.4).

Patient 021, described in detail earlier in this chapter (4.1.2), underwent studies with LSD, mescaline, and chloralose (Monroe, 1957).

Under d-LSD 25, Patient 021 complained of numerous somatic symptoms such as nausea, blurred vision, head and backache. She became depressed and cried throughout the observation period, constantly struggled to get up, and was completely uncooperative. Periodically she became angry, striking out at the doctor or attendants and expressed accentuated paranoid referential ideas. She again hallucinated that her children were standing at the foot of the bed with a condemnatory attitude.

Electrograms (Fig.12) revealed paroxysmal, high amplitude bursts in the alpha-theta range, appearing in the right hippocampus and a dramatic increase in diphasic spikes in the left hippocampal area. A subsequent study with mescaline revealed paroxysmal electrographic changes but these occurred rarely (Fig. 12).

During this study the patient had numerous somatic complaints, such as chills, shivering, difficulty in breathing, and the sensation that her legs were drawing up. However, there were no hallucinations, and no outbursts of rage, although at times she appeared frightened and irritable.

On a third occasion she was given alpha-chloralose. In this instance the paroxysmal activity was even more dramatic, with high amplitude delta and theta occurring predominantly on the right, but ultimately involving both deep and cortical leads bilaterally. Sharp spiking activity was a prominent feature in both the right and left hippocampal areas (Fig. 12).

At this point the patient became extremely agitated, so rageful that she began tearing off her clothes and again hallucinated her husband and children. The children appeared frightened and cringing, while her husband was admonishing her for her rageful behavior.

Animal studies seem to support the observation that the rhinencephalic structures are particularly sensitive to d-LSD 25 (Killiam, 1956; Monroe, 1961) while arousal patterns were markedly depressed in the limbic system by chlorpromazine (Killiam, 1956b).

4.1.4 *Electrographic correlations with focal injection of drugs.* A more sophisticated and precise method for studying drug effects on the central nervous system is the instillation of minute amounts of drugs in selected areas of the brain through a chronically implanted micropipette (Heath, 1961; 1965). Detailed behavioral studies utilizing this technique have not been published, except for one describing two patients with epilepsy who also had episodic behavioral disorders (Heath, 1965). This report is particularly important for two reasons. First, a correlation was established between the episodic behavioral disorders and rhinencephalic paroxysmal activity. However, during periods of acting out, with the patient escaping from the ward and running to the roof of the hospital where he threatened suicide because he had been refused a pass to leave the hospital, there was no EEG abnormality. On the other hand, during a period when there was marked septal dysrhythmia, his behavior was characterized by diffuse emotions and disorganized behavior without precise motivation or direction. For example, he drove his fists through a window and struck out recklessly without provocation at hospital personnel. During this episode he had a "glassy stare" and was disoriented. These two brief descriptions by Heath would be differentiated at the phenomenological level in our terms as instinct dyscontrol in the latter and acting out in the former. They could also be differentiated by subcorticograms, but not by routine EEG's. As we will discuss in more detail in Chapter 9, we can also distinguish between the two at the phenomenological and dynamic level: instinct and impulse dyscontrols are primitive, diffuse, explosive acts with undisguised intentions; acting out is a more subtle coordinated act with a disguised intention.

The second contribution of this study (Heath, 1965) was the discovery of marked differences in the response of epileptic patients and schizophrenic patients to acetylcholine (ACH) injection through the micro-cannula system. ACH introduced into the septal region caused high amplitude 18 per second spindling in epileptics, but not in schizophrenics. With the appearance of this activity, there was a shift in the epileptic patient's mood from dysphoria to euphoria, in the schizophrenic there was neither EEG nor behavior changes. This suggested to Heath a basic metabolic difference between the two disorders. However, the epileptic patients Heath described showed episodic behavioral disorders which are often diagnosed as schizophrenia. It would seem that our distinction of two types of schizophrenia—one persistent and chronic, the other intermittent and in some instances epileptoid, is supported by neurophysiologic data.

4.1.5 *Intracranial self-stimulation.* Interest in the technique of intracranial self-stimulation (ICSS) as applied to humans followed the original animal studies of Olds (1954) and Delgado (1954).* Olds found that he could delineate a "pleasure" ("reward" or "start") system paralleling the median forebrain bundle; the lateral hypothalamus being a particularly potent area for eliciting this "pleasure" response. This was also true to a varying extent in other limbic areas. The area that would elicit a "punishment" ("aversive" or "stop") response occurred in the midbrain reticular formation, ventromedial portion of the thala-

---

* For reviews of the animal studies on subcortical stimulation and ablations, see Kaada (1951), McCleary (1965), and Smythies (1966).

mus, medial caudate nucleus, dorsal hippocampus, lateral amygdala, and ventral system of the hypothalamus. Between these two areas there was a large region of mixed response. Olds indicated that electrical stimulation of 35 percent of the brain area is associated with pleasure or "approach" behavior, 5 percent with pain or "avoidance" behavior, and the remaining 60 percent of brain area seemed neutral in this regard. The response appeared similar in most characteristics to the responses of animals working for an external reward or avoiding an external punishment. Olds also felt that he could distinguish with ICSS a separate food-rewarding and sexual-rewarding area (Olds, 1958).

Human studies on ICSS were first reported by Sem-Jacobsen (1960); the only other studies are those reported by Heath and associates (Bishop, 1963; Heath, 1963b). Bishop, reporting on a study of one schizophrenic found that the head of the caudate, septal region, amygdala, intralaminar nuclei of the thalamus, midhypothalamus and posterior hypothalamus all gave reward responses at varying thresholds which, if increased from 25 percent to 100 percent would then elicit an aversive response. Only the septal region gave no aversive response (reward threshold tested from 3.5 milli-amp up to 12.5 milli-amp), while the tegmentum of the mesencephalon elicited an aversive response, even at the lowest possible level of stimulation (0.2 milli-amp). Studies were also reported on two other patients, one with narcolepsy and the other with psychomotor epilepsy and episodic behavioral disorder (Heath, 1963a). In the first patient stimulation to the mesencephalon was alerting but aversive; hippocampal stimulation was mildly rewarding; septal stimulation was most rewarding and also the most alerting. In the latter area the patient subjectively was aware of sexual feelings, as if building up to an orgasm which he could never attain. This led the patient to push the button frequently in an effort to reach this orgastic climax. (The fact that no orgasm occurred may be explained by McLean's studies of sexual response in animals to stimulation in the limbic system [1962a and b]. He pointed out that there seem to be two separate sexual areas, one for erection and one for ejaculation.) Heath's epileptic patient found both septal and mesencephalic stimulation "good," but the latter was not accompanied by sexual thoughts as was the former. In this patient the most aversive area was in the hippocampus. It is obvious from this study, as well as the studies of Sem-Jacobsen (1960, 1968) that self-stimulation might be encouraged by other than straightforward pleasure responses. For example, one of the patients would stimulate at a maximal level because the stimulation elicited the feeling that he was going to recollect an important memory. As the memory was never recalled the patient would frequently push the button to see whether it was possible to accomplish this. From our point of view one of the most interesting findings was that the epileptic patient, during an episodic psychotic reaction manifest by agitation and violent psychotic behavior, instantly became happy and euphoric with stimulation to the septal region. The importance of failure of pleasure emotions in psychotic behavior will be discussed in Chapter 9 and has been the subject of a symposium (Heath, 1964).

In view of the animal studies that show 35 percent of the brain as pleasure-eliciting areas as opposed to 5 percent of the brain that is aversive, it is surprising that epileptic auras are not more often pleasurable. There are two possible explanations. First a question arises whether even in animals there might be motivations other than "pleasure" leading them to rewarding behavior. Second, as pointed out by Bishop (1963), rewarding and aversive responses can be elicited from the same area, the threshold for positive reward being lower than that for aversive behavior. Perhaps in epileptics the excitation exceeds the pleasurable response threshold, and reaches aversive levels.

4.2 STUDIES UTILIZING ACUTE AND SUBACUTE ELECTRODE IMPLANTATIONS

Acute or subacute studies from the surface and depth of the temporal lobes are not only hard to compare with the chronic implant patients because of the limited period of observation but also because in the more acute studies the array of implanted electrodes is limited and precise localization is often not reported. Also, almost all patients studied in this way are epileptics. But the studies remain valuable for us because most had associated episodic dyscontrol or episodic reactions. The investigators using these techniques have consistently noted that seizural activity can take place in subcortical structures without corresponding activity on the cortex. Likewise they report low hippocampal-amygdala convulsive thresholds. They find that stimulation of the deep areas of the temporal lobe sometimes does and other times does not induce seizures that are typical for the individual patient. Other responses reported with stimulation are auras (Chapman, 1954, 1960; Rand, 1964), hallucinations (Chapman, 1954, 1960), euphoria (Delgado, 1954; Chapman, 1954, 1960), amnesia (Rand, 1964) and recollection of past experiences, déjà vu (Rand, 1964) and sexual excitement (Delgado, 1954). Delgado reported that the onset of seizural discharge seems to correlate with the reporting of auras, while Chapman noted that the seizural activity when limited to the amygdala region was correlated with only slight sensory or somato-motor phenomena, whereas if the after-discharge spread to involve the cortical area then typical seizural behavior occurred.

Chapman (1960) studied six epileptics, two with typical psychomotor seizures and four with grand mal seizures and periodic rage reactions. He stimulated the amygdala between the third and sixth post implantation day (before electrocoagulation of the area). In the two subjects with psychomotor epilepsy stimulation reproduced their attacks. In one of the other four subjects the only finding was a brief comment by the patient that "something is different." The remaining three demonstrated automatisms, amnesias, and confusions with stimulation. None repeated their assaultive behavior, nor did they seem to be rageful or angry. In fact they did not even report fear or the dysphoria as reported by Heath (1955b). One patient at times reported a pleasurable response. Chapman also noted that subcortical seizural activity could be present without reflection on the cortex, but reported no consistent relationship between subcortical abnormalities and behavior in his epileptic patients.

The complexity of making mind-brain correlations is detailed by Higgins (1956). An analysis of his data is complicated by a number of factors. First, the patient studied was an 11-year-old boy, and there was no extensive preoperative introspective data supplied. Probably, like most 11-year-olds, he did not give such data. Second, the stimulations occurred in the second to sixth postoperative day and it is obvious that the patient never attained his preoperative pattern of behavior. Third, only the approximate locations of the electrodes were known. Fourth, only the temporal lobe was explored. And, fifth, the period of observation was so short that spontaneous changes in behavior were limited. It is not surprising that the findings were often inconsistent. But the important observation for our present consideration is that certain stimulations produced pleasurable, even sexual sensations in this subject. At times the stimulation seemed to disturb the balance between drive and defense with defensive functions less operative, due either to the increased drive or to a decrease in inhibitory anxiety (e.g., he would express otherwise denied passive, feminine, sexual strivings). Another detailed study by Groethuysen (1957), who recorded from the rhinencephalon during psychiatric interviews, revealed that in a patient with no history of epilepsy but a long history of schizophrenia, forcing the patient to think about an adolescent seduction by her father, culminating in the question "you wanted to kill him, didn't you?," elicited waveform abnormalities from the region of the amygdala followed 11 minutes later by a generalized seizure.

The crucial question then is not clearly answered; that is, how frequently and under what conditions does seizural activity in the limbic system (particularly involving the hippocampal, amygdala and septal regions) correlate with observed behavioral changes? There seems to be some evidence that it can occur in epileptic patients without obvious behavior changes until it spreads to the cortex. Heath believes this is true for epileptic patients if the seizural activity is limited to the hippocampal-amygdala area, but not involving the septal region. On the other hand, psychedelic drug studies suggest a correlation with behavioral changes and paroxysmal hypersynchronous activity limited to the hippocampal-amygdala regions, but these studies were done with schizophrenic, not epileptic patients.

Further data reflecting on this problem is provided by Sherwood (1960), whose subcortical studies have the limitations of being acute and performed while the patient was under anesthesia. He made the following generalizations: patients subject to frequent fits showed paroxysmal activity in diffuse and widespread patterns. Patients suffering from fits as well as episodic psychotic reactions showed localized paroxysmal activity limited to the rhinencephalon and related regions of the temporal cortex. Patients with rare seizures only, but with psychotic episodes that would fit our episodic behavioral disorders, had widespread synchronized paroxysmal activity, predominantly involving the basal frontal cortex and anterior median parts of the temporal lobe, with less conspicuous involvement of the amygdala and hippocampus. He also identified a fourth group of chronic "residual" schizophrenics showing subcortical abnormalities without any consistent pattern or localization. Thus, again we have some evidence that there is a basic neurophysiologic difference between those patients who show the episodic behavioral disorders and those who show more chronic schizophrenic patterns.

4.3 Behavior Changes with Ablations and Cortical Stimulation

In general, unilateral temporal lobectomy, either limited to the temporal cortex or including the anterior portion of rhinencephalic structures underlying the temporal pole, has been successful in alleviating seizures in 50 percent of epileptic patients (Rasmussen, 1958). If significant complicating behavioral disorders are not present, most postoperative behavioral changes are transitory. However, if the deep structure of the temporal lobe are involved, 10 percent of the subjects develop some recent memory impairment, even with a unilateral operation (Walker, 1957). When the lesion and the operation are on the dominant hemisphere there is also some deficit in the patient's ability to retain verbal material. Milner (1959) observes that this deficit is demonstrable preoperatively and only augmented by the operation. In the same way lobectomized patients with lesions on the nondominant side show some impairment of visual recognition, but this never approaches anything like visual agnosia (Milner's discussion, in Baldwin, 1958).

It was during lobectomy operations that Penfield (1941, 1951, 1952, 1954a) made his classic studies of evoked recollections by stimulation of the cortex in the conscious epileptic patient. He summarized 20 years of work in this contribution to the symposium on Brain Mechanisms and Consciousness (1954b). In many areas of the cortex, stimulation elicited little or no response (frontal area) or negatively had an effect only in interfering with ongoing functions (speech area over dominant hemisphere), or elicited only crude sensations and crude motor responses (motor and sensory areas). However, in a relatively well-demarcated area over the superior and lateral surface of the temporal cortex, complex psychic phenomenon were elicited in many of the epileptic patients. Here stimulation evoked vivid recollections of the recent or remote past which included visual and auditory (and apparently concomitant emotional) reenactments as if the past events were going on in the present. The subject usually maintained dual orientation inasmuch as no matter how vivid the experience, he recognized that they were at the moment in the operating room undergoing a surgical procedure. These recollections or memories were not generalizations of experience, but a single experience being relived in all its detail. The same experience was usually elicited from repeated stimulation of the same point, although at times stimulation of the same point might elicit a different but probably related "memory." Although Penfield often refers to these as hallucinations, they were not what the psychiatrist would call hallucinations in that they were recognized as a recollection and not current reality. However, he mentions one patient who, having heard music upon stimulation, was convinced that a radio was playing in the operating room. This experience sounds more like what the psychiatrist would consider a true hallucination. He also mentions that temporal stimulation may alter the patient's current interpretation of his ongoing experience but it is my impression that this is a crude alteration, just as crude, for instance, as the sensory or motor responses elicited by stimulation of the sensory and motor cortex, both being recognized by the individual as outside his volition.

The patient also may have the feeling that what is going on has happened before or that it is strange and absurd. He may seem far off from reality, lonely, or afraid. To Penfield these responses indicated that the temporal cortex was important in the individual's judgment, which depends on comparing present experiences with past recollection, a process we will suggest is deficient in the episodic behavioral disorders (Chapter 9). However, again we would interpret the responses elicited during electrical stimulation of the temporal cortex as crude in comparison with the subtle behavior defects observed clinically.

Many authors have held that serious behavioral disorders associated with psychomotor epilepsy contraindicate temporal lobectomy. However, Hill (1957) concludes that if the operation includes the underlying rhinencephalic structure, that is the uncus, amygdala, and anterior portion of the hippocampus, there will be dramatic improvement in behavior, particularly in a lessening of hostility or episodic aggressive rage reactions. According to his findings typical schizophrenic patients and psychopaths did not do well but only a few patients showed an inverse correlation between seizure and behavioral disturbance. Generally speaking, the patients who showed most improvement in terms of decreased frequency of seizures also showed the most behavioral improvement. In 18 of the 27 patients he found a reduction in aggressiveness and an increased tolerance for frustration, or what he called a "training influence." Accompanying this there might be a turning of rage onto one's self with depression and hypochondriasis which responded readily to electroshock therapy, although in turn this improvement might be accompanied by an increase in paranoid hostile attitudes. In our terms the episodic behavioral reactions were ameliorated but the underlying neurosis and psychosis was either unmasked or perhaps augmented. Of 16 patients, 13 demonstrated increased sexuality, two showed no change in sexual behavior, one became impotent, and one showed an increase of deviant or perverse sexual behavior. There was also a considerable increase in warmth and closeness in social relationships, demonstrated by more concern for others. Eleven of the 27 patients were completely free of seizures and 14 had only occasional seizures. When hysterical symptoms or psychopathy are not influenced by operation, further data would probably indicate that these behavior patterns were learned adaptive patterns; hence one would predict that they would not be influenced by any operation, unless the operation was so radical as to induce pronounced behavioral retardation.

Others too have reported improvement in behavior when the rhinencephalic structures were removed, although the improvement is inconsistent and hard to predict (Hulley, 1955; Morris, 1956). Morris states that in his series there was a 66 percent chance of attaining freedom from disturbing psychiatric complaints, and an 86 percent chance of gaining economic independence. Again, we see evidence for a significant difference between the classic schizophrenic response and the response of patients demonstrating episodic psychotic reactions. Morris reports that the former tend to show little change in personality, while the manic-depressive, the unclassified psychotic and those with personality disorders are likely to show a marked improvement in mood, increased tolerance for others, less irritability, and more interest in their job. Unfortunately, the psychiatric data in most of these reports are too sketchy to ascertain precise recovery rates for those demonstrating what we have defined as the episodic behavioral disorders.

An attempt has been made to improve the behavioral disorders either with or without epilepsy through a bilateral operation, yet avoid the severe defects of the Kluver-Bucy (1937, 1939) syndrome (Scoville, 1957). The literature on this subject has been reviewed by Terzian (1958). In an earlier report Terzian (1955) gave the most valuable detailed information on a dramatic failure in such an attempt. This concerned a patient with psychomotor epilepsy and frequent severe homicidal and suicidal behavior. He was subjected to bilateral temporal lobectomy with complete removal of the temporal lobes anterior to the vein of Labbe, thus the uncus, the anterior part of the hippocampus and the amygdala were removed. The outstanding changes in this patient were the lack of emotions. Although he had previously been quite dependent upon and affectionate towards his mother, he now addressed her as "Madame" and his father as "Sir." When taught later to call them mother and father, this was said without emotion. Everyone was treated with equal indifference, although previously the appearance of doctors, nurses and other people in his environment might have elicited a violent rage reaction with homicidal intent. Only once after the operation did he show any facial expression, and that was when he looked into a mirror. His voice was monotonous without emotional coloring. Other changes were equally dramatic. There was a failure to recognize friends and relatives, a reduction in motor activity, distractability, imitative behavior, and a peculiar difficulty in following any conversation through to completion. However, he could be put back on the track and the conversation reinitiated by giving a stereotyped clue such as stroking one's face as if stroking a mustache. The patient would indiscriminately and superficially inspect all objects in his environment (but would not do this orally as do monkeys). He developed an insatiable appetite, demanding food constantly, bolting it down when it was given to him, and licking his plate voraciously when the food had been consumed. He also showed alexia and developed sexual exhibitionism, as well as an interest in homosexuality, although he never aggressively pressed this interest. There was a severe impairment of memory, disorientation, an obsessive preoccupation with his belongings, and a complete lack of any particular vegetative changes. In essence we see then that the human equivalent of the Kluver-Bucy syndrome in monkeys was obtained. The author states that the patient appeared to be a "dement who could read, articulate letter by letter, but could not understand the meaning of the words; who could write spontaneously only his name; who could speak only in order to satisfy the most urgent needs of his immediate present. He could not remember anything of the past and could make no plans for the future."

Milner (1959) reported that patients showed severe memory impairment after bilateral removal of the hippocampus as far posteriorly as 5½ to 8 cms, behind the temporal pole, including the removal of the amygdala, uncus, and the medial temporal cortex. No new learning was retained. The patient could read an article many times without recognition of familiarity. There was no practice effect in doing jigsaw puzzles, and once a new task was introduced there would be a total amnesia for the immediately preceding one. There was a retrograde amnesia of up to three years' duration. At the same time the I.Q. otherwise was intact, and the attention span as measured by digit recall unimpaired. The fact that this response occurred only if the posterior aspect of the hippocampus was removed in association with other structures suggests that the posterior hippocampus is somehow related to the consolidation of experiences into meaningful memory. This consolidation in the central nervous system may take a surprisingly long time to develop if it is related to the extent of the retrograde amnesia. There appears to be a correlation between these findings of Milner and those reported earlier in the chapter by Lesse (4.1.2) on the spontaneously induced fast activity in the hippocampus when affectively meaningful memories of the distant past were recalled. (For a review of hippocampus and learning see Meissner, 1967).

Other undesirable deficits after bilateral ablations have been reported as extreme childish regressions, exaggerations of catatonic withdrawal, occasional intensification of anger, loss of social consciousness, and increase in sexual deviancy. It is thought by most workers that the usual taming effect of the bilateral ablation with a disappearance of impulsive aggressiveness does not compensate for the rather severe personality deviations induced by bilateral ablations.

However, there are some studies which suggest that bilateral procedures might be devised to avoid such defects. Narabayashi (1963) reports that unilateral or bilateral stereotaxic amygdalectomy resulted in improvements in 85 percent of his subjects, most of his patients manifesting irritability, easy excitability, uncontrollable labile moods, difficulty in concentration, and a tendency to attack people or destroy property. Many of them were children so uncontrollable that they could not be tolerated at school. Bilateral operation was felt necessary in a significant number of the patients to adequately control the extreme behavioral disorder.

During the surgical procedure Narabayashi made subcortical recordings from the amygdala, finding hypersynchronous activity in both the patients showing aggressive behavior and in those showing typical psychomotor epilepsy. He too emphasized that the abnormality cannot be recorded from the cortex or, in his experience, even from sphenoidal electrodes. Fourteen of the subjects had no history of seizures. Reorganizing the data, it is apparent that 10 of these 14 showed either marked or moderate improvement in behavior after bilateral amygdalectomy. A dissenting report by Sawa, mentioned by Terzian (1958), found an intensification of anger and infantilization of emotions and behavior as well as many of the Kluver-Bucy symptoms in his series of bilateral amygdalectomies.

Another technique reported as successful is that of Turner (1963), who bilaterally sectioned the tracts leading from the isthmus of the temporal lobe. This virtually abolished attacks of uncontrolled rage and violence. However, again the chronic psychotic behavioral disturbances were not influenced, e.g., paranoid mental conditions remained. The two positive reports on bilateral operations suggest that with refinement of neurosurgical procedures and psychiatric diagnosis we might develop a successful bilateral operation with minimal postoperative defects but beneficial to the extreme episodic dyscontrol patients.

In conclusion we should mention several reports of behavioral changes with subcortical pathology. Vaillant (1965) describes a woman with a temporal lobe arterio-venous malformation with symptoms of schizophrenia which early in its course was episodic. Zeinan (1958) reports four cases of tumors of the septum pellucidum and adjacent structures which lead to emotional instabiltity and bursts of violence, uncontrolled anger, verbal abusiveness, and homicidal behavior.

4.4 SUMMARY

What kind of generalization can we draw from the data on subcortical studies on the limbic lobe? Smythies (1966) discusses theories on the function of the limbic system in his publication,

"The Neurological Foundations of Psychiatry." He points out that Herrick, in 1933, suggested that the limbic system was a non-specific activator of all stimuli influencing the internal apparatus of general bodily attitude, disposition, and feeling tone; while Kleist in 1934 suggested that the limbic structures were the basis for emotional behavior, attitudes and drives, subserving the search for food and sexual objects. In 1937 Papez involved the limbic system in his now famous circuit which was concerned with the higher elaboration of emotions. Certainly these broad generalizations seem pertinent in the light of more recent studies. Can we say anything more precise on the basis of our recent knowledge? Gloor, as reported by Smythies (1966), suggests that the amygdala is concerned with "motivating reinforcement of behavioral patterns," with the defect produced by lesions resulting in disturbances in the motivating mechanisms necessary for the selection of behavioral patterns appropriate for a given situation. This, if true, is a very meaningful statement for us, because this is precisely one of the faulty mechanisms we identify in episodic dyscontrol (Chapter 9).

More comprehensive generalizations have been proposed by others. Delgado (1954) suggests that the specific sensory system carries information regarding the internal and external stimuli while the reticular formation functions as an arousing and alerting mechanism with the limbic system, concerned with motivation. Olds (1954) suggests that the specific sensory system subserves selection and coding of information; the hippocampus fornix epithalamus, learning and memory; and the amygdala hypothalamic region, motivation. Smythies (1966) suggests that the hippocampus is important in the "laying down of memories"; the amygdala with the hippocampus may determine what memories are laid down; while the reticular system subserves the complex switching in general program organization. The cortex then is a specialized computing subsystem to deal with problems of a higher order of complexity than the subcortical nuclei can manage.

These are high order speculations and generalizations that have to be accepted warily, and they are proposed only tentatively by their advocates. For our purposes it would seem safe to say that the rhinencephalon is intimately associated with emotional behavior and the balance between both painful emergency behavior (fear and rage) and pleasurable emotion (oral, sexual). It must play some role in controlling and integrating these emotions, mediating between the higher cortical functions and the lower diencephalic midbrain functions. The emotional component of behavior, from psychiatric and psychoanalytic observations as well as from some neurophysiologic studies, is obviously important in the realistic interpretation of the environmental situation, in the storing of appropriate information in the form of memories, and in the recollection of past significant experiences. In one way or another these functions are impaired in the episodic dyscontrols and the episodic reactions. We will attempt a more detailed psychodynamic and neurophysiologic synthesis of this data and that presented in the next three chapters in Chapter 9.

5 Epilepsy and Behavioral Disorders

In the preceding chapter we examined the studies of a relatively select group of patients intensively studied with subcortical electrograms. In this and the following two chapters we will examine mind-brain correlations in a large group of subjects. In this chapter, we will select patients with specific EEG abnormalities or typical epileptic symptoms that are associated with excessive neuronal discharges, and look for behavior correlates.

5.1 DEFINITIONS

There is a current attempt to establish a generally acceptable international classification of epilepsy and a strict definition of the EEG manifestations. This as yet has not been accomplished, although a classification of seizures has been proposed (Gastaut, 1964). It is necessary therefore to define some of the terms that will be used in this and subsequent chapters. We will use the term *temporal lobe epilepsy* when patient selections has been based on scalp EEG criteria, indicating temporal lobe abnormalities. We will refer to *psychomotor epilepsy* when the selection of the patient was based primarily on the clinical manifestations of the disorder, demonstrating the triad as described by Lennox (1960) as (1) automatism; (2) subjective psychic seizures; and (3) focal increase in muscle tone, arrest of mentation, stupor states with impaired awareness, and subsequent amnesias. In referring to seizures other than typical grand mal and petit mal epilepsy, we will describe the seizures as well as name them. The word *seizure* will be applied to any stereotyped pattern of behavior that occurs precipitously and is characterized by a disturbance of consciousness and by changes of motor activity and/or mentation. This will be called epilepsy or ictal behavior if it is associated with, or presumably associated with, excessive neuronal discharge within the central nervous system. In the EEG this is seen as wave forms which are clearly observable because of the sudden alteration in frequency and/or amplitude. This activity will be labeled paroxysmal if it occurs intermittently and is sustained for a significant period of time; that is, a minimum of at least one second. In this way we will distinguish between the more sustained yet intermittent bursts of abnormal wave forms, and the isolated hypersynchronous spike or spike and slow wave occurring in patients with a predisposition to seizures. The period when only these isolated wave forms occur or presumably occur will be referred to as the interictal period and the behavior manifest by the subject at that time will be referred to as interictal behavior. Whenever we propose that the episodic behavioral disorders are an ictal phenomenon, that is, correlated with a sustained excessive neuronal discharge somewhere in the central nervous system, but the behavioral change is not a typical seizure, we will refer to the behavior as epileptoid.

5.2 DISCRIMINATING BETWEEN ICTAL AND INTERICTAL BEHAVIOR

The assumption behind the differentiation of epileptic behavior into ictal and nonictal phenomena is that ictal behavior is a reflection of a massive, excessive neuronal discharge within the central nervous system, while prodromal, aura, postictal and interictal behavior, although reflecting disturbed neuronal function, are not the result of this excessive neuronal discharge per se. Subcortical recordings reported in the last chapter reveal that this is a naive and oversimplified assumption. We have seen, for example, that localized excessive neuronal discharge, electroencephalographically characteristic of seizural discharges on the cortex, can occur in the septal-hippocampal-amygdala region in association with symptoms that have previously been considered prodromal, such as mounting irritability, tension, insomnia, or excessive sensitivity. We have also noted in other instances that the onset of the subcortical paroxysmal hypersynchronous activity reflecting this excessive neuronal discharge is correlated with the phenomenon of auras or "warnings" which may or may not be followed by typical seizures. These behavioral responses then should not be called preictal, peri-ictal, or interictal, but, rather, behavior responses due to "partial"or "circumscribed" excessive neuronal discharges.

One of the characteristics of the excessive neuronal discharge is supposedly the relatively short duration of the discharge. Hence, a definition of epilepsy as proposed by Critchley (as reported by Strauss, 1959) is "the periodic appearance of recurring patterns of behavior characterized by *short-lived* disturbances of consciousness and typically accompanied by unrestrained motor activity." However, more refined EEG techniques reveal that sustained behavior disorders can represent a form of status epilepticus; that is, petit mal status or status epilepticus temporalus (Gastaut, 1953b). We cannot then indiscriminately relegate prolonged behavior disturbances to the phenomenon of interictal behavior disorders.

Many of the behavioral disorders of epileptics have been attributed to the postictal period. During this stage neuronal elements are supposedly in a state of "exhaustion," following a period of excessive discharge usually reflected in the EEG not as high amplitude spikes or spike and wave, but by either flat records or high amplitude very slow waves. It was felt that this represented a refractiveness of neurons resulting in a disturbed balance between excitatory and inhibitory systems. This was the explanation for the patient's behavior which was sometimes one of sleep, sometimes one of considerable altered awareness with confusion, and at other times a release of more primitive behavioral patterns. However, we will see that this behavior too can be a manifestation of subcortical circumscribed excessive neuronal discharges.

In evaluating interictal behavior even if a truly interictal state can be established the problem will still be complex. We would like to be able to determine what, if any, behavioral deviations are correlated with the relatively isolated and intermittent excessive neuronal discharges or hypersynchrony, such as the single spike or spike and slow wave which occur in epileptic patients during intervals between the repetitive discharges associated with typical ictal response. We would also like to determine what behavior characteristics differentiate the epileptic with diffuse central nervous system damage from the epileptic patient without diffuse central nervous system involvement. Finally, we would like to be able to discriminate between these behavioral patterns and the learned, reparative, behavioral patterns that develop secondarily as a result of the epileptics' adaptive limitations or as a reaction to society's attitude towards his seizural symptoms. We have learned from our subcortical studies the hopelessness of determining whether the behavioral phenomenon is associated with excessive neuronal discharge on the basis of scalp EEG recordings alone. Activation studies may increase the sensitivity of scalp recordings (see Chapter 7) but they usually indicate only the potentiality for abnormal neuronal discharges, not whether at any given moment such a discharge is taking place.

5.3 DISCRIMINATING BETWEEN ICTAL AND NONICTAL BEHAVIOR

The problem of determining which of the episodic behavioral disorders are epileptoid and which are not is unresolved, and precisely the reason for this monograph. At the extremes of typical grand mal seizures on the one hand and the complex acting out of a psychoanalytic patient on the other, such differentiation is not difficult. But as Lennox (1960) states, there is a broad grey area in which it is impossible to be sure. As a clinician Lennox makes a distinction on the basis of the following criteria: did the change of behavior come abruptly without obvious cause or explanation? Did the period of disturbed behavior end equally abruptly? Did the person who suffered the attack have only fragmentary or no knowledge of what transpired? Is there a family or personal history of more typical epileptic seizures? Is there an abnormal EEG? Did the patient respond to anticonvulsant medication? If the answers to these questions are affirmative in each instance, Lennox feels it strongly suggests epilepsy. Yet we have already presented data and will present even more later which convincingly demonstrate that these criteria singly or in combination do not give absolute assurance in making the diagnosis. We will propose other criteria for the differentiation at the end of Chapter 10.

In our discussion of subcortical recordings we pointed out that intermittent hypersynchronous activity in the rhinencephalic structures was correlated with disturbed behavior in a significant number of patients. If the hypersynchronous activity is paroxysmal and of sufficient duration, the behavior deviations are even more dramatic. We have also pointed out that this may or may not be reflected in scalp recordings, but if it is, the scalp abnormalities are likely to be localized in the temporal region. This is not surprising in view of the close proximity and demonstrated connection between the temporal cortex and the immediately underlying rhinencephalic structures. These observations are congruent with others, suggesting that those individuals with temporal lobe abnormalities also demonstrate a high incidence of interictal behavior disturbances. In fact, it has been stated that the study of psychomotor epilepsy has resulted in a truly multidisciplinary meeting place involving the neurologist, neurosurgeon, psychiatrist, psychologist, electroencephalographer, neurophysiologist, neuroanatomist, and most recently, the biochemist (Baldwin, 1958). There have been a number of symposia devoted to this subject, including Colloquiums in Marseilles in 1952, 1954, and 1956, as well as a follow-up sponsored by the National Institutes of Health in Washington in 1958 (Dongier, 1959; Baldwin, 1958). Reviews of the subject, particularly on the relationship between temporal lobe epilepsy and the behavioral disorders, have also been published (Bingley, 1958; DeHaas, 1958; Cazzullo, 1959) so that the literature will only be selectively considered here, limited to data pertinent to the discussion of episodic dyscontrol and episodic reactions. This particular orientation was also used in a concise review by Hans Strauss (1959).

What is meant when it is said that temporal lobe epilepsy is frequently correlated with behavioral disturbances? Behavioral disturbances do not usually refer to the ictal behavior itself, many aspects of which are similar to symptoms found in nonepileptic behavioral disorders. The ictal phenomena in psychomotor or temporal lobe epilepsy are much more complex and variable and much less stereotyped and repeatable than the seizures of grand mal or petit mal (Gibbs, 1948), so that the distinction between ictal and nonictal behavior is more difficult. A condensation of symptoms based on the original classification of Gastaut, as modified by Lennox (1960) follows:

I. Sensorial symptoms
   A. From external stimuli: respiratory, olfactory, auditory, vertiginous, visual, somatesthetic
   B. Involving autonomic symptoms; abnormal sensations of the mouth, pharynx, epigastrium, abdomen, genitals, precordium; with or without nausea, sense of asphyxia, palpitations, sensations of heat or cold, hunger or thirst; impulse to urinate or defecate

II. Mental symptoms
   A. Changes in consciousness, ranging from normal to complete loss
   B. Perceptive manifestations: unusual clearness; illusions with macropsia, microacusia, macroacusia, déjà vu, incoherence, strangeness, depersonalization, etc.; hallucinations, always complex and dynamic, suggestive of events in a dream
   C. Ideational manifestations; sudden blocking of thought, or compulsive thinking; panoramic memory
   D. Affective manifestations: fear, sadness, anger, joy

III. Motor symptoms
   A. Related to external stimuli
      1. Abnormal simple movements

      (a) Clonic

      (b) Tonic; invariably hypertonic, resulting in deviation forward, backward, or to one side, or rotation of head or trunk

   2. Complex movements

      (a) Orientation and investigation

      (b) Walking or flight; procursive epilepsy

      (c) Gestures in response to impressions, such as scratching of the nose, placing the hand on head or stomach

      (d) Gestures of a confusional state, such as rubbing the body, arranging clothes, or coordinated occupational activity

B. Autonomic manifestations

   1. Respiratory, with hyperpnea or apnea

   2. Circulatory, vasomotor, cardiac

   3. Digestive, masticatory, salivatory, with or without discharge of urine, gas, feces

   4. Pupillary, mainly dilation

C. Movement involving speech

   1. Aphasic manifestations

   2. Expression of sensations such as "feel sick," "I am afraid"

   3. Incorrect, inappropriate speech or flow of words

It is obvious that many of these symptoms are closely related to those seen in the neurotic, psychosomatic, or psychotic patients without epilepsy. Despite this, in the more typical cases of psychomotor epilepsy both the physician and patient can clearly distinguish the seizures from other disordered behavior. What makes this distinction possible? One is the precipitous onset and equally precipitous remission of such symptoms. The other is a subjective sense of "drivenness," or alien quality experienced by the person with psychomotor seizures. They describe the experience as an "attack" or "spell." These patients are often aware of the illusory or unreal quality of the experience, even during the episode itself ("mental dyplopia" of Jackson). To the trained observer there is a qualitative difference between the hallucinations, depersonalizations, or illusions experienced during a psychomotor attack, and those which occur in acute schizophrenia. In the former these symptoms are simple or fragmentary. They are brief, repetitive, and have a primitive quality with comparatively little conceptual elaboration. The episodes are generally associated with altered awareness, although seldom complete amnesia. The sensory, motor, and autonomic manifestations have a stereotyped quality which is also true of the fragmentary speech that may occur during such seizures. In discussing the behavioral disorders associated with temporal lobe epilepsy we will propose that at least some of the supposed nonictal behavioral disturbances in temporal lobe epilepsy, particularly those with precipitous onset and remission are ictal phenomena. Subcortical studies seem to support such an interpretation. We will also assume that an ictal phenomenon does not have to be of short duration but can persist for hours, weeks, even months, and what indicates that it is ictal is this precipitous onset and equally abrupt remission, whatever the duration (see Patients 019 and 021).

5.4 CHRONIC BEHAVIORAL DEVIATIONS: THE EPILEPTIC PERSONALITY

In our systematic evaluation of the association of personality disorders with epilepsy it will be simplest first to investigate the chronic or persisting personality deviations, leaving until later the more episodic, hence possibly ictal disturbance. This leads directly into the subject of the so-called "epileptic personality," which has been characterized as poverty of ideas, one-track mind, stubbornness, combativeness, introversion, preoccupation with somatic symptoms and perseveration. Speech is generally described as slow and marked by circumstantiality. Religious ideas seem to be cultivated. These individuals are often irritable and depressed. They supposedly manifest narrow-mindedness and a selfishness that strains all of their interpersonal relationships. To quote Schorsch (1960): "Stubbornness and abnormal suggestibility, quite marked respect for authority and a need for obtrusive familiarity without any sense for distance, devout at times with sugar-coated manners, solemn formality, exaggerated politeness towards others, and the uninhibited use of foul language as well as outbursts of reckless brutality, arrogance and submissiveness" characterizes the epileptic personality.

Most of these descriptions originate with the reports of nineteenth-century German psychiatrists whose observations were made on institutionalized epileptic subjects. Lennox (1960) feels that this selection of patients and the lack of effective therapy during this period have given a distorted view of the relationship between personality deviations and epilepsy. His findings in a modern neurologic practice is that somewhat less than 50 percent of the epileptics show character deviations which he lists in order of frequency as follows: irritability, depression, overactivity, emotional instability, seclusiveness, hesitancy, egotism, and hypersensitivity. There are two classic descriptions of famous epileptics, one in the essay by Freud on "Dostoevski and Parricide" (Freud, vol. XXI) in which he describes the contradictory personality of the epileptic due to the struggle between conscience mechanisms and the threat of repetitive uncontrolled acts. The other famous epileptic with episodic dyscontrol was supposedly Van Gogh, and his illness was discussed by Gastaut (1956). Strauss (1959) provides one of the best psychiatrically oriented discussions of this subject in Chapter 54 of *The Handbook of Psychiatry*. He points out that there are two diverse implications in the concept of the epileptic personality. One, represented by the German school of Minkowsky, Kretschmer, and Mauz, implied that there was a common hereditary predisposition for both seizures and a particular personality development. The second point of view just describes phenomenologically the association between certain character traits and epilepsy without a specific hypothesis as to the interrelationship between the two.

Two recent mongraphs systematically investigate this problem. Guerrant (1962) dismisses previous clinical studies as reflecting fads or clinical biases that could be historically related to the development of psychiatry at the time. Thus, he interprets the pre-1900 era as one that emphasized the concept of "deterioration"; the 1900–1930 era as one that emphasized the "epileptic character"; 1930–1948 as the era when the epileptic was seen as "normal"; and finally since 1948 the period which has emphasized the deviant personality peculiarly related to psychomotor epilepsy. Although there may be an element of truth in what he says, this explanation applies to the interpretation of the clinical observations but neglects the observations themselves. On the other hand, Delay (1958) points out that regardless of the theoretical orientation, almost all clinicians and psychologists have agreed that epileptics usually show "explosive viscosity and egocentricity," but beyond that there is little agreement.

Guerrant's study included one group of temporal lobe epileptics, a second of ideopathic grand mal epileptics, and a third group of patients with a variety of chronic medical illnesses. Each group numbered 25 to 30, and all were selected from a university outpatient clinic. He concluded that psychomotor epileptics (temporal lobe epileptics by our definition) did not display a greater incidence of functional psychiatric disorders than did grand mal or nonepileptic patients. However, 90 percent of the patients in all three groups showed significant "functional" psychiatric disorders. Two criticisms of the study can be made. Although the experimental design is rigorous, the established criteria for selection of groups seriously limits the clinical value of the findings. For example, the psychomotor group was limited to patients with seizures that lasted no longer than five minutes; without sensory, motor, or coordination dysfunctions on neurological examinations; without EEG abnormalities in any area other than temporal lobes; and without x-ray evidence of intracranial abnormalities. It is obvious then that most of the problem cases that the clinician deals with were excluded from this series. At the same time, for reasons that are unclear, there was an extremely high incidence of minor psychological deviations, such as anxiety, fatigue, depression, irritability, impulsiveness, social withdrawal, stubbornness, social insensitivity, anger, and egocentricity, in all of the patients, even the nonpsychiatric group. The second criticism of the study is that although he collected considerable information the data were superficially evaluated. For example, the psychiatric ratings were based on only one or two hour interviews, and the data were recorded on rating scales and then converted for a subsequent statistical analysis to a dichotomous score of either normal or exceeding normal. Likewise, a number of psychological tests, including the Bender-Gestalt, Draw-a-Person, memory span for objects, Wechsler memory scale, Kent EGY scale, the CVS, the MMPI, and Rorschach tests were utilized; but usually the tests were merely evaluated for signs of "organicity" without any other possible breakdowns in the data. For instance, the Rorschach data were rated only on Piotrowski's organic signs plus a global evaluation of the extent of psychopathology; this unfortunately does not allow for a comparison between Guerrant's data and the more detailed analysis by Delay (1958).

However, some of his suggestive correlations confirm previous studies. Clinical evaluation did show that the grand mal group had memory difficulty and psychomotor patients were egocentric. The epileptic patients, in general, showed impaired attention and concentration, slowed speech, lability of affect, and a tenaciousness of ideas, although psychological data did not support these clinical observations. They were slightly more disturbed than the chronically ill group, and within the epileptic groups those with psychomotor epilepsy demonstrated more organic signs. In some ways the chronically ill group was more neurotic, the grand mal group showed more personality disorders, and the psychomotor epileptics fell somewhere in between, except that in this group psychotic reactions were more likely to occur. Guerrant found (and this is supported by the report of Milner [1959]), that there was some difficulty in tests of immediate recall among epileptic patients. In ratings on the level of social adaptation, epileptics showed serious difficulties in nearly all important interpersonal contacts, including those with spouse, parents, siblings, and employer. Guerrant implied that this reflected the attitude of society towards individuals with seizures, but in view of Delay's findings one must consider the alternative possibility that the epileptic personality alienates those closest to them.

Delay (1958) studied 50 epileptics with a much broader range of symptoms and etiologic mechanisms. Twelve of the 50 had severe personality disorders similar to the episodic behavioral disorders described herein. They showed marked impulsivity with outbursts of rage and aggressiveness, as well as intense depressive reactions accompanied by suicidal attempts. Seventeen other patients had milder disturbances of a similar type, and 21 patients were considered "normal." In this sense the group composition was consistent with the clinical observation of Lennox in that half of Delay's epileptic patients also had relatively normal personalities. Delay concluded that epileptics did show personality deviations, although temporal lobe epileptics were only slightly more likely to show severe personality disorders than the other epileptics. In fact, such personality deviations were even more likely to occur in what she called "symptomatic epilepsy." Sixty-five percent of the patients showed Piotrowski's organic signs, which Delay felt reflected an organic component, independent of the etiology and localization of the excessive neuronal discharge. The epileptics showed a reduction in creative intellectual productivity both in terms of quantity and quality; a reduction in imaginative capacity; and ideational perseveration with a relative awareness of this incapacity and consequent lack of confidence in their abilities. Of course these traits are common to many organic syndromes with or without seizures. Ross, as quoted by Delay, expresses the relationship between organic signs and epilepsy as follows: "epileptics are more neurotic than organic patients and more organic than neurotic patients."

A second dimension Delay identified as specific for epileptics was that these patients could be grouped around two opposite poles; one labeled coarctative, where the individuals are described as rigid, conventional, cold, calculating, pedantic, and meticulous. When these patients do show aggressiveness, it is deliberate and sadistic, but they do tend to make a more satisfactory social adjustment and are often not considered to have personality disturbances. The opposite pole was labeled extratensive. This group are described as passionate and forceful with live affectivity, openly expressed hostility, and spontaneous im-

pulsive aggression. They make a poor social adjustment. The coarctative group was commonly seen in the ideopathic epileptics
while the extratensive group was more common in the traumatic
and psychomotor group. Delay admits the possibility that these
extremes in character structure may be related to the site of abnormal central nervous system activity and thus have a neurophysiologic explanation, but suggests a dynamic alternative: that
the epileptic attempts to control his impulsiveness by constriction
of his personality. Thus we can identify two groups, those who
succeeded in the secondary control mechanisms by developing a
coarctative personality; and those who have failed in this defensive maneuver and maintained the explosive labile personality.

Szondi, as reported by Delay, came to a similar conclusion in
suggesting that the "gluey viscous" affectivity represented a safety
device in view of the threatening emotional instability and in
this sense is a defensive maneuver to avoid murderous impulses.
A similar thought is expressed in Freud's description of Dostoevski: "the contradiction is resolved by the realization that Dostoevski's very strong destructive instinct, which might easily have
made him a criminal, was in his actual life directed mainly
against his own person and thus found expression as masochism
and a sense of guilt . . . Thus in little things he was a sadist towards others and in bigger things a sadist towards himself, in fact
a masochist—that is to say, the mildest, kindest, most helpful person possible" (Freud, vol. XXI). It is likely that there is an interplay between the focus of an excessive neuronal discharge and the
dynamic mechanisms that protect the individual against the behavioral consequences of excessive neuronal discharge. We will
discuss this in more detail in Chapter 10, but our proposal is that
if such a discharge involves rhinencephalic structures, the more
likely will the behavioral response be significantly influenced by
intense affects; precisely because these affects are intense, defense
mechanisms based on constriction of the personality are less effective.

Of the 70 patients discussed in detail in Chapter 8, 19 had an
unquestionable history of typical epileptic seizures and treatment with anticonvulsants. Six patients had EEG abnormalities

of the bilateral paroxysmal slow variety elicited by activation, twelve had focal temporal abnormalities and one had typical 3 per second bilateral synchronous spike waves. Twelve of the 19 had predominantly grand mal seizures, six had predominantly psychomotor seizures and one had petit mal attacks (see Table 8). All had significant emotional problems, enough so that they required psychiatric hospitalization, at least for diagnostic purposes. Sixteen of the 19 patients had a full psychological test battery. Most showed significant evidence of anxiety and depression on this evaluation, but it was not greater than that shown by the total group of 70 patients. What is significant is that only five had evidence of an organic brain syndrome while nine had evidence of "schizophrenic thinking" and 14 had evidence of paranoid thinking. These latter two findings will be referred to in the discussion of Slater's (1955, 1965) observations that schizophrenia, particularly paranoid schizophrenia, often appears as a delayed complication of epilepsy (5.6). Ten of the 16 subjects tested had definite evidence for obsessional control but only rarely was this the extreme type noted by Delay (1958) as coarctative. The following patients seem to fit Delay's personality description of epileptics.

Patient F223 had been seen off and on in the psychiatric outpatient department over a three-year period with a chief complaint of forgetfulness, inability to concentrate, daydreaming, clumsiness, inferiority feelings, tiredness, sleepiness, sweating of his hands, and occasional insomnia and nightmares. During his childhood he and his family had been prisoners in a Nazi concentration camp; both parents were killed there, and the patient, when released, was hospitalized for two years to recuperate. He had two types of seizures. One, occurring during childhood, seemed to be rather typical petit mal, that is, momentary lapses of consciousness; the other was a more prolonged episode lasting from 10 to 30 seconds when he was aware of what was going on but could not respond in any way.

He described his life as though it was a drab, dull existence. He was preoccupied with a menial job far below his

intellectual capabilities, had few friends, and no close heterosexual relationships. For our present purpose what is important is the psychologist's evaluation, which was summarized by saying, "Mr. —— has even better intelligence
than his rating on the test shows. There is no evidence of
organic impairment. He seems to be a compulsive, meticulous, pedantic person who tries to avoid all emotional en-
tanglements."

Patient F247 is said by the psychologist to discharge her
hostility in a childish fussiness about detail and a negative
arbitrariness. It was also noted that this patient showed evidence of a brain syndrome, paranoid ideation, and schizophrenic disorganization of thinking. However, she had been
hospitalized for diagnostic evaluation because of her seizures
and accompanying depression. Her seizures were typically
grand mal and poorly controlled by anticonvulsants. Several
times recently she had suddenly begun screaming and yelling
at herself in a self-derogatory way but there had never been
any aggressiveness or acting on impulses.

Patient F271 was reported by the psychologist to be per-
fectionistic in trying to meet the expectations of others and
self-critical to the extent that her ability to express herself
verbally was completely paralyzed. She was noted as a hyper-
sensitive person, "pollyannaish" in her outlook. It is probably significant that the psychologist reported that, despite
her perfectionism, she appeared to be basically an impulsive
rather than a compulsive person. Her social adjustment reflected this with very long periods of control, depression,
and spells of ataxia and uncoordination. These alternate
with periods of instinctual and impulsive acts of an extremely aggressive nature during which time she becomes
either homicidal or suicidal.

Two of these three patients seemed to represent the polar extremes reported by Delay (1958). That is, F223 would be the coarctative individual with obsessional controls of his impulsivity
or what we have designated episodic inhibitory behavior, while

patient F271 at least periodically showed episodic dyscontrol or disinhibitory behavior. Patient F247 would fall somewhere between these two extremes. It is important to note the interplay between the basic personality structure and the type of episodic behavior.

In analyzing the group of patients who had definite evidence of seizures, it is surprising to discover that only five of the sixteen revealed evidence on psychological evaluation of impulsive behavior, although clinically three gave evidence of instinct dyscontrol, one of impulse dyscontrol, and two of acting out. Five others were diagnosed as showing seizure dyscontrol. Inasmuch as the frequency of instinct dyscontrol, impulse dyscontrol and acting out is considerably less in this group than in the nonepileptics with activated EEG abnormalities, it would seem that seizures protect against other forms of episodic dyscontrol to some degree. This is further confirmed by the fact that, if one would add together the total number of seizure dyscontrols and those of instinct, impulse, and acting-out dyscontrol, the frequency of episodic dyscontrol would be about the same in the epileptic group as in the nonepileptic group. This may explain why some observers have reported no greater or even less tendency for epileptic patients to show aggressive behavior, a point discussed further (6.1.2).

5.5   EPILEPSY AND EPISODIC BEHAVIORAL DEVIATIONS

We cannot make a definitive correlation between the EEG and behavior until two basic questions are answered: what are the neurophysiologic and biochemical mechanisms underlying the excessive neuronal discharge and do scalp EEG recordings indicate the primary focus of this excessive neuronal discharge? For example, does a focal temporal spike indicate a superficial cortical irritability with a relatively limited focus of hyperexcitability, or does it represent the cortical expression of a more widespread subcortical hypersynchronous activity involving rhinencephalic or diencephalic structures? As we still cannot make a reliable inference as to the primary focus on the basis of our EEG findings, nor do we fully understand the biochemistry of the excessive neuronal discharge, it is unlikely that we will find a one-to-one correlation between the clinical EEG and behavioral deviations.

However, two questions which are answerable with our present techniques of statistical analysis are the following: is the incidence of behavioral abnormalities higher in the epileptic than in the nonepileptic population and is any particular group of epileptics more likely than others to show these behavioral abnormalities? We have already reported conflicting data regarding the presence of personality deviations in the psychomotor epileptics as compared with normal persons or other epileptics. Also, there is considerable discrepancy in reports of the prevalence of episodic behavioral disorders among patients with various convulsive patterns. For example, contrary to the 50 percent figure reported by Lennox (1960) and Delay (1958), DeHaas (1958) in his group of over 1,100 epileptics could find only five percent who showed significant behavioral deviations. Generally, the estimates of behavioral disorders in psychomotor epileptics vary between 30–60 percent (Lennox, 1960; Gastaut, 1953; Dongier, 1956; Gibbs, 1951), but several studies suggest much higher incidence (Ervin, 1955; Treffert, 1964). Obviously such discrepancy must reflect either overt or covert variations in sampling, and differences in defining epilepsy or defining behavioral disorders. Although it is important for us to try to establish the prevalence of behavioral disorders with epilepsy, our immediate interest is to scrutinize epileptic patients who do show behavioral disorders to see whether these fit our description of episodic dyscontrol or episodic reactions.

A related question is whether the episodic disorders, when they do occur, are truly an ictal phenomenon, that is, associated with excessive neuronal discharges. The evidence overwhelmingly supports the fact that many of these episodic disorders are ictal, although not recognized as that. We have already seen that what we call impulse dyscontrol, characterized by a long period of mounting tension and irritability before the dyscontrol act itself, has many of the characteristics of what has heretofore been called an epileptic prodromal (4.1.2). From our subcortical studies we have seen that it is more likely that this is a partial or limited epilepsy, with the excessive neuronal discharge limited to rhinencephalic structures. We will see later how many explosive rage or fear reactions are probably ictal manifestations. We will document evidence for aggressive acts characteristic of instinct dyscontrol and impulse dyscontrol being ictal phenomena and not just postseizural confusional behavior or interictal disturbances of behavior. In fact, it is not hard to identify the postseizural disinhibitions and distinguish them from ictal aggressions. The former disorders do not present a social problem, because such responses are usually poorly coordinated, diffusely directed acts of relatively short duration. They are accompanied by such extreme impairment of consciousness that the acts are ineffectual, in that the primitive homicidal, suicidal, or sexual intentions are not successfully completed. However, it will be our contention that even some of the higher hierarchial levels of episodic dyscontrol, that is, those which are socially effective in terms of their homicidal, suicidal, or sexual intent, are also epileptoid phenomena directly related to undetected excessive neuronal discharges in the central nervous system.

As the typical epileptic patient demonstrates a propensity for excessive neuronal discharges, it is reasonable to look for evidence that such atypical epileptoid phenomena occur frequently among this group. Undoubtedly some of the episodic disorders and episodic reactions are related to this excessive neuronal discharge and some are not. As we cannot easily detect the excessive neuronal discharge on the routine scalp EEG, it is not possible to use this criteria as a definitive diagnostic aid. What we have to establish is a phenomenological symptomatic distinction between the epileptoid and the motivated episodic dyscontrol. This has obvious therapeutic implications in the prevention and treatment of the episodic reactions. As clinicians faced with treating individual patients, we are not generally concerned with the frequency that such epileptoid disorders occur in the general population, but with the fact that we have such a patient in our office at the moment and we have to do something for him. If it is primarily an ictal phenomenon what we do about it will be quite different than if it is primarily a motivated behavioral pattern. (Jonas, 1965). These issues will be discussed further in Chapters 9 and 10.

5.5.1 *EEG recordings during episodic reactions.* Correlations between scalp EEG and episodic behavioral disturbances will depend upon how meticulous both the EEG and psychologic data have been collected. We should have at least one EEG recording prior to the acute behavioral disturbance, one or more during the height of this disturbance and several after the disturbance has remitted. The problems of completing an accurate EEG recording during the height of disturbed behavior makes this a formidable task perhaps now solvable by the use of telemetry. As far as I know, there have been only two such studies on an extended series of patients reported in the literature (Landolt, 1958, and Dongier, 1959). Landolt divided 107 epileptics into four categories distinguished on the basis of characteristic EEG pattern, and each characteristic pattern seemed to correlate with a specific behavioral change. His classification is as follows:

I. Post-paroxysmal twilight states. In this group of patients EEG recordings reveal diffuse delta-theta dysrhythmias over both cerebral hemispheres. The episodes often follow seizures. There is a decrease in consciousness with a response to simple primitive stimuli, but not to complex ones. There is also confusion, slowness, as well as aggressiveness if the patient is forceably restrained. There can be yelling, running, and other obvious defensive reactions. The behavior disturbances tend to recede as the awareness increases. From his brief description it seems obvious that if dyscontrol acts occur during this post-paroxysmal twilight state, they tend to be low in our hierarchial level; that is, either seizural or instinctual acts.

Patient S228 is a fourteen-year-old boy who has had grand mal epilepsy since the age of eight months, the attacks most often occurring at night. When they do occur during the day usually they are associated with extremely aggressive outbursts. Anticonvulsant medication never completely controlled the attacks, the minimum being one per week. Because of the behavioral problems, he had been followed in the outpatient psychiatric clinic for two years prior to his admission, which was precipitated by the following episode. The father found the patient having a seizure. When his father tried to loosen his belt, the boy suddenly jumped up, threw his father against the wall, began beating him, and indiscriminately breaking up furniture. He desisted only when interrupted by another seizure and had three more grand mal seizures that day. The episode was so frightening to the family that they decided on hospitalization. He had been restless and agitated for the previous several months, and considerably upset by incestuous thoughts regarding his mother as well as guilt regarding masturbation. In the hospital, seizures followed by aggressive instinct dyscontrol became so frequent and so frightening to the personnel that it was necessary to transfer the patient to maximum security ward at the state hospital. Sometimes these episodes were characterized by frantic escape attempts rather than aggressive attacks. Several EEG's were not significant except for moderate amplitude slow waves noted diffusely and some build-up with a rapid return to normal during hyperventilation. Chloralose activation was somewhat unusual in this patient in that it elicited a positive response of a high amplitude synchronous paroxysmal slow wave with posterior, rather than the usual anterior predominance.

Psychological evaluation at the time of his admission to the hospital revealed not only definite signs of "organicity," such as perseveration, confabulation, and stimulus-bound perceptions, but also an extremely infantile personality with markedly autistic thinking and poorly organized paranoid feelings.

At the time of follow-up he had been out of the hospital for two years, his seizures finally brought under control by anticonvulsants. The patient is now working and plans to go to college.

II. Petit mal status. In this condition the EEG is accompanied by continuous bilateral synchronous spike and wave complexes with more variation in wave forms and amplitudes than one sees in the typical petit mal attack. There is an obvious disturbance in consciousness with slowed thinking, limited perception, a tendency towards mental and verbal perseveration and a general lack of initiative. There is an increase in reaction time, disorientation, and faulty motor performance. Although habitual activities may be performed correctly, they usually are performed at the wrong time or in unsuitable situations. The attacks can be precipitated by an unexpected or alarming stimulus, even such things as suddenly being called upon to perform in class, and they can be temporarily interrupted or permanently terminated by external stimuli, calling of name, and so on. For these reasons they are often misdiagnosed as hysterical reactions. In our nosology these reactions would be characteristic of what we have called *episodic inhibition*.

If Dongier (1959) is correct, this type of response would only be found in children, and at least this was true of our small series. None of the 70 adult patients seemed to display this syndrome. In fact, only one of the 16 children fit this category, although to have been absolutely certain we would have had to have had an EEG during the episode itself.

The patient 407 is an eleven-year-old boy whose baseline EEG was normal, but after alpha chloralose activation, he showed occasional bursts of high amplitude rhythmic 3 to 4 per second activity with low amplitude sharp forms. This was bilaterally synchronous and diffuse, but showed an anterior predominance. Since the age of three and a half he had suffered from a number of phobias and hypochondriacal preoccupations, but the outstanding problem prior to hospitalization was difficulty with school work. He was apathetic, a poor reader, unable to concentrate or sustain his attention, and noted to suddenly "stare off into space." He was described as shy and retiring, preferring the company of adults rather than peers and "unable to fight back." This passivity was striking in view of the findings on projective tests, namely that in his fantasy life he was constantly occupied with sadistic, homicidal violence directed towards his environment, particularly his parents. There was also evidence for both organic and schizophrenic thought disorder.

III. Productive psychotic episodes. In these instances, although the EEG between episodes may show diverse abnormalities, according to Landolt (1958), during the attack itself there is a "normalization" sometimes forced by antiepileptic medication. The clinical features are diverse; the patient may be restless, continuously excited, and in constant motion with flight of ideas, inability to concentrate, and distractability. In the past this syndrome has been called *epileptic mania*. There may be hallucinations, illusions, delusions, and compulsive acts. Dysphoric feelings, particularly intense fears such as the fear of dying, can accompany this syndrome. Instead of being apathetic these patients are impulsive with intense mood swings. One important feature is that these individuals often recognize the morbidity of their behavior even during the episode itself. Unlike the two previous conditions, which are associated with relatively complete amnesia, there is little or no amnesia with these attacks. The amnesias that do occur are more related to psychotic preoccupations or limited apperceptions due to intense affects. Generally there is a complete absence of epileptic seizures during these episodes. Landolt states that the EEG abnormalities seen between attacks are often, but not always, associated with focal discharges over the temporal lobe. Landolt feels that there is a true normalization of the EEG during the episodic reactions, while others (Dongier, 1959) suggest that this may be a spurious normalization; that is, during the acutely disturbed period all one gets is an artifact record, unlikely to reveal focal abnormalities. In support of this idea of true normalization is the absence of typical epileptic seizures during psychotic periods. As Landolt says, "there would seem to be epileptics who must have a pathological EEG in order to be mentally sane." In his discussion of this issue he sites a number of investigators who support this view.

Dongier reports that there is a group of patients with catatonic or hebephrenic symptomatology who would fall in this EEG category. Although nine of our sixteen epileptics who had psychological tests that showed evidence of schizophrenic thought disorder, only two presented clinical evidence for this (S202 and F213), and only F213 was a clear cut example of the combination of schizophrenia and epilepsy. It is clear, then, that our patients with overt seizures and focal EEG's were less likely to show the secondary symptoms of schizophrenia, than were those without typical epilepsy.

Patient F213 is the only epileptic who received a primary diagnosis of schizophrenia. Since the age of eight months this nineteen-year-old girl has had grand mal and petit mal seizures. Until recently they were well controlled by medication. Development was normal, but it was reported that she was a nail biter and enuretic until age eight. She was always shy and retiring, daydreamed a lot, had very few friends, and felt that those she did have were talking and laughing about her behind her back. Four months before hospitalization the patient became restless and complained of insomnia. One month before hospitalization she ignored her nineteenth birthday, expressing a number of fears regarding "getting old." She also began having auditory and visual hallucinations and bizarre sexual preoccupation that a boy in a black cape was going to be her lover. One week before hospitalization she was raped, although at first both her family and police thought this was a psychotic fantasy. Medical examination confirmed the rape, however, and since that time the patient had frequent episodes of acute abdominal pain during which she would double up, sweat profusely, shake with anger, and then burst into paroxysms of sobbing.

Upon admission to hospital her speech was disconnected and incoherent, her emotional response either bland or inappropriately silly. Three EEG's during this period revealed not only irregular mixed frequencies with excess of slow and fast activity, but on two occasions left anterior and mid-temporal spike and sharp waves and on the third a similar focal abnormality this time limited to the left posterior temporal region.

At the time of follow-up she had been continuously hospitalized for four years. During the first year her condition fluctuated widely from regressed disorganized behavior to rather apathetic passive cooperativeness. She had twelve grand mal seizures during that period. Following treatment with ECT, phenothiazines, and anticonvulsants her behavior gradually improved so that at the time of follow-up she had had no seizures for one year and no hallucinations for the preceding eight months. She was on a convalescent ward, making frequent home visits and anticipating discharge in the near future. At that time she was receiving thioridazine (Mellaril) 50 mg. t.i.d. diphenylhydantoin (Dilantin) 0.1 gm. q.i.d. She remained emotionally flat, childish, apathetic. It is noted by hospital personnel that she cannot sustain any interest or follow through with any long-term plans. There was no indication in this patient of an inverse relationship between her seizures and her psychosis.

Although as previously mentioned, nine of the 16 epileptics showed evidence for schizophrenic thought disorder on psychological testing, only one other patient was even seriously considered to be a schizophrenic on clinical grounds, and this diagnosis was ultimately discarded.

Patient S202 is listed in the present diagnostic schema as an example of instinct dyscontrol. Psychological testing revealed that under stress the patient's thinking became loose and her perception distorted. She had an intense desire for a symbiotic relationship as well as wish-fulfilling autistic preoccupations. However, all of this was dominated by emotional lability and basic hysterical character traits. She was hospitalized because of episodes of confusion with partial amnesias during which time she would misidentify people, thinking they were her parents, and then begin attacking them, becoming even more belligerent when restrained. Sometimes these outbursts were precipitated by visual and auditory hallucinations with voices telling her to be aggressive or to act out sexually. However, since these episodes lasted only for a few minutes or at most several hours, she was considered as an example of episodic dyscontrol rather than of episodic psychotic reaction.

It is probably significant then that, according to our classification, only one epileptic patient, F213, would have been diagnosed as schizophrenic, one as having a psychotic depression (S239), and one as having a chronic brain syndrome (F227). Thus, only three of the 19 patients with seizures could be considered psychotic. In the past, six other patients would probably have been considered psychotic, largely because of the deficiencies in the official nomenclature. Instead, under our new classification, three of these patients were labeled with instinct dyscontrol, one with impulse dyscontrol, and two with acting out dyscontrol, because the alleged psychotic behavior was characterized by isolated bizarre acts rather than any sustained disorganization in thinking.

IV. Psycho-organic episodes. In this group of subjects the EEG is more abnormal during the episodic disorder. This group should be differentiated from the postictal twilight states (category I) and the petit mal statuses (category II). The symptoms of the psycho-organic episodes, aside from impulsiveness, would be primarily organic dementias; that is, intellectual defects and memory impairment typically seen in chronic brain syndromes. These symptoms may be due either to excessive medication or to an underlying organic process which is the common etiology for both epilepsy and the organic intellectual impairment. As might be expected, the EEG is often characterized by diffuse slow waves.

Patient F227 had been hospitalized four times during eight years, the first time allegedly for multiple sclerosis. Her EEG showed diffuse 4 to 7 per second activity plus 3 to 5 per second activity with hypersynchrony in the left anterior and the left mid-temporal region. For ten years she had had intermittent grand mal seizures, which were controllable by diphenylhydantoin (Dilantin) and phenobarbital. The last three hospitalizations had been precipitated by lethargic behavior and depression, with questionable suicidal attempts through the excessive use of her medication. Inasmuch as she was not closely supervised regarding this medication and showed considerable memory impairment as well as confusion, it is hard to evaluate whether these were true suicidal attempts, inappropriate self-medication during confused states, or abuse and dependency on drugs.

As the acute toxic symptoms subsided, the chronic brain syndrome became obvious, particularly the memory impairment covered by confabulation. At the same time she became obstreperous, aggressive, antagonistic, and demanded her discharge, usually successfully. Psychological examination revealed paranoid ideation, depression, withdrawal from inter-personal contacts, as well as an infantile egocentric orientation. There was also clear evidence for the central nervous system involvement.

This classification system proposed by Landolt has been supported at least in part by the findings of Dongier's (1959) statistical analysis on 516 epileptic patients with 536 episodic psychotic reactions reported by participants of the 1956 Conference on Psychomotor Epilepsy in Marseilles. These cases were submitted by 19 investigators, including Landolt. Dongier reported that the petit mal status was most often found in children and, like Landolt, emphasized the confusional state without affective lability or other psychiatric symptoms. Dongier also mentioned that these episodes frequently terminated with grand mal seizures. The adults who showed similar behavioral deviations, that is, confusion, restlessness, and a noticeable dullness of affect, seemed to be in postictal confusional states often following a seizure. Dongier's third group of subjects, comparable to what Landolt called his productive psychosis, were subdivided into two groups, one whose episodes were predominantly affective deviations, that is mood swings, depressive episodes, maniacal episodes; and a second with characteristic symptoms of dissociative phenomena marked by hebephrenic, paranoid, or catatonic behavior, with hallucinations and systematized delusions.

Dongier also reports a number of patients whose EEG's became normal during these episodic psychotic reactions, but, reanalyzing the data, she found that this occurred in only about 30 percent of the patients and concluded that this was a spurious finding since one fails to obtain a relaxed or drowsy recording in acutely disturbed individuals and it is precisely in this relaxed drowsy state that focal abnormalities of the temporal type are most likely to occur. Dongier mentions that in those patients whose EEG's tended to normalize there was usually an increase in depression and sometimes paranoid ideation.

There was a statistically significant correlation between the confusional reactions and centrencephalic EEG patterns during the episodes, while correlations between noncentrencephalic patterns and the affective ideational psychotic disturbance were of borderline significance. Correlations between behavior and the EEG patterns recorded between episodes did not show statistical significance. Vislie (1958) in his study of 162 patients agreed with Dongier to the extent that his group with EEG patterns associated with centrencephalic disturbances were also associated with "dementia," whereas the noncentrencephalic group were associated with neurotic or psychotic symptomatology.

5.5.2 *Behavioral abnormalities associated with specific Interictal EEG patterns.* In a double blind study comparing a selected sample of 25 patients with clear clinical features of psychomotor epilepsy with 25 patients with classical clinical and interictal EEG findings of centrencephalic seizures, Small (1962) quantified the psychological data in terms of personality rating scales along dimensions of anxiety, passivity, depression, hysteria, and impulsivity. She was not able to demonstrate a statistically significant difference in psychopathology or personality characteristics between the two groups, nor were there any significant differences in the psychiatric diagnoses in the two groups. The negative findings in this study, as well as in another by Stevens (1959) using similar techniques, are at variance with most reports in the literature and the overwhelming clinical impression. These findings must therefore be examined closely. It is their contention that double-blind methodology, combined with rigorous statistical analysis, prevents conscious or unconscious distortion of data. However, one must also consider the possibility that under these conditions the collection of data is relatively superficial and may be distorted by the use of these rating scales. Also, Small and Stevens limited their studies to a small, select patient group (epileptic outpatients in a university center) which may have significantly influenced the result. Third, the data of Dongier (1959) suggest that correlations between behavior and the EEG will occur only if the EEG is taken during acute episodic disturbances. In the studies of both Small and Stevens there is no consideration of episodic behavioral disturbances, so one must presume that these were overlooked or dismissed in view of the frequency with which such episodic behavior has been reported by others. The study of 100 patients by Stevens (1966) found that in the psychomotor group with correction for age, there was no difference in the frequency of psychiatric disorders as measured by admission to mental institutions when compared with other epileptics. However, this study did support the observation that psychomotor epileptics were more likely to show syndomes similar to acute schizophrenia with dysphoria, anxiety, compulsions, impulsiveness, and withdrawn behavior, while the slow apathetic reaction correlated with grand mal seizures. Like Landolt she noticed a large proportion of psychomotor epileptics who, with control of seizures, developed psychotic manifestations (10 of 13 patients).

If one traces historically the reports on the incidence of behavioral disturbances and epilepsy, particularly psychomotor epilepsy, one can see increasing evidence that interictal behavioral disturbances tend to occur in all forms of epilepsy, whether the epilepsy is defined in terms of the clinical manifestations of the seizures or in terms of the locus or type of interictal EEG abnormalities (Small, 1962; Dongier, 1959; DeHass, 1958; Benet, 1965; Revitch, 1954; Bruens, 1963). Qualitatively, however, there seems to be a difference in the episodic disturbances when correlated with the EEG abnormalities during the episodic behavior itself (Dongier, 1959). We can distinguish two groups of disorders. One group represents prolonged centrencephalic ictal response (Goldensohne, 1960; Putnam and Merrit, 1941) or a prolonged postictal response (Levin, 1952). In this group the outstanding clinical symptoms are confusion, negativism, withdrawal, and apathy. The duration of the abnormality can last considerably longer than we usually associate with ictal or postictal reactions, persisting for weeks or months. The second group of behavior disorders *not* accompanied by centrencephalic EEG abnormalities or grand mal seizures display intense affect, emotional instability, and psychic disturbances similar to "functional" psychosis (including hallucinations and delusions). These episodic psychotic reactions are also associated with altered levels of awareness. Such episodes usually have been considered as interictal, preictal or subictal rather than ictal responses. Subcortical recordings suggest that when this behavior appears precipitously and remits in the same manner, it probably represents a circumscribed or partial ictal phenomenon in the rhinencephalon. It seems better to reserve the terms "interictal," "subictal," or "preictal" behavior for the more chronic behavioral deviations which were described as the "epileptic personality" (5.4). The ictal response should be reserved for those periods when the sustained paroxysmal hypersynchrony occurs and would refer to the precipitous behavior changes concurrent with this excessive neuronal discharge. Unfortunately, to document this objectively we would need both cortical and subcortical studies and simultaneous behavioral observations. From a practical clinical point of view then, we are forced to infer the excessive neuronal discharge on the basis of clinical phenomenon. However, the genetic studies of Mitsuda (1967) support a relationship between family histories of epilepsy and atypical psychoses.

5.5.3 *Temporal lobe epilepsy and behavioral disorders.* Gibbs (1952) reports that 90 percent of the patients with anterior temporal lobe abnormalities show psychomotor epilepsy. Excluding the behavioral abnormalities he believed associated with the seizure itself, he says that 15 percent of these patients have demonstrated psychotic symptoms, 40 percent personality disorders and 10 percent fear or rage reactions. Gastaut (1953b) states that more than half the epilepsies are psychomotor, and again it is in this group that marked behavior deviations occur during the intervals between attacks. According to his observation, these are characterized by either retardation or impulsive behavior. Ervin (1955) made a careful psychiatric evaluation of 42 patients with focal temporal lobe spiking. I also evaluated most of Ervin's patients. All 42 patients showed some personality deviations; 34 were classified as schizophrenics, with 24 of these showing secondary symptoms. Twenty of the patients never sought psychiatric help, but careful evaluation of this group revealed significant psychopathology. For example, on three independent psychological measures of disordered behavior, every member of this group deviated as much as, or more than, patients attending a psychiatric outpatient clinic. This reveals the severe limitations of studies that assume psychiatric disorders only if the patient has previously received psychiatric help. In the group of 20 patients who had not previously sought help, it was noted that the degree of deviation from normal was least in those who had no seizures, intermediate in those with grand mal, and greatest in those with psychomotor seizures. Ervin distinguished between acute psychotic reactions and chronic psychosis, differentiating both from episodic ictal behavior, although the criteria he used for establishing acute psychotic reactions might be considered by others as indicating an ictal response. Of the chronic psychotic reactions with secondary symptoms, 23 of the 24 showed paranoid referential hypochondriacal behavior. This has added significance in light of the report by Slater (1955) who found that a number of years after the onset of epilepsy a patient might develop a paranoid reaction (5.6). Characterologically, all the patients studied by Ervin showed infantile, poorly organized personalities. He points out that the hypochondriacal preoccupation may evolve from the frequency of episodic visceral disturbances that occur in this group, which in turn are probably ictal phenomena. The extremely high incidence of behavioral disorders in this group cannot be explained, although examination of the referral source to the EEG laboratory might have clarified the issue. The assumption often expressed by critics is that a large number must have been psychiatric referrals.

Treffert (1964) compared a group of hospitalized psychiatric patients showing temporal spikes but without a history suggesting psychomotor seizures (Group A); a matched group controlled for age, sex, and diagnosis of hospitalized psychotic patients (Group B); a group of hospitalized patients with temporal spikes plus psychomotor epilepsy (Group C); and a random group of hospitalized psychiatric patients (Group D). All groups came from the same institution. In 10 of the 17 temporal spike patients without a history of psychomotor seizure (Group A) the reason for hospitalization had been acting out of aggressive impulses, including two murders. Such intense aggressiveness was characteristic of only four of the ten matching patients (Group B). In fact, combining the two groups with focal EEG abnormalities in the temporal lobes (Group A and C), Treffert found that these patients, as compared with the nonepileptic patients (Groups B and D), were much more likely to show homicidal, suicidal, and assaultive behavior; episodic rages; and clouded sensorium and organic findings. Both the focal epileptic groups (A and C) were assaultive, but those who showed overt psychomotor seizures were more likely to show hallucinations, while the presence of delusions statistically distinguished the matched nonepileptic group (Group B and D) from those with temporal abnormalities (Group A and C). Contrary to these reports by Ervin and Treffert is one by Mulder (1952) on 100 patients with neurological and EEG evidence of temporal lobe lesions, but whose presenting complaints were predominantly psychiatric. Schizoid traits were diagnosed in only 20 of these subjects, and only four were considered overtly psychotic. Unfortunately, Mulder did not provide the clinical details that might clarify the difference between these findings and those of Ervin and Treffert.

Glaser (1963) reports on 22 patients with psychomotor-temporal epilepsy, all with seizures and all having one or more acute psychotic episodes distinguishable both from the seizural phenomenon and from classical schizophrenia. The acute psychotic reactions, although prolonged, were characterized by a fluctuating disorder of mental functioning; the onset often followed a relatively prolonged build-up in tension and anxiety. Glaser did not notice the "normalization" of the EEG during the psychotic episodes, as was reported by Landolt. Instead, the records were more likely to show some increase in abormality or no change at all. Again these studies revealed that what is recorded in the scalp EEG has little relation to the behavioral disorders, and probably little to do with what is going on in the subcortical regions. The fluidity of the symptoms suggests that these may reflect a waxing and waning excessive neuronal discharge, either in terms of the magnitude of the discharge or the area involved. This may be one of the reasons why the psychological studies, even when meticulously carried out, give such contradictory results.

In a small group of "specific" EEG abnormalities (18 of 70 patients discussed in detail in Chapter 8) 14 had focal temporal abnormalities, and 12 of these 14 had seizures. As already mentioned, only two of the twelve were overtly psychotic. Four others, however, had evidence for schizophrenic-type thinking on psychological testing; that is, "subclinical" psychosis. Thus, our findings were more similar to those of Mulder's than either Ervin's or Treffert's. The two patients with temporal lobe focus on the EEG but no evidence of seizures were severely disturbed individuals with a unique kind of psychosis that deserves illustration.

F283 is a twenty-nine-year-old married, white, female housewife and office clerk, who at the time of evaluation for this study was in the hospital for the fifth time over a period of four years. Each hospitalization had been precipitated by some serious dyscontrol episodes. She accepted hospitalization as necessary to establish restraints on her behavior. During the intervals between hospitalization she was seen in intensive individual psychotherapy and also participated in a group therapy program. Following this hospitalization I saw her, her husband, and occasionally the children in family therapy. Despite the severity of her disorder there had never been any overt hallucinations or delusions. Her affect was marked by extreme lability with rapid swings from elation to depression, rage to panic. On the wards she was manipulative and demanding, constantly harrassing and baiting the staff. Symptoms other than the episodic dyscontrol and emotional lability included periods of depersonalization and feelings of unreality lasting from a few hours to a few days. Episodic psychophysiologic reactions, including constipation, diarrhea, stomach pains, generalized edema, menstrual irregularity, headaches, dizziness, and bladder difficulties, also occurred. Because of the episodic depression and panic, she had received at one time or another phenothiazines and antidepressants. She often took excessive amounts of these drugs and for extended periods controlled her dysphoria by keeping herself chronically inebriated.

Since early childhood she had aggressively coerced and manipulated her family. She was intensely rivalrous with her younger brother and hostilely competitive with her mother, while idolizing an alcoholic, inadequate father. Relations with peers were always intense but strained because of her overwhelming extractive dependency. She married a passive, somewhat effeminate, professional person and immediately established an ambivalent dependent relationship without any true affection or sexual interest in him. Two children resulted from this union, a boy and a girl who were largely neglected; she was overtly seductive with the boy and cold and rejecting towards the girl, often having homicidal fantasies towards her and sometimes acting sadistically. Family life was characterized by constant bickering with at least daily explosive rage reactions followed by depression and withdrawal. She reneged on even the simplest house-wife-mother-spouse responsibilities. On the other hand, she would develop consuming interests outside the house, including rescue involvements with emotionally sick, usually psychopathic males. Once such a relationship was underway, however, she became so extractive that she drove even these people away.

The episodic dyscontrol included seductive sexual behavior and repeated self-mutilations, particularly slashing her arms and legs with knives. She made frequent coercive threats of suicide which frightened friends and relatives alike. As already mentioned, she had homicidal impulses towards her daughter and her husband.

Three of the four EEG's, including two chloralose activations, were normal, but the fourth revealed a left temporal focus of slow and hypersynchronous activity. She also reported transitory episodes of a peculiar taste in her mouth ("metallic-like") often accompanied by an indescribable but unpleasant odor. Because of this she was placed on a trial therapeutic regime of diphenylhydantoin (Dilantin) 0.1

gram t.i.d. and continued on this medication for a period of over one year. The gustatory sensations ceased and the depersonalizations became less frequent, in fact almost nonexistent. There was also improvement in the impulse dyscontrol acts. However, it must be pointed out that during this same period she was receiving intensive individual, family, and group psychotherapy. At the time of the last follow-up she had spontaneously discontinued her medication with no return of the symptoms.

The second patient (F201) is similar in many ways to the above, particularly in terms of the incapacitating yet confusing nature of the psychopathology. During the four years she was followed she also had been in the hospital five times. She too was unable to cope with either her wifely or her maternal duties, having separated from her husband, moved back with her mother, and relegated the care of her children to mother and other relatives. Unlike the previous patient, who rushed into the world to solve her problems through action, this patient tended to withdraw into a childish, autistic fantasy. She too never manifested overt hallucinations or delusions. At the time of her hospitalization she appeared vague, circumstantial, emotionally labile and perplexed, complaining of peculiar episodes which she could not describe but which were apparently frightening periods of depersonalization. In the hospital emotional instability was marked with sudden bursts of tears and depression and equally sudden outbursts of raucous laughter. She occasionally showed explosive outbursts of aggressive behavior, but they were only in the family setting directed towards her mother or children. Two hospitalizations were precipitated because the patient's mother was frightened for the well-being of herself and her grandchildren.

On the psychological tests this patient, as well as the one described above, revealed a hysterical character structure, oral dependency, narcissism, and sado-masochistic preoccupations, as well as schizophrenic type thought disorder. Both of these patients were bright, sensitive, and creative.

This patient had a normal baseline EEG but with chloralose activation developed not only diffuse bilateral paroxysmal high amplitude slow activity, but also bursts of paroxysmal slow activity in the left anterior temporal region.

Her past history revealed disturbed behavior since infancy. She presented a severe feeding problem during the first five years of her life. She was intensely jealous and impulsively aggressive at the time of the birth of her young brother. She was competitive with her mother, in fact disturbed in her relationships with all adult females, particularly female teachers. She was cold and aloof in relationships with peers, seldom having any close friends. At 16 she became pregnant and during the several months before the decision to marry the boy had repeated "emotional storms" with aggressive impulsive acts. Following her marriage, she never made an adequate sexual adjustment and occasionally showed rather bizarre attitudes. For instance, she not only insisted that she nurse her children, but also coerced her husband into nursing at the same time.

Both patients represent syndromes of what might be called an episodic pseudoneurotic schizophrenia (Hoch, 1949) or the atypical psychoses of Mitsuda (1967). That is, they manifested predominantly the primary symptoms of Bleuler and were severely incapacitated by these symptoms. Although both these patients showed impulsive acts, in the first patient this was much more prominent, the difference between the two apparently representing that vague characteristic alluded to as an "alloplastic readiness to act."

5.5.4 *Behavioral disorders with both rhinencephalic and centrencephalic abnormalities.* Is there a possible combination of centrencephalic and rhinencephalic seizural activity, and if this occurs, would the behavioral response be merely a combination of the confusional apathetic state of the former and the "productive psychosis" of the latter? Or, would such a combination lead to new symptoms not particularly prominent in either the confusional state or the productive psychosis? Gastaut (1953b) has proposed that it is in precisely this group where impulsive acting out of homicidal, suicidal, or sexual impulses is most likely to occur. Logically this makes sense because we know that in some ictal and postictal confusional states uninhibited aggressive and impulsive behavior does occur. If in such instances there were also an accompanying excessive neuronal discharge in rhinencephalic structures responsible for intense affects, generally of a dysphoric nature, would not the combination be more likely to lead to the uninhibited expression of these affects? We have already postulated that in episodic dyscontrol there is either an excessive intensity of instinctual urges or some impairment in inhibitory controls or a combination of both. The data presented in this chapter suggest that these two possible neurophysiologic dysfunctions, one resulting in inhibition of higher integrated control mechanisms (centrencephalic) the other reflected by intense dysphoric affects (rhinencephalic), could be just the combination responsible for the most dramatic and deviant episodic acts.

A somewhat analogous combination of neurophysiologic dysfunctions which might lead to severe episodic dyscontrol would be the following. Epilepsy can be symptomatic as well as cryptogenic (idiopathic). In symptomatic epilepsy the seizure is only one symptom of a chronic brain syndrome where definite, diffuse cellular pathology can be demonstrated. If the cellular damage is diffuse, it also may be reflected in diffuse EEG abnormalities, and obvious at the psychological level in terms of the usual organic syndrome of memory impairment and intellectual deterioration, particularly impaired abstract reasoning. This organic syndrome is often characterized by forms of emotional instability and deficient inhibitory control. Again, if such diffuse cortical changes are combined with excessive rhinencephalic neuronal discharges, we have the neurophysiologic substrate for an increase in instinctual urges and a simultaneous deficit in higher inhibitory mechanisms—a combination we suggested is responsible for some of the extreme forms of episodic dyscontrol. An example of this would be Patient S228.

What kind of evidence is there to support or contradict such a hypothesis? Vislie (1958) in his study of 190 epileptic patients stated that impulsiveness and outbursts of rage, as well as mental slowness and severe personality disorders occurred in those subjects with evidence of diffuse lesions of the central nervous system, either neurologically or electroencephalographically. Unfortunately, he did not compare the patients that showed diffuse cortical lesions alone with those that showed diffuse cortical lesions plus a temporal focus. However, by reanalyzing his tables, one can conclude in support of this hypothesis that there was a trend among those showing the combination of lesions to be more spontaneous, irritable, and anxious. Rodin (1957) reports on 23 patients with focal temporal abnormalities accompanied by background recordings slower than 8 cycles per second in 50 percent to 75 percent of the EEG record after eliminating all periods when the patient was drowsy. In ten of the 23 there was a history of epilepsy, but in all instances the behavioral abnormalities were so outstanding that epilepsy was a secondary diagnosis. It is noteworthy that in almost every patient these symptoms were incapacitating enough to interfere with work adjustment. By far the most frequent disturbances were deviations in affect, most often depression. Eight patients showed disorientation and confusion, and six suffered from memory impairment. Unfortunately there was no analysis of impulsivity or aggressiveness, and the data presented were collected from hospital records and not patient contact.

Our own series of 19 epileptic patients does not reveal any significant differences when we compare those having organic signs on psychological tests (5 subjects) with those that did not have organic signs (14 subjects); or those having temporal abnormalities alone (8 subjects) with those having temporal abnormalities plus frontal abnormalities (3 subjects); or those having focal abnormalities alone (6 subjects) with those having focal abnormalities plus generalized paroxysmal slow activity (6 subjects). However, the two children who had both temporal foci and generalized spike-wave abnormalities after chloralose activation were dangerously aggressive patients (6.1.1).

5.5.5 *Fourteen cycle and six cycle per second positive spikes and behavioral disorders.* Recently there have been many reports relating behavioral disorders to the presence of 14 and/or 6 cycle per second positive spikes. The controversy regarding this subject was reviewed by Henry (1963) and Hughes (1965a). For this reason an exhaustive review will not be repeated here. But the subject is important because of the alleged behavioral manifestations of impulsive rage and homicidal reaction, irresistible impulses, and other episodic symptoms supposedly associated with this EEG abnormality. The average incidence of typical epileptic attacks is only 41.5 percent in patients with positive spikes. However, correlations with other episodic phenomena not usually considered epileptic either in terms of altered awareness or the primitive sensory and motor responses that usually accompany seizures are much higher. The autonomic symptoms associated with 14 and 6 positive spikes appear epileptoid in that they appear abruptly, are of transitory nature, and disappear equally precipitously. The behavioral episodes, although impulsive and explosive, are usually characterized by a skilled, well-planned and coordinated behavior. This sets these episodes apart from the usual psychomotor automatism and "furors" that might appear as ictal or postictal phenomena. Hughes (1961) reports that in the group of 14 and 6 positive spike patients, 90 percent had clinical manifestations of behavior disorders and/or autonomic dysfunctions. However, most observers do not feel that the 14 and 6 abnormality per se is an ictal phenomenon, that is, a manifestation of concomitant excessive neuronal discharge.

Many of the problems that made this subject controversial following Gibbs's original observations in 1951 have been resolved. These concerned whether the EEG findings were merely an artifact. This in part was due to the difficulty in recording the phenomenon, which requires for its most obvious recognition monopolar recordings during the drowsy stage or specifically arousal from light sleep. The abnormality is usually seen in recordings over the posterior temporal or occipital areas. The second controversy centered on the primary localization of the abnormality. It was originally proposed by Gibbs, on the basis of the wave form, that this reflected a thalamic or hypothalamic focus, this being supported by a number of observations of pathology in the diencephalon accompanied by similar positive spikes. So far there is little experimental evidence for this, others proposing that the abnormal focus might be limbic, particularly in the hippocampal region (Neidermeyer, 1962; Refsum, 1960). Grossman (1954) suggests that the peculiar EEG pattern may be due to "transient laminar blocking of inhibitory mechanisms" in the superficial layers of the cortex, and that this blocking of cortical inhibitory mechanisms may be the reason for the expressions of uncontrolled rage and assaultiveness precipitated by underlying autonomic responses, a possibility similar to the one we have already proposed for a combination of centrencephalic and temporal lobe epilepsy.

Originally the 14 and 6 per second positive spikes were emphasized as a disorder found in children. Thus they might have been eliminated from our present consideration which is focused on adult behavior disorders but for certain characteristics which make it particularly pertinent to our studies. Subsequent analysis of age distribution indicates that it does occur in adults and is particularly marked in adolescence. In unselected populations the rates of positive spiking vary from 1 percent to 3 percent, but in sleep records this increases to 12 or 13 percent. In children and adolescents with psychiatric referrals, the typical reported incidence is 30 percent and it has been reported as high as 58 percent among problem children in schools and 72 percent in impulsive children (Hughes, 1965a).

Most investigators readily admit that patients with positive spikes who also show behavior disorders have a history of psychological trauma. They suggest that the underlying pathology responsible for the 14 and 6 cycle per second abnormalities makes this group unusually susceptible to psychic trauma. Hughes (1965a) shows that such 14 and 6 patients have an exaggerated reaction to stress and do not easily recover from this as compared with groups with normal EEG's or even groups with abnormal EEG's of a different type. This is similar to a proposal we will suggest later for those showing paroxysmal slow activity after activation (Chapter 7). In fact, Kellaway (1960) and Shimado (1961) found that positive spikes might be related to just such paroxysmal slow activity. Others have noted the inverse age relationships with temporal spiking and suggest some of the 14 and 6 patients may develop temporal spiking when they mature (Hughes, 1965a). Long-term studies are needed to prove these points.

Gibbs (1963a, b) indicates that personality disorders are more likely to be found in the positive spike group than among any other group with EEG abnormalities, except for those showing anterior temporal discharges. The symptoms most likely to be characteristic of patients with 14 and 6 cycle per second EEG's are headache, dizziness, stomach ache, nausea, vomiting, blurred vision, paresthesias, mild behavior disorders, and, less likely but still significant, temper tantrums, rage attacks, and severe acting out. Although Gibbs reports on a large number of subjects, detailed clinical material, particularly on the psychiatric aspects, is lacking. Other authors have reported similar findings, some emphasizing such symptoms as syncope and others emphasizing the behavioral abnormalities (Hughes, 1961, 1965a).

A clinical observation that the episodic autonomic reactions have responded to antiepileptic drugs seems to support the view that this is an epileptoid response. Behavioral changes are less responsive to anticonvulsants, but they too have been reported to respond not only to antiepileptic drugs, but to tranquilizers and to chlordiazepoxide (Librium) (Hughes, 1965a; Boelhouwer, 1968). The reports of behavioral abnormalities as a major complaint vary from 12 percent to 72 percent of those showing positive spikes. What would be most pertinent from our point of view is not just the incidence of such behavioral disorders but more details regarding the quality of these behavioral disturbances.

Regarding this, Yoskii (1964) provides us with some data. In comparing a group of habitual offenders he found that the group with 14 and 6 had more complaints of a vegetative nature and more often committed acts that were sudden in onset, directed against persons and followed by a lack of affect. This was also similar to those who had other EEG abnormalities but different from those with normal EEG's who were more likely to have gotten into difficulty because of petty larceny, truancy, and absconding. Walter (1960) felt that previous studies might be distorted because of retrospective interpretation of the clinical data by an investigator who knew the EEG findings. His blind study, comparing patients who had normal EEG's with those with 14 and 6 positive spikes alone, and those with 14 and 6 positive spikes plus other abnormalities, found only two statistically significant differences. In contradistinction to almost all other reports, the group with 14 and 6 abnormalities had less emotional difficulty than either the normals or the subjects with combined abnormalities. This is so different from the consensus in the literature that one wonders whether the study, which was rigorously designed to eliminate bias, could have also eliminated useful clinical data. For example, were the rating scales sensitive enough to reflect behavioral differences, or was the group with normal EEG's particularly select; that is, patients who had been referred for EEG's because of behavioral problems? Again, what is important from our point of view is not simply an evaluation of the prevalence of behavioral disorders in patients with 14 and 6 per second positive spikes, but, if they do occur, can they in any qualitative way be distinguished from the behavioral disorders of other groups? Walter did find, and this may be important in view of the finding reported by Yoskii, that those patients with 14 and 6 per second positive spikes plus other abnormalities demonstrated more aggressive behavior than did either the patients with other EEG abnormalities or those with 14 and 6 abnormalities alone. Antisocial behavior with this EEG pattern has been reported by Schwade (1960) but not found by Friedlander (1964). Both Dietze (1963) and Yoskii (1964) have suggested that it is not the 14 and 6 cycle per second abnormality per se that is associated with aggressive behavioral disturbance, but the central nervous system damage, the 14 and 6 positive spike being just one of several possible indications of this. It is the extent of this damage, usually associated with other EEG abnormalities, that determines how aggressive the patient is.

Unfortunately much of the clinical data which could give us a sense of the quality of the behavioral deviation is reported in such a cursory way that it is difficult to evaluate. Generally it has been mentioned that these patients show chronic states of tension, anger, and resentment with frequent expressions of cruelty and destructiveness. Other patients with these findings, however, seem to be particularly compliant and obedient, perhaps failing to express normal assertiveness prior to their explosive outbursts. It is rather consistently reported that when rage and destructiveness are expressed it is done so in an explosive way, usually as the result of a relatively insignificant stimulus, and the aggressive acts are carried out with a considerable degree of skill or precision. Such a description would fit well with what we have designated as episodic dyscontrol of the higher hierarchial levels; that is the impulse dyscontrol or acting out. (Compare this, for instance, with our previous observation that most often expression of aggression in psychomotor automatism or postepileptic confusional state is more characteristic of the lower hierarchial levels, which we have labeled seizure or instinct dyscontrol.) It would seem then that in the 14 and 6 cycle per second group, control mechanisms are overwhelmed by excessive instinctual urges so that there is an explosive expression of rage and destruction with an apparent impossibility to stop the act once initiated. The completion of the act is accompanied by relief of tension and followed by little expression of remorse (Schwade, 1960). This lack of remorse, which is emphasized as accompanying the 14 and 6 abnormalities, also occurs with childhood and adolescent homicidal acts (Bender, 1953). Thus it may not be a significant differentiating factor, but one more characteristic of the periods—childhood and adolescence—in which 14 and 6 abnormalities are most likely to occur.

Although it is risky to generalize from individual cases, it may be significant that Gibbs (1952) reports that the four murderers from his epileptic series all had positive spikes. Eleven other childhood or adolescent homicidal acts occurring in patients with 14 and 6 abnormalities have been reported in the literature, including several instances of matricide (Schwade, 1960). It has been remarked that these murders were usually committed with little or no motivation. However, it is quite obvious that evaluations regarding motivation would require rather detailed clinical contact with the subject, which is not usually indicated in the reports. Perhaps it would be a more cautious statement to say that homicidal acts were committed without obvious motivation. It is probably significant that the victim often is a member of the family. However, in several reported cases the victim has been a total stranger.

In the series of 70 adolescent and adult patients reported in Chapter 8 only three, all adolescents, showed 14 and 6 positive spikes. This is less than 15 percent of our series who were under twenty years. Among the 16 children also studied, three, or slightly under 20 percent, had this pattern. In view of the type of patient we were studying, this is a surprisingly low incidence of 14 and 6 compared with other reports in the literature. It is important to note that none of the three children gave any history suggestive of epilepsy. The three adolescents gave a history of "spells," but these were not typically grand mal, petit mal, or psychomotor seizures. There was another significant difference between the adolescents and the children with regard to manifestations of episodic dyscontrol. The children as yet had not, or only very rarely, demonstrated dyscontrol acts, although projective tests revealed a preoccupation with loss of control. The adolescents demonstrated overt impulsivity. Only one of the patients with 14 and 6 abnormalities gave other evidence for organic central nervous system involvement, but five of the six showed evidence of schizophrenic thought disorder on psychological testing. All had a history of psychological trauma prior to their hospitalization, and all had evidence for episodic psychophysiologic reactions. Aside from the above similarities, the symptoms and clinical course of these patients were markedly different, and so deserve detailed reporting.

Patient 406 was a nine-year-old girl. Three days before hospitalization she was first seen by a psychiatrist at which time she was screaming uncontrollably that she had done something "terribly wrong." What she had done was reluctantly revealed in time as masturbation, thinking dirty words, wanting to look at breasts and penises, sticking a bottle up her vagina while pretending it was a penis, and so on. What is striking is that she had apparently not felt guilty about this behavior which had been going on for some years until the onset of the present illness. She was anxious, depressed, unable to sleep, preoccupied with being dirty, constantly washing her hands, and begging the doctor to cure her, or put her in the hospital. She was also preoccupied with the idea that she had "killed somebody."

The family had not noted any marked deviations in behavior before this, although in retrospect they mentioned that she was somewhat overweight, sickly, and had suffered from allergies and asthma during her early years. She also tended to boss and manipulate her playmates. Psychological tests contributed the additional observations that she had many paranoid ideas, problems in maintaining her identity, oral-erotic preoccupations, and concerns about homosexuality. She was extremely phobic and obsessive, very dependent, but because of her intelligence struggled against this dependency.

With chloralose activation, the EEG revealed high amplitude diffuse, paroxysmal slow waves plus several short bursts of 6 per second positive spikes in the right posterior quadrant.

In the hospital the patient made rapid improvement, almost immediately dropping her acute symptoms, trying hard to please everybody and establish herself as the favorite patient. She energetically attended school and participated in all ward activities. With individual psychotherapy she resolved most of her guilty sexual concerns and overcame her phobic obsessive traits. Both her behavior and psychological tests revealed better control over her impulses. She was discharged home six months later having received no specific medication.

The above patient is quite different from patient C400, an eight-year-old boy admitted because he was having difficulty in learning and following directions in school. He was a quiet, complaisant, reserved child, never showing his feelings and mistrusting everybody. The EEG revealed two short bursts of 14 and 6 positive spikes in the left posterior quadrant. In the hospital he never openly expressed his feelings, nor did he establish any kind of relationship with his peers or the staff. Six months later he was discharged from the hospital, having shown no improvement, to be transferred to a special training school. Psychological tests however revealed preoccupation with control over his impulses.

402 was an eight-year-old girl who, although withdrawn, was provoking and domineering with other children. She had numerous physical complaints, particularly vomiting. The reason for her hospitalization was her parents' concern that she would hurt another child or be hurt herself during one of her rare but extremely fierce acts of dyscontrol. Psychological tests revealed evidence of a central nervous system involvement, but also revealed intense fears of her own aggression as well as fears of expected retaliation. She was defeatist about being loved and pictured being loved as being orally devoured or otherwise destroyed.

After chloralose activation she showed several short bursts of 14 and 6 positive spikes in each posterior quadrant, sometimes independently with a right-sided predominance and at other times bilaterally synchronous.

By the time of her discharge, one year after admission, she had developed considerable impulse control, although she accomplished this by inhibiting her emotions and withdrawing from interpersonal relations.

The following three patients are adolescents who demonstrated the 14 and 6 per second positive spikes.

Patient F272 is a fifteen-year-old boy who was admitted to the hospital after he impulsively ran from the house following an argument with his father. He sat on the street curb, planning to throw himself under the seventh car that passed by because it was the seventh day of the month (it was actually the sixth day of the month). He had to be physically restrained by his father to keep him from carrying through with his plan (perhaps he selected the seventh car because his father had not arrived by the sixth). Several weeks earlier he had impulsively threatened, in the presence of his mother, to throw rocks through a store window. He proceeded to do this in a daring, defiant way and then went into the store, paying for the window by giving the owner his coin collection ("I paid $100 for a $10 window.") Thus, though his acts had an explosive, impulsive quality, there was a coldly calculated, planned element in them. For the six months preceding these episodes, he had been restless, irritable, and rather suddenly began doing poorly in his schoolwork. He was emotionally unstable, frequently talked about suicide and in past years had had a series of illnesses including allergies, colds, nausea, vomiting, diarrhea, and anorexia. Because he was always "sickly," his mother babied him in what must have been a seductive manner; in fact she occasionally slept in his bed. The patient had no friends, spending his time in solitary pursuits. He seemed remote and indifferent when describing his recent behavior.

The EEG revealed short bursts of 6 per second positive spikes in the right posterior quadrant and, after chloralose activation, paroxysmal, high amplitude rhythmic slow waves with an anterior predominance. The only possible epileptoid phenomenon uncovered was that, during interviews with the doctor, he would suddenly stare off into space for a few seconds, and when asked what was going on he would say "the world seems to be fading away into a general blur." He also admitted to unformed visual hallucinations of brilliant colors assuming vague changing shapes, and also indistinct voices which he could neither identify nor understand. Psychological tests revealed feelings of low self-esteem with compensatory grandiosity, depression and intense oral needs.

The follow-up psychiatric interview, which came ten months after his discharge from the hospital but while he was still receiving outpatient psychotherapy, revealed that he still had dyscontrol acts at which time he would be overwhelmed by anger, resentment, or depression, pounding the table or walls (what we would call instinct dyscontrol). He said he was doing well in school although it was hard to believe on the basis of the interview, because he was so rambling and preoccupied with petty details that it was almost impossible to follow his train of thought.

The second adolescent, patient F246, had 14 and 6 per second spikes in the left posterior quadrant. Her impulsive acts included running away, but this had a calculated quality in that she flew to Puerto Rico after first pawning all her belongings to pay for her fare. When she arrived, she immediately picked up a policeman and lived with him several days, supposedly marrying him later when she felt overwhelmed by guilt regarding her behavior. The symbolic nature of this act was described previously in that she was fleeing from an Oedipal temptation, with the act itself an unconscious solution to this frightening prospect. Twenty-six months after hospitalization and six months after she had discontinued outpatient psychotherapy, she was working regularly, having completed a beautician's course, sublimating her acting out by living a conventionally rebellious "hippie" existence, which her family learned to tolerate. She still had frequent transitory depressive reactions preceded by mounting irritability, but had only two aggressive explosive acts which were just momentary verbal expressions of rage with pounding of the table. The only possible epileptic symptom that this girl had were several "falling spells" where she suddenly collapsed and was unable to move, although she was still aware of what was going on around her.

The third patient, F211, is a sixteen-year-old girl who reported spells consisting of generalized weakness, falling to the ground, a short period of motionless behavior, and then a thrashing about of all extremities lasting up to 30 minutes, with supposed amnesia for these spells. The spells were often preceded by vague abdominal and chest pains. Abdominal pains in the past had been a problem, leading to a negative surgical exploration some years before. Although her present hospitalization was precipitated by a suicidal gesture following a disturbed group therapy session, this episodic dyscontrol was not characteristic, her main problem being that she was isolated, withdrawn, cold and indifferent. The father, apparently a paranoid schizophrenic, sexually accosted his daughter on repeated occasions. Psychological tests revealed in this girl, as well as in five of six other 14 and 6 patients, schizophrenic thinking. She also showed a hysterical character structure, obsessive compulsive intellectualizations, isolation, and withdrawal. The EEG revealed 14 and 6 per second positive spikes in the right posterior quadrant and, with chloralose activation, high amplitude paroxysmal slow waves, but in this instance there was a posterior rather than the usual anterior predominance found in our series.

5.6 EPILEPSY AS A PRECURSOR OF "SCHIZOPHRENIA"

Slater (1955) in his monumental article on schizophrenia-like psychoses of epilepsy reported on 69 cases of psychotic reactions appearing some years (mean 14) after the onset of seizures. His conclusion was that every cardinal symptom of schizophrenia is exhibited at some time by these patients. Detailed clinical data were given to support his conclusions. Patients were included in this series only if they had prolonged psychotic reactions without confusion. Unfortunately, this last criterion may have eliminated a number of patients who would interest us as demonstrating episodic psychotic reactions. However, as will be described below, even with this preliminary screening, many of the patients did show characteristics of episodic psychotic reactions.

Slater distinguished between four groups of schizophrenic patients, 11 in the series demonstrating chronic psychoses which had been preceded by repeated occurrence of short-lived confusional episodes. Forty-six of the patients demonstrated more typical paranoid schizophrenia without the preceding confusional episodes. A third and fourth group, combined in the analysis of the data, consisted of eight patients with hebephrenic reactions and four patients with histories of petit mal epilepsy (the rationale for combining the two groups is illustrated by the fact that five of the eight hebephrenic patients had EEG evidence of centrencephalic epilepsy). My analysis of this last group would be that they represent the apathetic group with a bland or silly affect described by Landolt (5.5.1). Slater, however, does not emphasize confusion as one of the symptoms in his patients, as did Landolt.

In Slater's total group he noted that the premorbid personality tends to show normal variations, except in those patients with an early onset of epilepsy. In this latter group there was an early appearance of personality characteristics sometimes identified with epilepsy, such as irritability, aggressiveness, stubbornness, obsessional traits, pedantry, circumstantiality, and rigidity. These occured in 14 of the 19 subjects whose epilepsy started before age 15. In the group of 46 patients who showed paranoid psychotic reactions, there was an inverse fluctuation in paranoid symptoms and seizures. The onset in the group as a whole was insidious, except that those patients with episodic confusion were more likely to show an acute onset of their schizophrenic reaction, indicating that the characteristics of this group must have been similar to those we have labeled episodic psychotic reactions.

In terms of symptoms, all but two of the patients had delusions; 52 of the 69 hallucinations; 31 had thought disorders of the schizophrenic type; 28 had loss of affect; 40 had bizarre behavior; and 13, impulsive or bizarre acts. However, there were other symptoms, presumably episodic; 34 patients had periods of irritability and aggressiveness, and 33 had episodic depressions. The depressions, he notes, were short-lived but very severe and often accompanied by suicidal attempts. Twelve patients reported euphoria. Gross catatonic behavior was unusual in this group. It is obvious then that even though he eliminated the psychotic patients with confusion, by our definition a large but undetermined number of subjects showed episodic behavioral disorders. His conclusion that the ultimate development of psychotic reactions was related to temporal lobe epilepsy is a point debated by other observers. In fact, Stevens (1960) misquotes Slater's findings, saying that only 65 percent of those who became psychotic demonstrated temporal lobe or psychomotor epilepsy, this being the approximate frequency of psychomotor epileptics among epilepsy in general. Slater noted, however, that 55 patients, or 80 percent, had evidence of temporal lobe or psychomotor epilepsy.

Slater concluded that the psychosis, although phenomenologically similar to schizophrenia, was etiologically different; that is, a schizophreniform psychosis of purely epileptic causation. He did make the point, however, that there are some differences between the schizophreniform reaction and classical schizophrenia; there is less tendency for the affect to disappear in the former as well as the likelihood that the psychosis will remit, suggesting again that even this group may fall into our episodic psychotic reactions category. Slater pointed out that with remission there is also a greater chance that the personality will remain intact, except for symptoms of organic brain disease which he believed to occur as a late complication of epilepsy.

In his follow-up study (a mean of 7.8 years after the onset of psychosis), the data reported suggest a tendency for considerably better remission than one would see in the usual chronic schizophrenic reaction. With this tendency for remission there was also a similar tendency for recurrence, and ultimately half of the patients had some social handicap due to the organic syndrome. Thirty of the 60 patients followed-up were living entirely at home and 16 others mainly at home; 20 were employed full time and four more part time; 33 were described as socially adequate. This too suggests the episodic nature of the psychotic reaction.

In a subsequent publication, Slater (1965) summarized the data and discussed the implication of these findings. He rejected the possibility that the finding of epilepsy in schizophrenia is merely coincidental, nor did he consider that the psychotic reaction is just the ultimate expression of a disturbance in reality resulting from many exposures to psychotic-like auras preceding the ictal phenomenon. He held that the more likely explanation is that both epilepsy and this particular type of schizophrenia are manifestations of some common underlying process, an early symptom being epilepsy and a later one psychosis. The frequency with which he found evidence for central nervous system damage in this group suggests that cellular damage may be the common cause, although he said that it may not be so much the result of the dead cells as the dying ones. Again, these findings support what we have already mentioned and will repeatedly refer to in later chapters: there appear to be two large classes of what are generally labeled schizophrenic reactions, one episodic and more related to epilepsy, while another is typically chronic and unremitting, probably not related to epilepsy (Rodin, 1957).

In our long-term study of 70 patients, we noted that among the

16 subjects with seizures who had received extensive psychological evaluations, 14 showed significant paranoid thinking that at the time was not clinically obvious even upon careful detailed psychiatric evaluation. Nine of the 16 patients had definite evidence of schizophrenic thinking, although only one showed overt symptoms of schizophrenia. The patients' adjustment in this group, although disturbed enough to require hospitalization at least for diagnostic evaluation, was not bizarre, nor would it have been considered schizophrenic. This raises the issue that a possible explanation for Slater's findings is that the schizophrenia does not truly follow the epilepsy but is concomitant with it, just less overt until later life. Patients F211, F285, F247, F287, S239, and F206, all described elsewhere in this book, substantiate this possibility. Only long-term follow-up will prove or disprove this, but Mitsuda's (1967) and Otsuka's (1967) findings seem to support this point of view.

5.7 SUMMARY

The data in this chapter support much of that reported in the last chapter on subcortical recordings, particularly the importance of ictal discharges as a possible mechanism behind many of the episodic behavioral disorders. The data indicate that we have to be cautious in labeling behavior as preictal, ictal, postictal or interictal. Many behavioral abnormalities, in the past not considered ictal, are probably just that, being manifestations of what is more appropriately called "partial" epilepsy, that is, an excessive neuronal discharge limited to subcortical structures, hence not recorded on scalp EEG's.

From the mass of data presented in this chapter are there any more specific generalizations we can propose at least tentatively? It seems that the following generalizations are legitimate, at least as working hypotheses.

1. If the behavioral disturbance is associated with grand mal seizures or simply automatisms, the more likely the episodic behavior will be disorganized; that is, what we call seizure dyscon-

trol or instinct dyscontrol. This behavior is seldom useful or effective, even though it may provide the individual with subjectively appreciated tension relief without the disastrous consequence of the higher level dyscontrol acts characterized by more coordinated and direct instinct gratification.

2. There is some evidence that if the patient has typical grand mal, petit mal, or automatisms, other behavioral disorders will be less frequent or less intense. The question of a true inverse relationship between epilepsy and schizophrenia or psychosis is still not established.

3. One of the persisting clinical notions that should be discarded is that ictal phenomena are necessarily of relatively short duration. There is evidence that they can persist for months. The most distinguished feature of the ictal phenomena is the precipitous onset and remission of behavioral deviations.

4. There are two possible behavior patterns associated with excessive neuronal discharges, one representing what we have called episodic inhibition and the other episodic disinhibition.

a. Episodic Inhibition is characterized by torpor, apathy, lack of initiative, and dulling of affect. There is also usually confusion and disorientation. This pattern of behavior is likely to be associated with ictal or postictal EEG recordings characteristic of centrencephalic epilepsy, even though there may be no clinical evidence for typical centrencephalic seizures.

b. Episodic disinhibitions are characterized by behavior that is more typical of what we call episodic dyscontrol or episodic reactions. Individuals with these syndromes manifest intense affect, impulsive actions dictated by these affects, and often such psychotic symptoms as hallucinations, delusions, and depersonalizations. Again there are altered states of consciousness or levels of awareness. These patterns of behavior are more likely to be associated with rhinencephalic dysfunctions and are more likely to represent higher hierarchial levels of episodic dyscontrol, such as the instinctual or impulsive acts or even acting out.

5. This inhibited and disinhibited episodic behavior may also influence the persisting character traits of the individual indenti-

fiable during the period between episodes, the first manifesting what Delay (1958) calls the coarctative personality and the latter the extratensive personality.

6. Although it has been reported that combinations of centrencephalic and rhinencephalic dysfunction with reflections at the behavioral level of loss of inhibitory control and excessive instinctual urges results in the most severe behavioral disorders, our own data (which is limited) do not convincingly support such a hypothesis.

7. We are beginning to see evidence, supplemented in later chapters, that there may be two classes of patients now labeled as schizophrenic, one whose condition is perhaps mechanistically related to epilepsy, the other not. In the former, overt signs of schizophrenia may not appear for many years after the onset of epilepsy. It may be that the schizophrenia related to epilepsy may be identical to the syndrome we have designated the episodic psychotic reaction, particularly the subgroup episodic acute brain syndrome.

8. Certain EEG abnormalities, such as the 14 and 6 cycle per second positive spike, may be associated with a hyperreactivity and/or an abnormal persistence of automatic response to external stimuli, which in turn may play a part in the development of episodic behavioral disorders. The episodic dyscontrol associated with this type of abnormality may not be concurrent with an excessive neuronal discharge. This is suggested by the fact that the manifest behavior, no matter how explosive or impulsive, is usually highly organized and skillfully carried through to completion, representing the highest hierarchial levels of our episodic dyscontrol, either impulse dyscontrol or acting out. It has been reported that these patients respond favorably to anticonvulsant medication.

6 Electroencephalograms and Episodic Behavior

In Chapters 4 and 5 we considered the electroencephalogram as the dependent variable, with behavior as the independent one. In this chapter we will look at the data in the reverse, that is, identifying psychiatric syndromes and/or symptom complexes and looking for associated EEG abnormalities. We have mentioned already that scalp EEG's are crude and at times unreliable measures of what is actually taking place in the central nervous system, and our evaluation in the previous chapter was further complicated by the fact that epilepsy is such a heterogeneous syndrome. We will have similar problems in this chapter, but they will be compounded tenfold.

We must briefly consider some of these problems. First, correlations between EEG patterns and broad diagnostic categories are destined for failure because the diagnostic categories are so vaguely described that there is a disappointingly low consensus even among trained observers as to what label to apply to a given patient (Conference on Classification, 1965; Cooper, 1969). One can instead define groups more simply by labeling them with their social settings, such as prisoners, patients in psychiatric hospitals, nonpsychiatric patients, or individuals not under medical or psychiatric care. But, as yet, we are not quite sure of all the social, psychological, and physiologic forces that have led to a given social status, even as a patient. Even at best, such grouping can provide correlations at a statistical level and, even if the correlations are statistically significant, their meaning is not clear nor are the data particularly useful to the clinician evaluating a specific patient in his office. Symptoms and symptom clusters provide more meaningful psychological data, and it is precisely this that we are attempting in this book by defining subcategories of the episodic behavioral disorders at the phenomenological level (Introduction, Chapters 1–3). It is believed by some that computerized data allowing for a multivarient analysis will reveal significant correlations, but there is spurious objectivity in this technique because subjective psychological observations must be reduced to numbers. Such reductionism in no way magically confers objectivity on the data (Symposium on Classification, 1965). Others hope that more dynamic physiologic techniques such as toposcopic analysis, frequency analysis, "functional" electroencephalography, sedation thresholds, differential drug responses, and evoked potential studies will provide reliable correlations, but these techniques either have not lived up to their proponents' expectations, or are too new to have been proven clinically useful. In this chapter we will limit our discussion of electroencephalographic correlations with behavioral disorders to areas pertinent to episodic dyscontrol and episodic reactions. There have been reviews on EEG's and psychiatry by a psychiatrist (Hill, 1963), a psychologist (Ellingson, 1954, 1956), and an electroencephalographer (Kennard, 1956), as well as a published symposium on this subject (Wilson, 1965) to which the interested reader is referred.

6.1 CORRELATIONS WITH ANTISOCIAL BEHAVIOR

6.1.1 *Childhood behavioral disorders.* It has been suggested that there is a detectable maturational lag that can be identified by EEG patterns that correlate with a psychological maturational defect. Children's records tend to be more "poorly" regulated than adults, showing a predominance of slow frequencies. In adolescence and early adulthood the regulation usually improves and the slow theta activity disappears (Pond, 1963). In some children this EEG maturation is delayed; it is precisely this group that is believed to show a high incidence of behavior disorders (Kellaway, 1965; Cohn, 1958). As the behavioral disorders of children often manifest symptoms which we have labeled episodic dyscontrol, or episodic reactions, the data supporting this maturational lag and its correlations with behavioral disorders in children deserve attention, as do possible behavioral correlations with typical interictal EEG abnormalities.

Ellingson (1954) points out that in most studies of behavior disorders in children, the frequency of EEG abnormalities cluster between 50 and 60 percent. Unfortunately these abnormalities may reflect a number of different phenomena. First, they may include epileptic recordings, with typical seizure discharges in subjects with no history of clinical seizures, but with episodic behavior. Because the predominant symptoms do not fit any of the usual adult diagnostic categories, the wastebasket diagnosis of "behavioral disorders" is utilized (Rey, 1949; Dagchi, 1955; White, 1964; Goldman, 1962; Gottshalk, 1953). For example, in an unpublished study of 233 epileptic children seen consecutively at the Maudsley Hospital, London, Edward J. A. Nuffield found that children with temporal lobe foci were significantly more aggressive than similar children with three per second spike and wave patterns (the latter being more neurotic); and the children with temporal foci were also more aggressive than those children showing other paroxysmal EEG abnormalities. As our clinical material is primarily limited to adults, we have not further complicated the subject by a detailed evaluation of abnormalities in children with epilepsy. The interested reader should refer to the articles by Green (1961); Glaser (1955); Bray (1962); Kemph (1963); and Pond (1961). It is important to note, however, that other EEG abnormalities in children with behavioral disturbances are thought to represent a maturational lag in the developing central nervous system rather than a potential for "excessive neuronal discharges" characteristic of typical epilepsy. Davis (1942) sees most of the behavioral disturbances in children associated with abnormal EEG's as "psychic epilepsy"; that is, the result of an excessive neuronal discharge rather than a reflection of this maturational lag. She suggests, in accordance with our thesis, that these neuronal discharges involve predominantly rhinencephalic structures, represented by EEG abnormalities most often located in the posterior temporal region, in contrast to the more characteristic abnormalities in the anterior temporal region of psychomotor epilepsy.

Returning to the concept of maturational lag as diagnosed by the EEG and its supposed correlation with behavioral disorders of children, we are confronted with the difficulty in establishing age standards against which such abnormalities can be discerned. (For example, consider the complications in interpreting 6 cycle per second waves in children as described by Mundy-Castle [1947]). This is particularly important because most of the studies reviewed by Ellingson (1954) do not give appropriate control data, but in the three that do, there was a significant difference in the frequency of EEG abnormalities between the children with behavioral disorders and normal children, normal children showing rates of all types of EEG abnormalities at the level of only 5 to 15 percent, compared to the 50 to 60 percent in those with behavior disorders. As one reaches adolescence this difficulty in determining what is normal for age diminishes and there is evidence that theta rhythms thought to represent maturational lag are correlated with aggressive behavior (Pond, 1963).

A third possibility is that the EEG abnormalities in behaviorally disturbed children are reflections of diffuse brain pathology with demonstrable structural alterations. For example, many of these patients show syndromes described by Kahn (1934) as "organic drivenness," manifested as hyperkinetic, impulsive, and compulsive behavioral patterns sometimes associated with outbursts of sudden unprovoked aggressive and destructive behavior that is quite typical of our instinct or impulse dyscontrol. In these instances the correlations between EEG abnormalities and behavior disorders might be an extraneous finding valuable only to the extent that it reflects what can otherwise be demonstrated by pneumoencephalography, angiograms, or neurological signs as central nervous system pathology. Epilepsy, if it occurs at all, is then just one of the many symptoms of diffuse brain pathology.

In our study of 16 consecutive admissions to a small prolonged (six months to four years) residential treatment service for children, we found the following types of EEG patterns: four showed no abnormalities, even after alpha chloralose activation; three manifested 14 and 6 per second positive spikes; two developed focal spikes associated with high amplitude slow waves after activation; and the remaining seven showed high amplitude, paroxysmal, bilaterally synchronous slow activity, in two of which there were occasional sharp forms in the same distribution. All were severely disturbed children, but none had a medical history suggesting epilepsy, and only two of the 16 showed EEG abnormalities that were unequivocally seizural activity (Patients 405 and 413). Both of these patients were episodically aggressive. The four who showed no abnormalities with EEG activation did not demonstrate overt aggressive behavior, although they had aggressive fantasies (Patients 403, 411, 412 and 415). The children with 14 and 6 positive spikes similarly did not show significant overt aggressive behavior, although they were very much preoccupied with the control of aggressive impulses. The patients who showed the high amplitude, paroxysmal, bilaterally synchronous slow abnormalities with activation were likely to show overt aggressive behavior, comparable to those with the seizure records. We will see later in discussing our adult series that it was this last group that was the most aggressive among adult patients (8.1). Clinical examples to illustrate these observations follow:

Patient 405 was one of the two patients who showed a seizure EEG. During the resting EEG, bursts of low to moderate amplitude, single to multiple spikes mixed with high amplitude slow waves appeared bilaterally and essentially symmetrically, although on occasion there was a definite left temporal predominance. After alpha chloralose activation these abnormal findings were augmented and during the final hyperventilation there were frequent bursts of spike and slow wave combinations. This patient is a 7-year-old boy who was admitted because of a history of aggressively attacking his peers so severely that they required medical attention and on several occasions hospitalization. Other symptoms were that, despite his rough behavior ("everything he touches breaks") he liked to dress in girls' clothes, play with dolls, and do feminine dances, including a striptease. Moreover, he soiled his pants, was restless, distractable, and hyperactive in school.

He was the youngest child in a family with three older female siblings. He was their "baby doll," slept with his sisters, and his mother had been observed clutching him to her breasts and tickling or openly masturbating him. The father was a taxi driver seldom at home, but when he was, there was little interaction with the rest of the family, except to fight with his spouse. Psychological evaluations confirmed the clinical impression that this boy enjoyed and was rewarded for infantile behavior. He was of dull-normal intelligence and primarily used the defense of denial. He was depressed, felt helpless and fearful of those older than himself, and sadistic towards those younger. He had no real identity and his modus operandi seemed to be a cautious, passive, dependent, symbiotic relationship with safe female figures.

Away from his family in an atmosphere that did not encourage the infantile symbioses, nor provide excessive stimulation, and yet one that did provide guidelines for independent behavior, he showed considerable improvement. Restless and destructive behavior ceased, as did his soiling. However, he never developed any real identity of his own nor any close emotional attachments to personnel or peers. His family insisted that he be discharged and six months after hospitalization he regressed to his old behavioral pattern.

Despite the aggressiveness and severe personality disorganization, all the available evaluations suggested that this was a "neurotic reaction." This would seem to fit with the findings of Nuffield that those with spike waves were more likely to be neurotic. However, this patient also had a temporal lobe focus and again, the extreme aggressiveness would be compatible with Nuffield's findings.

Patient 413 also showed a temporal lobe focus, and random sharp spikes and sharp waves, sometimes mixed with high amplitude slow waves, bilateral and synchronous in the posterior quadrant, but with a definite left posterior temporo-occipital predominance. Alpha chloralose activation exaggerated this abnormality. This was a seven-year-old boy who was hospitalized for a period of eight months because of multiple phobias, clinging to his mother or female teachers, and destructive behavior directed towards the belongings of other children. He was born by breech delivery into a chaotic, disorganized family. His early care was left haphazardly to relatives and babysitters. At two and a half he was described as a wild, uncontrollable child, pulling everything from the tables, ripping plaster off the wall, breaking up furniture. His behavior became so uncontrollable that three years before admission he had to be institutionalized in a children's home because the family could not cope with him. During his present hospitalization he was hostile, defiant, and threw one temper tantrum after another. He was incontinent of urine, smeared feces, and bedeviled the other children, yet was phobic regarding showers, toilets, and storms. He was restless in school, showing a short attention span. Psychological tests revealed an average IQ with some evidence of brain damage. He appeared lonely and sad, seeing no significant adults in his environment. He perceived the environment as filled with aggressive destructiveness, which he had to respond to with aggressiveness on his own part. There was no evidence for psychotic thinking, and he too was considered neurotic.

With strict limit-setting, his behavior was easily controlled and many of his symptoms improved. Unfortunately the family situation was such that even concentrated attempts by social agencies to provide a stable home environment were unsuccessful. Upon discharge from the hospital he had to return to the institution from whence he had come. His adjustment there, however, was much improved, with advice given on how to handle the boy, particularly in terms of setting limits, as well as efforts directed towards increasing the frequency of family visits.

What seems to distinguish these two patients from the others was that the difficulties of both were considered to be neurotic disturbances, whereas in most of the patients described below, the diagnosis of psychosis was a serious consideration. The destructive nature of the symptoms dominated the picture in these two boys, which is in marked contrast to the patients without abnormal activation patterns. A question arises as to whether the extremely aggressive behavior in these two children resulted from concurrent rhinencephalic and centrencephalic dysfunction, as has already been discussed (5.5.4).

A clinical synopsis of the four patients with normal EEG tracings follows:

> Patient 411 was an eight-and-a-half-year-old boy hospitalized because he was "babyish," socially inept, and a slow learner. His EEG was normal and there was no evidence of central nervous system involvement on physical or neurological examination or psychological evaluation. Psychological tests, however, did reveal that he was of dull-normal intelligence, withdrew from interpersonal contacts into autistic fantasies, and perceived himself as either helplessly passive and dependent, or as an aggressive monster. He apparently had decided on the former "style of life."
>
> The child's parents had recently separated and he had taken the blame for this separation. At the same time various mannerisms and tics became exaggerated. These, plus his babyish behavior, led his mother to say ambivalently "he is all I have" and, on the other hand, "he is driving me crazy."
>
> This boy has been continuously hospitalized for over four years and has shown slow but definite improvement. He had only one short period of aggressive outbursts while working through his death wishes towards his father. He now generally functions on a more mature level with increase in his intellectual performance, less autistic withdrawal, and none of his former clinging dependency. There is also considerable lessening in his tics and mannerisms.

Patient 403, with a normal EEG even after activation, is an eleven-year-old boy admitted because of hypochondriacal preoccupations and fears of death, which developed following his father's death when he was eight years old. He was a love-starved boy with many aggressive feelings because of his frustrations, but these were rigorously controlled.

Another child with a normal EEG is Patient 412, an eight-year-old girl who was referred to the hospital because she could not learn, wandered away from home, did not seem to relate to anybody, and was hyperactive and confused. Despite the normal EEG, there was definite evidence of organic involvement on psychological evaluation. This also revealed psychotic disorganization of a schizophrenic type. Although on admission she would provocatively slap other children, with simple limit-setting this was easily controlled. In this patient, too, there was little difficulty with aggressive outbursts.

Patient 415, a seven-year-old boy who was admitted with a diagnosis of childhood schizophrenia (autistic), demonstrated a surprising capacity to relate to other people, for one with this diagnosis. He improved in therapy, until he showed predominantly phobic and depressive features. Although initially he demonstrated a number of temper tantrums when not getting his own way, these immediately disappeared upon hospitalization and like the other patients with a normal EEG, there was no sustained aggressive instinctual or impulse dyscontrol. At the time of discharge there was little evidence of psychotic thinking, although psychological tests again showed a preoccupation with aggressive impulses.

Among the seven children who demonstrated paroxysmal slow waves under alpha chloralose activation, almost all showed dramatic examples of acting on aggressive impulses.

The least aggressive of this group was Patient 404, whose aggressive dyscontrol acts were always directed towards herself. At the same time there were fantasied preoccupations with aggressivity, and concern over loss of control. For instance, she would often look at the therapist and say, "hit me, hit me," and then begin striking herself because of guilty feelings regarding her angry fantasies. Unfortunately, projective tests were not completed, so that evidence for latent aggressive fantasies cannot be documented.

Patient 407 was an eleven-year-old schizophrenic. There was some evidence of organic central nervous system involvement on psychological testing. He showed aggression only in protracted play therapy and on projective tests, which revealed that he was preoccupied with extremely aggressive, sadistic fantasies and feelings of explosiveness within himself. He saw himself as a monster and in play therapy his games were marked by destroying objects and killing people. He would angrily bite and chew, and otherwise destroy the play dolls or other toys, but unlike the others of this group he did not display this aggression in other than the therapeutic setting.

Patient 408 was a ten-year-old boy who was considered schizophrenic in addition to displaying some evidence of brain dysfunction. He was admitted because of repeated temper tantrums, threats of suicide, and physical violence towards his parents. He also had a number of paranoid delusions and visual hallucinations.

Patient 409 was a nine-year-old boy whose condition was diagnosed as a childhood adjustment reaction. He was admitted because of lying, stealing, temper tantrums, running away from home, and finally threatening his brother with a knife.

Patient 410 was a six-year-old schizophrenic boy who showed evidence of central nervous system impairment. His aggressive outbursts were described as "going berserk," which meant that he angrily destroyed furniture and defaced property, and verbally attacked his family and friends.

He, too, was preoccupied with destructive games in play therapy.

Patient 414 was a ten-year-old boy with evidence on psychological evaluation of both schizophrenia and organic involvement of the central nervous system. He was uncontrollable at school, hitting the other children and having repeated, sudden, unexplained temper tantrums. There was restlessness and "drivenness" as well as distractability in his behavior, but also, a symbiotic psychotic pattern, with no true self-identity and no meaningful communication with others.

All these children show paroxysmal high amplitude slow waves after alpha chloralose activation. In this small series it would seem that this group was only slightly less aggressive than those patients with temporal lobe abnormalities. However, most of these children had evidence of associated diffuse brain damage, so we will have to turn to our adult series for an evaluation of whether the paroxysmal slow activation shows a better correlation with aggressive behavior than do focal abnormalities in the temporal lobe (8.1). Aggression with 14 and 6 per second abnormalities have been described previously (5.5.5).

Retrospective clinical observations suggest that patients manifesting episodic dyscontrol also have a history of excessive stimulation, either sexual or aggressive, in their early life. We are cautious in relying on such data because of the dangers of retrospective falsification in reporting. However, data from our children, where such retrospective falsification would be less likely to occur, seem to reinforce this observation. Among the seven patients with overt aggression, five were subjected to extreme overstimulation, most often sexual, during their early developmental years. As already mentioned, one mother cuddled her son while openly tickling and masturbating him. Another boy was constantly exposed to nude female bodies and cuddling in bed, not only by his mother but by his three older sisters. A third patient was encouraged by his mother to fondle her breasts, play with her navel, or explore her vagina. Another boy was subjected to his mother's aggressive lovers and repeatedly exposed to orgastic scenes. One mother, a masochist, had had three alcoholic husbands who were physically abusive to her as well as to the children. Among the patients with overt aggression, only one family seemed reasonably normal, while another, although completely unable to cope with parenthood, was not excessively stimulating. Of the three children who showed overt expression of aggression, but only in the protected therapeutic environment, two had family situations which provided considerable overstimulation. One had a hostile, aggressive, paranoid, schizophrenic mother and the other extremely punitive parents who physically abused their children.

On the other hand, among the six patients who showed aggression only in their fantasy life, two seemed to have reasonably normal families. One other had an overprotective, restrictive family; one had a family that went through but resolved a crisis during which there was some physical abuse by father, and one had a mother who placed the child in constant "double bind." The last child came from a cold, isolated family that had withdrawn completely from their unwanted daughter. Thus in this small series there would seem to be some relationship between those children subjected to overstimulation, particularly sexual, and those children who showed overt aggressive symptoms. All the children who showed overt, undisguised aggression were males; this has been reported also by other observers (Symposium on Acting Out, 1963).

Our series of children was too small to prove or disprove Nuffield's contention that posterior abnormalities in the EEG were correlated with severe aggressive behavioral disorders. Three of our patients (other than those who showed 14 and 6 positive spike abnormalities) did show this posterior focus (Patients 408, 410, and 413), and all these were particularly aggressive patients. Four other aggressive patients did not show such a posterior localization.

6.1.2 *Sociopathic behavior in adults.* What are often designated as behavioral disorders in children and early adolescents become categorized as psychopathic or sociopathic behavior in late adolescence and adulthood. It may be significant, then, that there is a consistency in the figures reported for EEG abnormalities among the psychopaths, and those for behavioral disorders in children. Ellingson (1954), in summarizing these studies, reports a surprising consistency of 47 to 58 percent EEG abnormalities among adult psychopathic personalities. In contrast to this figure of approximately 50 percent, reports have indicated abnormality rates from 5 to 20 percent in controls, 2 to 35 percent in psychoneurotic disorders, and 9 to 60 percent in schizophrenia (Ellingson, 1954). In our far from random sample of seventy patients of mixed diagnosis, 30 percent showed abnormalities in the resting EEG while 80 percent showed abnormalities after chloralose activation.

It is important to investigate this high rate of EEG abnormalities among sociopathic patients because episodic dyscontrol may result in antisocial behavior and hence be loosely categorized as psychopathic or sociopathic behavior. In episodic dyscontrol we have postulated a disturbed balance between urges of a primitive, homicidal, suicidal, and sexual nature versus higher control mechanisms. We also mentioned that if the loss of impulse control is so frequent as to become a way of life for these individuals, the world then appears discontinuous and inconstant. Moral values, however, to have meaning, depend on stability and continuity (Shapiro, 1965). It would not be surprising, then, that patients demonstrating frequent episodic dyscontrol might also be characterized by psychopathic or criminal behavior (Smith, 1965).

Psychopathic behavior is diverse, hence probably needs further refinement in order to see whether EEG characteristics would be more likely to correlate with specific behavioral deviation. Hill (1942) distinguished between an aggressive and an inadequate group of psychopaths. The aggressive group had histories revealing either determined suicidal attempts, violence to others regardless of the consequences, repeated destruction of property, or combinations of such aggressive and impulsive behavior. These patients were usually described as having uncontrollable outbursts of temper during early life. At times they were able to discuss their behavior with insight and detachment. At other times they pictured themselves as products of hostile circumstances or victims of harsh fate, being surly, morose, resentful, contentious, and sarcastic. Their hostility would either be narrowly directed against a few people or against the world at large. They showed evidence of inner tension in the form of tremor, tachycardia, excessive flushing, and peculiar "blocking" of self-expression. These individuals were usually hospitalized following several acts of violence. There was also a history of frequent brawling or resisting arrest. In this study, while 48 percent of the total psychopathic group had abnormal EEG's as opposed to 15 percent of a normal control group, the incidence of abnormalities increased to 65 percent of the 66 aggressive psychopaths, as compared with 32 percent of the 38 inadequate psychopaths. In this study, then, Hill emphasized the association of EEG abnormalities with aggression, denying that there was any particular association between abnormal EEG's and delinquency in general. In later studies by Hill (1944, 1952) of these aggressive psychopaths with abnormal EEG's, 59 of 80, or 74 percent, showed bilateral slowing in the 4 to 6 cycle per second range, either in the parietal or post-central area. In 49 this was the only abnormal EEG pattern and only two of the aggressive group had EEG recordings typical of epilepsy. Thus Hill speculated that the aggressive act may not be so much a manifestation of seizural behavior as a release from cortical inhibition.

Although some of the EEG patterns that Hill designated as abnormal might now be considered of borderline significance, there have been a number of studies confirming this early finding. In a study of adolescents, Jenkins (1943) agreed that the abnormal EEG's were more likely to be found where the delinquency was characterized by assaultive tendencies resulting from emotional instability, irritability, and poor self-control. In school this group was reported as showing rebelliousness, distractability, short attention span, inability to concentrate, and intolerance of inactivity.

A particularly pertinent study is that of Stafford-Clark (1949), who reported on EEG records of prisoners charged with murder. He found that the EEG was much more likely to be abnormal in those prisoners who committed motivationless murders, or who were psychotic at the time of the murder, when compared with those subjects whose homicidal act was accidental or those whose acts were premeditated. Murder associated with sexual offenses fell somewhere in between these two groups. Colony (1956) compared 1,000 schizophrenic patients with 474 patients with nonpsychotic behavioral disturbances. He found no significant difference in abnormalities between the two, but 27.7 percent or 18 patients diagnosed as asocial or amoral with aggressive personalities had abnormal EEG's. In most of the above studies the statistics on the EEG abnormalities are based on pooling all types of abnormalities, although the vast majority are relatively diffuse, predominantly theta activity, either generalized or with posterior predominance, which may be bilateral or may be dominant over one or the other posterior temporal areas. This type of abnormality was referred to by Hill (1952) as a maturational defect. Paroxysmal slow waves or hypersynchrony, either generalized or focal, which is more suggestive of epilepsy, was a relatively rare occurrence. For instance, in Stafford-Clark's (1949) series, only 8 of the 64 patients showed this pattern. However, none of the eight were in the group of accidental murderers. Two included in the group of premeditated murderers were borderline examples that might have been considered motivationless, and the other six were among the motivationless murders.

Not all observers agree with this correlation between EEG abnormalities and aggressive behavior (Arthurs, 1964; Knott, 1943). Nor for that matter do all observers report an unusually high incidence of EEG abnormalities among psychopaths in general (Simons, 1946; Gibbs, 1945). Such a disparity in results reflects differences in defining psychopathic behavior as well as the EEG deviations. Kennard (1955), utilizing frequency analysis, found an increase in abnormalities among psychopathic subjects.

This, of course, leads us into the possible relationship between crime and epilepsy, a heatedly debated subject. Livingston (1964) denies any connection between epilepsy and murder. Lennox (1960) says that in thousands of cases he has seen there was only one questionable incidence of murder during an epileptic attack. Both refer to a study by Alstrom (1950), reporting a Swedish survey that shows only a slightly increased prevalence of epileptics in the criminal registry as compared with the prevalence of epilepsy in the general population. Gibbs (1952) also reports that the only murderers he has encountered were among those patients with 14 and 6 per second positive spikes. Lennox (1960) feels that the epileptic furors reported by physicians during the last century might have been due to inadequate treatment, particularly with the bromides.

Bleuler's description of the aggressive epileptic as quoted by Hill (1944) might be an appropriate description of the epileptic furor: "The irritable types (psychopaths) react to influence from without in a very acute and exaggerated manner, which takes the form of attacks of rage lasting mostly a few hours, despair with suicide, anxiety attacks, or stupor states. During the attacks, reflection is altogether inadequate. Some cases are practically in a twilight state, the memory is later clouded; jealousy and alcohol are especially frequent causes for the precipitation." We emphasize that many of the episodic dyscontrol acts may be related to "excessive neuronal discharges" somewhere in the central nervous system and might respond to anticonvulsant medication (Monroe, 1965b). As Lennox (1960) says, "the last word on this subject has not been spoken."

Can we make sense out of this disparity of opinion? Often, as typical epileptic seizures become more frequent, the emotional disturbances decrease. This is particularly true if the typical seizures are grand mal or psychomotor epilepsy with simple automatisms. In our own series of patients, however, this occurred only occasionally (see Patient F242). We have observed that in petit mal status the behavior change is usually marked by apathy and lack of initiative, which would mitigate against antisocial, or in fact, any acts. The best example of this in our series would be Patient F223. In postictal confusions when an attempt is made to restrain the patient, manifest aggressive behavior is poorly coordinated and diffusely directed, so not likely to lead to any effective antisocial behavior. Turner (1962) described five possible epileptic episodes associated with antisocial acts from a series of 337 patients referred by the courts for psychiatric evaluation. The referral was made because it was thought that the crime might have been associated with "mental aberration." However, his brief histories would hardly convince the skeptic, nor was the author convinced himself of the connection between crime and epilepsy.

The correlation depends to some degree on how one defines epilepsy. For instance, in three of four patients, all homicidal, reported by Winkler (1959), there was no history of typical seizures but in all instances there was paroxysmal hypersynchrony on EEG examination. The act of violence was out of character for the individual and would be categorized by us as either instinct dyscontrol or impulse dyscontrol. All of the episodes were associated with amnesia and in two of the three there was an aura just before the period of amnesia in which the violent act was committed. Should these patients be considered epileptics? Any statistics comparing epilepsy and acts of violence will depend on how one interprets such data. Similar patients were reported by Brown (1942), Stevenson (1963), Fenton (1965), Smith (1965).

The behavioral disorders we are studying are characterized by precipitous or explosive expressions of primitive impulses of a rageful, fearful, or sexual nature that are recognized by the individual and/or society as being inappropriate, and are often recognized in retrospect by the individual himself as ego-alien. A review of the literature suggests that it is precisely this group of patients who are most likely to have abnormal EEG's, particularly of a paroxysmal nature, usually associated with an altered level of awareness and sometimes (the exact incidence unknown) typical epileptic seizures. It is obvious from the data, however, that many people with EEG abnormalities such as those found in the psychopath do not show psychopathic behavior, and almost all careful studies of psychopaths with abnormal EEG's reveal a dramatically disturbed family and social relationship during the subject's early life, marked by parental dissension, separation, emotional deprivations, and cultural and economic privations. This combination has been emphasized by many investigators (Silverman, 1943; Jenkins, 1943; Schachter, 1955; Arthur, 1964; Hemmi, 1967); thus it would seem that the ultimate expression of aggressive behavior might depend upon a combination of "faulty" equipment and "faulty" learning. The psychoanalyst is even more specific regarding early childhood experiences and impulsivity, suggesting a close correlation between this impulsivity and experiencing excessive stimulation of a sexual or aggressive nature. In our 70 patients, 24 did give such a history, and 17 of the 24 manifested overt aggressive, sexual, or suicidal dyscontrol acts. The gene-environment effects are complex. The balance between the nature-nurture influence on this problem is further confounded by the observation of a high incidence of EEG abnormalities in families of patients showing episodic aggressive behavior (Knott, 1965; Mitsuda, 1967).

6.2 Correlations with Psychotic Behavior

The figures relating EEG abnormalities and schizophrenic patients vary from 9 to 60 percent, thus showing much less consistency than we found in the behavioral disorders of children and psychopathic disturbances of adults. One of the earliest findings reported by P. Davis (1942) was the "choppy" rhythm of low voltage frequencies in the 25 to 50 cycle per second range in schizophrenic patients. Other equally vague abnormalities include disorganization of the fundamental rhythms, absence of alpha dominance, and the presence of delta rhythms (Kennard, 1957).

In view of the rather specific hypersynchrony reported from subcortical recordings in schizophrenics by Heath (1954) and Sem-Jacobsen (1955), it is surpising that more specific cortical abnormalities have not been noted in this group of patients. In one of the earliest studies on this subject, Gibbs (1938) felt that there was a correlation between schizophrenia and the EEG patterns of psychomotor epilepsy. This subject has already been reviewed in Chapter 5 and was discussed in a paper by the present author (Monroe, 1959). Aside from the complex schizophreniform behavioral deviations manifested by psychomotor epileptics, paroxysmal EEG abnormalities have been noted in recurrent catatonias, particularly low voltage bilaterial spikes, fast spikes and waves, and paroxysmal slow waves at 4 to 7 cycles per second wth a posterior distribution. However, these changes are not consistently found in catatonia and not even consistently found in the same individual with recurrent catatonia; nor are they related quantitatively to the severity of the symptoms (Ando, 1959; Hill, 1963).

Statistical correlations are of little use in individual diagnoses, although such correlations have been used by a number of authors to support belief in the "organic" etiology of schizophrenia. Kennard (1956) thinks that these abnormalities increase with chronicity of schizophrenia, but Mitsuda (1967) finds this true only in the atypical psychoses. Kennard also points out that the EEG improved with clinical improvement. This raises the question of whether the EEG changes are a psychophysiologic reflecttion of the disturbed homeostasis known to exist in schizophrenia, hence only a secondary reflection of the illness, rather than an objective measure of the underlying neurophysiologic disturbance which is causally related to the appearance of the syndrome (Barker, 1950). This subject is discussed further in Chapter 9.

Liberson (1944) suggested that rather than look for differences on routine resting EEG's, one should utilize "functional" studies, such technicques allegedly providing better differentiation between schizophrenics and normals (Fedio, 1961; Salamon, 1965). Utilizing the Drohocki integrator, Sugerman (1964) differentiated between chronic schizophrenics and normals, but these techniques as yet have not been confirmed by others.

The reason we discuss schizophrenia at all is that what we have labeled episodic behavioral disorders, particularly certain types of episodic psychotic reactions, are often diagnosed as schizophrenia, usually being referred to as remitting, recurrent, reactive, atypical, or peripheral schizophrenia or oneirophrenia. The primary characteristic of the episodic reactions is the precipitous onset and equally precipitous remission. A detailed phenomenological description is one of the purposes of this monograph, but we have already noted such discriminating characteristics between this group and typical schizophrenia as acting out or impulsivity, intense emotions (generally fear, rage, or sexual feelings), altered awareness, relatively high level of performance during the periods of remission, and a tendency to recur. We also postulate that there should be a higher incidence of seizures in this group and frequent paroxysmal hypersynchrony in the EEG, particularly if activating techniques are used (Monroe, 1959). These findings are strikingly similar to those of Mitsuda (1967). As already mentioned, the routine EEG is not too reliable in identifying this group. For instance, Levy (1953) reports data on the incidence of paroxysmal EEG abnormalities in the behavioral disorders. He studied four groups of subjects, including: (1) behavioral problems confined to a hospital; (2) behavioral problems confined to a prison; (3) sex psychopaths confined to a hospital; and (4) schizophrenics confined to a hospital. All patients having a history of epilepsy, blackout, head injury, recent shock therapy, or birth injury were eliminated. Only a small number in each group (6 to 9 percent) showed paroxysmal recordings of the type generally considered presumptive evidence of epilepsy. This is probably higher than one would expect in the general population, but patients with this type of EEG were not more likely to fall in any one of the above diagnostic groups. Theta activity, on the other hand, which also has been related to epilepsy as well as to the "maturational lag," was more likely to appear in patients with behavior problems, whether in the hospital (10 percent), or in the prison (24 percent), as compared to the hospitalized schizophrenics (0 percent).

What evidence do we have in the literature that episodic psychotic reactions show higher incidences of EEG abnormalities, seizures, and paroxysmal hypersynchrony? Unfortunately not much, because, although the distinction between persisting and remitting schizophrenia is frequently made, there have not been EEG comparisons between the two groups. However, Japanese studies are exceptions (Sawa, 1957; Yamada, 1960; Mitsuda, 1967).

Sawa (1957) studied twenty-eight cases of "endogenous psychosis," fifteen of whom had shown epileptic seizures, although in four the seizures had occurred only during childhood, and in eight only subsequent to electric shock therapy. All the patients, however, had paroxysmal EEG abnormalities, either generalized, irregular, atypical spike-wave patterns of 4 to 6 cycle per second slow waves; or high voltage slow wave and small spikes; or sporadic spikes over the temporal lobes. These abnormalities occurred either spontaneously or after metrazol activation. In these patients the metrazol thresholds were low (4.5 milligrams per kilogram), a point which will be discussed in some detail in the next chapter. The illness in these patients was cyclic or recurrent with periods of relatively good remission. Ten patients showed symptoms characteristic of schizophrenia, eight showed manic-depressive psychosis, and the other ten a mixture of manic-depressive psychosis and schizophrenic reactions. Particularly prominent symptoms were "turbidity of consciousness, hypermotility colored with anger or excitability, or hypomotility, or a fitful episodic psychic syndrome." With this background we can evaluate the extensive study by Yamada whose rationale was quite similar to ours (Monroe, 1956a, b; 1957; 1959; 1961; 1965; 1967a, b).

Yamada (1960, 1967a) studied 111 unquestionably schizophrenic patients divided into a nuclear group (23 mild and 27 severe) and a peripheral group (61 subjects). By nuclear schizophrenic he meant those patients in whom the predominant symptomatology was regression due to the disintegration of the personality, associated with "dissoluation of the ego" and emotional blunting. The course was usually chronic and progressive, with a relatively strong tendency to "mental deterioration." The peripheral group consisted of those with incoherent stupor or oneiroid states, hallucinations and delusions that were "delirium-like," and a course marked by periodicity. The classification was based on that of Mitsuda (1967), whose work was mentioned in the Preface. Yamada found a clear-cut differentiation between EEG patterns of the two groups. For example, with resting EEG's, 10 percent of the nuclear group showed abnormalities or borderline records, paroxysmal dysrhythmias being quite rare. On the other hand, in the peripheral group, 42.6 percent showed abnormalities, and in 29.6 percent this abnormality was paroxysmal. Activation with metrazol or megimide increased this differentiation: only 2 percent more showed abnormalities in the nuclear group after activation, while 57.2 percent of the peripheral group showed abnormalities with 43.5 percent now showing paroxysmal hypersynchrony. In looking for correlations with specific symptoms or course of illness, he found that the normal EEG tended to correlate with gradual onset, a chronic course, and deterioration, whereas the abnormal EEG group was characterized by subacute or intermittent course, a tendency towards inpaired consciousness, and no mental deterioration. Monroe (1967), using chloralose as the activating agent (see Chapter 7), found an incidence of paroxysmal abnormalities in 47 percent of consecutive psychotic admissions to an acute treatment center, compared with 21.7 percent in a normal contrast group. In this study, except for alcoholics (who apparently develop a tolerance for chloralose) all behavior deviations showed elevated abnormality rates after activation, but the more disturbed the behavior, the greater was the occurrence of abnormalities. The highest rate (except in those with epilepsy and neurological disorders) was found in female schizophrenics (67.7 percent), which was considerably higher than the male schizophrenics (36.4 percent). This makes one question whether the breakdown by sexes would have modified Yamada's findings inasmuch as there were 32 males and 18 females in his nuclear group and 21 males and 40 females in the peripheral group. Why this disparity exists between sexes is itself an interesting problem. Monroe (1967) suggested that the precipitating event which led to hospitalization in the female patients who activated, would probably have led to imprisonment in the male group. Stated in Yamada's terms this would mean that a significant group of males with peripheral schizophrenia might end up in jail instead of the hospital. Although Monroe (1967) expected to find, like Yamada, that the group with abnormal EEG's was characterized by acute remitting reactions, this was not true as interpreted from a retrospective evaluation of clinical records alone. He did find, however, a correlation between the activated EEG abnormalities and those patients showing the triad of negativism, destructiveness, and anger, and to a lesser extent anger, acting out, and conceptual distortions (see 7.4, 7.5). Taking the literature as a whole, it seems that if a differentiation is made between acute remitting schizophrenia and insidious chronic schizophrenia, one might find significant differences in the incidence of EEG abnormalities, with the highest rates found in acute remitting schizophrenics.

6.3 CORRELATIONS WITH AFFECTIVE DISORDERS

As Ellingson (1954) points out in his review, there have been only a few reports attempting to establish EEG abnormalities in affective and involutional psychosis. There seems to be no statistically significant correlation between these diagnostic categories and the EEG. However, there have been several reports on ictal depressions and fears that deserve mention (Macrae, 1954; Williams, 1956; Stevens, 1957; Weil, 1959; Yamada, 1960, 1967b). There is also the possibility of an atypical manic-depressive reaction with an epileptoid mechanism (Asano, 1967). Clinically, Yamada differentiates what he calls ictal from nonictal depression. The ictal depression is of acute onset and equally acute remission, lasting for relatively short periods, that is, several hours to several days. Although he points out that ictal depressions may last longer, to clarify the issue in his study he limited himself to those subjects with short-lived depressions. The ictal depression is usually associated with intense anxiety, but little motor retardation. Feelings of inferiority and guilt are relatively mild when compared with nonictal depressions. However, hypochondriasis, depersonalization, and compulsive behavior of a simple type, such as compulsive crying and laughing are more common in the ictal depression, as are disturbances in memory, hypermetamorphosis and olfactory hallucinations. With pentylenetetrazol (metrazol) or B, B-methylethyl glutamide (Megamide) activation, all the ictal depressions showed some paroxysmal abnormalities, 13 of 15 showed paroxysmal high voltage delta, and seven either spikes, or sharp wave abnormalities; whereas in the nonictal group only four of the 15 showed paroxysmal high voltage delta and none had the spike or sharp wave combination. These findings are compatible with those of Macrae (1954), who reported that fear and concomitant depression was a frequent aura to epileptic seizures, and Monroe (1965a, 1967a), who mentioned the association between depression and spike abnormalities. Macrae points out that if the aura is not followed by a seizure, the ictal characteristic of the affect is easily overlooked. Thirty-seven of his 44 patients had abnormal EEG's and 29 of the 37 had focal abnormalities limited to the temporal area. Weil (1959) gives us some clue as to the frequency of ictal emotions. In a study of 388 subjects with symptomatic epilepsy, 132 of whom had clinical or EEG evidence of temporal lobe epilepsy, 28 subjects complained of ictal emotions, that is 7 percent of the total group and 28 percent of the temporal lobe group. Unfortunately, he gives no figures on ictal emotions in the nontemporal epileptics, nor in the idiopathic epileptics, but Gibbs (1952) has reported rates that are very low. Although depression and fear were frequently related, Weil thought that there was some difference between the syndromes when one emotion clearly dominated the others. Both were invariably associated with a number of visceral sensations and feelings of unreality, déjà vu, as well as paranoid ideation. However, the fears were of shorter duration than the depressions and more often associated with seizures. Weil believed that the more localized lesions of the temporal cortex were likely to be associated with ictal fear, while lesions involving the hippocampal-amygdaloid temporal complex were responsible for depressions. In both the fear and the depression syndromes there occurred episodes of explosive rage (five patients). Thus, we see represented in these patients with temporal lobe epilepsy the fear-flight-fight sequence reported by Stevens (1957), but a surprising lack of pleasurable or sexual responses, which one might have predicted on the basis of MacLean's (1959) characterization of the limbic system's relation to the two basic life principles of survival of the individual and survival of the species. One explanation of this has already been suggested in Chapter 4, where the data on subcortical self-stimulation in humans suggest that, as the stimulus intensity increases, there is a change from reinforcing to avoidance responses (Bishop, 1963). A study by Terzian (1958) to determine cerebral dominance by injecting sodium amytal into the internal carotid arteries revealed that if the injection was on the left there was a momentary depressive episode, while an injection on the right was accompanied by a momentary euphoric response. As far as I know, however, there has been no clinical evidence to support this experimental finding that disturbances of affect depend on the laterality of the lesion.

6.4   CORRELATIONS WITH OTHER PERSONALITY DEVIATIONS

Correlations between the EEG and neurosis or milder personality deviations are certainly unconvincing or not pertinent to the subject at hand. This has been reviewed by others (Hill, 1963; Ellingson, 1954; Kennard, 1956; Wilson, 1965), so will not be exhaustively reviewed here. The problems in differentiating epilepsy from hysteria in the days before the EEG are illustrated by the review article by Notkin (1930). With the help of the EEG, current reports on the subject emphasize the diverse symptoms attributable to an ictal phenomenon (Jonas, 1965; Von Sheyen, 1963). Epstein (1956, 1964, 1966) reports on the psychodynamic significance of the seizure content in psychomotor epilepsy. Epstein (1964) notes that one of the striking characteristics of the dreams of psychomotor epileptics was their catastrophic quality. Generally the feeling tone was one of unpleasantness and the theme one of annihilation; fear, terror, anguish, with only occasional struggles or attacking rage, were the usual affects. In the subsequent clinical material, we will point out the frequency with which the stereotype catastrophic repetitive dream occurs in patients showing episodic behavioral disorders. The relationship of depersonalization to psychoses, neuroses, and epilepsy is considered by Tsuda (1967). In our previous discussions we have also pointed out the frequent occurrence of visceral sensations in the

psychomotor epileptics as well as in those patients showing episodic behavioral disorders. Ging (1964) reports a significant relationship between paroxysmal EEG abnormalities in multiple
physical complaints as scored on the MMPI test. These findings
support a hypothesis originally posed by Ervin (1955) that the
frequency of hypochondriasis found in his patients with temporal
lobe spikes might be a concomitant of the ictal visceral sensations
these same individuals experience. Shimoda's (1961) vast study of
2,500 patients with episodic somatic disturbances who revealed a
high incidence of paroxysmal EEG abnormalities suggests the
importance of a largely unrecognized group of disorders, the episodic physiologic reactions, associated with an ictal phenomenon
(see 5.5.5). In fact, historically it is of interest to review Deutsch's
(1957) fifty years follow-up of Freud's Dora. Dora, too, suffered
from episodic physiologic disturbances, including migraine,
coughing spells, hoarseness, palpitations, and multiple gynecologi-
cal complaints which kept "everyone in the environment in con-
tinual alarm." As one informant said, she was "one of the most
repulsive hysterics he had ever met."

6.5 SUMMARY

Because of the lack of precision in defining and describing behavioral disorders and the inevitable high incidence of false negatives on the EEG, as well as an unestablished number of false
positives, correlations between the EEG and behavior are only
possible at a statistical level. Such correlations may have value
in increasing our understanding of the dynamics and the etiologic
mechanisms of the episodic behavioral disorders, but clinically
this means that the routine EEG is of little use as a diagnostic
instrument. Attempts at reducing the false negatives without
substantially increasing the false positives, thus making the EEG
a clinically useful instrument, will be discussed in the next chapter. There is ample evidence that both behavioral disturbances
and diffuse EEG abnormalities are likely to occur with specific
structural damage to the central nervous system. This is so well

recognized that the literature was not reviewed in the present monograph nor the issue discussed in any detail. Our primary interest was focused on the possible correlation between paroxysmal changes in the EEG and episodic reactions of a sociopathic, psychotic, neurotic, or psychophysiologic nature, and between such EEG changes and episodic dyscontrol acts.

There is substantial, although still inconclusive evidence that there is a frequent correlation between paroxysmal EEG's and episodic reactions or episodic dyscontrol. The further point as to whether the paroxysmal EEG's represent a maturational defect or lag, or whether they reflect an ictal "excessive neuronal discharge" or a potential for this excessive neuronal discharge remains unanswered. This, too, will be discussed further in Chapter 7.

We see evidence, however, from the data presented on the EEG and behavior, that there are at least two large groups of patients now generally diagnosed as schizophrenics. One of these groups would seem to be more closely related to epilepsy and to what we have designated the episodic psychotic reaction, the other to the more chronic *nuclear* or *process* schizophrenia. The former is characterized at the neurophysiologic level by low convulsive threshold and a high incidence of EEG abnormalities. There is also evidence of ictal emotional states, particularly precipitous and unexplained appearance of fear and depression, which, aside from these characteristics, can at times be differentiated from motivated emotional states at the phenomenological level, in that the depressions are particularly intense yet have little of the guilty conceptual elaboration of the more typical depressive states. In the same way, there may be a similar atypical manic-depressive group characterized by low convulsive thresholds and EEG abnormalities.

What appears at times to be hypochondriasis may be the result of somatic auras or episodic psychophysiologic reactions. Also there is mounting evidence that may of the bizarre, and at least superficially appearing motivationless aggressive acts, may be related to this "excessive neuronal discharge" or the potentiality for such.

7 Electroencephalographic Activation of the Episodic Behavioral Disorders

We have emphasized the fallibility of the routine, clinical EEG as a diagnostic instrument. This has been discussed in some detail in Hill and Parr's published symposium on electroencephalography (1963b). In 1943 Gibbs, utilizing the techniques of that day in a study of 1,000 controls and 1,200 epileptics, concluded that the EEG was of little or no use in making a diagnosis in 42 percent of the cases. By 1963 there had been such improvement in techniques (temporal recordings and physiologic activating techniques) that Lennox could report that diagnostic seizural discharges could be elicited in 45 percent of grand mal epileptics and 94 percent of petit mal epileptics. False negatives, however, remain a problem. In fact, in a study of EEG recordings during metrazol-induced seizures in unquestionable epileptics, a significant number of seizures occurred without any preictal, ictal, or postictal changes in the EEG (Ajmone-Marsan, 1957). This underlines the fact that, no matter how extreme the activating technique in an attempt to elicit seizural discharges from the brains of even known epileptics, the EEG will never be 100 percent reliable as a diagnostic tool.

Of course, any correlations between EEG abnormality and epilepsy depend on definitions of both the EEG abnormality and the clinical syndrome. In Gibbs's early studies defining EEG abnormalities not only on the basis of paroxysmal rhythms but also

176

on the basis of deviant frequencies, he found 13 percent of epileptics with normal rhythms and 15 percent of the controls with abnormal rhythms, but only 38 percent of the epileptics had paroxysmal seizural rhythms. It is assumed that with repeated and prolonged interictal recordings in unquestionable epileptics, sooner or later a significant number (between 60 and 90 percent depending on the type of epilepsy) would demonstrate paroxysmal hypersynchronous abnormalities as recorded from routine scalp electrodes. As such prolonged studies are not clinically feasible, it was hoped that some kind of *activation* technique would be discovered as a clinically useful substitute for prolonged or repeated recordings.* The interested reader is referred to reviews on EEG activation techniques (Kaufmann, 1949; Buchthal, 1953; Symposium, 1954; Preswick, 1965). We will focus on the use of such techniques in differentiating the epileptoid from the motivational episodic behavioral disorders.

In this chapter we will review activating procedures under the following categories: first, we will consider sleep activation, either spontaneous or drug-induced, the latter apparently being equally as effective as natural sleep, except when the EEG record is obscured by drug effects such as barbiturate spindling; second, we will consider activation utilizing analeptics, usually metrazol or Megamide, which are convulsant drugs even in nonepileptics. They must be interpreted on the basis of thresholds or unique responses in both the epileptic and nonepileptic. In these procedures, most often the goal is to elicit clinically useful EEG data while avoiding the seizure itself. This has been most often attempted by combining techniques, such as metrazol and photic stimulation or metrazol and barbiturates, or slow injection of

---

* *Activation* as used here refers to any procedure or manipulation, either physiologic, psychologic, or pharmacologic, utilized to elicit latent EEG abnormalities in order to reduce the number of false negatives, and at the same time (this has been less well studied) without significantly increasing the number of false positives. Unfortunately the word *activation* is also used in an entirely different context to refer to the "arousal" pattern or desynchronization of the EEG during period of alertness. In fact, the term often refers to a theory of behavior, combining physiologic and behavioral observations reflecting, for example, the inverted U-shape curve of a behavioral efficiency with levels of arousal (Malmo, 1959).

metrazol (Ulett, 1955). Third, we will consider the use of miscellaneous activating drugs, which have a significant effect on central nervous system excitability, though not properly classified as either sedatives or analeptics. Most of our attention will be focused on alpha-chloralose, which may have specific value in differentiating between the epileptoid and the motivational episodic behavioral disorders. The last part of the chapter will be devoted to a discussion of a particular type of elicited abnormality characterized by bilaterally synchronous high amplitude paroxysmal slow waves (3–7 cycles per second) that, while usually generalized, often show a frontal predominance. Also, to evaluate activating procedures properly, one has to consider possible "false positives." To do this we will briefly review the literature on activation techniques in normal populations.

The possibility of psychological stress "activating" EEG abnormalities will be discussed in Chapter 10. Other attempts at using the EEG to differentiate psychiatric disorders, sometimes referred to as activating techniques, include the pentothal "activation" of schizophrenia proposed by Goldman (1962a, 1964) and evaluated by Sila (1962); sleep thresholds of Shagass (1956, 1959); evaluated by Kawi (1960); and evoked cortical potentials (Shagass, 1965). These will not be discussed in detail.

7.1 SLEEP ACTIVATION

The most natural way to enhance the reliability of the EEG examination is by recording under varying degrees of alertness: resting record with eyes open, resting record with eyes closed, drowsy states, light sleep, and deep sleep. Proponents of sleep activation stress the importance of such recording during drowsy and light sleep when both the characteristic epileptic hypersynchrony is enhanced and the obscuring background activity diminished (Gibbs, 1947). Fuster (1953) points out that as long as drug-induced sleep acts slowly, so that drowsy and light sleep is recorded, such sleep is equally as effective as natural sleep. Fuster concludes that 87 percent of epileptics will show epileptiform activity if sleep records are taken, while only 47 percent show such abnormalities in the awake record alone. These figures are similar to Gibbs's (1947) figures of 82 percent and 36 percent respectively. Sleep activation is particularly effective in the group that interests us, the psychomotor or temporal lobe epileptic. It is not of value in eliciting the abnormalities of the petit mal states. In the previous chapter we mentioned how crucial sleep recordings are for eliciting the 14 and 6 cycle per second abnormalities. It is hard to understand why other studies have been so contradictory. For example, although Pupo's (1956) report is too brief to be properly evaluated, he stated that 29 percent of awake records of epileptics were abnormal, while sleep increased this only to 38 percent, hyperventilation to 68 percent and metrazol to 75 percent. Others also have maintained that sleep recordings are less useful (Silverman, 1958; Gastaut, 1953a). However effective sleep is in activating the EEG, it presents a particular problem for the behavioral disorders, as so often these patients are tense and unable to attain even a relaxed state, let alone drowsiness or light sleep. If one resorts to sedatives, these patients require high doses, often showing paradoxical excitement or sudden shifts from an agitated state into deep sleep, so that stages of drowsiness and light sleep so necessary for proper activation are missed. According to Kennard (1958) this is not true for schizophrenic children and children with behavioral disorders on the basis of an organic syndrome. She found that such children were more likely than normal children to become drowsy or to sleep during the EEG procedure.

7.2 ANALEPTIC ACTIVATION

We have already alluded to the complexities involved in pentylenetetrazol (metrazol) activation, inasmuch as one wants to obtain a meaningful EEG pattern without inducing convulsions (Merlis, 1950). Much of the confusion regarding metrazol activation has been clarified by the detailed study of Ajmone-Marsan (1957), who for both experimental and clinical reasons elected to induce seizures in his unquestionably epileptic subjects. During the procedure he carefully monitored both EEG and clinical phenomena. The goal was not so much to diagnose epilepsy as to secure additional information regarding the particular type of epileptic seizure. In answer to the critics who feel that metrazol seizure is an artifact even in the epileptics, he found that 90 percent of the metrazol-induced seizures were characteristic of the patients' spontaneous seizures. In 76 percent of the patients metrazol reproduced the habitual aura. Surprisingly, in 30 percent of the patients, particularly in those developing automatisms, there was no preictal paroxysmal EEG change, so that on the basis of most metrazol-activating procedures, these would have been considered negatives, but in reality they were false negatives. Eighteen percent of his patients actually had no ictal EEG manifestations, and 15 percent no postictal changes. Such false negative reactions occurred in all types of epilepsy.

He divides the paroxysmal changes into two types: one "aspecific" and the other "useful." The aspecific reactions are highly variable but their topography is characteristic inasmuch as they are bilateral and more or less synchronous and symmetrical slow waves. As a rule, they are diffuse but maximal over the frontal region. They consist of high voltage slow waves, brief bursts of moderate high voltage sharp waves, or groups of multiple spikes. From his description as well as illustrations, the response is usually similar to the type of activated abnormalities obtained frequently with alpha-chloralose. This aspecific reaction was common in (1) bilateral temporal lobe epileptics; (2) mixed temporal lobe epileptics (those with temporal lobe focus but only grand mal seizures, or on the other hand automatisms without temporal focus); or (3) cases of unlocalized cerebral seizures . He points out that some forms of this aspecific pattern also can be a specific pattern for certain epileptics, such as centrencephalic epilepsy. He notes that this aspecific response most often occurred when the resting EEG was inconclusive. He assumes that the EEG patterns and clinical syndromes which were likely to show this aspecific pattern shared a number of characteristics with centrencephalic epilepsy, such as not only the frequency of elicited aspecific patterns but also the low convulsive thresholds and high incidence of generalized seizures. This response was in contrast to the "useful" patterns, that is EEG abnormalities which either had more precise and characteristic wave forms, such as the regular 3 per second spike and wave or focal abnormalities. We will discuss this aspecific response later in the chapter and review further studies on metrazol and B, B-methylethylglutamide (Megamide) activation.

7.3 ACTIVATION IN NORMAL SUBJECTS

Before discussing alpha chloralose as an activating agent, we will look at the data on possible false positives revealed by studies on nonepileptics and nonpsychiatric populations. Ulett (1952, 1953, 1959) compared photic stimulation, hyperventilation, and sleep activation on adult male college students. He found that 8.8 percent showed marked response to photic stimulation, 15.2 percent to hyperventilation, and 10.2 percent to sleep activation. Activation was not predictable from photic stimulation to hyperventilation to sleep, nor was it dependent upon the classification of the resting EEG, except that those students whose resting EEG's were mildly to moderately irregular were more likely to show paroxysmal responses (also reported by Kennard, 1958). On repeated examination of the same individual, Ulett (1959) found that activation by photic stimulation was most consistent, whereas hyperventilation and sleep were less so. He reports that in the original group of college students there was no correlation with neurologic or psychologic factors, but he added that this was a particularly homogeneous sample regarding these factors. For instance, in a study of 30 schizophrenics and 23 nonschizophrenics who had neurotic or sociopathic behavioral disorders, he found an activation rate of 23 and 26 percent respectively, considerably higher than their control group (Ulett 1955, 1965). It is obvious that a significant number of any control population will show paroxysmal response of this aspecific type, which is not related to clinical epilepsy. The possible relationship to behavioral disorders will be discussed later in the chapter (7.5).

7.4 Alpha-Chloralose Activation

Although alpha-chloralose has been used periodically as an EEG activating agent since 1949 (Baruk, 1949; Bercel, 1953; Verdeaux, 1954; Schneider, 1954; Monroe, 1956c; Muratori, 1956; Monroe, 1967a), it has never been widely accepted as a useful clinical procedure. One of the reasons is the unpredictable side effects of the drug, which, although benign, can be disruptive in a clinical EEG laboratory. An early review of the drug effects, particularly in clinical use, was made by Joubert (1954) and a more biochemical, physiologic, and pharmacologic, as well as clinical review, was made by Balis (1964). Because it has been the predominant activating procedure used with the subjects in this monograph, and because of its unique effects in psychiatric patients, we will pursue this subject in detail. Inasmuch as the drug has sedative properties, inducing sleep without any specific obscuring drug effects, has a stimulant or analeptic effect in that it induces myoclonus and augments the hyperventilation reaction, alpha-chloralose is unique in possessing properties of all of the more common types of activating agents or procedures. Even though the complications or side effects may be disturbing to the onlooker, there is rarely any retrospective awareness of discomfort by the patient, as may occur with metrazol. In over a thousand studies, the author has experienced only two instances in which the subject adamantly refused to repeat the procedure. In view of these advantages one might wonder why it is not utilized more often. One reason is that, because of the drug's relative insolubility, parenteral administration is difficult (Monroe, 1963a); hence oral administration necessary. This means a delay in response as well as a certain unpredictability of response. The patients seldom show any effect during the first half hour, maximum effect occurring in the next hour, and rarely there may be a delayed response two or more hours after the drug has been given. Used routinely then, it requires at best between two to three hours to complete a full clinical study, a period that is uneconomical for most busy clinical EEG laboratories. However, new studies of effective solvents for chloralose may allow a more expeditious method (Braude, 1965).

The fact that the drug may induce, at the height of activation, an acute behavioral disturbance of a type similar to our episodic behavioral disorders, which requires barbiturate sedation, further complicates its use as a routine procedure. However, it is precisely this effect that originally aroused our interest in the drug in the study of the episodic behavioral disorders (Monroe, 1956a,b). Just as Ajmone-Marsan considers that metrazol is a true activator of epilepsy because the metrazol-induced seizure recapitulates the spontaneous seizure, we are impressed with the fact that 50 percent of the episodic psychotic reactions activated by alpha-chloralose–scopolamine combination developed similar episodic reactions at the height of the EEG response (1956a). Subsequent studies have indicated that the precipitation of these episodic psychotic reactions is much less frequent using pure alpha chloralose rather than with the chloralose-scopolamine combination. In only rare instances, however, does this psychotic reaction outlast the effect of the drug (four to five hours), and in these instances there is evidence that the patient was entering a psychotic phase before the drug was given.

Balis (1964), after reviewing the literature on alpha-chloralose, said that the results of pharmacologic studies are so contradictory that a unitary hypothesis seems inadequate to explain its effect. Moruzzi (1950) stated that in chloralose anaesthesia the cortical neurons were in a subconvulsive state, but Gastaut (1953) pointed out that the neuronal response to individual stimuli was increased (as with metrazol), while the recuperative time increased (as with the barbiturates). Monroe (1963a) found that in rats and subsequently in other species, chloralose induced progressive sedative, hypnotic, and anaesthetic responses not preceded by true activation, and furthermore that it actually had a marked anticonvulsant potentiality, despite the spontaneous jerks produced during preanaesthetic states and the more generalized clonic movements induced by abrupt stimuli during light chloralose anaesthesia. Braude (1966) has shown in operant studies (Variable Interval and Fixed Interval schedules) the effects of chloralose are similar to those of chloral hydrate, and that phenobarbital synergizes the chloralose response.

Subjective sensation in the early stages of chloralose action is one of pleasant relaxation with slight euphoria and disinhibition; individuals often voluntarily express affectionate, warm, or even sensuous attitudes, while quite aware of the fact that previous inhibitions have disappeared.

> This effect was charmingly described by one of our control subjects, Number 326, a mature but unmarried secretary, who said, "I don't feel particularly sexy, I don't want to break up any marriages, I just wish there were somebody I could darn socks for." Others describe the feelings as wanting to be "cuddly" or to rest quietly in someone's arms. Another control subject, Number 321, a male who could not urinate if anybody else was in the washroom, was surprised to discover that under the effects of the drug, he had no inhibitions regarding this.

Relaxation, together with mild ataxia and slight dysarthria, give the impression of inebriation, and the relaxation is followed by sleep from which the individual is easily aroused and kept awake by minimal external stimuli. The impression one gets is that the individual is in a twilight state; that is, cognition is slowed, there is a feeling of haziness or a dreamlike state, followed by a partial amnesia or difficulty in spontaneous recall. If left alone, the individual will sleep uninterruptedly, although there may be slight twitching of the thumbs, and in some instances more generalized clonic responses in the extremities. This clonic response can become marked with deep unresponsiveness, which gives the impression of the clonic phase of a major motor seizure. In those instances where this occurred while being monitored by the EEG, there was no evidence of seizural discharge on the cortex. However, in several instances (and in these unfortunately the EEG was not being monitored) the patients' clonus disappeared with the injection of phenobarbital and at the same time they awakened abruptly. At no time during EEG monitoring has it been possible to make a correlation between the EEG response and the myoclonic jerks. We have never observed a typical grand mal seizure preceded by a tonic phase, nor seen a post-

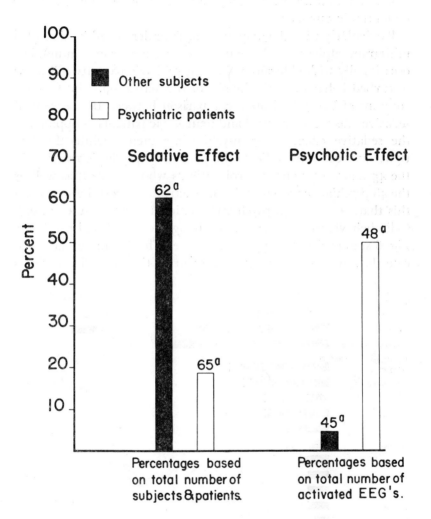

Fig. 5. Behavioral response to activation

Source: R. R. Monroe, G. Jacobson, and F. Ervin, "Activation of psychosis by combination of scopolamine and alpha-chloralose," *A.M.A. Arch. Neurol., Psychiat.* 76:541, 1956.

ictal record. However, this may be because there were few classic epileptics in our series.

Particularly with the scopolamine-chloralose combination (500 milligrams alpha-chloralose and 0.5 milligrams scopolamine), but occasionally with chloralose alone, psychiatric patients will show disturbed behavior at the height of the activation. The two left columns of Fig. 5 indicate a comparison between the percent of sedative effect in 62 control and neurologic patients as opposed to the sedative effect in 65 psychiatric patients, while the two right-hand columns indicate the percent of psychotic reaction in the 45 neurologic and control patients who activated, as well as the 48 psychiatric patients who also activated. It can be seen from this that 24 of the 48 psychiatric patients showed an acute episodic behavioral disorder severe enough to be labeled psychotic. Fig. 6 summarizes the type of response. The top three bars indicate that in approximately 70 percent of the impulsive patients

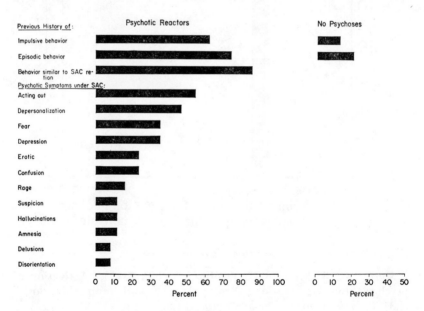

Fig. 6. Psychotic response to activation

Source: R. R. Monroe, G. Jacobson, and F. Ervin, "Activation of psychosis by combination of scopolamine and alpha-chloralose," *A.M.A. Arch. Neurol. Psychiat.* 76:542, 1956.

and 80 percent of those who showed prolonged episodic behavioral deviation, a psychotic reaction was induced, and when it was, the behavior was similar to the patients' spontaneous episodes in 90 percent of the induced reactions. The frequency of the symptoms manifest during such an activated psychotic reaction are also listed in the same figure. Thus, under the alpha-chloralose–scopolamine combination there is an acting out of primitive, aggressive-suicidal behavior or overt sexual solicitousness. We would now call this instinct or impulse dyscontrol. The most frequent symptoms are depersonalization and expressions of fear, depression, or erotic feelings. Less frequent are severe confusion, rage, suspiciousness, hallucinations and delusions. As already mentioned, at the height of the response there is slowed cognition and afterwards there is impaired spontaneous recall, though rarely complete amnesia. Perhaps it is this frequent psychotic response that explains the many contradictory reports in the European literature on the clinical use of the drug, with some investigators describing it as an excellent sedative, and others reporting it as toxic (Joubert, 1954). We have never seen a psychotic reaction without accompanying EEG changes. This, plus the fact that many individuals will experience dramatic relaxation and disinhibition without manifesting psychotic behavior, suggests that the clinical response we are observing is not just a specific psychotomimetic action, but a release of latent potential for such psychotic behavior.

Patient S288 (Appendix 4) dramatically illustrates this response. At the height of the activated abnormality of paroxysmal bilateral synchronous slow waves, she sat up on the couch with a faraway preoccupied look, failing at first to respond when questioned. Then she said, "I'm having those feelings like I often do, the strong force within me." Later she described the feelings of strangeness and unreality, and at the same time strained to hear distant voices that were calling her.

On the basis of our own clinical observations as well as the review of the literature, we agree with Dell (1960) that a likely hy-

pothesis is that chloralose exerts a temporally and spatially differential depressant action which disrupts the negative feedback
of the reticulo-cortico-reticular loop. Such a disruption is brought
about by an early depressant action on the cortex which results
in the elimination of descending inhibitory influences on the
thalamic and mesencephalic reticular formation. At this stage
cortical depression manifested as sedation, slowness of thinking,
and increased convulsive threshold is not accompanied by the
usual depressant action on subcortical structures such as characterizes barbiturate anaesthesia. On the contrary, there is a
facilitation of subcortical structures, either directly or through
release of these subcortical structures from cortical inhibitory
tone. This means that, despite sedation, there is evidence of
motor hyperexcitability, increased evoked associative responses,
preservation of the facilitatory effects of reticular stimulation on
evoked cortical potentials, and arousal reaction to sensory stimuli.
There is some evidence that at higher does levels such a selective
facilitation tends to disappear; thus, a diphasic dose response may
contribute to part of the confusion in the literature regarding the
pharmacologic actions of the drug (Balis, 1964).

In Bercel's (1953) report on the activating potential of alpha-
chloralose, he indicated that 22 of 30 epileptics with normal baseline recordings showed abnormalities after activation, 10 with a
focus and 12 with bilateral discharges. In 22 subjects with abnormal EEG's, the abnormality was exaggerated in seven subjects
who showed only diffuse slowing in the baseline, with the patients demonstrating a focus after activation. He also noted that
the bilateral paroxysmal slow activations were similar to those
elicited in the same patients by metrazol, while the focal abnormalities were more characteristic of sleep recordings. High amplitude slow activity and hypersynchrony elicited during hyperventilation in the baseline recording appeared earlier and was
prolonged after alpha-chloralose. These bilateral discharges were
apparently similar to what Ajmone-Marsan has called the "aspecific" response to metrazol.

Verdeaux (1954) reported on chloralose activation in two
groups, one consisting of 121 hospitalized epileptics, 86 under

Subjects	Diagnoses	Baseline EEG	Activated EEG	Behavioral Change
I. 31 psychotic patients in hospital	18 schizophrenics 3 epileptics with behavior disorder 4 schizophrenics with epilepsy 6 character disorders suggesting psychoses	24 normal 2 normal buildup on hyperventilation 2 slowing after hyperventilation 1 bilateral occipitoparietal theta 1 generalized theta 1 random spike	4 no change 8 generalized low-amplitude theta-delta 2 focal theta 2 spike 15 paroxysmal high amplitude theta-delta (9 with focal abnormality)	no change aura 1 lost consciousness 9 clouding sensorium 7 psychotic all dramatic emotional outbursts
II. 15 volunteers	6 laboratory workers 9 outpatients, psychiatric clinic with no evidence of psychoses or epilepsy	11 normal 2 normal buildup on hyperventilation 1 slow activity after hyperventilation 1 frontal theta	11 no change 4 paroxysmal high amplitude theta-delta	no dramatic change
III. 8 patients with intracranial electrodes	6 schizophrenics 1 cancer with cerebral metastasis 1 periodic psychotic behavior	6 normal 2 occipital theta	all activated (see text)	2 no change 2 clouding 2 psychotic 2 emotional

Fig. 7. Summary of EEG and behavioral correlations with activation

Source: R. R. Monroe, R. G. Heath, W. Miller, and C. Fontana, "EEG activation with chloralosane," *EEG Clin. Neurophys. J.* 8:280, 1956.

treatment with anticonvulsants and 35 not. Activation occurred in 60 percent of the former and 83 percent of the latter. Most often the activation consisted of either spikes or spike and slow wave abnormalities. In a second group of 124 psychiatric patients with a history of doubtful seizures but character disturbances or psychasthenias, 73 activated. Forty-eight of these showed bursts of bilateral paroxysmal slow activity that will be the subject of discussion later in this chapter. One inconsistency with our findings, although it may be explained by the large group of epileptics Verdeaux studied, was that alpha-chloralose induced ten grand mal seizures in 121 studies on epileptics. He mentions the possible correlation between activation in psychiatric patients and what the French call "larval epilepsy of Morel," a syndrome that would generally fit our episodic psychotic reactions. Verdeaux does not mention any particular behavioral disturbances

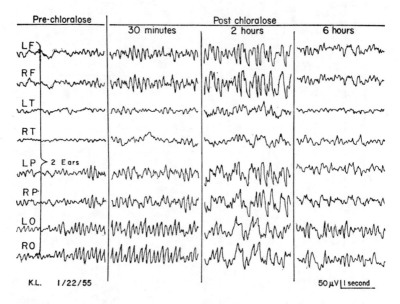

Fig. 8. Typical EEG response to chloralose activation

Source: R. R. Monroe, R. G. Heath, W. Miller, and C. Fontana, "EEG Activation with chloralosane," *EEG Clin. Neurophys. J.* 8:281, 1956.

during activation, even though he was using the alpha-chloralose–scopolamine combination, except that one of the epileptics developed an epileptic "furor." Without detailed psychiatric data, it is hard to determine the characteristics of this group and compare them with our episodic disorders.

In my first study of chloralose-scopolamine activation, I found that 19 of 31 psychotic patients activated, with 15 showing the paroxysmal high amplitude theta-delta activity, while nine had focal abnormalities either alone or in combination, with paroxysmal slow activity. (See Fig. 7.) In a contrast group of 15 volunteers, nine of whom were receiving outpatient psychiatric care, four demonstrated this paroxysmal high amplitude theta-delta activity, and all four of these showed some abnormality in their baseline resting EEG. A generalized low amplitude slowing of the records occurred in eight patients after alpha-chloralose, but it

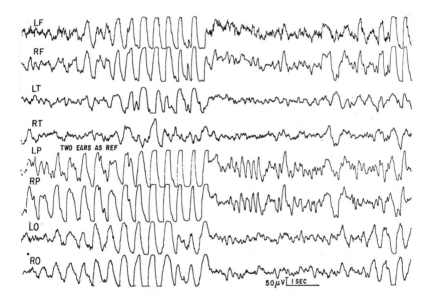

Fig. 9. "Aspecific" chloralose activation pattern

Source: R. R. Monroe and W. A. Mickle, "Alpha chloralose activated electroencephalograms in psychiatric patients," *J. Nerv. Mental Dis.* 144:64, 1967.

was thought, and subsequent studies confirmed, that this diffuse slowing is a nonspecific reaction to the drug when it induces relaxation and drowsiness. Two examples of the bilateral paroxysmal high amplitude slow activity with a frontal predominance, with or without associated spikes or slow waves, and the frequency of the slow waves varying between three and six cycles per second, are demonstrated in Figs. 8 and 9.

In a subsequent study of 200 consecutive admissions to a mental hospital accepting predominantly acute psychiatric problems, 164 had normal baseline EEG's, with 78 or 47 percent of these patients activating (Monroe, 1967a). In 55 the "aspecific,"

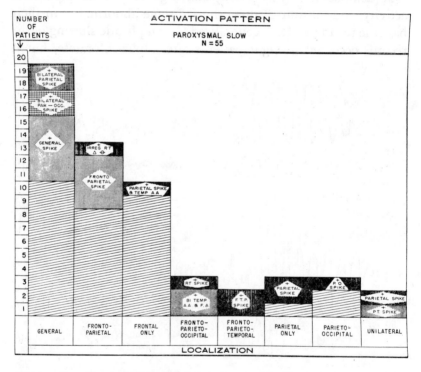

Fig. 10. Localization of paroxysmal slow activation patterns

Source: R. R. Monroe and W. A. Mickle, "Alpha chloralose activated electroencephalograms in psychiatric patients," *J. Nerv. Ment. Dis.* 144:63, 1967.

bilateral paroxysmal high amplitude slow activity with frontal predominance occurred. Figs. 10 and 11 summarize the location of the activated abnormalities with a notation on the presence and location of spikes or sharp wave activity if it occurred. Fig. 10 indicates that in 19 of the 55 who developed paroxysmal slow activity, this was generalized, but even when generalized it first appeared and remained maximal in the frontal areas. Thus in only eight of the 55 patients was this frontal predominance lack-

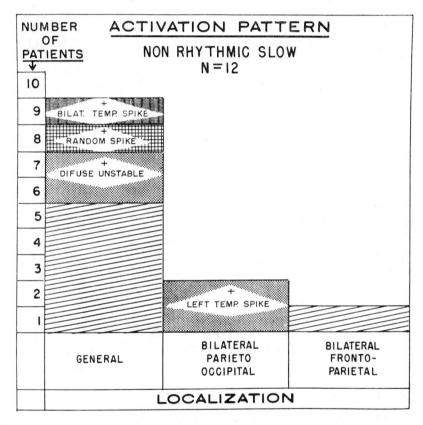

Fig. *11*. *Localization of nonrhythmic slow activation pattern*

Source: R. R. Monroe and W. A. Mickle, "Alpha chloralose activated electroencephalograms in psychiatric patients," *J. Nerv. Ment. Dis.* 144:63, 1967.

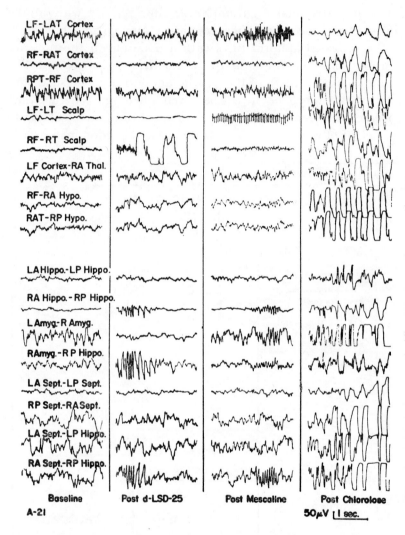

Fig. 12. Electrographic response to LSD, mescaline, and chloralose

Source: R. R. Monroe, R. G. Heath, W. A. Mickle, and R. C. Llewellyn, "Correlation of rhinencephalic electrograms with behavior (a study on humans under the influence of LSD and mescaline)," *Electroencephal. Clin. Neurophys. J.* 9:632, 1957.

ing. Fig. 11 presents the EEG patterns in twelve patients who showed high amplitude nonrhythmic slow activity, a pattern characteristic of various levels of sleep, except that this slow activity occurred during periods when the patients were awake and responding. Other abnormalities recorded were as follows:

1. Nonparoxysmal, rhythmic, slow activities (one each)
   Generalized
   Generalized with bilaterial parietal spike
   Bilateral frontal
   Bilateral parietal with left temporal spike
   Parieto-occipital
2. Spike only (one)
   Bilateral parietal
3. Unclassified (five)

Studies utilizing alpha-chloralose activation were also conducted on eight patients with subcortical implanted electrodes and compared with the subcortical effects of d-LSD and mescaline (Monroe, 1957). There was no clear-cut pattern of involvement in comparing the cortical response with those of the septal, hippocampal, and amygdala areas (only three subcortical areas were investigated in all subjects). Fig. 12 illustrates that the response to chloralose was quite different from that of mescaline and LSD, being high amplitude slow activity rather than the fast sharp waves recorded with the latter two drugs. The response was also much more diffuse, and not limited to the hippocampal-septal-amygdala recordings as it was with LSD and mescaline. The patient's response during these EEG recordings has already been reported (Patient 021).

Although the number of experiments was much too small for reliable interpretations, Fig. 13 represents a tentative evaluation of the data. If the chloralose activation was accompanied by diffuse nonrhythmic slow activity, a pattern already mentioned as characteristic of sleep (although in most instances under chloralose there is a dissociation between the sleep EEG pattern and the clinical behavior), the patient is relaxed and drowsy. If on the other hand, the record demonstrates paroxysmal activity in both

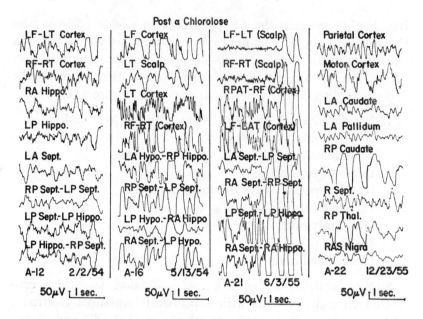

Fig. 13. Different EEG activation patterns

Source: R. R. Monroe, R. G. Heath, W. A. Mickle, and R. C. Llewellyn, "Correlation of rhinencephalic electrograms with behavior (a study on humans under the influence of LSD and mescaline)," *Electroencephal. Clin. Neurophys. J.* 9:634, 1957.

subcortical and cortical areas, the behavior is dominated by altered levels of awareness; that is, regardless of the behavior, there is accompanying confusion, disorientation, and relatively extensive amnesia, as well as slowness of cognition and difficulties in spontaneous recall. If this paroxysmal response is predominantly limited to the subcortical structures without prominent changes in the cortex, the confusion is less even though behavioral disturbance is equally marked.

What kinds of subjects show activation patterns? Fig. 14 summarizes our findings in an early study. In interpreting the graphs it should be remembered that all abnormal and borderline resting baseline EEG's show augmentation after chloralose and are therefore rated as "activated records." We see from this figure

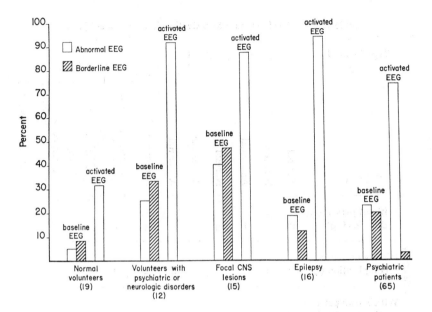

Fig. 14. Activation response in different subjects

Source: R. R. Monroe, G. Jacobson, and F. Ervin, "Activation of psychosis by combination of scopolamine and alpha-chloralose," *A.M.A. Arch. Neurol. Psychiat.* 76:540, 1956.

that approximately 90 percent of those with epilepsy and focal CNS lesions activated. A similarly high rate occurred in a volunteer group with a history of psychiatric and/or neurologic disorder. It is noteworthy that this group had a high incidence of baseline abnormality or borderline records, even higher than the epileptic group. In this early study over 30 percent of the volunteers also activated, but in later studies where the normal volunteer group was screened to eliminate all abnormal or borderline resting EEG's, this figure was 21.7 percent (Monroe, 1967a). In the 65 psychiatric patients, 75 percent activated. Table 1 summarizes both the EEG response and the behavioral reactions to activations in this group. Again the high frequency of the episodic psychotic reaction among the psychiatric patients as opposed to such a response in the volunteer and the neurologic patients should be pointed out. The behavioral characteristic of this

Table 1. Behavioral response to activation in different subjects

Experimental group / Subgroup	Baseline EEG			Activated EEG			Behavioral Responses					
	Normal	Borderline	Abnormal	Normal	Borderline	Abnormal	Relaxation	Minimal change in behavior	Clouding of sensorium	Seizure	Recurrence of discrete symptoms	Psychotic behavior
Volunteers												
Without personality disorder (19)	16	2	1	13		6	14	2	3			
History of neuro. complication (4)	2	2				4	2	2				
With known personality disorder (8)	3	2	3	1		7	3	4				1
Total = 31	21	6	4	14		17	19	8	3			1
Neurologic patients												
Focal lesion (15)	2	7	6	2		13	11	3	1			
Epilepsy (16)	11	2	3	1		15	8	3	1	2	1	1
Total = 31	13	9	9	3		28	19	6	2	2	1	1
Psychiatric patients												
No drugs (44)	23	8	13	10	1	33	12	10	2		2	18
On drugs (21)	14	5	2	5	1	15		13	2			6
Total = 65	37	13	15	15	2	48	12	23	4		2	24

Source: R. Monroe, G. Jacobson, and F. Ervin, "Activation of psychosis by a combination of scopolamine and alpha chloralose," *A.M.A. Arch. Neurol. Psychiat.* 76:539, 1956.

episodic psychotic response has already been described above and was summarized in Fig. 6.

Twenty psychiatric patients who activated were studied in some detail and reported by Monroe (1959). The diagnostic impressions for these twenty patients are summarized below.

Schizophrenia		19
Sociopathic personality		17
Antisocial	10	
Alcoholism	3	
Sexual deviation	4	
Adjustment reaction adolescent		2
Psychomotor epilepsy		4
Dissociative reaction		4
Passive-aggressive		2
Manic-depressive		1
Psychotic depression		1
Acute brain syndrome		1
Malingering		1
		—
Total number diagnostic possibilities considered (20 patients)		52

What is striking is the diagnostic confusion, inasmuch as 52 possibilities were entertained for these twenty patients. In only five instances was it even suggested that epilepsy or an acute brain syndrome should be considered. This is even more strikingly revealed in a clinical summary of these patients, which indicates that nine had occasional symptoms suggesting epilepsy and 13 had significant periods of disorientation and/or amnesias.

Baseline EEG (20 pts.)	
Normal	17
Borderline	3
Psychiatric symptoms (20 pts.)	
Aggressive	19
Homicidal	7
Depressive	19
Suicidal	10

Impulsive acting out 15
Disorientation or amnesia 13
Depersonalization 9
Hallucinations 7
Delusions 9
Symptoms suggestive of epilepsy (9 of 20 pts.)
   Grand mal 3
   Minor motor 6
   Automatisms 2
History of previous episodic behavioral disturbances
   (18 of 20 pts.)
   Psychiatric hospitalization—16 admissions 6
   Other hospitalization with behavioral disturbances .. 8
   Episodic behavioral disturbance not requiring
      hospitalization 4
Abnormal personality (20 pts.)
   Schizoid 10
   Paranoid 5
   Other (immature, sociopathic) 5

This emphasizes that the behavioral disturbances are so over-whelming when compared with the symptoms suggestive of an acute brain syndrome that the latter diagnosis is seldom entertained. The episodic quality of the illness is emphasized in the clinical summary above, which shows that only two of the patients gave no history of previously disturbed behavior. In fact, six patients had had a combined total of 16 previous admissions. It is obvious then that the symptoms of these patients were generally characteristic of what we now call the episodic behavioral disorders. Many of the symptoms were characteristic of episodic dyscontrol, that is, there was an instinctual, impulsive or acting out of aggressive or sexual urges. There was also a high incidence of depersonalization. A significant number of patients showed more overt psychotic manifestations such as hallucinations and delusions. As we can see, all of these patients had persisting nonepisodic personality deviations, predominantly described as schizoid or paranoid character traits.

I thought that it would be important to determine the incidence of activation in a relatively unselected patient population in order to check whether such behavioral characteristics as mentioned above really correlated with activation records.*

Two hundred consecutive admissions to an acute treatment center were studied with the activation procedures. Generally, patients considered to have a bad prognosis or to require merely chronic custodial care were not admitted, although, because of political pressure, this was not always the case. Two thirds of the patients came from a rural and suburban area and one third from a large metropolitan community in a southern state. The latter group had been hospitalized for a period of at least one month in an acute care general hospital where they awaited a complicated legal commitment procedure. During this month they were actively treated, and many such patients improved enough so that they could be discharged before the commitment was completed. This probably eliminated a significant group of patients with what we call episodic reactions. Twenty of these patients were between the ages of 11 and 20 years of age while ten were over 55; 63 percent were females and 47 percent males. Table 2 summarizes this group with regard to diagnosis and sex. Table 3 indicates the activation response for the 200 patients. In the first column we see that 164, or 82 percent, were considered to have a normal resting baseline EEG with 9.5 percent abnormal and 8.5 percent borderline records. Although the borderline and abnormal records are slightly high, it is not beyond the range of abnormalities reported in the literature for a general population. In Table 3 it is also noteworthy that, as in previous studies, those with the abnormal or borderline resting EEG's tended to activate (35 of 36 patients). Table 4 shows a breakdown by diagnosis of the activation rates among patients with normal baseline EEG's as well as a normal group of 46 volunteer, screened nonpatients

* It is almost impossible to get a completely heterogeneous psychiatric population because numerous selective processes are covert in any patient sample. Many such factors remain obscure even after careful scrutiny because we have yet to identify all the reasons why a person becomes labeled a psychiatric patient (Brody, 1967). Such factors undoubtedly influence the experimental result and probably cause the inconsistency of activation studies reported in the literature.

Table 2. Diagnostic and sex distribution of 200 "unselected" patients
subjected to activation studies

Diagnosis	% Men (N = 74)	% Women (N = 126)	% Total (N = 200)
Personality trait disorders	10.8	1.5	5.0
Sociopathic personality and addiction	16.2	6.3	10.5
Neurotic reactions	4.0	3.9	4.0
			19.5
Acute brain syndrome (alcohol)	8.1	0.0	3.0
Chronic brain syndrome	4.0	2.3	3.0
			6.0
Affective psychosis	13.5	5.5	8.0
Involutional psychosis	2.7	15.8	11.0
			19.0
Schizophrenic reactions			
Chronic undifferentiated	8.1	24.6	18.0
Catatonic	8.1	8.7	8.5
Hebephrenic	0.0	1.5	1.0
Paranoid	20.2	20.6	21.0
Schizo-affective	4.0	8.2	7.0
			55.5

Source: R. R. Monroe and W. A. Mickle, "Alpha chloralose activated electro-encephalograms in psychiatric patients," *J. Nerv. Ment. Dis.* 144:60, 1967.

whose baseline EEG's were normal and who had no history suggesting either neurologic disorder or psychiatric problems. The activation rate for the 164 subjects was 47.6 percent and for the 46 controls 21.7 percent. Although these groups were not completely matched with regard to age and sex, so that the significance has to be interpreted cautiously, this represents a statistical significance at the level of $P<.01$.*

Several important points are revealed by this table. First, the alcoholic group, whether acute or chronic, failed to activate at a

* The problems in establishing control groups for EEG and behavioral studies have been investigated by Brockway (1954) and Perlin (1958).

Table 3. Activation response of 200 unselected subjects

EEG	Total (N = 200)	No activation[a]	Positive activation[b]	Exaggerated activation[c]
Normal	164 (82%)	86 (53%)	78 (47%)	
Abnormal	19 (9.5%)	1 (5.3%)	2 (10.5%)	16 (84%)
Borderline	17 (8.5%)		10 (59%)	7 (41%)

Source: R. R. Monroe and W. A. Mickle, "Alpha chloralose activated electroencephalograms in psychiatric patients," *J. Nerv. Ment. Dis.* 144:61, 1967.

[a] No change from baseline recording.

[b] Abnormalities when there was a normal baseline, or abnormalities of a different type from baseline recording.

[c] An increase in amplitude or duration of a baseline abnormality.

level that was significant (P<.001). Such a finding has been suggested by the clinical reports summarized by Joubert (1954), who indicated that the alcoholic developed a tolerance for alpha chloralose so that it was not too effective as a sedative. Second, the table reveals that as the personality disorders become more severe, the activation rates tend to increase, from 37.5 percent in the nonpsychotic disorders to 59.3 percent in the schizophrenics. Previous studies indicating that the activation rates are high in those with CNS lesions and sociopathic reactions are supported by this study, although the patient groups in this category were small. The correlation of activation pattern with age was at the level of .01<P<.02 and the difference between activation rates in males and females, 34.8 percent for men and 56.1 percent for women, was significant at the level of P<.02. In contrast to other reports that women might be more sensitive to activating agents than men (Sellden, 1964), our data revealed no significant difference between activation rates in males and females, except in the schizophrenic group. Table 5 summarizes the findings in the schizophrenic group labeled "pure," in that not only all patients with abnormal baseline EEG's have been eliminated, but also

Table 4. Correlation of activation pattern and diagnosis

Group	Diagnosis	N	Activated[a]
Group I: Alcoholic	Acute brain syndrome	6	16.7
	Chronic alcoholism	16	6.2
	Subtotal	22	9.1
Group II: Normal	Volunteer, screened nonpatients	46	21.7
Group III: Nonpsychotic	Neurotic reaction	7	28.6
	Personality trait disorder	9	44.4
	Subtotal	16	37.5
Group IV: Affective psychosis	Affective psychosis	15	40.0
	Involutional psychosis	18	44.4
	Subtotal	33	42.4
Group V: Schizophrenic reaction	Schizo-affective	10	50.0
	Catatonic	15	53.3
	Paranoid	37	62.2
	Chronic undifferentiated	24	62.5
	Subtotal	86	59.3
Group VI: CNS[b] lesion disorder	Chronic brain syndrome	3	66.7
Group VII: Acting-out disorder	Sociopathic personality and addiction (nonalcoholic)	4	75.0
	Total	164	46.6

Source: R. R. Monroe and W. A. Mickle, "Alpha chloralose activated electro-encephalograms in psychiatric patients," *J. Nerv. Ment. Dis.* 144:65, 1967.

[a] Percent activated according to sex: men (N = 66), 34.8%; women (N = 98), 56.1%. Percent activated according to secondary diagnosis: medical, other than epilepsy. (N = 14), 75.0%; neurological disorder (N = 3), 66.7%.

[b] CNS = central nervous system.

patients with any history even vaguely suggesting epilepsy, neurologic disorder, or other significant medical illnesses. Because the groups are small, it is difficult to obtain statistical significance, but at the level of $P<.05$ there is a difference between female and male schizophrenics. In an attempt to determine why such a

Table 5. Sex distribution of activation response

Group	Activation[a]		N	% Activated
	Yes	No		
Male schizophrenic	8	14	22	36.4
Female schizophrenic	32	16	48	67.7
Male nonschizophrenic	8	9	17	40.0
Female nonschizophrenic	9	11	20	45.0
Total	57	50	107	53.3
Male	16	23	39	41.0
Female	41	27	68	60.3
Schizophrenic	40	30	70	57.1
Nonschizophrenic	17	20	37	45.9

Source: R. R. Monroe and W. A. Mickle, "Alpha chloralose activated electroencephalograms in psychiatric patients," *J. Nerv. Ment. Dis.* 144:66, 1967.

[a] Female schizophrenic vs. female nonschizophrenic: $x^2 = 1.93$; one degree of freedom; p not significant. Female nonschizophrenic vs. male nonschizophrenic: $x^2 = .04$; one degree of freedom; p not significant. Male schizophrenic vs. male nonschizophrenic: $x^2 = .17$; one degree of freedom; p not significant. Female schizophrenic vs. male schizophrenic: $x^2 = 4.49$; one degree of freedom; $p < .05$.

difference might occur, the charts of these groups were again reviewed. This revealed that 24 of the 32 schizophrenic women who activated were hospitalized following acute episodes characterized by behavior which, if it had occurred in males, probably would have led to incarceration in jail rather than hospitalization. For example, one patient was hospitalized because she had stolen her neighbor's clothes and poured boiling water on her husband; a second, for fighting; a third, for walking down the street cursing and abusing the neighbors; a fourth, for threatening to kill a neighbor; a fifth, for having stolen some figurines from a store; a sixth, for physically abusing her children; a seventh, for disrobing in front of her neighbor's house. Such behavior was not true of any of the 16 female patients who did not activate, nor for the male schizophrenics; although because the groups were small, the difference between the male schizophrenics who activated and the nonactivators was not clear. But the data reported by Ostow (1946) and discussed below (7.5), indicating a high incidence of spontaneously occurring paroxysmal slow activity in a prison population, would seem to support this view. This has been mentioned earlier (6.1.2) and will be discussed again in Chapter 8.

Unfortunately, for practical reasons the clinical psychiatric data in this study were abstracted from hospital records. Data collected this way did not reveal statistically significant correlations between any single symptom and positive activation, nor did it reveal a correlation that had been expected between the frequency of hospitalization and activation. However, there was a consistent trend in the directions predicted from the previous study of 20 patients (Monroe, 1959), which was reported earlier in this section. There was, however, a clinically significant correlation when negativism, destructive behavior, and anger were grouped together, and a correlation that approaches significance for the cluster of anger, acting out, and conceptual distortions. A spot check on the patients through personal interview by one of the authors suggests that episodic behavior was overlooked or not emphasized by the hospital staff when they recorded their data, probably because such observations heretofore were not thought to be clinically pertinent.

As most of the early studies (Bercel, 1953; Verdeaux, 1954; Monroe, 1956) have been done with combinations of alpha-chloralose and scopolamine, Burns (1961) repeated activation studies on a group of epileptics, neurologic, and psychiatric patients, with a small group of controls having peripheral neurologic lesions, utilizing pure alpha-chloralose. He found this was equally effective in eliciting abnormalities in neurologic and epileptic patients with normal baseline EEG's, and again emphasizes the potency of alpha-chloralose alone in eliciting abnormalities in patients with abnormal or borderline baseline EEG's. His activation rate of 48 percent in the psychiatric patients seems compatible with the findings of Monroe (1967a). Although he does not go into sufficient detail in describing these patients to indicate how many demonstrated characteristic symptoms of the episodic behavioral disorders, he does report that the highest rate of activation (63 percent) occurred in a group that he labeled "hysterical" and described as "excitable, unstable, unpredictable patients who thrive on secondary gains and only rarely demonstrate true conversion symptoms."

In summary, then, we can see that alpha-chloralose is an effective activating agent for patients with epilepsy or central nervous system lesions. What is important from our point of view is that it activates a large number of patients with psychiatric problems. Despite its limitations as a practical clinical procedure, it has a decided advantage in being a drug which is readily tolerated by the subjects so that repeat studies present no problem. After our discussion in Chapter 8 of 70 patients who received chloralose activation, it will become more obvious that this activation procedure should be used extensively in research studies to determine epileptoid versus motivational disorders of behavior. The ultimate heuristic value of this procedure as a clinical diagnostic aid will depend upon whether subjects who show positive activation will also respond to specific therapeutic regimens. Studies suggesting that this is true have already been reported by the author (Monroe, 1965a, b, and 1967b), and will be discussed further in Chapter 11.

7.5 SIGNIFICANCE OF BILATERAL PAROXYSMAL SLOW WAVES

We have repeatedly noted the frequency with which the appearance of bilateral paroxysmal high amplitude slow wave activity in the range of 3 to 7 cycles per second occurs in the activation of psychiatric patients. This paroxysmal slow wave activity may be associated with spikes and/or sharp waves, but often is not. Many times the waves take on an almost sinusoidal characteristic (see Fig. 9). In most instances there is also a frontal predominance of such activity. In fact, it may be limited to this area, but even if it becomes generalized it first appears in the frontal area and is usually of maximal amplitude and regularity there. Despite variations as to the description of this activity, this type of paroxysmal hypersynchrony has been noted frequently, occurring either spontaneously (Ostow, 1946; Kennard, 1958) or with activation (particularly metrazol activation). The various labels that have been applied to this pattern are the "mteeg" response of Ziskind (1947), the "aspecific response" of Ajmone-Marsan (1957), response "B" of Sellden (1964), the "high voltage bursts" of Ades (1962), or the "bisynchronous paroxysmal slow activity" of Ostow (1946). The consistency in all these descriptions is the bilaterally synchronous paroxysmal slow waves with frontal predominance. Most often such a finding is looked upon as presumptive evidence of epilepsy, or, if it accompanies activation procedures, it is described as "positive" activation. On the other hand, some investigators feel that this is a nonspecific drug effect reflecting the unreliability of the activating procedure used. Others describe the finding as indicating "a lability of cerebral electrogenesis" or low convulsive thresholds (Gastaut, 1953a). We have already discussed the findings of Ajmone-Marsan (1957), who points out that this response occurs most frequently when the metrazol-induced seizure will be grand mal and is less likely to ocur when the seizure is an automatism. These same patients show a low and high seizural threshold respectively. In the group with normal resting EEG's this "aspecific" reaction was found alone in 35 percent of Ajmone-Marsan's patients, and was associated with a specific focal activation in 25 percent. It appeared much more frequently in the bilateral temporal lobe epileptic than in the unilateral temporal group. The variability of its appearance in different forms of epilepsy or in patients with different abnormalities in the baseline EEG make it difficult to explain this response as just a nonspecific drug effect. Ajmone-Marsan believes that it correlates with centrally located subcortical foci, but not with scalp abnormalities. This interpretation would seem to be supported by the finding of Lesny (1960) who notes a similar pattern with eserine activation, particularly in children with centrencephalic epilepsy. While a small control group did not show this pattern with eserine activation.

Other evidence indicates that this is not just an unexplained and clinically unimportant response to drugs. Shimoda (1961) studied a group of 2,500 patients complaining of paroxysmal or periodic symptoms, using a number of EEG activating techniques. Eliminating the cases of grand mal and petit mal epilepsy as well as those with central nervous system defects, he found 814 patients showing paroxysmal EEG's. Unfortunately, he gave no correlations between such EEG responses and the various activating procedures used, which included not only metrazol but also diphenhydramine (Benadryl), sleep and hyperventilation. Shimoda noted that many of these patients had symptoms suggestive of psychomotor epilepsy, but that the EEG characteristics were not typical of that disorder. He also reported a high incidence of paroxysmal response among those episodic disorders which are usually labeled psychophysiologic responses. In a subsequent study (1961) he reported that 69 percent of 135 patients with 14 and 6 per second positive spikes also demonstrated this paroxysmal slow activity. He did not analyze this particular group as a separate entity but in the total group of 14 and 6 activators, 22.3 percent had convulsions, 14.8 percent headaches, 12.6 percent behavioral problems, and 10.4 percent abdominal disorders, all episodic. The paroxysmal slow activity was generally activated by metrazol or Megamide, although sometimes by natural sleep and Benadryl.

Kershman (1949), in studying what he called (after Gowers) "the borderline of epilepsy" found a group of subjects activated with hydration and pitressin who showed bilateral 6 per second rhythms, 3 per second spike and wave or 3 per second spike and wave variants who had histories of no more than three seizures throughout their life, but whose seizures were precipitated by alcohol (3 per second spike and wave) or were associated with stress (6 per second waves). Szatmari (1955), using atropine-prostigmine or acetylcholine as activating agents in a small group of patients (7 epileptics, 8 schizophrenics, and 3 controls), induced sleep EEG's, as well as the paroxysmal responses we are considering, in 12 of 18 subjects. Unfortunately, one can only surmise from the few clinical examples given that this paroxysmal activation pattern was found in a group of patients with symptoms similar to our episodic behavioral disorders. All of the epileptics and half of the schizophrenics had such a pattern. Kershman thought that the epileptics and those schizophrenics who activated were similar in other ways; that is, in both, sleep was induced and sympathetic hyperactivity as measured by the mecholyl test noted. On the contrary, a group of four schizophrenics did not show the paroxysmal change and did not show sleep or sympathetic hyperactivity.

What makes Kershman's study noteworthy is a fact we have repeatedly remarked upon in this monograph: that perhaps what we now label as schizophrenia can be divided into at least two diagnostic groups, depending on the central nervous system reactivity, a point also emphasized by Mitsuda (1967). A similar point of view is expressed by Driver (1962). In reporting on his metrazol-photic activation studies in schizophrenics, he says, "40% of the patients with schizophrenia show a photo-convulsive end point which might suggest that some of them have diencephalic factors in common with subcortical epilepsy." This view is also shared by Gastaut (1950). In an early, brief report, Browne-Mayers (1953) activated three groups of psychiatric patients with metrazol, one group having minor EEG abnormalities, a second described as having acute rage reactions or disturbed perceptions of self but with normal baseline EEG's, and a third without either of the above. The first two groups were much more sensitive to metrazol in terms of elicited abnormalities and thresholds than the last group.

What about the occurrence of this type of activity among epileptics and in a general population without drug activation? It has generally been considered a characteristic finding in idiopathic epilepsy (Echlin, 1944; Jasper, 1941) and is frequently a familial response. Gibbs (1943) reports an incidence of such patterns in the general population as less than 1 percent, 6 to 8 percent in posttraumatic epilepsy, 39 percent in "idiopathic" epileptics, 6 percent among relatives of epileptics, and 1.2 percent among patients with organic neuropsychiatric disorders. Pacella (1944) found this type of discharge in 14 of 31 neurotics.

Ostow (1946) studied the incidence of such patterns in a heterogeneous prison sample, including neurotic, psychotic, physically ill, and presumably "normal" prisoners. What he labels "bisynchronous paroxysmal slow" activity, occurring predominantly in the frontal areas and with an amplitude at least as great as the resting activity with frequencies at either 3 or 6 cycles per second, was a frequent finding in this prison group. He mentions that hyperventilation was usually required to elicit this response, particularly the 3 per second wave. He found that patterns occurred in 85 percent of the confirmed epileptics, 50 percent of the suspected epileptics whom he considered either malingerers or hysterics, 50 percent of those prisoners who had encephalopathies with seizures, and in 20 percent of those with encephalopathies without seizures. Among the psychopathic patients, the incidence varied between 25 and 40 percent. It occurred in over 20 percent of the "obligatory" homosexuals, but less often in what might have been called "situational" homosexuals. It occurred in about 15 percent of the schizophrenic patients but, surprisingly, was present in 40 percent of the conscientious objectors who had been imprisoned because they refused even conscientious objectors' status during the war. He noted that these individuals were particularly rigid and negativistic, with less than one third willing to submit themselves to EEG procedures. These figures are surprisingly high when one considers that he used nothing more than physiologic activating techniques and routine resting EEG's. Ostow believed that the pattern elicited was associated with unstable individuals likely to manifest their instability through criminal behavior or through neurotic defenses against such behavior. He did not believe, however, that the EEG patterns themselves were directly related to episodic disturbances, that is, were evidence of an ictal phenomenon.

Gibbs notes a high incidence of paroxysmal high amplitude rhythmic 6 per second activity during drowsy states in children and young adults, particularly among six to twelve year olds. This pattern, he assumes, is a normal response for the age; it gradually disappears until by age 30 it is virtually nonexistent. Kennard (1958), however, seems to reverse this interpretation. In a study of 100 patients, 7 to 18 years of age, admitted to a state hospital, she notes a correlation between the "tendency toward drowsiness" and abnormal EEG, particularly of the paroxysmal slow wave type. This, in turn, she correlates with certain behavioral disturbances. Unfortunately, her data are not presented in such a way that we can evaluate whether these "frontal dysrhythmias" or other EEG abnormalities are correlated with sleep just because they are sleep-activated, or whether there is actually an increased tendency towards drowsiness in those patients with this type of EEG pattern. This becomes particularly important because the frontal dysrhythmias noted in younger age groups were irregular, high voltage, slow and fast activity, very sensitive to hyperventilation and sleep. What she describes does not completely coincided with Gibbs's drowsy pattern, but with its location, reactivity, and age association one wonders whether or not it is at least related. Kennard's interpretation is based on a number of other clinical observations. For example, she has noted that adult patients with regular resting EEG's show less tendency to become drowsy during routine recordings than adult patients with irregular resting EEG's. She has also noticed that children with schizophrenia or severe organic personality disorders, both having irregular abnormal resting EEG's, are more likely to sleep during the recordings than children with more stable baseline EEG's. She also reports studies on monkeys which show that if regular resting EEG's are converted to irregular ones by temporal or frontal lobectomies, the tendency to drowsiness is considerably increased. Among the patients studied by Kennard, the children with normal EEG's were far less likely to be delusional and far less perseverative and hyperactive than those with frontal dysrhythmias. The dysrhythmic group were not only more likely to be delusional, but otherwise demonstrated disturbances in thought content (obsessive ruminations, phobias).

Finally, we mention several other observations that concern bilateral paroxysmal frontal slow activity. Goldman (1964) points out that it occasionally appears during pentothal activation of schizophrenics. Hollister (1963) found it in patients receiving thioridazine and haloperidol. (Phenothiazine-induced abnormalities of this type will be discussed in Chapter 11 on drug therapy). Rogina (1962) also reported a high incidence of behavior disorders that we would call episodic dyscontrol in patients with typical spike-wave complexes that were not associated with centrencephalic epilepsy. In his group of 16 patients who showed behavioral disorders, nine, or 64 percent, showed this paroxysmal activation with photic stimulation, while in his group without behavioral disorders 14 of 50 responded to photic stimulation with the paroxysmal response.

Another significant observation regarding this type of EEG pattern was reported by Sem-Jacobsen (1955), who noted paroxysmal rhythmic bursts of high voltage 2 to 5 per second waves, usually bilaterally, in 23 of 40 psychotic patients studied with depth electrodes. This finding was questionably present in three others and absent in 14. It was most often maximal in the medial orbital portion of the frontal lobe and did not appear in the cortex. He found that it varied in a single patient from recording to recording. Eight other patients with minimal cortical abnormalities also had this deep paroxysmal slow activity. Despite a relatively high incidence of paroxysmal slow activity, in such select populations as those reported by Ostow in prisoners and Kennard in youngsters admitted to a mental hospital, this finding of Sem-Jacobsen's suggests that significant abnormalities may be present deep in the frontal region without appearance on scalp recordings. This reemphasizes our contention that if correlations are going to be made between behavioral disorders and EEG recordings it will require more than routine clinical EEG's usually in the form of some activating technique or subcortical recordings.

We have already discussed the frequency of this pattern with alpha-chloralose, metrazol, and photic activation. Unfortunately too few studies have been done on a large number of control subjects utilizing activation techniques. Of course, such studies are necessary if we are to determine the incidence of false positives. We have mentioned the figure of 4.4 percent for photic stimulation and 16 percent for hyperventilation found by Ulett (1959) in 100 college students and 21 percent with alpha-chloralose activation by Monroe (1967a). In a much larger sample and using more drastic activation techniques, Buchthal (1953) studied metrazol activation in a population of 682 air force applicants. Most of his subjects were between 18 and 22 years old, none had a history of epilepsy, and only 16 had histories suggestive of central nervous system involvement. However, in 36 there were definite neurologic findings on physical examination, 12 had questionable neurologic findings, and ten had a family history of epilepsy. On the basis of such criteria Buchthal designated 77 individuals as "neurologically involved." In the total sample of 682, 203 were rejected on medical or psychiatric grounds and 479 were accepted for training. One third of the latter group, or 167, were dismissed before completing their training. In this total group Buchthal found that the percentage of normal EEG's was 84.9 percent at rest, 82.3 percent after hyperventilation, 79.5 percent after hyperventilation plus photic stimulation, and 64.4 percent after metrazol. What is most striking is that with three nonmetrazol procedures he elicited 5.5 percent paroxysmal responses and 3.5 percent more were questionably paroxysmal. However, after metrazol, 22.4 percent showed this paroxysmal response. At first glance it would seem that there is such a high incidence of paroxysmal response in this supposedly normal population as to render such a response clinically meaningless. A number of other observations would suggest quite the contrary. The incidence of metrazol-induced paroxysmal response was directly proportional to the extent of the abnormality seen on the resting EEG record; that is, 15 percent of those with a completely normal record showed the paroxysmal response, while 50 percent of those with a resting abnormal baseline showed a paroxysmal response after metrazol activation. The paroxysmal patterns occurred eight times more frequently in the subjects listed as "neurologically involved," and twice as often in those refused admission to training for psychiatric or medical reasons (24 percent versus 12 percent). Comparing these findings with studies of 100 grand mal epileptics using similar activating techniques, Buchthal found that in subjects with normal resting EEG's, only 15 percent of the normals as compared with 80 percent of the grand mal epileptics developed paroxysmal EEG's with metrazol. Corresponding figures for photic stimulations were 1.4 percent and 15 percent respectively.

An important study by Ades (1962) is quite revealing regarding the possible importance of this "aspecific" activity. He investigated EEG correlates with the rate of accidents among naval pilots, an experimental group that is ideal for such a study because of the occupational requirement of coordinated motor activity and acute perceptual awareness. At the same time, this group is subjected to unusual physiologic and psychologic stress. He defined the EEG abnormalities as varying from a highly impressionistic category such as "poor regulation" to the rather precisely defined "prolonged hyperventilation reaction." In between these he identified resting slow records, and records with "high voltage bursts." All of these deviations were higher in the accident-prone pilots than in the nonaccident pilots. If the "high voltage burst" group (the type of EEG under discussion) had been eliminated from flight training, it would have eliminated 75 percent of those pilots who had episodes of unconsciousness during flights and 52 percent of those who had flying accidents. The same criteria would have eliminated only 15 percent of the nonaccident group. These findings are supported by Sem-Jacobsen's (1963) telemetry studies during flight.

A precise and carefully analyzed series of studies of the nature of changes in awareness in centrencephalic epilepsy has been published by Mirsky (1960a, b, and 1965). The most sensitive test he utilized was the continuous performance test (Rosvold, 1956), which incorporates reception of information, motor output, and the integrative process between. This test requires the maintenance of a constant state of vigilance, and he found performance was significantly impaired during burst activity, more so if the waves were well organized, of maximum amplitude, symmetrically located in the fronto-central region, and superimposed on normal background rhythms. There was a suggestion that failure in performance probably correlated more with subcortical midline paroxysms, which are usually, but not invariably, accompanied by cortical abnormalities. Failure in performance occurred significantly more often in patients predisposed to such EEG abnormalities even during nonparoxysmal EEG periods as compared with a contrast group of patients with focal abnormalities. It seems that the receptive aspects of performance were impaired before the appearance of cortical bursts, and tended to subside before the cortical burst activity disappeared. On the other hand, motor performance deficiencies appeared only after the paroxysmal activity was observed on the cortex, and persisted beyond this period of cortical paroxysmal activity. Another test which was designed to evaluate the integrative function indicated impaired performance even if a burst of paroxysmal epileptiform activity was limited to the interval between the stimulus and the response. What is somewhat surprising in view of the other data is that the group of patients with background-slowing, variable bursts in terms of symmetry and wave form, and bursts of slower frequency (e.g. 2 cycles per second, a group similar to what Gibbs would call a petit mal variant), was not nearly as deficient as the pure spike and wave or polyspike group, although showing a significant decrease in performance when compared with a focal epileptic contrast group. Those showing focal epilepsy, particularly temporal lobe focus, did not show this deficiency (Mirsky, 1960a). There was some evidence, however, that the temporal lobe epileptics, particularly if the epilepsy was of long duration, showed a memory deficit. Chlorpromazine, sleep deprivation, and, to a lesser extent, barbiturates depressed performance on the continuous performance test, while dexedrine counteracted the deficiency in performance induced by sleep deprivation. Thus, Mirsky postulates some correlation between attention or vigilance and the EEG frequencies. The more desynchronized and faster the activity, the more vigilant the individual and vice versa.

A number of other investigations, beginning with the one by Schwab (1947), have been devoted to this subject. Briefly summarizing these reports, it has been found that disorganization in the EEG, if induced by photic stimulation in normals (Johnson, 1960) or even epileptics (Milstein, 1961), is not associated with impairments in levels of performance, although Davidoff (1964) does report a deficit if the photic stimulation response induced is of the same duration as the spontaneous epileptic one. In most studies, however, this spontaneous paroxysmal activity, particularly as these approach the more typical petit mal patterns, and regardless of whether the seizures are clinical or subclinical, is accompanied by measurable defects in performance in terms of changes in reaction time, errors of omission, or errors of commission (Tizard, 1963; Kooi, 1957; Yeager, 1957; Goldy, 1961). Yeager (1957) emphasizes that there can be a significant intellectual impairment without other signs of clinical seizures and that although these are unrecognized by the individual himself or even by the trained observer, they may have serious psychological consequences.

Other studies on the prevalence of EEG-activated abnormalities in normal and nonepileptic groups are quite variable. Cure (1948) found a somewhat similar rate to ours of 15 percent of the normals who activated. Schwab, however, in a study of a small control group of military personnel, decided that metrazol was not specific enough to use as a diagnostic instrument because 40 percent of his controls showed a paroxysmal response. Sellden (1964), using another analeptic, megamide, found that 33 per cent of the normal females and 40 percent of the males developed this paroxysmal response. He speculated as to why this response sometimes was associated with spikes and sometimes not, referring to a study by Pollen (1963), who elicited bilateral waves and spikes from thalamic stimulation in animals, the appearance of spikes seemed dependent upon the level of arousal of the animal.

Some as yet unpublished data from our laboratory are also pertinent for our understanding of this paroxysmal slow activity with a frontal predominance.* In the course of study on the anaesthetic effects of gamma-hydroxybutyrate, we noticed that a significant number of patients showed paroxysmal hypersynchrony before developing typical sleep patterns; this is quite typical of that seen with alpha-chloralose. Gamma-hydroxybutyrate is reported to be endogenous in the brains of rats, cats, and men (Bessman, 1963). This substance has been reported to induce a sleeplike state, identical with natural sleep (Laborit, 1960). Similarly Winters (1965a,b) noted intermittent short hypersynchronous $2\frac{1}{2}$ cycle per second bursts, as well as continuous

* This study was done in collaboration with Dr. Gerald Klee, Dr. Robert Vidaver, and in association with Drs. Samuel Bessman and T. C. McAslan.

2½ cycle per second hypersynchronous activity, spikes with poly-phasic bursts, and varying periods of electrical silence in cats. He also noted, as we have with alpha-chloralose, that sensory stimula-tion induced large evoked responses and mild clonic jerking. Bessman reported that gamma-hydroxybutyrate was converted in the body to gamma-butyrolactone, and that gamma-butyrolactone is apparently an active metabolite acting on the central nervous system with elevated brain levels closely paralleling the duration of "sleep." In 20 subjects whom we studied, all but one obtained levels of at least light sleep, 11 showed the appearance of this paroxysmal slow activity, generally four to five minutes after the intravenous injection of 45 milligrams per kilogram gamma-hydroxybutyric acid. Three others demonstrated a questionable response, one diffuse, nonparoxysmal, nonrhythmic slow activity, and five no changes except those correlated with induced sleep. The individuals who showed marked paroxysmal slowing also showed behavioral responses similar to those reported for alpha chloralose. Preliminary studies in animals also suggest that fol-lowing pretreatment with 100 milligrams per kilogram of chlora-lose dissolved in carbo-wax there was an increase in gamma-hydroxybutyric acid and gamma-butyrolactone in rats at one half hour and again at four hours following injection of chloralose.* These findings suggest that our understanding of the significance of this paroxysmal slow activity might depend upon further investigation of gamma-hydroxybutyric acid and in the interre-lationship between this and activating drugs.

In summary then, the importance of paroxysmal bilateral synchronous slow activity with a frontal predominance remains controversial. However, our review of the literature strongly suggests that it does have significance, although complex and probably not yet completely delineated. It definitely is not just an analeptically induced drug response occuring in most if not all individuals. We have seen that it occurs most frequently in epileptics (60–80 percent), particularly those with grand mal seizures, or those with a suspected focus in the midline subcortical

---

* This study was done in collaboration with Dr. Monique Braude.

structures. We have also seen that among patients with neurological lesions but without epilepsy the incidence is high (eight times normal), as well as in those patients whose resting EEG's have shown borderline or definite abnormalities (25–50 percent). It is higher among control subjects who have a history of neurologic disease, trauma, or epileptic heredity, and it is also higher in those who were rejected for air cadet status for psychiatric or neurologic reasons. It is high in pilots who black out or who have accidents. Next to the epileptic patients, the frequency of this pattern is highest in adult patients with severe psychopathology, and it has been recorded from frontal lobe depth electrodes in a number of psychotic patients. It occurs frequently in the drowsy state in children and adolescents and perhaps is higher in the behavioral disorders in this same group. When epileptic and neurological patients, those with behavior disorders, and the very young are ruled out, the frequency of appearance in the EEG in the general population is anywhere from 0 to 20 percent, depending on the selection of the population and the activating procedures used. However, with analeptics as the activating agent the incidence in nonpatient controls has been reported as high as 40 percent. We have seen that this activity is not a seizural discharge in the usual sense, although some studies indicate subtle impairments in adaptive performance during the paroxysms themselves.

It is obvious then that such a finding is not pathognomonic of any presently indentifiable disorder or syndrome, whether neurologic or psychologic. Such a response probably represents an instability or an immaturity of the central nervous system that may occur spontaneously or be elicited by stress. There is evidence that the combination of this response with other factors, such as an epileptogenic focus or a psychologically traumatic environment, may be significant. As a working hypothesis based on considerable but still circumstantial evidence, we would like to propose the following: *if an individual is destined, for whatever reason or combination of reasons (heredity, brain lesion, psychic trauma) to develop disordered behavior, it is more likely to be episodic if accompanied by bilateral paroxysmal slow activity with a frontal predominance, and that eliciting this electro-graphic pattern often requires drug activation.* This is an over-simplification, but despite exceptions, laboratory and clinical data seem to make such a hypothesis tenable.

We have discussed the diverse reasons why one may get false positives and false negatives with any EEG procedure. Among the seven patients diagnosed as having nonepisodic disorders, we had one classic example of this false positive. According to our hy-pothesis this patient having shown a positive activation with alpha-chloralose, should have demonstrated, but did not, some episodic behavioral disturbance superimposed on her basic schizo-phrenia.

> Patient S232 was a twenty-six-year-old, married, Negro housewife. She showed unquestionable activation with a minimal amount of alpha-chloralose. There was present 2½ to 3 per second activity, most prominent in the anterior quadrant.
>
> She was followed over a period of two and a half years during which time there was no particular evidence of epi-sodic behavioral disorder, nor did a reasonably reliable and detailed history indicate such behavior in the past. Her ill-ness was an insidiously developing paranoid psychosis, char-acterized by referential and persecutory ideas involving her husband and her own family, with hospitalization precipi-tated by two rather halfhearted suicidal attempts, the only possible evidence of dyscontrol acts. On admission to the hospital there was some depression, but this abated over the next three months, following which she was discharged. Her paranoid referential behavior was sublimated following hospitalization because of a legal battle regarding separation and custody of the children, with the patient showing a tend-ency to defy the court rulings that awarded custody of the children to her husband. Her appearance at the time of follow-up was that of a disheveled, disorganized woman with considerable tension and hostility, as well as evasiveness, al-though she tried to maintain a superficial air of cooperation. She talked in a pompous, stilted manner and adopted a rather haughty, condescending attitude towards the inter-

viewers. It was felt by the observers that she was covering up more overt delusional and perhaps even hallucinatory material. An attempt was made on several occasions to get her to cooperate with projective psychological testing, but she persistently refused to do this.

From all the available data then it would seem that this patient, despite the definite activation pattern, gives no indication of episodic behavioral disturbances; thus, the activation pattern must be considered a false positive. However, her evasiveness and lack of cooperation with psychological testing limits the reliability of the data obtained.

What appeared to be a false negative occurred in Patient 0236, a schizophrenic patient who showed numerous episodic symptoms while not showing a positive activation with alpha-chloralose. Instead of immediately assuming that this was a mistake in EEG categorization, that is a false negative, analysis of the clinical data might suggest other possibilities.

Patient 0236 is a twenty-three-year-old, white, female, college student, who had been in and out of trouble for seven years, during which time she was receiving some form of psychotherapy, either as an outpatient or as a hospitalized patient. She was frequently suspended from school for drinking, vandalism, drag racing; or hospitalized because of suicidal attempts by shooting, overdose of sleeping pills, hanging, and slashing of her wrists. This patient had psychological evaluations at the onset of her illness, and three, five, and eight years after the onset. Although she has never shown any delusional or hallucinatory symptoms, I would identify the underlying process as schizophrenic because of the consistent observation in all of these evaluations of her retreat into a fantasy world, failure in her ability to abstract and conceptualize, and paranoid trends. However, there were other outstanding behavioral deviations; that is, strong hysterical and depressive features, extreme anxiety with a low tolerance for frustration as well as a tendency to defend herself through denial or counterphobic impulsivity. There were also depressive features and confused identifications.

As one observer put it, "very few of her satisfactions or gratifications seemed directly related to interactions with the outside world. Rather she seemed to have developed a life-long
pattern of attempting to fend off excessive stimulation from
this outside world."

In this instance it would seem reasonable to interpret the impulse dyscontrol and occasional episodic antisocial behavior as
motivated, occurring in a patient who is overwhelmed by external stimulation, and involved in an exceptionally difficult
adolescent identity crisis, in part due to the underlying schizophrenia and basic hysterical character. Thus, in this patient as
in the other patients who showed episodic behavioral disorders,
but failed to show activated abnormalities in the EEG, close
scrutiny of the data convincingly revealed that the episodic behavior was largely motivational rather than epileptoid. In this
sense then, this was not a false negative, but confirmation by
physiologic examination of the psychodynamic impression. There
were two exceptions, however, and these appeared truly false
negatives.

Patient 0260, a forty-two-year-old woman was admitted to
the hospital after severely slashing both wrists. In the hospital she experienced a number of precipitous panic reactions with rapid onset and remission; acting out some of her
impulses, she several times signed out against medical advice,
only to change her mind before discharge was actually completed. On one occasion she made another suicide attempt
by hanging. Another important factor was the chronic depression that had been continuous for some months, in part induced by an overwhelming environmental situation in that
she was deserted by her husband and left to care for her
small children without adequate resources. She attempted
to counteract a basic depressive dysphoria by excessive alcoholic intake, so much so that she was considered a chronic
alcoholic.

The activation record was an example of the borderline
response to alpha-chloralose, which had to be arbitrarily as-

signed to either the no activation or positive activation group. Fifty minutes after the drug, her record was mildly and diffusely slow, containing considerable low amplitude 3 to 7 per second activity, bilateral and symmetrical. However, was considered, therefore, to be a nonspecific toxic effect.

In this false negative activation study we see a record that might have been placed in the positive activation group. However, the most important factor is that a true activation pattern may have been obscured by the already reported tolerance which patients seem to develop if they use alcohol to excess. This has been such a frequent observation in our studies that we feel activation studies are unreliable in alcoholic patients.

The most clear-cut and unexplained example of false negative activation is the following:

Patient 0281 is a twenty-three-year-old twin who was continuously hospitalized during the period of our present study with a diagnosis of chronic undifferentiated schizophrenia. Despite the fact that he had overtly expressed no secondary symptoms such as hallucinations or delusions, such were revealed on psychological tests. His overt psychosis, which waxed and waned and thus superficially appeared to have remitting or periodic quality, was predominantly characterized by dyscontrol acts and bizarre regressive behavior (copraphagia). Most of the acute episodes were ushered in by typical instinct or impulse dyscontrol acts, such as stripping off his clothes and running around nude, or viciously attacking his father and twin brother.

Again this was a borderline record with diffuse, irregular, slow waves resembling those seen in drowsy states appearing 45 minutes after alpha-chloralose, with one or two bursts of single high amplitude 2 per second waves. Because there was no build-up on hyperventilation, and even though the patient did not cooperate well for this, the record was arbitrarily placed in the no activation group. Unfortunately, because of his own physician's reluctance to repeat the study, serial EEG's were not obtained.

False negatives are sometimes determined by a lack of persistence in repeating the EEG activation studies. Experience with normal contrast groups show that the activation pattern is usually consistent from one study to the next. However, as reported in the clinical histories, subsequent studies of some of our patients who have shown negative activation initially have revealed dramatic and unquestioned abnormalities, either of the focal "specific" type or the "aspecific" type (Patients F250, F283, and S217).

8 Symptoms and Course of the Episodic Behavioral Disorders: An Evaluation of Seventy Patients

With the present state of empirical knowledge regarding the episodic behavioral disorders, we can learn more from a detailed study of individual cases than from larger clinical samples. Studies of relatively large groups, however, will probably offer some modifications of the hypotheses derived from individual patients and may point to areas that have been neglected or overlooked (Monroe, 1967a). This chapter then is devoted to the phenomenological characteristics of 70 acute psychiatric patients all of whom I saw at least once; all had detailed EEG evaluation, all were extensively observed during a minimum of one month of hospitalization or in intensive outpatient psychotherapy, and most underwent a battery of psychological tests. Ten of the 70 were my private patients seen in psychoanalysis or psychoanalytically oriented psychotherapy, two to five times a week for a period of two to five years.

Follow-up study ranged from 12 to 60 months after the initial contact. It included an interval history, a mental status examination and Inpatient Multidimensional Psychiatric Scale (IMPS) (Lorr, 1963) rating by two psychiatrists.* The selection of pa-

* Dr. Myron Eichler, assistant professor of clinical psychiatry and Mrs. Kathleen Hughes Wise, instructor in psychiatry (psychiatric social work), The Psychiatric Institute, University of Maryland School of Medicine, cooperated in this study.

tients was unsystematic, so the following data cannot be used to determine the prevalence of the episodic behavioral disorders. (For a discussion of this see 7.4 for the report on 200 consecutive admissions to a psychiatric hospital.) All cooperating physicians were requested to refer for special EEG study any patient that met the following criteria: They would be hospitalized for more than one month, scheduled for a full battery of psychological tests, and available for follow-up studies. Physicians were asked not to refer known epileptics or patients with unequivocal evidence of abnormal EEG patterns. The fact that 14 patients did show baseline EEG abnormalities suggests that a number of the referring physicians were in fact referring epileptic patients with severe behavioral disorders despite my request to the contrary. My own orientation or bias played little part in the collection of most of the data used in this analysis, because the personnel, psychiatrists, psychologists, and nurses were either not aware, or only vaguely so, of the specifics regarding the author's hypothesis.

EEG recordings from the prefrontal, frontal, premotor, motor, parietal, occipital, and anterior, middle, and posterior temporal regions, utilizing four minute runs (12 channels with five different montages, both monopolar and bipolar) ending with a four minute period of hyperventilation, were included in the baseline record. Then 6.5 mg./kg. alpha chloralose, suspended in a small amount of warm water, was given orally. Three quarters of an hour later, EEG recordings were restarted repeating the baseline montages for a minimum of three quarters of an hour or continued until the drug effect had begun to wane. At three quarters of an hour, or one and one half hours after the drug was given, a repeat hyperventilation was performed. Sleep recordings were usually obtained after the administration of alpha chloralose. Following the discontinuation of the recordings, objective and subjective data were collected on the clinical effects of alpha chloralose. In a number of instances, repeated activation studies with alpha chloralose were made. Sometimes such studies were supplemented by other activating procedures, usually metrazol. In two of the 70 patients, baseline abnormalities were so marked that activation procedures were unnecessary or unwise.

The patient group was divided into three categories on the basis of EEG findings. The first consisted of 24 patients listed as "no activation," including 18 subjects with absolutely no change after the administration of alpha chloralose. All but one of these patients had normal baseline recordings. Six other patients had minimal changes; that is, the appearance of low amplitude slow waves, but these were not paroxysmal bursts, nor did they meet the criteria for either the specific or aspecific abnormalities as defined below. In analyzing the data, these two groups were first considered separately, but no clinical differentiation between the two seemed apparent, so patients with no change and minimal EEG changes were later considered as one group.

A second group of 25 patients showed activation patterns characterized by "aspecific" bilateral paroxysmal slow activity (discussed in detail in 7.5). This pattern was defined as a sudden change in frequency to a lower range, that is 3–7 cycles per second with an amplitude of at least twice that of the baseline activity; the bursts were not considered significant unless they lasted for a minimum of one second, although they might continue for seconds or even minutes. What gives them the paroxysmal quality is the sudden change in frequency and amplitude. The patterns were usually bilateral, synchronous and generalized, although often showing a frontal predominance. Hypersynchronous or sharp forms in the same distribution would occasionally occur with these patterns (3 of the 25).

EEG's of a third group of 21 subjects who showed "specific" or focal abnormalities are summarized in Table 6; "h" refers to hypersynchrony, that is spikes or sharp waves, and "s" to slow waves. The table also indicates the baseline recording as well as the presence or absence of the "aspecific" response to activation. Patient F284, who showed generalized, paroxysmal, slow waves with hypersynchrony, might have been listed with the aspecific paroxysmal slow activators. However, as this was markedly present in the baseline recording, regular in wave form and frequency, and did not change significantly in form with chloralose activation, it was listed as a "specific" abnormality considered characteristic of centrencephalic epilepsy. Ajmone-Marsan (1957)

Table 6. "Specific" activated abnormalities

Pa-tient	Front		AT		MT		PT		14&6	Gen parox. slow	Base-line	Diagnoses
	R	L	R	L	R	L	R	L				
201				h/s		h/s		h/s		+	N	Episodic reaction (schizophrenia)
206						h/s		h/s		+	N	Seizure dyscontrol
211									+	+	N	Acting out
213				h/s		h/s		h/s		o	A	Schizophrenia with seizures
221			s			s				+	A	Acting out
222				h/s		h/s				+	A	Paranoid person, with seizures
223						h/s				+	A	Obsessive-compulsive person with episodic inhibition
227				h/s						+	A	Brain syndrome and seizures
242			h	h	h	h	h	h		o	N	Instinct dyscontrol
246									+	+	N	Acting out
247	h	h				h				o	A	Seizure dyscontrol
250			h	h	h	h	h	h		o	A	Episodic reaction (depression)
267	h	h								+	A	Episodic reaction (schizophrenia)
271	h			h		h		h		+	A	Impulse dyscontrol
272									+	o	A	Impulse dyscontrol
275	h	h				h				+	N	Seizure dyscontrol
276	s	s								o	A	Tics with brain syndrome
283			s	s	s	s	s	s		o	A	Impulse dyscontrol
284	general		parox. slow-h							+	A	Episodic reaction (anxiety)
285	general		spike wave							+	A	Seizure dyscontrol
287					s	s				o	A	Instinct dyscontrol

h = hypersynchrony.
s = slow wave.
A = abnormal baseline augmented by activation.
N = normal baseline.

discusses the difficulty in making such a distinction. The same table reveals that 15 of the 21 subjects with specific abnormalities had temporal foci.

For contrast purposes, the same subjects were regrouped into four other categories differentiated on either clinical, historical, or psychological test criteria. The first included 26 patients in whom evidence of schizophrenic thought disorder was found on psychological testing; a second group of 14 subjects showed evidence of "organicity" on psychological testing; a third group of 16 patients had clinical histories which revealed no evidence for significant episodic behavioral disorders; and a fourth group of 19 subjects had histories of typical epilepsy including treatment with anticonvulsants. Whereas the EEG groups were mutually exclusive, the latter four groups were not. A patient might be included in more than one group. These four groups were selected because the criteria were reasonably rigorous and clear-cut, and because they provided an appropriate contrast for those groups differentiated on the basis of EEG criteria.

Table 7 summarizes the identifying characteristics of the total group of 70 patients as well as each subcategory in terms of sex and average age, length of hospitalization, number of hospitalizations, months of follow-up, educational level and I.Q. This table reveals that the age for both the specific and the paroxysmal slow activation group is somewhat lower than for any of the others, except for those with seizure. In view of the fact that there is some evidence for higher rate of activation among younger age groups, this will introduce some cautiousness in interpretation of the data regarding activation patients.

Table 7 also shows that 18 females as opposed to only seven males showed the "aspecific" paroxysmal slow activation. In no other group was there such a marked sex differential; in fact, in the nonactivators the ratio was almost reversed (15 males and 9 females). Such a sex differential has already been reported in previous studies and discussed earlier (7.4). Two factors that might lead to such a sex differential are the younger age groups among the females and a higher incidence of diagnosed schizophrenia (Monroe, 1967a), but neither of these adequately explains

Table 7. Characteristics of subgroups of seventy patients (ranges in parentheses)

	Groups	Age	Male	Female	Length hospital- ization in months	Number of hospital- izations	Number months follow-up	Years education	IQ
EEG criteria	Nonactivators N = 24	29 (16–45)	15	9	3.4 (0–14)	1.6 (0–4)	20 (6–45)	11.1 (9–16)	104 (89–117)
	Specific activators N = 21	26 (15–47)	10	11	4 (1–19)	1.8 (1–5)	20 (3–48)	12 (9–16)	105 (91–124)
	Paroxysmal slow activators N = 25	25 (14–47)	7	18	6 (0–30)	1.5 (1–2)	28 (12–60)	11 (6–16)	109 (72–136)
	Total group N = 70	26	32	38	4.6	1.5	24	11	106
Clinical Criteria	Schizophrenic thought disorder N = 26	29	10	16	6.2	1.4	25	11.5	108
	"Organicity" N = 14	30	9	5	4	1.8	22	11.5	105
	Diagnosed nonepisodic N = 16	29	12	5	2.3	1.3	22	11	100
	Seizural N = 19	26	9	10	3.1	1.5	22	12	110

the difference. Another explanation might be that males who commit aggressive acts are more likely to be jailed than hospitalized (Monroe, 1967a). Among the males showing paroxysmal slow wave activation two of seven were transferred from jail to the hospital, and with two others incarceration in jail was seriously considered; these few individuals therefore would tend to support such a hypothesis.

Another finding shows that the group with paroxysmal slow activation was hospitalized for a longer period of time than either the specific or the nonactivation groups, or in fact longer than those showing evidence of organicity, those diagnosed as nonepisodic, or those with seizures. The length of hospitalization was similar to that of patients who showed schizophrenic thought disorder, although the paroxysmal activation group did not contribute disproportionately to the diagnosis of schizophrenic thought disorders. Interpretation of this finding on the basis of a study of individual cases, particularly adolescent patients, reveals that the problems leading to hospitalization for those showing this "aspecific" paroxysmal slow activation are as severe as the problems of those who show schizophrenic thought disorder. They interfere equally with socialization and rehabilitation outside the hospital even though the symptoms are qualitatively different (see Patient S202). In terms of average educational level and I.Q. there did not seem to be any significant difference between the groups.

8.1 CLINICAL SYMPTOMS

Table 8 gives an overall summary of the clinical symptoms for the total patient group as well as the three subgroups determined by activation patterns and the four groups differentiated on the basis of psychological testing or clinical data. First, 32 of 70 patients showed epileptoid phenomena. Nineteen had typical seizures; 12 with predominantly grand mal seizures, six with predominantly psychomotor seizures, and one with petit mal epilepsy. As might have been predicted, 16 of the 21 patients with

Table 8. Predominant clinical symptoms of subgroups

	Subgroups	Grand mal	Psychomotor	Petit mal	Atypical	"Blackouts"	Aggressive	Suicidal	Transitory hallucination	Depersonalization	Conversion an issue	Excessive stimulation
		\<Seizure\>					\<Dyscontrol act[a]\>		\<Symptoms\>			\<Anamnesis\>
EEG criteria	Nonactivators N = 24	0	0	0	5	1	6	6	3	4	7	6
	Specific activators N = 21	8	4	1	3	0	1[b]	8	2	3	12	7
	Paroxysmal slow ("nonspecific") activators N = 25	4	2	0	2	2	13	8	10	16	10	11
	Total N = 70	12	6	1	10	3	20	22	15	23	29	24
Clinical criteria	Schizophrenic thought disorder N = 26	7	1	0	3	1	7	7	5	10	11	3
	"Organicity" N = 14	5	1	0	4	1	2	7	2	3	9	5
	Nonepisodic N = 16	0	0	0	0	0	2	6[c]	1	2	4	2
	Epileptics N = 19	12	6	1	0	0	3	6	0	5	13	7

[a] Precipitated hospital admission or therapy.
[b] Seven other aggressive acts in past.
[c] All insincere attempts.

specific EEG abnormalities had a history of "spells," with 13 of the 16 having had typical grand mal seizures or simple automatisms. Atypical seizures were most likely to occur in those patients without specific EEG abnormalities, probably reflecting the importance of motivational elements behind the symptoms. While it might not be surprising that 11 of the 14 patients with signs of "organicity" also had seizures, it is surprising that 12 of the 26 with psychological evidence of thought disorder of schizophrenic type also had a history of seizures. The high incidence of seizures in this group undoubtedly reflects selection factors in obtaining the 70 patients, but it may have important clinical significance in view of Slater's findings (1965) that overt psychotic symptoms often appear some years after the first signs of epilepsy (5.6).

The incidence of aggression and suicide was over 80 percent in the paroxysmal slow activation group and approximately 50 percent in all other groups. Twenty-one of the 25 patients who showed paroxysmal, slow activation were admitted to the hospital following serious aggressive acts (13) or serious suicidal attempts (8). The small number of patients with specific abnormalities whose hospitalization was precipitated by aggressive acts is in part an artifact, because many of these patients were allegedly hospitalized for diagnostic purposes; however, seven of them had a history of assaultive behavior. Even taking this into account, aggression seemed to be less common in those patients who either showed specific EEG abnormalities, or those who did not activate as compared to those with "aspecific" EEG abnormalities. Although 12 of the 24 nonactivators showed some kind of aggressive or suicidal acting out, the qualitative difference between the dyscontrol acts of this group compared to the dyscontrol acts of the "aspecific" activation group is striking. Among the nonactivators in only four instances were the aggressive acts toward self or others serious ones. Two were serious suicidal attempts, and two were homicidal rage reactions; the other eight were obviously fake or impotent aggressive acts: four patients manifesting typical adolescent rebellion, one showing adolescent sexual promiscuity, and three making patently fake suicidal attempts. It is of note that in this series, those patients who showed evidence of organicity on the psychological battery were not particularly aggressive. This is the opposite of what we found in our small series of children (6.1.1).

Since almost all patients in all groups gave both clinical and psychological test evidence of anxiety, depression, and sexual conflicts (over 90 percent in every instance) these were omitted from Tables 8 and 9. However, there was a difference between those showing transitory hallucinations and depersonalization; ten patients among the paroxysmal, slow activators had hallucinations while only two of the specific activators and three of the nonactivators reported such symptoms. Inasmuch as none of the seizure patients reported transitory hallucinations, this phenomenon then was not related to the auras or prodromata of typical epilepsy. There was a similar differentiation in terms of transitory depersonalization; 16 of the paroxysmal slow activators reported this symptom while only three of the specific activators and four of the nonactivators did. Inasmuch as these symptoms were vague and transitory, they were not judged as sufficient criteria for making the diagnosis of an episodic psychotic reaction, unless there was evidence for other characteristic symptoms of the acute schizophrenic reaction or acute brain syndrome.

The problems of conversion or hysterical defenses is a confusing issue, partly because it exists in all groups whether identified electroencephalographically, clinically, or on projective criteria. Approximately one quarter to one third of the nonactivating group were identified as manifesting hysterical defenses, increasing up to one third to one half in all other groups. It is not surprising that over one half of the seizure patients and those with specific activated abnormalities were considered by at least some observers to manifest conversion reaction. Projective tests (Table 9) support the clinical impression, namely that hysterical defense mechanisms although highest in the patients who show paroxysmal slow activation are also high in those with specific EEG abnormalities. It is worthwhile to note the high frequency of hysterical defenses, even in those patients with definite evidence of "faulty" equipment (organic and epileptic group). However, when compared with evidence on the psychological tests, the clinician appears to overemphasize hysterical mechanisms in patients with epilepsy, probably because he considers atypical seizures a conversion reaction.

In earlier chapters, we mentioned the psychoanalyst's proposal that acting out and impulsivity may be related to excessive stimu-

Table 9. Psychological test findings of subgroups

	Subgroups	Poor impulse control	Hysterical defense	Oral dependency	Identity problem	Narcissism	Sadism-masochism	Schizophrenic thought disorder	"Organicity"
EEG criteria	Nonactivators N = 19	9	6	5	6	3	4	8	3
	Specific activators N = 17	8	7	12	9	6	8	8	7
	Paroxysmal, slow ("nonspecific") activators N = 25	13	12	11	9	6	8	11	4
	Total N = 61	29	25	28	24	15	20	26	14
Clinical criteria	Schizophrenic thought disorder N = 26	13	14	13	10	7	7	26	6
	"Organicity" N = 14	9	6	10	3	6	4	6	14
	Nonepisodic N = 12	4	5	4	4	3	2	5	1
	Epileptics N = 16	5	6	12	4	4	6	9	5

lation during childhood. We presented data offering some support for this hypothesis when discussing children (6.1.1), at the same time pointing out that an adult's retrospective evaluation of his early childhood is usually unreliable. In our series of adults, there were 24 patients in whom there was clear-cut evidence of either sexual or aggressive overstimulation. Although the schizophrenic patients represented over one third of our total sample, only three patients with a history of such overstimulation were schizophrenics. The nonepisodic patients represented slightly less than one fourth of the total group, and only two of the patients with a history of overstimulation during childhood fell in this group. To look at it another way, only two patients (0238 and 0280) who were subjected to overstimulation failed to show episodic behavioral disorders. Somewhere between one third to one half of the patients in the specific activation group and paroxysmal slow activation had a history of being subjected to overstimulation. These observations also suggest that overstimulation during childhood may be a contributory cause of the episodic behavioral disorders.

8.2 DIFFERENTIATION BY PSYCHOLOGICAL TESTS

Most patients selected for study had previously been administered a full battery of psychological tests as part of their initial diagnostic work-up, independent of their subsequent inclusion in the study. Such diagnostic testing was conducted by staff psychologists as part of their usual service function, on the basis of individual referral from the resident and staff physicians, via individual testing sessions that ranged from a minimum of two to more than six hours per patient. The particular test battery varied somewhat from case to case, from the minimum of Rorschach, Bender-Gestalt, Figure Drawings, and Thematic Apperception or Sentence Completion to the wide range of tests for central nervous system deficit. The majority of patients also had been administered at least portions of the Wechsler Adult Intelligence Scale. While there was considerable variability in the particular reasons for referral and in the questions posed by the referring person, the resulting test report uniformly took the form of a narrative comprehensive psychological evaluation with assessment of the patient's functioning in cognitive, affective, and interpersonal spheres, as well as broad formulations of underlying psychodynamics. Table 9 summarizes the frequency of typical statements in the narrative interpretation.

Our operating hypothesis was that such a psychological test battery would not clearly identify those with a propensity for dyscontrol acts. To test this, each of the psychological evaluations was examined for specific statements regarding the presence of impulsive or acting-out behavior as revealed by testing; and such indications were related to the independent clinical evidence *for* such behavior. These comparisons are reported in Table 9. Thus among those patients with paroxysmal slow activity, although 21 gave clinical evidence for impulsiveness, in only 13 was such a propensity identified on projective tests. In the specific activation group, 16 showed clinical evidence for impulsivity while only 8 demonstrated such on projective tests. In the no-activation group, 12 showed clinical evidence for impulsivity and 9 of the 12 gave evidence for this on the projective tests. A detailed analysis of the correlation between the clinical observations of impulsiveness and the psychological test evidence for such revealed no false positives; if impulsivity or acting out was suggested on the projective test, it always occurred in the clinical behavior of the patient. Among the nonactivators, the correlation between projective test and clincal observations was high. In the three cases where psychological tests failed to predict impulsivity, there was questionable clinical evidence of impulsiveness. However, such a correlation does not stand up in the specific abnormality or paroxysmal slow groups. It would seem that if the patients show an activated EEG abnormality, either of the "aspecific" paroxysmal slow type, or a specific focal abnormality, projective tests are not a reliable prognosticator, or put another way, projective tests will predict correctly in only one half the cases in which there is significant clinical impulsiveness. As might have been assumed then, projective test evidence for impulsivity identifies best "motivational" impulsivity and not the impulsivity related to significant epileptoid phenomena.

In our psychodynamic considerations, we mentioned that the factors supposedly characteristic of the impulsive patient were oral dependency, identification problems, narcissism, and sadomasochism. Examining our patients for such factors, at least as interpreted from projective tests, we see little difference between groups, except for a suggestive increase in "oral dependency" in those with specific abnormalities and organic brain syndromes. Another possible difference is a slight increase in "sado-masochism" in the specific abnormality group, which we will discuss in Chapter 10. As relationships might be obscured by inappropriate grouping, we compared the 26 patients who showed episodic dyscontrol with the 12 patients with nonepisodic disorders. No difference appeared between the groups with regard to hysterical defenses and narcissism and only a slight excess of oral dependency and identity problems in the episodic dyscontrol group. However, sado-masochism was three times more common in patients with episodic dyscontrol than it was in the nonepisodic group. Another analysis of the data removed from the episodic dyscontrol group all patients who were considered to be primarily motivated. Then, hysterical defenses, oral dependency, identity problems, and sado-masochism were now twice as frequent in the epileptoid episodic dyscontrol group when compared with the nonepisodic group. This suggests that these factors correlate better with those patients whose etiologic mechanisms are significantly epileptoid rather than motivational. Narcissism, however, was equally prevalent in the two groups.

Time estimation studies as well as the Porteus Mazes are both supposed to test anticipatory mechanisms which we postulate as important for developing inhibitory controls (9.2.2). Over half the patients in this series underestimated time, but except for the group with specific abnormalities and "organicity" who almost all underestimated time, there were no distinct trends. It should be pointed out that time estimation studies and the Porteus Maze test were all done during a follow-up period when most of the patients were in remission; these tests during the height of the acute episodes might give a different result. The reason for utilizing tests during a period of remission is that the value of any psychological test or battery of tests for diagnosis and prognosis depends on its predictive capacity, that is, its usefulness in uncovering a potential for dyscontrol acts during a period of remission. As yet, we are not able to predict impulsivity by psychological testing when epileptoid mechanisms play a significant role.

8.3 DIAGNOSTIC DISTRIBUTION

Detailed case histories are included in the Appendixes, and most clinical examples utilized in this book (200 series) were selected from this group of patients. Tables 10, 11, 12, and 13 illustrate the distribution of the 70 patients in terms of the diagnostic categories we have defined.

Twenty-seven of the 54 patients demonstrating episodic behavioral disorders were categorized under the heading episodic dyscontrol, and 16 under episodic reactions. Eleven were given a primary diagnosis other than episodic behavioral disorders, but still considered to have significant episodic disturbances, while 16 subjects were considered to have nonepisodic reactions. In the case of the episodic dyscontrols and episodic reactions, a determination of the relative importance of epileptoid and motivational elements was made on the basis of evidence in the baseline (nonactivated) EEG, neurological and physical examinations, laboratory tests, psychological evaluation, and clinical history. Of the 11 subjects whose conditions were diagnosed as episodic dyscontrol or episodic reactions with a predominance of epileptoid elements, nine had focal abnormalities on the activated EEG's while the other two had activated "aspecific" abnormalities in the form of paroxysmal slow activity. At the other extreme, ten subjects were considered to be primary motivational and seven of the ten showed no EEG abnormalities, even after activation. The three who did activate showed the "aspecific" paroxysmal slow activity, and none showed focal abnormalities. In 22 subjects, there was considered to be a mixture of epileptoid and motivational elements, four of these showing focal abnormalities, 16 paroxysmal slow activity, and two no EEG abnormalities, even with activation. These data indicate that activation patterns can give us clues in weighing the importantce of epileptoid and motivational factors.

8.3.1 *Episodic dyscontrol.* Considering first the lowest hierarchial level of episodic dyscontrol, seizure dyscontrol (Table 10), one notices that these four patients had focal or specific abnormalities. Three of the four showed temporal foci, and the fourth a generalized spike wave pattern. At the next hierarchial level, instinct dyscontrol, two of the subjects had focal temporal abnormalities, one an aspecific paroxysmal slow activation, and two no abnormalities, even after activation. In these two last

Table 10. Classification of episodic dyscontrol patients (N = 27)

Diagnoses	Etiologic mechanism	Episodic disorder	Episodic neuroses	Episodic act
Seizure dyscontrol (N = 4)	Epileptoid ↑↓ — — — — — — — — — — — — — — — — Motivated	F285		F247 F275 — — F206 —
Instinct dyscontrol (N = 5)	Epileptoid ↑↓ — — — — — — — — — — Motivated		F287 — S202 — O264	— F242 — O258
Impulse dyscontrol (N = 14)	Epileptoid ↑↓ — — — — — — Motivated	{ O260 S210 S286 O214	F272 S254 S219 F283 } S290	F271 S228 — — — O225 O208 S204
Acting-out dyscontrol (N = 4)	Epileptoid ↑↓ — — — — — — Motivated	F221 — F246	— — F211	— S288 —

patients, the instinct dyscontrol was felt to be predominantly motivational.

By far the largest group of episodic dyscontrols were diagnosed as impulse dyscontrol (14 subjects); however, only four of the 14 showed impulse dyscontrol alone; ten had accompanying seizural, instinctual, or acting-out dyscontrol. They were categorized under impulse dyscontrol either because this was the predominant form of episodic dyscontrol, or if several types of episodic dyscontrol were equally prominent, the highest hierarchial level was arbitrarily selected as the diagnosis. A further breakdown of this group reveals that two of the 14 also had seizural and instinct dyscontrol; four also had seizure dyscontrol; three had instinct dyscontrol; and one of the impulse dyscontrol patients also manifested acting out.

All patients showing acting out also demonstrated either specific or aspecific paroxysmal slow wave patterns with activation. Although this was a small group (four subjects), other patients showing occasional acting out, but not as the primary condition (F246, S286, F289), also had activated abnormalities. This strongly suggests that at least a large percentage of the patients who manifest acting out, which we have already suggested is predominantly the result of "faulty learning" rather than "faulty equipment," have some evidence of central nervous system instability, if this instability is measured by EEG activation procedures.

8.3.2 *Episodic reactions.* The activation pattern in the episodic reactions also gives us clues regarding the importance of epileptoid and motivational factors (Table 11). Eight patients were diagnosed as having episodic psychotic reaction. By strict "Bleulerian" criteria, five of the seven with nonaffective psychoses, even though manifesting symptoms typical of schizophrenia, would not have been considered as schizophrenic because of significant "clouding of sensorium," which would alert one to possible organic or toxic factors. The fact that the usual exogenous or endogenous toxins were lacking, as well as the rapid clearing of awareness without residual amnesia, lead the casual clinical observer to overlook this "clouding." Two of the three patients whose EEG showed no response to activation showed "pure" episodic schizophrenic reactions without clouded sensorium. This is why we feel it is important to distinguish between true episodic schizophrenic reactions (e.g., Patients O262, O274, F201), and what should more properly be called an episodic acute brain syndrome (e.g., Patients S229, S243, S249, and F267). We

Table 11. Classification of episodic reactions (N = 16)

Diagnoses	Subclassification	Epileptoid ←		→ Motivated
Psychoses N = 8	Schizophrenia		F201	O262 O274
	Brain syndrome	F267	S229 S243 S249	
	Depression		S216	
Neuroses N = 5	Anxiety-depression	F284 F250	S251	
	Conversion		S278	
	Dissociation		O289	
Other N = 3	Physiological	S218		
	Sociopath		S212	S282

have already mentioned that vague and fleeting episodes of depersonalization and hallucinations are not considered adequate evidence for the diagnosis of an episodic psychotic reaction.

Four patients are listed (Table 11) as having episodic depressive reactions (one psychosis, three neurosis), but again, there are frequent transitory depressive spells in the other episodic groups. As a reflection of this, 22 of the 70 patients were hospitalized because of suicidal attempts. The fact that one quarter of those with no activation, one third with paroxysmal slow activation and one third with specific abnormalities were admitted following suicidal attempts suggests that only a qualitative analysis of the depression would show a significant difference between the depressive affects in the episodic behavioral disorders and the non-episodic disorders (previously discussed in 6.3).

Episodic conversion reaction was a primary diagnosis in only one patient, and episodic dissociative reaction in one other patient. Yet in 29 patients conversion was considered a possibility and in 25 (of 61 subjects tested) hysterical defenses were identified on projective testing. However, to emphasize this hysterical potentiality or to overemphasize the importance of secondary motivational mechanisms is to miss the importance that central nervous system instability plays in the complex of symptoms.

Only two patients were given a diagnosis of an episodic sociopathic reaction, but 42 of the 70 patients showed aggressive dys-

Table 12. Primary diagnosis nonepisodic; secondary diagnosis episodic (N = 11)

Primary diagnosis	Patient number	Secondary episodic diagnosis	Epileptoid◄————►Motivated		
Schizophrenia	S205	Episodic anxiety		X	
	F213	Seizure dyscontrol	X		
	O236	Episodic sociopathic			X
	S248	Impulse dyscontrol		X	
	S257	Instinct dyscontrol		X	
	O281	Impulse dyscontrol			X
Personality disorder	F222	Seizure dyscontrol		X	
	F223	Episodic inhibition	X		
Neurotic depression	S239	Seizure dyscontrol		X	
Brain syndrome	F227	Seizure dyscontrol	X		
Involutional depression	S269	Episodic schizophrenia			X

Table 13. Diagnosis of nonepisodic behavioral disorders
with no evidence for episodic behavior (N = 16)

Diagnosis	Patient number
Schizophrenic	S232
Psychotic Manic Depressive	O220, O238, O255
Involutional psychoses	O256
Brain syndrome	F276, O265, O277
Neuroses	O217, O273, O279, O280
Personality disorder	O203, O263, O266, S259

control acts directed towards themselves or others, and 20 were seriously assaultive or homicidal (Table 8). It may be important that 13 of the 20 assaultive acts which precipitated hospitalization ocurred in those who showed the "aspecific" paroxysmal slow wave activation, only six occurred in those with no activation and only one in those with specific EEG abnormalities.

The problem of whether episodic physiological reactions are a significant category of the episodic behavioral disorders remains unanswered. Only one patient was given this as a primary diagnosis (S218); however, several others showed episodic psychiologic reactions to a lesser degree (S205, 0203, F250 and 0279). Inasmuch as two of the five patients are in the nonactivation group, our data give contradictory evidence as to the importance of epileptoid mechanisms behind such symptoms.

8.3.3 *Primary nonepisodic diagnosis with and without superimposed episodic behavioral disorders.* Eleven patients with a significant history of episodic dyscontrol and episodic reactions were nevertheless given a primary diagnosis of a nonepisodic nature. From Table 12 one will see that there is a range of episodic behavioral disorders represented in this group. The primary diagnoses were also varied; six schizophrenia, two personality dis-

Table 14. Activation pattern in episodic and nonepisodic disorders

	Episodic	Nonepisodic	Total
Nonactivation (O)	11 (20%)	13 (81%)	24
Focal or specific activation (F)	20 (37%)	1 (6%)	21
"Aspecific" activation (S)	23 (43%)	2 (12%)	25
Total	54	16	70

orders (obsessive-compulsive and paranoid), one chronic brain syndrome, one involutional psychosis, and one neurotic depressive reaction. In comparing these patients with the group of 16 subjects who were also given a primary nonepisodic diagnosis, but who did not show the superimposed episodic behavioral disorder (Table 13) the most significant finding is the difference in activation pattern between the two groups. Only two patients, for example, in the former did not activate (those with O before the number), while only two in the latter did (those with F or S before the number). We have already described (7.5) examples of false positive and false negative EEG response (Patients S232, 0236 and 0260).

Patient F276, the other exception, is one who activated, but who was considered to represent a nonepisodic reaction. The bilateral frontal slow activity found during baseline EEG recording, suggestive of brain damage, was augmented with alpha chloralose; hence was listed as a positive activation. The diagnosis was unclear, but most often given as Gilles de la Tourette disease. His symptoms were generally chronic with a waxing and waning quality, and therefore did not fit our category of episodic reactions. However, at times there were precipitous exacerbations of his symptoms so perhaps he could have been considered as an example of superimposed episodic behavioral disorder.

Table 14 summarizes the presence or absence of activated EEG abnormalities in the episodic and nonepisodic disorders in the study of 70 patients. The finding that 80 percent of the epi-

Table 15. Follow-up status (N = 64)

Subgroup	Work	Idle	Hospital	Suicide	Excited	Hostile	Intropunitive	Retarded	Motor	Conceptua	No drugs	Abuse of drugs	Anticonvulsant +	Anticonvulsant −	Phenothiazines +	Phenothiazines −	Benzodiazepines +	Benzodiazepines −	?
EEG criteria																			
No activation N = 23	15	4	4	0	16	19	40	20	14	3	11	3	0	1	6	2	0	0	0
Specific activation N = 16	10	2	3	1	21	22	38	28	16	4	2	3	5	2	0	0	2	0	2
Paroxysmal, slow activation ("nonspecific") N = 25	18	4	2	1	26	33	36	16	14	4	8	2	3	0	2	3	5	0	2
Total group N = 64	43	10	9	2	21	26	38	21	14	4	21	8	8	3	8	5	7	0	4
Clinical criteria																			
Schizophrenic thought disorder N = 26	19	3	2	2	29	29	37	23	13	6	6	6	2	0	5	4	3	0	0
Organicity N = 13	7	1	4	1	24	30	45	7	7	1	1	3	4	1	3	0	1	0	0
Nonepisodic N = 16	11	3	2	0	11	21	37	26	20	2	7	3	0	1	4	1	0	0	0
Epileptics N = 19	13	2	3	1	24	22	32	18	9	3	1	3	7	1	0	1	4	0	2

sodic group had activated abnormalities as opposed to only 18 percent of the nonactivated group emphasizes the importance of epileptoid mechanisms in the episodic behavioral disorders as well as the usefulness of the activating technique in identifying potentially episodic patients.

8.4 FOLLOW-UP STATUS

As already mentioned, the median time of follow-up was 24 months with a range from 12 to 60 months. Follow-up data were obtained on 64 of the 70 subjects. Table 15 summarizes the data. Two thirds of the subjects were out of the hospital and working at the time of follow-up. They were placed in the work category if they were working, attending school regularly, or functioning effectively as housewives. Ten were considered idle, that is out of the hospital and able to care for their personal needs, but not gainfully employed, nor helping significantly around the house. Nine were rehospitalized or still hospitalized at the time of follow-up, and two had committed suicide. There is no significant difference in the distribution of the follow-up status between the nonactivators, "specific" or "aspecific" paroxysmal EEG groups, nor is there any difference between these groups and the group of patients identified as having schizophrenic thought disorder by psychological test battery, or clinically as nonepisodic disorders. There is slight evidence that fewer of those patients with psychological evidence for "organicity" or with a clinical history of seizures were functioning, but in view of the small size of this group, this is of questionable significance.

At the time of follow-up, most of the patients were given mental status examinations, including rating their behavior on the IMPS (Inpatient Multidimensional Psychiatric Scale), although these patients were not inpatients at the time of evaluation. However, three symptom complexes showed what seemed to be important differences. Those who showed paroxysmal slow activation tended to have higher scores on the excitement and hostility scales than those with specific activation patterns or those with no activation. On the other hand, those individuals with specific activation patterns tended to show definitely greater motor retardation compared to the activation group.

Comparing the groups differentiated by EEG criteria with the groups differentiated by clinical or projective test data, we see considerable similarity in the IMPS syndrome listed in the paroxysmal slow and the schizophrenic groups. There was also a similarity between the no-activation group and the nonepisodic group, which is not surprising in view of the fact that these two groups overlap. Despite the overlap between the specific abnormality group and the organic group, there is a high retardation score in the former and a low retardation in the latter. This results from the fact that those patients manifesting what we have previously described as an inhibitory "psychosis" (5.5.1) were more likely to appear in the specific abnormality group. This is not true of those who showed "organicity." The best explanation of why the organic patients with a high level of hostility and little retardation were not more overtly aggressive seems to be indicated by the high intrapunitive (guilt) score in this group, supported by the relatively high incidence of serious suicidal attempts (seven of fourteen in the same group).

The drug response at the time of follow-up will be discussed in detail in chapter 11 and only briefly referred to here. Twenty-one patients received no drugs; eight patients appeared to abuse the drug by becoming habituated or at least episodically taking excessive amounts. The rest of the groups are too small to give any decisive answers, but they do fit in with our observations that in general the episodic dyscontrol patients respond poorly to phenothiazines, at least when they are given alone (three patients); two patients who did well on the phenothiazine were chronic psychotic patients with superimposed episodic disturbances, and it was the chronic symptoms that improved. The episodic behavioral disorders, particularly episodic dyscontrol, tended to do better with anticonvulsants, or benzodiazepines or a combination of the two. Otherwise, drug response was what one would predict, the epileptics and organics doing best on anticonvulsants, the schizophrenics and nonepisodic disorders on phenothiazines.

In summary, an evaluation of 70 patients, 64 of whom were available for follow-up studies two to five years after therapy began suggests the following: activation studies, despite occasional false positives and false negatives, are an aid in weighing the relative contribution of epileptoid and motivational factors in patients with episodic behavioral disorders. Also the incidence of activated abnormalities is much higher in the group showing episodic symptoms as compared with those showing nonepisodic symptoms. Patients showing high amplitude paroxysmal slow activation are more likely to be seriously aggressive towards themselves or to others than those who show specific or no EEG abnormalities. Typical epileptic seizures and "organicity" seems to reduce the possibility of effective aggressive acts. Projective tests predict the possible clinical expression of impulsivity when such impulsiveness is predominantly motivated, but underestimated by 50 percent such impulsivity if there is significant evidence for epileptoid or maturational lag mechanisms. As yet, we have found no individual psychological test or test battery that will correct this important prognostic deficiency. As psychiatrists we tend to overemphasize the motivational elements of atypical epileptoid phenomena seeing these as a "conversion." There is however a surprisingly high incidence of hysterical defense mechanisms identified in this group by psychological test battery. There is also a high incidence on projective tests of schizophrenic thought processes in the seizure patients, an even higher incidence than for organic brain damage in the seizure patients.

There is evidence to suggest that the exposure to excessive aggressive or sexual stimulation during early childhood was a contributing, but certainly not sufficient cause for the subsequent development of episodic behavior. Statements in the literature that oral dependency, identification problems, narcissism and sado-masochism are associated with impulsivity appear to be inappropriately broad generalizations. In our group, oral dependency was highest in the "organic" patients, and sado-masochism tended to be three times more frequent in patients with episodic behavioral disorders than in the nonepisodic group. Patients with paroxysmal slow wave activation patterns tended to be hospitalized longer (similar to schizophrenic patients) than the specific EEG-organic-seizural groups, but there was some evidence that once discharged, they adjusted better than the latter groups.

Part Three Psychodynamic-Neurophysiologic Synthesis

9 Psychodynamic-Neurophysiologic Mechanisms

In this chapter we will try to integrate the observations reported in preceding chapters. No matter how thorough we are, the result will inevitably be distorted. But we do hope to make some generalizations to aid us in making meaningful etiologic diagnoses, and to provide guidelines for an effective therapy as well as a reliable prognosis. The psychodynamic-neurophysiologic synthesis should indicate what somatic or psychotherapeutic techniques should be utilized, and the degree to which we must rely on one or the other; that is, to what extent we must modify or substitute for "faulty equipment," and how much we must rely on reeducation to alter "faulty learning." We hope that this synthesis will allow us to predict whether an individual is or will be a danger to himself or society. Of course, our ultimate medical ideal is to identify predisposing factors which then can be eliminated in a preventive psychiatric program. This will require an epidemiological analysis of the disorders. However, no such analysis can be made until we have rigorous criteria for identifying specific disorders with common etiologic mechanisms (Monroe, 1967d).

9.1 THE "ACT AS A UNIT"

Fig. 15 is an attempt to represent schematically the process of the human organism responding to an environmental stimulus with

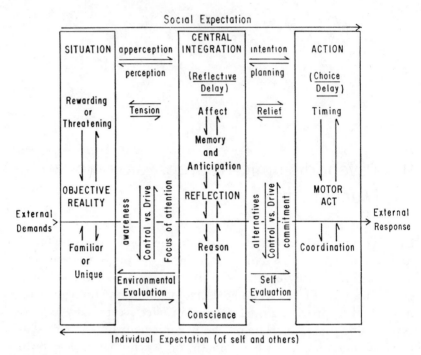

Fig. 15. The "act as a unit"

a motor act. It represents a homeostatic or transactional equilibrium between the demands of the external situation on the left, the internal integrative mechanisms in the center, and the goal-directed motor behavior on the right. Because we are concerned with disordered acts, we want to locate what goes wrong between the perception-apperception of the external situation (left) and the planned intentional act (right). We arbitrarily dichotomize the process between affect (above) and reason (below). Affect is represented by the sequence of a perceived rewarding or threatening situation eliciting tension, determined by and/or resulting in a kind and degree of affect demanding either immediate or postponed relief (timing) through a motor act. At the bottom of our diagram we have familiarity and uniqueness of the objective reality determined by intellectual evaluation dependent upon reason, memory, and conscience, with a self-evaluation

weighing alternative courses of action against personal competence, and finally, a commitment to a coordinated motor act.
Our vertical homeostasis, as opposed to the horizontal ones just
discussed, represents the equilibrium between what we call drives
or affects with their need for gratification balanced by reality
testing and control. The adaptive value of the motor act is dependent not only upon the perception of the objective reality
and the coordination of the motor act, but upon varying degrees
of integration or what we have called reflection, that is, thought
as "trial action." This depends not only on the secondary intellectual processes, but also on hindsight (memory) and foresight
(anticipation of future consequences). If the act is to take place,
there must have been perceived an external demand for some
action (far left) and following the act there will be as a consequence an external response to that demand (far right). The
chain of events from demand to action must include an awareness of the demands of the objective reality, a selection of stimuli
with a determination as to what is important and what is unimportant, a reflection which results in a consideration of various
alternatives with a commitment as to the most appropriate act,
and finally an awareness of the external response to that act.
There can be an internal demand for action in terms of tension,
affects, and need for relief or gratification, as well as external
demands for action. The finesse of the act depends not only upon
how well the motor behavior is carried out (coordination), but
also the appropriateness of the act after consideration of a number of alternatives. It goes without saying that any imbalance in
one of the vectors represented on the diagram will be reflected
as an imbalance in all others, but we hope it will be useful to
describe the disturbances in action as representing pressures first
exerted at one point or the other.

The ultimate determination of whether the act is considered
adaptive or maladaptive is in terms of the social or external
expectation represented by the arrow at the top border of our diagram, as well as the individual's expectation of both himself and
of others, represented by the arrow at the bottom of the diagram.
It is these expectations which give the action a cohesive unity. In

the broadest sense, the acceptability of the act is determined by its adaptive quality for society and for the individual, with three possibilities. The first is that what is good for one (society) is also good for the other (the individual). The second is that either society or the individual at the moment take precedence over the other (e.g., society over the individual in times of war). The third possibility may be a compromise of both (e.g., sub rosa sexuality during the biologically mature but economically dependent decade).

We have repeatedly mentioned that the broadest dynamic interpretation we can make regarding the episodic behavioral disorders is that there is an imbalance in the urge-control mechanisms at the extremes, either intense urges overwhelming normal control mechanisms, or normal urges unrestrained by inadequately developed control mechanisms. At the phenomenological level, the act, to qualify as one of our episodic phenomena, must have an abrupt or precipitous onset and be out of character for the actor as well as inappropriate for the situation. These factors will be the guidelines for our psychodynamic-neurophysiologic considerations.

9.2 ABSENT REFLECTIVE DELAY: PRIMARY DYSCONTROL

It is our contention that if the act is maladaptive due to an inhibition or deficiency of reflection, the disorder of action will be characterized by what we have labeled either seizure or instinct dyscontrol. This is in contradistinction to the formulation of Fenichel (1945b), who feels that the "alloplastic readiness for action" is the sine qua non of impulsivity. We have suggested that this readiness for action in itself is not pathological, but characterizes both the spontaneous act and the spontaneous personality. The man of action, assuming an adequate integrative function, is not only an effective member of society but usually a leader. Thus, for understanding the disorders of action we must look elsewhere for the basic disturbance. What differentiates this man of action from the contemplative man who must also act, and even from the inhibited neurotic whose life is also one of action, no matter how timid, indecisive or inappropriate? Again, referring to our original classifications on episodic disinhibition (see Introduction), we have used the word "precipitous" to describe these acts. There is an abrupt, quick, even explosive quality to the act, with a short time span between the perceived situational demand and the responding motor behavior. A second characteristic is the overt, relatively undisguised expression of affect or need, with the act itself leading to relief of tension or a gratification of the need. If these acts are pathological, there is lack of consideration for the needs of the environment, generally referred to as the narcissistic quality of the act or the individual. In our scheme it would seem that the tension-affect-relief balance becomes exaggerated or intensified, overwhelming either a normal or perhaps deficient evaluation-reason-competence control system. However, excessive urges that overwhelm control mechanisms characterize our episodic dyscontrol at all hierarchial levels, as well as other disordered behavior which is not generally considered episodic disinhibition. A further characteristic of the primary dyscontrol (seizure and instinctual acts) is that the deficient control is primarily related to a lack of integrative reflection. Only through such reflection can the consideration of the needs and gratification of others be made. Again, the most fundamental disturbance in the seizure and instinctual dyscontrols is a failure in this integrative reflection, usually manifest by the lack of delay between the environmental stimulus and the responsive act to that stimulus. This is not a surprising conclusion, in fact, it is one arrived at by many other observers.

Patient S202 illustrates such a lack of reflective delay. In a controlled and repeatable environmental situation, namely psychological testing, when the stimulus, usually the projective test, would elicit overwhelming anxiety, particularly with regard to her relationships with her father, she would suddenly jump up and tear up the cards. Immediately after-

258 | 9 MECHANISMS

wards she would be contrite and complain that she had no forewarning she was going to do this, nor idea why she carried the act through.

However, our scheme does clarify a point largely overlooked in the literature: that the delay between the environmental stimulus and the act itself consists of two types, or at least there are two facets to this delay. The first is what we have called "reflective delay," that is the time involved in trial action through thought, the time needed for establishing the uniqueness and familiarity of the external reality by associative connections with past experiences, the time necessary to contemplate a series of alternative courses of action, the time necessary to project into the future and predict the outcome of alternative actions. Depending upon the complexities and the novelty of the situation and the range in possible choices of action, this reflective delay could last anywhere from a fraction of a second to hours or days.

The neglected second aspect of the delay mechanism is what we call "choice" delay. This choice delay implies postponement of immediate gratification for long-term rewards. It is a decision regarding possible devious actions or preparatory actions; that is, waiting for the "opportune time" or "biding one's time." The "choice" delay assumes that the reflective delay has taken place, but the reverse is not necessarily true. For example, one can conceive of integrated and appropriate reflective delay followed by a lack of appropriate "choice" delay, particularly where there is an imperative quality to the urges which leads the individual to seek gratification, the consequences be damned. In this instance, the individual has elected to "take his chances," "pay the price," or "suffer the consequences," but does so with varying degrees of realistic awareness of the possible harmful consequences of his act. Such failure in "choice" delay without impairment of reflective delay certainly characterizes a group of sociopathic individuals whose behavior is often referred to as acting out or impulsive. This would not be labeled episodic dyscontrol or episodic reactions according to our scheme, because in this instance the actions would not be out of character for the individual but part of his "life style." On the other hand, it is obvious that if the reflective, integrative process were lacking, postponement or "choice" delay would also be absent. Refining our evaluation further, then, we will say that the sine qua non of the group of disorders we have labeled seizure or instinct dyscontrol (primary dyscontrol) must be an inhibition or deficiency in reflective delay with consequent failure in "choice" delay. As we will see later in this chapter, it is only at these two lower hierarchial levels of episodic dyscontrol that the "alloplastic readiness to act" is an appropriate description, but we reiterate that this readiness to act should not in itself be considered pathological.

Again referring to our diagram of the "act as a unit" we can see many possibilities for distortions in this reflective delay, such as reflective recall based on affective associations rather than logical ones, reason distorted by misdirected conscience mechanisms, distorted or absent anticipatory mechanisms; but all this implies not an absence of reflection but a distortion of reflection. Reflective delay takes place but it functions in a maladaptive way. We will see below that such is probably the case in what we have categorized as secondary dyscontrol (acting out and impulse dyscontrol). Our immediate focus is not on these distortions, but on the complete lack of reflection, hence lack of delay between stimulus and action. These disturbances are pure inhibition-disinhibition disturbances, a too much, too little balance: too much action, too little reflection. With such a simple dichotomy, we are more likely to find examples of seizure and instinct dyscontrol in patients who have "defective equipment," that is, deficiency in this mechanism due to disturbed neuronal function. Those patients with distorted reflective delay and disturbed "choice" delay are more likely to have learned disorders, or if there is a disturbance in neuronal mechanisms, these disturbances are considerably modified by superimposed "faulty learning" (see Fig. 2).

A relatively complete lack of any one of the facets of reflective delay, namely affect, memory, anticipation, reason, or conscience, would mean no reflective delay. However, we will have to postulate that a lack of any one of these facets of reflective delay may in turn be the result of a superabundance of another. For example, overwhelmingly intense affects, such as fear, or blind rage, that elicit fight-flight reactions as a response to even the most crude environmental stimuli overwhelm all memory, anticipation, and reason mechanisms. At the other extreme, although not quite as obvious, when there is an overwhelmingly severe conscience mechanism, it too can so overwhelm reason and memory that even the most benign urges cannot be expressed except by an impulsive act without characteristic reflective delay.

9.2.1 *Neurophysiologic mechanisms: paroxysmal disorders.* What evidence do we have for specific neurologic dysfunctions that would knock out affect, hindsight, foresight, reason, or conscience mechanisms, either one alone or all together? Of course, it will be useless to try to localize such complex functions to any one area of the brain. But we do see evidence that certain loci are sensitive areas for some of these component functions of the reflective delay. For example, temporal lobectomy studies reveal the importance of an intact hippocampus, at least on one side, for the preservation of recent memory and immediate recall. If an intact hippocampus is lacking bilaterally we see very little delay between the stimulus and response as shown by the distractability and hypermetamorphosis manifested by these patients. This lack of delay between stimulus and response does not lead to the dramatic impulsivity usually associated with seizure or instinct disorders, because with the bilateral temporal lobectomies which usually accompany such lesions there is also a severe reduction in affect. On the other hand, what would happen if this recent recall were impaired at the same time as excessive neuronal discharges in other parts of the limbic system were leading to excessive affects, particularly fear and rage? We have also noted that stimulation of the amygdalal region leads to confusion and altered levels of awareness, suggesting that perceptions as well as intellect are seriously impaired. The combination of intense affects, plus impairments in recall and reason could be a disturbance in function attributable to excessive neuronal discharge in the temporo-limbic area. As we have already pointed out (4.3 and 5.5.3), this area is important for recording immediate impressions, comparing these impressions with past memories, and deducing the current reality from such a comparison. If the temporo-limbic area is malfunctioning, seizure or instinct dyscontrol with little or no delay between stimulus and motor action would be likely.

Patient 021 particularly illustrates this point. She had subcortically implanted electrodes so that electrographic activity in the rhinencephalon could be monitored. Orientation was checked during a time when she showed excessive paroxysmal discharges in the hippocampal-amygdala area (Fig. 4). She was asked "Where are you?" Her reply, "Charity Hospital" (correct). "What floor are you on?" She replied, "Third floor" (correct). "In what city?" She replied, "Monroe, Louisiana" (incorrect). What is important is that there is a Charity Hospital in Monroe, Louisiana, and she had been hospitalized there one time in the past. But what is probably more significant was that at the moment she was talking with Dr. Monroe. It is probable, then, that she was making a faulty connection between her past memories and immediate impressions, therefore coming to an erroneous conclusion regarding her immediate environment.

What about the anticipatory mechanisms that are so important in this reflective delay? Again we have at least circumstantial evidence of impairment in this function with accompanying instinct dyscontrol, correlated with a specific neurological lesion. Those patients with radical frontal lobotomies, and the frontal lobe with the temporal cortex is considered by some as part of the cortical projection of the limbic system (MacLean, 1959), show irresponsible, impulsive, antisocial behavior as if they did not care for the future consequences of their immediate response to a given stimuli (Pribram, 1961). As one of Freeman's patients (as reported by Pribram) said, "now that I have done it, I can see that it was not the thing to do, but beforehand I couldn't say whether or not it would be right." This response may be socially unimportant, if at the same time the affects have been severely blunted. If not, however, such patients can show dangerous impulsive behavior.

From a dynamic point of view we can assume that one reason the human animal develops both "reflective" and "choice" delay is what we will call "inhibitory anxiety." As humans we worry about the consequences of our act, first as young children in terms of parental disapproval, withdrawal of love, and the implementation of restrictive punishment. With maturation this anxiety should concern itself with social acceptance, social reward, freedom of action, social responsibility and personal self-fulfillment. Emphasis is usually placed on internalization of the fear of punishment, as the basis for this anticipatory anxiety or conscience mechanism. But the capacity to anticipate or project into the distant future is equally important.

It might be presumed that because this impulsive behavior without apparent anticipation of future consequences is often associated with at least some reduction in affect, it is this lack of affect, particularly inhibitory anxiety, which is responsible for the failure in anticipatory mechanisms. However, it is just as logical to consider the reverse possibility, that the capacity for foresight extended into the distant future is necessary for the development of this inhibitory anxiety. This is supported by the observation that the inferior medial and more anterior frontal lobotomies, while reducing anxiety, have little effect on anticipatory self-control mechanisms. We have reported a number of studies that suggest that if EEG abnormalities localized in the temporal lobes are associated with general cortical slowing (particularly frontal cortical slowing), the associated behavioral disturbances are more likely to be episodic disinhibition (Rodin, 1957a,b). Although undoubtedly it is an oversimplification of a complex phenomenon, it is clinically useful to say that if the limbic-temporal-frontal complex is disturbed, there is impairment in reflective delay, with defects in the anticipatory mechanisms. When accompanied by intense affect (also a result of rhinencephalic dysfunction) this leads to episodic dyscontrol of the most primitive and severe type. Unfortunately at present we have no clear-cut neurophysiologic correlate with this impairment of anticipatory mechanisms. Although there is no more reason for assuming that frontal cortical slowing might reflect this than a similar slowing in the posterior quadrants, in our own series of 70 patients (reported in Chapter 8) we could demonstrate no increase in impulsivity in those showing both frontal slowing and temporal lobe abnormalities. This, then, remains a hypothesis still unsupported by our clinical data in adults. The clinical findings in two of our children, however, would suggest such a possibility.

Patient 405 showed bursts of single and multiple spikes mixed with high amplitude slow waves bilaterally and symmetrically, with occasional left temporal focus. His aggressiveness towards his peers was so intense that he sometimes seriously injured them enough to require hospitalization.

Patient 413 had random spikes and sharp waves mixed with high amplitude slow waves bilaterally and symmetrically in the posterior quadrant. But again, a left posterior temporal focus was often seen. He was described as a wild, uncontrollable child, pulling everything from the table, ripping plaster off the wall, and breaking up the furniture, to such an extent that it was necessary to hospitalize him.

9.2.2 *Neurophysiologic mechanisms: maturational delay.* Aside from an overall increase in brain mass as one ascends the evolutionary scale, there has also been a proportionately greater increase in the prefrontal area, the very area we have suggested is in some way vital for the anticipatory function. To the psychologically oriented anthropologist, there can be no doubt that one of the distinguishing characteristics of homo sapiens, and even of the hominides, is a widening range of anticipation until the human animal can anticipate not only his own inevitable death but beyond his death (suggested in prehistoric burial rituals) and that this has been crucial for man's acculturation (Hockett, 1964). What is generally overlooked is that this takes place not only relatively late phylogenetically but also ontogenetically. Anticipatory mechanisms of looking into the future are obviously quite rudimentary in the preschool child. What is equally true is that such anticipation does not develop fully until late adolescence and early adulthood, perhaps not until the resolution of the adolescent "identity crisis." At the same time we emphasize that this anticipation is essential for reflective delay. If this anticipatory mechanism is still not developed fully in adolescence when affects are particularly intense and labile, may not this explain at least in part the so-called "phase specific" episodic dyscontrol during this period? Of course, there is much more to adolescent impulsivity than the failure in anticipatory mechanisms, but this is beyond the scope of our present study, although briefly discussed later in this chapter. The point we wish to make here is that a number of studies, particularly that of Hill (1963), have noted that the EEG in many adolescents show instability and slow theta activity, particularly in the posterior quadrants. This is more characteristic of early childhood, hence is thought to reflect an immaturity of neurophysiologic development in the adolescent. Is such an immaturity reflected at the psychological level by delay in the development of this anticipatory mechanism? The data would seem to suggest that this concept is a useful one because of the high incidence of just such signs of immature brain activity in subjects who behave impulsively.

> Patient S282 is a seventeen-year-old boy. Although his baseline EEG was normal, with activation he showed paroxysmal, bilaterally diffuse slow waves. To illustrate our present point, he was fighting an oedipal attachment with his mother and rejection of a rather meek, ineffectual stepfather. He identified with a caricature of his real father, whom he knew only by the resentful comments of his mother. He saw "father" as a rough, tough, hard-drinking, fighting, antisocial man, and whenever he felt deserted by mother and stepfather, he reverted to this behavior himself.

9.2.3 *Motivational mechanisms.* It would be folly to doubt the proposition that a failure in reflective delay could also result from faulty learning in an individual with a completely unimpaired nervous system. We have previously reported considerable clinical observations of the reciprocal relationship between the "alloplastic readiness to act" and verbalization or thinking. As one dominates the picture, the other recedes (1.1.3). In "Totem and Tabu," Freud pointed out that in both primitive man and children there is little differentiation between the thinking and the doing, with thought passing directly into action (Freud, vol. XIII). Freud contrasts this disinhibition in action to the inhibition of the neurotic when the thought becomes a substitute for action. In his earlier paper on "Two Principles of Mental Functioning" (1911), he said, "restraint upon motor discharge (upon action) which then becomes necessary was provided by means of the process of thinking. Thinking was endowed with characteristics which made it possible for the mental apparatus to tolerate an increased tension of stimulus, while the process of discharge was delayed" (Freud, vol. XII). This statement raises many questions. How, for example, does thinking increase this capacity to tolerate tension and to postpone gratification? Or, in still other terms, what process goes on in the development of the child so that he can give up the "magic of action" for the reality testing of the "trial action through thought"? Understanding this phenomenon requires more than psychoanalytic or motivational analysis. Piaget's concept of the sensory-motor theory of intelligence offers a possibility for answering this question—that is, how thinking evolves from the earliest reflexive response. This has been summarized by Wolff (1960). Piaget tried to understand how the child, starting with only a repertory of stereotyped reflex behavior, by eighteen months is "capable of searching for an object after it has disappeared from vision; of inferring unobserved causes from observed results; of constructing spatial relationships in thought; of arranging a sequence of actions into means-ends relations." Using Piaget's concepts, Malone (1963) discusses the development of impulsivity and acting out. For example, in children whose initiative is severely impaired by overprotective and restrictive mothers, the causal relationship between intention and action is distorted, giving action an isolated identity of its own without appropriate connection with one's intention (the magic of action), but it is this concern for the intention which demands reflective delay. The important part that words play in the development of intentional thought is through generalization by common intentions (e.g., all pencils are something to write with). The need for consistent communication between the child and his environment to make these intentions predictable are discussed by Lidz (1963) in the same symposium. The clinical correlation to this speculation is the severe speech disturbance often seen in children (Gardner, 1963) and adults (Greenacre, 1950; Michaels, 1955) who demonstrate impulsive behavior and an inverse relationship between speech and acting-out (1.1.3). Undoubtedly, the shift from the sensory-motor experience to thought and speech as trial action depends to some degree on a basic genetic endowment, or intellectual capacity, as well as on the environmental rewards for thought and speech.

In the later development of thought as "trial action" and the reflective delay between stimulus and response must also depend in large part on inhibitory anxiety arising from consistent parental discipline; an optimum level of such anxiety is a prerequisite for appropriate delay between the urge and the act, while too much results in the inhibitory neuroses (phobias and compulsions), and too little in our episodic disinhibitions.

> Patient S288 dramatizes this inverse relationship between episodic dyscontrol and verbalizations (as well as meaningful introspection). During therapy, when impulse dyscontrol and acting out were at a maximum, she either could not communicate, or rattled on with inconsequential minutiae. However, when the acting out and impulsivity were controlled by reserpine, she not only free-associated about conflictual attitudes, but dreamed frequently—dreams with little distortion or displacement. Oedipal dreams were quite overt (in bed with father who was naked). However, circumventing her defenses by the use of drugs was so anxiety-provoking that she also developed incipient psychotic symptoms, particularly feelings of depersonalization and intense depression, so that the regimen had to be discontinued.

It is not surprising that analysts have focused on the second year of life as the period of crucial trauma for the development of impulsivity and acting out. It is during this period that both motor behavior (walking) and thought (speech) are rapidly developing. It is here that we should be able to identify the roots of the "alloplastic readiness to act."

All infants demonstrate an ecstatic joy in action for its own sake, running aimlessly, seemingly without purpose except for the pleasure of pure movement. What happens if the value of the motor act becomes enhanced through environmental reward and encouragement, or perhaps the very opposite extreme—excessive restriction making action a forbidden, therefore more desired, mode of expression? David Levy (1962) reports that in the latter instance, when the restraint is removed, one sees a burst of activity; while if the restraint continues one sees the development of partial acts or tics. What if these environmental influences are in turn reinforced by genetic potential, that is the exceptional capacity for skilled coordinated movement? Are these factors important for the development of the "alloplastic readiness to act," and do they with other factors predispose one to episodic dyscontrol? A carefully controlled study with a comparison between the motor coordination skills of the disinhibited and inhibited disorders of action might give us some clues regarding this matter, but in lieu of this, we do have some circumstantial evidence that this is true. For example, Rexford (1963) observed that impulse disorders tend to predominate in well-developed, muscular children. Other suggestive evidence appears in the reports of Fries (1953), who maintained that hyperkinetic motility could be identified even in the newborn. Such hyperkinetic activity has been related to the development of impulsive behavior and sado-masochistic acting out (Rochlin, 1963). We have also seen that instinct dyscontrol characterizes children who develop hyperactive, distractable behavior following diffuse damage to the central nervous system (Kahn, 1934). Further support could be cited in the observation that impulsive patients tend to do proportionately better on the performance subtests of the

WAIS as compared with the verbal subtests (Abt, 1965). The idea of a relationship between highly cathected motility and acting out must have occurred to others, because the Study Group on Acting-out of the New York Psychoanalytic Society reports one patient who showed rather extreme joy in his motor behavior and yet suffered from an inhibitory neurosis (Angel, 1965b). One such observation on one patient would not rule out this possibility, particularly as a correlation has not been attempted with what we see as the more primitive disinhibitions in action (e.g., seizure and instinct dyscontrols).

There are other implications to be gathered from this period of newfound motility in the child's development which will be important for some of our subsequent considerations. It is obvious that the child uses motility in the service of the separation-individuation phase of development; that is, he runs away from mother and begins to establish his own personal identity, a process which at the same time reflects an increase in self-assertion, as well as a rebellion against passivity. This is the "I act, therefore I exist" formulation of Angel (1965a).

The magic quality of the act, then, has at least the following important aspects: the pleasure of movement for movement's sake; the act as a means of establishing intentions; the use of motility to establish personal identity; and the motor act as an expression of self-assertiveness. This is balanced against parental discipline with developing inhibitory anxiety and the reinforcement of thought as trial action, which assures rewards for planned acts while avoiding punishment for ill-conceived ones.

For the analysts who see disordered behavior as the result of infantile trauma with fixation, leading either to arrest or distortion of subsequent psychic development, or as a tendency to regress to the point of traumatic fixation, the genesis of this disinhibited action might be seen as follows: the most frequent observation, and one that seems to be established by considerable clinical data, is that in most individuals manifesting episodic dyscontrol there are identifiable in infancy and early childhood many situations which tend to arouse intense affects, such as overt sexual stimulation, viewing primal scenes, aggressive behavior between parents, aggressive behavior directed towards the child, or excessive bodily contact between child and one parent (Greenacre, 1963; Almansi, 1965). An example of such a patient in whom the early trauma is covered by a screen memory but reflected in a characteristic instinctual act (homicide) is reported by Rose (1960), and also found among the children in our series (6.1.1). If such overstimulation occurs at a period of a child's development when there are limited opportunities to discharge tension, either through coordinated motor acts or indirectly through speech and thought, or sublimated motor activity, the affects become traumatic in themselves. In these instances the affects will be cut short, either through avoidance of situations which elicit feelings, or through the immediate discharge of feelings before tensions can build up. Should the pattern become one of avoidance there is a withdrawal from all affect-producing situations with a pouting dullness and apathy which we would characterize as episodic inhibition. In our series of 70 patients only two patients reflect this.

Patient F267 was noted on psychological testing to compulsively rework anxiety-producing data, putting a distance between himself and others. Patient S288 (Appendix D) made a satisfactory adjustment by being the "belle of the ball" during adolescence, with many acquaintances but no intimate friends. This distant and superficial interpersonal contact broke down when she married and her husband insisted on closeness. Then severe psychopathology became obvious. Although her symptoms were often impulse dyscontrol and acting out, these alternated with pouting withdrawal, depression, and dullness. The psychologist reported that she was quite constricted in her emotional life, defending herself against strong affects by narrowing her scope of activities.

On the other hand, perhaps when motor patterns are more highly developed or allowed, the defensive pattern may be an immediate discharge of tension. This cuts short the developing affect. These individuals are seen as emotionally labile or shallow. If such a pattern is a life style, they would not be designated as exemplifying episodic dyscontrol. However, if this type of reaction is elicited only by occasional situations (which must have specific dynamic significance) then it would be episodic and would fit phenomenologically with what we call instinct dyscontrol. These individuals are often referred to as intolerant of frustration.

> Patient 0263 dramatically illustrates this point. Because certain pretty girls on the street elicit sado-masochistic sexual fantasies, with rapidly mounting tension, he aborts acting out of the tension by pounding his fists on the wall of the nearest building. He has done this so vehemently that twice he appeared in the emergency room to have his mangled hands bandaged. Such an immediate discharge of tension before he succumbs to uncontrollable acts was also noted on psychological testing. When he first approached the problem he did so in a clear, undistorted, unemotional manner. However, if the solution did not come immediately, he became anxious and disorganized, with surges of hostility and guilt. Again he seemed intolerant of the frustration required in any rumination or concentration on a difficult problem that could not be immediately solved in a direct and unconflicted manner.

If the excessive stimulation occurs at a time when thoughts (as trial action) are available as a way to release tension, the traumatophobic quality of the affect is less, the "alloplastic readiness to act" not so apparent, and reflective delay present, even though the ultimate action may be explosive and impulsive. In these instances, as we will see later, the act is more typical of what we describe as impulse dyscontrol or acting out. The fact that there is reflective delay does not necessarily mean controlled behavior. Environmental stimulation such as we are discussing may result in mounting tension which finally overwhelms control mechanisms, resulting in an explosive act often typical of what we call impulse dyscontrol or acting out. These acts then, are likely to be more intermittent and at the same time more intense than those demonstrating the traumatophobic reaction where the discharge of tension occurs immediately upon arousal.

Of course, in the above categorization, the definite syndromes with rather clear-cut and specific psychodynamics are simplified abstractions used for expository purposes; clinical experience seldom provides such clear-cut entities and dynamics. Most psychoanalysts today consider that the concept of traumatic fixation as an explanation for neurotic behavior is an oversimplification. Early trauma has a persisting influence only if reinforced by subsequent experience. Possible influences of this type are discussed in the Symposium on Acting-out held at the Thom Clinic (1963).

Seizure and instinct dyscontrol, however, are more primitive responses, probably less likely to be influenced by later learned behavior. We have presented some evidence that seizure and instinct dyscontrol may reflect strong genetic predisposition for such patterns, or that such patterns follow diffuse organic damage or accompany epileptoid "excessive neuronal discharges," particularly in the temporal, amygdala, hippocampal, or frontal areas. Overwhelming affects or learned fear of affects seem to be universally characteristic of these more primitive levels of dyscontrol, and alone or in combinations with dysfunctions in the memory-anticipatory mechanism, they lead to an immediate discharge of the affect through a motor act without reflective delay. If this is a learned pattern of response rather than due to neurophysiologic dysfunction, the traumatic experiences must have occurred at a very early preverbal age. What we have been discussing are some of the observations which lie behind the frequent comment that there is a "short-circuit between impulse and action." Organizing our observations within this framework, we see obvious diagnostic, prognostic, and therapeutic implications. The value of this scheme will of course depend upon the reliability of our predictions which are based on such a scheme.

There is one other observation we must consider at this point: whether patients with seizure and instinct dyscontrol might fall into two groups, or more likely along a spectrum ranging from those with intense anxiety, overt or covert (the traumatophobic reaction we have just discussed), to those patients at the opposite pole with too little anxiety, and, therefore, no inhibitory anxiety, even at the covert level (Cleckley, 1955). Data from Wechsler scales as reported by Blatt (1965) would suggest this possibility, as would some of the studies already mentioned by Kennard (1955). She found that regular alpha rhythms suggestive of a lack of anxiety were found in imprisoned sociopaths, while irregular rhythms with excessive beta, a sign of anxiety, where found in the sociopath confined to the mental hospital. One might also interpret the data of Weintraub (1964) and Eichler (1966) as supporting such a hypothesis, although details regarding their patient samples are lacking. Eichler's sample came from a unique correctional institution, and Weintraub's included impulsive patients from a psychiatric hospital. Both groups of patients probably manifested what we would call episodic dyscontrol. In studying these patients, the authors used an analysis of the form of verbalization without concern for specific content. Although there were a number of similarities in the two groups, the incarcerated group showed significantly less expression of feelings, less direct reference to the experimenter and more nonpersonal references. This could be interpreted as reflecting less "affect" in this group as opposed to the hospitalized impulsive patients. This will be discussed again later in this chapter and again in Chapter 12 on psychotherapy. In our own series, none of the patients could have been considered representative of the anxiety-free episodic dyscontrol patient. Perhaps this is because all our subjects were hospitalized or receiving outpatient psychotherapy. Detailed study of the incarcerated impulsive individual should clarify this point.

We have already suggested that an important part of "choice" delay, which follows reflective delay must be in some degree determined by inhibitory anxiety. If the inhibitory anxiety is lacking, the "choice" delay would be impaired and there would be no need for reflective thought delay, even though the capacity for such might be there. In this situation there would be little delay between the urge and the act. It would be interesting to know whether the patients identified by Rexford (1963) as having mothers who, because of their own needs, cannot tolerate frustrating the needs of their offspring, lack this inhibitory anxiety. Those individuals lacking this inhibitory anxiety would not necessarily be deficient in reflective delay, just not utilizing it because of deficient conscience mechanism. If such a differentiation can be made between the traumato-phobic primary dyscontrols and the anxiety-less primary dyscontrols, it would have important therapeutic implications.

9.3 DISTORTED REFLECTIVE DELAY: SECONDARY DYSCONTROL

Thus far we have focused on the psychophysiologic mechanisms, psychodynamics, and ontogenesis of primary dyscontrol (seizure and instinct dyscontrol), realizing that the crucial characteristic of this group of episodic disinhibitions is the so-called "short-circuit between impulse and action," what we prefer to describe as a lack of reflective delay. We will now consider what we have designated as secondary dyscontrol (impulse dyscontrol and acting out). In these disorders, particularly the former, the act itself may be little different from that which characterizes the instinctual act; that is an abrupt, often explosive expression of primitive impulses, frequently of a homicidal, suicidal, or sexually aggressive nature. Significant periods of premeditation, either conscious or unconscious, differentiate impulse dyscontrol and acting out from seizure and instinct dyscontrol. We have pointed out that the impulsive dyscontrol individuals consciously experience mounting tension with much thought devoted to the conflict between the need to relieve the tension and the dangerous consequences in so doing; hence, there is a varying period of reflective delay between the original impulse and the act itself. It would seem that during the reflective dely or even "choice" delay, tension mounts until it reaches a breaking point when the urges overwhelm the controls and trigger the explosive act with its release of tension. The differentiation between acting out and impulse dyscontrol is that in acting out, the delays, both reflective and "choice," are to a significant degree unconscious. The act usually does not have the explosive quality, but, if it did, we would further qualify it as impulsive acting out. Both these disorders, then, are examples of elaborate, although usually distorted and inappropriate controls being finally overwhelmed by mounting instinctual urges. Although we have classified acting out and impulse dyscontrol as episodic disinhibitions, usually the patient's life is characterized by inhibition of action. In this group there is an excessive reflection based on inhibitory anxiety with even ordinary day-to-day acting severely inhibited. Thus, acting out, from a dynamic point of view, is more closely akin to the inhibitory neuroses such as phobias and compulsions, while seizure and instinct dyscontrols, particularly with their primitive quality and primary process thinking, are more closely akin to the psychoses. The seizure and instinct dyscontrols are more likely to reflect neurophysiologic or neuropathologic disturbances, while inhibitory forms of action, such as acting out, are more often learned or motivated disorders of behavior. Some patients designated as having impulse dyscontrol will manifest this inhibition of action between episodes and others will not. Thus, this group of patients represents an intermediate form between instinct dyscontrol and acting out (see Fig. 2).

We have previously discussed the observation that gradually mounting irritability, restlessness, depression, fear, and even occasionally, sexual excitement can be prodromal to a characteristic grand mal or psychomotor seizure. Subcortical studies have also revealed that the mounting tension which patients subjectively perceive is sometimes correlated with localized excessive neuronal discharges in the rhinencephalic structures (Patient 021, and Patient 019). The build-up in tension correlates with a build-up in this neuronal discharge, thus representing what we call an epileptoid phenomenon. For diagnostic and treatment purposes, it is important to distinguish between the epileptoid impulse dyscontrol and the motivated impulse dyscontrol, recognizing that in clinical practice mixtures of the two ar more likely to be encountered than the pure polarities. Inasmuch as impulse dyscontrols are an intermediate form between instinct dyscontrol and acting out, let us first investigate the mechanisms of acting out, returning then to impulse dyscontrol. By examining the extremes our view of the intermediate form will be facilitated.

9.3.1 *Psychodynamic-neurophysiologic mechanisms of acting out.* We have previously indicated that an explosive act is not usually characteristic of acting out, nor does the "alloplastic readiness to act" usually characterize the person who acts out. To be sure, the act is the prime consideration in acting out, but it is not necessarily the tendency to action nor the frequency of action that makes the act the center of our attention, but the devastating consequences of the act, even if it is an isolated or rare event. We have implied that this "alloplastic readiness to act" is not only uncharacteristic of acting out, but in fact, the reverse is usually the case; even normal, everyday independent decisive acts are severely inhibited (Freud's Dora was hardly a girl of action, see Deutsch's postscript, 1957). We have proposed that the essence of acting out, however egosyntonic the act, is that retrospectively it is a surprise to the actor, either with regard to the form it has taken or the consequence that resulted. This is represented in our schema by the lower border of Fig. 15. We have mentioned that the act at times may be so thoroughly rationalized, denied, repressed, or projected that even in retrospect it appears egosyntonic to the actor, but even in these instances, according to our definition, the act would not be considered acting out unless it was seen as out of context and out of character at least to an objective observer who knew the actor well.*

* This point, already discussed in Chapters 1 and 2, is at considerable variance with the opinion of some observers. Bloss (1963) insists that even in retrospect, when the act becomes ego-alien, it should no longer be considered acting out, but a symptomatic act or a symptom. However, we prefer to limit the term symptomatic act to partial acts symbolically representing a conflict. We also feel it is not useful or generally possible to distinguish between a symptom and acting out, acting out itself being a symptom. We believe, as does Bloss (1963), that it is certainly important to identify clearly what is retrospectively ego-syntonic and what is retrospectively ego-alien, but we prefer to think of symptoms as being either ego-alien to the individual, alien to society, or both. This does leave, however, a crucial question untouched: the difference between neurotic action and acting out. We suggest that, however painful the neurotic pattern is to the individual and no matter how aware he is that this pain is self-induced, the neurotic does not often identify any particular isolated pattern of behavior as being the cause of his difficulty. The neurotic action which we would label acting out is a specific act which represents a sudden change in the style or pattern of the usual acts of the individual, whether the "usual" acts are neurotic or normal.

One might also ask, when does the ego-alien quality of the act become obvious to the actor? As we will see in subsequent patient histories, sometimes this immediately follows the act, while at other times it is delayed until the surprising consequences of the act become apparent. However, in acting out the act itself may be a complex series of behavioral patterns extending over a period of time. Sometimes the actor becomes vaguely aware of the ego-alien quality of his behavior, even before the act has been fully consummated. For example:

> Patient 102 was a rigidly puritanical female who seduced a reluctant male under conditions in which conception was likely. This was shortly after her husband had been found to be sterile. The husband, who was a pathologically jealous, paranoid person, was so upset by his recent "castration" that he was impotent at the time of her acting out. The seductive behavior occurred over a period of several days and several interrupted encounters. As success became imminent, she became increasingly aware of her unusual behavior and the dangerous consequences, but the compulsion to complete "the act" once started was overwhelming. Not unrelated to this acting out, was the fact that her analyst was out of town during this period and her sessions had been cancelled. When again on the couch, she was mortified by her infidelity, and panic-stricken regarding the possible consequences, anticipating quite correctly that if she was pregnant, not only her marriage, but also perhaps her life was in danger.

This example shows that the ego-alien quality of the act can be apparent even before the completion of the act itself. The surprise element to the actor was also reflected in a surprise element to the outside observer, in our scheme represented by the social expectation at the top of the diagram. Among her social group, a wife who was occasionally unfaithful would not be surprising, but it was quite a surprise that *this* individual would be unfaithful, everybody recognizing her extremely strict puritanical code. The act then is an abrupt disruption in the life style and the life flow of the patient, something that is out of character and out of context.

What is it then that goes wrong in terms of the mechanism schematically represented in Fig. 15? Returning to this patient, the reader may have already suspected a mishandled transference reaction, which was more than confirmed by her subsequent demands and associations.

> First, of course, was a demand that her therapist should make everything right by arranging for an abortion (even before she knew whether or not she was pregnant). If this caused him some anguish or inconvenience (such as losing his license) this would be just punishment for his desertion. It was expected that his own guilt could be expiated by proving his love in making such a sacrifice. In the end it was assumed that his jealousy over her intimacy with another man would be placated by her having his (the therapist's) baby.

Of course, none of this was conscious before the act, but an incompletely interpreted dream which preceded the act but followed her being informed of her therapist's temporary departure was:

> Father had returned unexpectedly early from a business trip and became enraged upon finding the dreamer (his daughter as an adolescent) petting with a boyfriend.

Thus, the present acting out was a carefully reflected, delayed response to the current situation, associatively connected with significant past experiences and leading to wish gratification, but all at the unconscious level and motivated by unresolved oedipal conflict. This is an example of how past experiences in acting out, whether actual or retrospectively distorted, can dominate present perceptions and apperceptions. The act becomes then a primitive form of memory dominated by emotional rather than rational connections and seems to be an insistence that the infantile or childish wish need not be abandoned. In essence, then, the act is not a token representation of a past experience, such as being flirtatious with her therapist as a father figure, but a repetition of the total experience or wished-for experience. (For a discussion of the therapeutic problems such acting out precipitates see Chapter 12.) In this chain of events there may be one or several distortions of reality, but working within this misperceived reality, the integrative functions are intact, and there is no lack of reflective delay. This is an important point, because again we would limit acting out to those patients in whom these central mechanisms are intact. If the same series of actions had taken place except that the patient delusionally misidentified the paramour with her therapist or her father or her husband, or misidentified the setting for her therapist's office, her father's bedroom, or her own bedroom, it would represent an "alloplastic readiness" for substituting action for delusion, but again we would not call this acting out; such acts we would consider "psychotic action."

Acting out, then, does not represent a "short-circuit" of reflective delay as we saw in the seizure and instinct dyscontrol, nor does it represent disintegration of the central integrative mechanisms as seen in psychotic action, but it is a misuse of the reflective delay, a misuse because the present situation is related to and inappropriatetly connected with a past situation, the inappropriate connection in turn related to the affectively charged memories of unresolved conflicts. Thus, the situation stirs up old tensions, distorting the apperception of the present, which mistakenly seems to offer relief for the old conflict. The apperceptions and intentions are distorted because of faulty (not lack of) reflection on the current situation. If there were any neurophysiologic mechanisms behind acting out it would be a mechanism related to repression. Nothing either in terms of epileptoid phenomena or the maturational lag gives us any clues to the neurophysiology of repression, so consideration of it remains in abeyance. It seems likely, that "faulty learning" must play a large part in most acting out. However, the fact that, as reported in Chapter 8, even patients considered to have acting-out disorders show paroxysmal abnormalities with activation suggests that neurophysiologic mechanisms may be contributing to the disordered behavior.

The dynamics of the act are, of course, as varied as the patients who demonstrate acting out, and even in the same patient the motivation for each acting out may have varying degrees of uniqueness. Here, however, we are interested in possible universals, leaving the uniqueness for our later consideration of individual patients. What is universal in acting out? We have already mentioned that in most "actor-outers" the ability to act decisively is in general inhibited. It is this change from inhibition of action to disinhibition of action that is crucial. Put in other terms, why is fantasy and trial action through thought suspended at this particular moment and the motor act now carried out? To answer this we must look again at the difference between trial action through thought and action itself.

Much has been made of the discharge of tension that accompanies trial action through thought and fantasy. However true this may be, the reverse is equally true. Trial action by thought can also increase tension, a prospect so obvious that socializing institutions such as the church emphasize one's responsibility for thoughts as well as deeds, implicitly recognizing, for example, that thoughts of fornication can often increase the need for fornication. Hence, the thought as well as the deed is a punishable sin. What is characteristic of the "actor-outer" in the period immediately preceding the act is that reflective thoughts, largely unconscious, have become so imperative and loaded with affect that the urge or need to discharge them overwhelms the usual inhibitory anxiety. This generalization must be particularly true for what we call impulsive acting out; that is, the pseudo-impulsivity that follows a long period of unconscious reflection. We have already mentioned that the same behavior, if it follows a period of conscious reflection, is designated as impulse dyscontrol.

More often than not, however, the acts in acting out are not explosive in quality, but a series of coolly calculated acts, modifiable in terms of form as the ongoing situation demands, but persevering in terms of the ultimate goal. Here the essential difference between acting out as opposed to trial action through thought is a *commitment*, the act representing a choice as well as a renunciation of all alternative choices. It is a decision, in a sense irrevocable and irretrievable (Strauss, 1966). There may be attempts to balance or negate the act by subsequent acts, and the subsequent acts may, if not neurotically inhibited, be determined by the response to the first act or the acting out, but nothing obliterates the act, not even the magic of the words, "I'm sorry." The act relieves the immediate tension. In fact, even the decision to act relieves considerable tension, that is the painful brooding doubt of indecisiveness. This is what Menninger was referring to when he formulated the episodic behavioral disorders within the framework of the psychoanalytic structural hypothesis (e.g., impulses escaping the restraints of the ego; see 3.2). Such a tautological explanation, however, has no practical clinical advantage, as an explanation should, by indicating a definite course of remedial action. Our formulation, on the other hand, does bring to light that to understand acting out, it is even more important to examine the dynamics of decision making than to clarify the content and meaning of the act itself. Why is it that at this particular moment the patient is able to commit himself irrevocably to an act? Such commitment of course is a necessary part of effective adaptive living. However inappropriate the act might be in acting out (and this would depend to a large extent on how much tension it would cause in the setting in which the patient lives), what may be important is an increasing maturity that leads to a newfound capacity to act decisively. This explains the frequent observation that acting out in neurotically inhibited patients takes place just when we have noted the most progress in therapy. The task of the therapist, then, becomes one of encouraging more appropriate actions without reinhibiting the will to act itself (Rosen, 1963). As Eckstein (1965) says, acting out is an attempt to resolve a conflict and should be treated as such rather than meeting it with regret and prohibition.

These matters will be discussed further in Chapter 12 on psychotherapy. Here we will mention only one other important aspect of the commitment: it represents self-assertion or taking a stand. In the "actor-outer" even everyday mundane self-assertion and stand-taking is fraught with doubt and fear because of inappropriate generalizations of neurotic inhibition. Every act becomes an unacceptable guilt-ridden one (such as killing mother and appropriating father) with possible catastrophic consequences. Retrospectively, no matter how unacceptable (ego-alien) the act is to the actor, one must remember that it is a disguised representation of an even more unacceptable act. There is in the action a self-deception with the disavowal of the true intention. Defenses are organized in such a way as to escape direct confrontation with the act. Rubin (1965) describes this matter in terms of ego psychology (ego function). As a substitute, the act never completely resolves the basic tension, but only temporarily alleviates it. Thus, until the act is seen for what it really is and the tensions resolve regarding the unacceptable act and denied intention of the act, the stage is set for a repetition of the act in the future. It is for this reason that acting out has its recurrent quality, regardless of the patent difference in eliciting situations. If ever the dictum of making the unconscious conscious is appropriate, it is in the treatment of acting out.

The manifold child-parent relationship which would lead to this alternating inhibition-disinhibition in self-assertive action can only be mentioned in passing, but was discussed in detail at the Thom Clinic Symposium on Acting-Out presented by the Division of Psychiatry, Boston University School of Medicine (Symposium, 1963). To mention only a few of the possibilities: there is a proposal by Rexford that children who ultimately develop the pattern of acting out are infantilized during their early development, while at the same time expected to exert adult controls; the infantilization or control by the mother is such that the child develops no sense of intention or responsibility; the inconsistency of parental attitudes is such that the child sees the world as capricious and, therefore, the child believes predictions of the future are useless; there is faulty introjection, hence inadequate superego controls because of a symbiotic relationship between mother and child. During adolescence, apart from the failure in anticipatory mechanisms that we have emphasized (9.2.2), there are also the problems of renunciation of previous object choices and previous identifications and the need to relate in new ways to the outside world as well as to rebel against dependency and passivity.

The psychodynamic possibilities of acting out are so varied that generalizations are inappropriate. Patient S282 demonstrates a combination of many of these factors and also shows some evidence of central nervous system dysfunction. To reiterate, however, the one generalization that we propose in analyzing acting out: we should pay particular attention not only to the content of the act but to the reasons for the commitment to act at any particular time and the lack of this commitment to act (indecisiveness) in other similar situations. At times we are hard put to identify motivations behind this new capacity to act. In such situations, particularly if they are associated with possible physiologic changes (premenstrual periodicity in acting out), one is tempted to suggest the possible hyperexcitability of the nervous system as explanation. Although we have indirect evidence that this is sometimes true, in that drugs seem to reduce the tendency for acting out, an emphasis on motivational elements is usually the most effective therapeutic approach.

9.3.2 *Psychodynamic-neurophysiologic mechanisms of impulse dyscontrol.* Impulse dyscontrol has in common with instinctual dyscontrol the abrupt explosive quality of the act itself, with an undisguised expression of primitive urges. In fact we have suggested that in impulse dyscontrol, the act often has a much more intense, explosive quality than characterizes instinct dyscontrol. On the other hand, in contradistinction to instinct dyscontrol but in common with acting out is the premeditation of varying degress that precedes the act itself. The distinguishing feature of the premeditation between impulse dyscontrol and acting out is the conscious premeditation that characterizes the impulse dyscontrol. The act itself in impulse dyscontrol is relatively unambiguous in comparison with acting out in that the object and the affect are much less disguised (e.g., killing mother's lover rather than father), while in acting out one or the other or both may be disguised (e.g., firing the governess as a substitute for killing mother). Thus, impulse dyscontrol on one hand is more primitive (less socialized) and on the other hand more mature (or less neurotic) inasmuch as it is less repressed. In this instance we see a clear reflection of Freud's hypothesis, stated in "Civilization and Its Discontents" (Freud, vol. XXI), that socialization is in some degree proportionate to neuroticism. Put another way, one can say that repressing forces in acting out are proportionate to the strength of conscience mechanisms, usually an unduly harsh or inappropriately childish conscience. On the other hand, conscience mechanisms in impulse dyscontrol are inappropriately weak or completely debilitated by the strength of the urges or the intolerance to mounting tension. Again, this differentiation has immense therapeutic implications discussed further in Chapter 12 on psychotherapy. In terms of our schematic representation, there is not only a distortion in integrative connections between the current situation with past experiences, such as occurs in acting out, but also a disproportionate balance between the affect and urges on one hand and the conscience mechanisms on the other. We have already mentioned and will discuss further in the next chapter patients whose mounting tension and irritability culminate in a seizure, either grand mal or a simple automatism, and we have seen in Chapter 4 that excessive neuronal discharge in the rhinencephalon can correlate with this period of mounting tension. If the act then, is a seizure, the epileptoid mechanism with a period of prodromal mounting tension is obvious. But what if the act is more coordinated and effective? Is this too an epileptoid phenomenon? Does the explosive act take place when there is final involvement of the cortex with loss of inhibitory functions, anticipatory mechanisms being impaired with the result that the consequences of the act are no longer perceived? Since recording during the act itself is seldom possible, EEG data are not readily available to prove these points. However, the high incidence of EEG abnormalities between episodes suggests that this is more than just a possibility. Our criteria for determining the predominence of epileptoid or motivational mechanisms will be discussed in the next chapter. Also, the findings reported in Chapter 7 that with alpha chloralose activation many of the patients (12 of 16—see Table 10) who demonstrate impulse dyscontrol or acting out had EEG abnormalities suggest that even in the higher hierarchial levels of episodic dyscontrol, epileptoid or maturational defects contribute to the basic mechanisms.

In some instances of impulse dyscontrol the basic mechanism must be relatively weak control over intense or intolerable urges, without any epileptoid or maturational defect of the central nervous system. As children, such patients were subjected to intense affective stimuli of a fearful, rageful, or sexual nature before being able to cope with such exposure. These stimuli, presented in the form of parental behavior usually of an inconsistent, explosive nature, not only left an intolerance to strong affects, but, as an inevitable corollary, failures in identification; hence the lack of stable persisting moral judgments necessary for the evolution of a healthy effective conscience or superego. Affects that are intense and persistent easily overwhelm the conscience that remains weak and unpredictable. This seems to be the sine qua non of impulse dyscontrol. However, some conscience mechanisms must be operating, otherwise there would not be the wavering and doubt during the period of premeditation.

Before leaving our discussion of impulse dyscontrol, we must mention another similarity between this group and those patients who act out. In this group of patients, as in the acting-out group, we usually see an inhibition in normal everyday assertive decisiveness. One other observation on impulse dyscontrol is worthy of note and that is the frequency with which impulse dyscontrol is a one-time affair. In such instances, despite the fact (or perhaps because of the fact) that the act is a severe transgression, even a heinous crime, there is immediate relief of tension and a lack of guilt after the act. This occurs more often in impulse dyscontrol than in acting out and must be in part related to the more direct and less disguised expression of the urge. The act is usually a retribution or an avenging of an imagined crime perpetuated against the actor, usually of a highly significant but symbolic nature. The "catathymic crisis" of Wertham (1949) is an example. It is probably significant that the guiltless reaction is more likely to occur in children and adolescents, perhaps because full development of anticipatory anxiety, hence conscience mechanisms, has not taken place.

At other times such an act, however, is followed by guilt and undoing, even to the point of self-destruction. We would modify the scheme of Weintraub (1963) to represent this as follows:

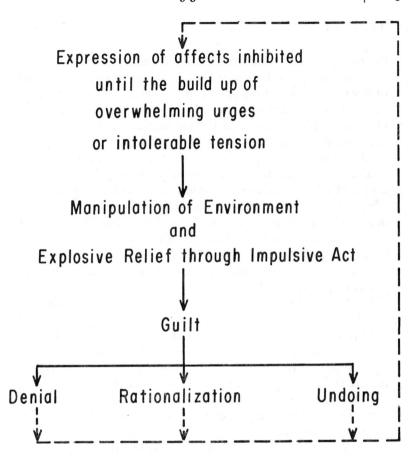

Fig. 16. Dynamics of impulse dyscontrol

Weintraub placed denial before manipulation. That this is partly true is obvious from the wavering doubt that occurs during the period of premeditation. In fact, the observation that impulse dyscontrol is associated with such wavering and doubt indicates that conscience mechanisms, however weak, are operating but are ineffective in aborting the act. Hence the denial, rationalization, and undoing are again necessary after the act has been completed. As an example, let us consider the following patient:

Patient S286 was seen at the request of the court because she had run down a man while he was getting into his car.

The first blow was a glancing one, the man running around
the car and up on the curb. She backed up her car, jumped
the curb, ran over him once, then backed up over him again
and only stopped when an onlooker managed to lift the hood
of her car and disconnect the spark plugs. She then rolled up
the windows of her car, locked the doors and read a Bible
until the police arrived. As the victim was being carried off,
she shouted, "Pray to God, Mac, that He will forgive you."
At the time of her apprehension she was calm and relaxed.

The victim had been her former paramour. Significantly,
they met when he, a used car salesman, sold her the car with
which she ran him down. At the time of her first contact he
made sexual advances which she resisted, but he persisted
and for a period of several months they lived together. This
arrangement was terminated when a fight over financial matters led to an appearance in court on charges filed by the
patient against her lover. He was acquitted, however, and
she returned to her mother's house where she brooded in
quiet sullenness for several months. Approximately one
month before the offense she became increasingly irritable
and explosive, saying such things as "75 percent of men
should be dead for what they do to women," and "God says
it's all right to kill." One day she saw him getting into his
car and had the impulse to run him down. This frightened
her, so she immediately went to church to pray. The impulse
became increasingly strong, and she traded cars with her
brother, hoping that if she did not have her own car she
would not commit the act. When this didn't relieve the tension, she left town for several weeks, but even this was of no
avail. The day before the homicide, she visited a sister who
had recently given birth to an illegitimate child. This further incensed her, so the following day she drove to the place
of her ex-paramour's work, waiting for him to leave in his
car for lunch. She still wavered in her resolve, decided that
she didn't have enough gas, so left to get the tank filled, at
the same time hoping he would leave before her return.
However, she did return and seeing him about to enter his
car, she went into a blind rage and ran him down. Several
thoughts occurred to her repeatedly before the act. One, that
she would not kill him but only maim him and then ulti-

mately he would kill her. The second was that she would miss him altogether, fall out of her car and be run over herself. Another thought was that whatever happened was God's will, and God willed that her boyfriend be punished and in fact even he himself wished for punishment.

The long period of mounting tension with wavering and doubt regarding the act is characteristic of impulse dyscontrol. We see evidence for both denial ("it is God's will") and undoing ("I will be killed instead") which took place during this period of wavering and doubt. After the act the main defense was a bizarre rationalization, namely that she was an agent of God, performing His will in committing the murder. The difference between the impulse dyscontrol represented in this woman's behavior and acting out is the fact that defenses of denial and undoing are in the latter replaced by repression and substitute gratification. The expression of affect and the intention of the act are much more direct in the impulse dyscontrol. Despite the lack of overt expressions of guilt in this patient, obviously guilt is operative because of the need for denial and undoing. Weintraub's (1963) data indicate how frequently adult patients feel guilty as reflected in their extremely apologetic behavior immediately after the act itself.

9.4   FAILURES IN CENTRAL INTEGRATION: EPISODIC PSYCHOTIC REACTIONS

The remaining group of episodic behavioral disorders which we will discuss are those designated as *episodic reactions*. Again, what this group has in common with the other episodic disorders is the precipitous appearance of disordered behavior. In this group, however, the abrupt interruption in life style or life flow is not limited to a single act, or to a closely related series of acts with a common intention, but extends over periods of days and months and may have elements of all types of episodic dyscontrol. In the episodic psychotic reactions, perceptual and conceptual distortions are of such a degree as to be labeled psychotic, usually schizophrenic reaction, affective psychosis, or paranoia. We also suggest that what is usually neglected or overlooked are altered states of consciousness. Psychoses accompanied by altered consciousness are often considered the result of an external toxin, hence an acute brain syndome. The very fact that in this group a history of such is seldom uncovered is probably one of the reasons that the importance of the altered consciousness is overlooked or underrated. Even in those instances where the episodic psychotic reaction is precipitated by alcohol it is usually noticed that the alcohol per se is not an adequate explanation for the precipitous behavioral change, but must function as a releasing agent in an abnormally predisposed or sensitized individual. Thus, the behavior has more of the characteristics of pathological intoxication than an acute brain syndrome.

Patient F250 (Appendix 6) is a classical example of this episodic psychotic reaction. He was seen in the emergency room with the smell of alcohol on his breath and a story that he had fallen off a bar stool and cut his head; this being the reason for having been brought to the hospital. For reasons discussed in the detailed case history, he reported in the emergency room that he was a chronic alcoholic. The fact that he was confused, disoriented, ataxic, and dysarthric "clinched" the diagnosis of inebriation and vague illusions suggested incipient delirium tremens. However, a detailed account from the bartender revealed that he had had only two martinis, and his family indicated that he had had nothing to drink for the preceding 24 hours and had not been drinking heavily before this. The fact that alcohol was an "activating" agent became established later with the finding of an abnormal EEG, the onset of seizures and subsequent tests proving that alcohol induced a seizural record.

From our neurophysiologic considerations we have seen that what is responsible for such disturbances of consciousness is not an exogenous toxin but an "excessive neuronal discharge." *

* The problem of endogenous toxins or disturbances of brain metabolism as responsible for excessive neuronal discharge has rather arbitrarily been considered as beyond the scope of the present work. In part, this is related

What do we mean when we refer to these reactions as psychotic? We are referring to the fact that the reported experiences of the patients are so individual or expressed with such a private language and logic that the observer has difficulty in empathically understanding the behavior in terms of his own inner awareness and experience. On the other hand, it has been pointed out that in episodic dyscontrol, no matter how much the behavior surprises the observer or the actor, it is understandable in terms of the observer's inner awareness and experience and even the actor's previous experience. Indeed, in this group, no matter how revolting the act may have been, there is some flickering recognition that such impulses do or have existed in all of us; nor are the affects felt by the actor as being unique or strange, except in their intensity.

9.4.1 *Neurophysiological mechanisms.* What is it then that can so disrupt the integrative functions of the organism that the perceptions and intentions become such a privately unique event that they cannot be empathically understood by most observers who have been in or can project themselves into similar situations? What is it that, at the same time, can disturb the level of consciousness to such a degree that it would appear as if the person were suffering from some exogenous toxin, even though a history of this is lacking? Our proposal is that this is, at least in many instances, because the episodic reaction is an epileptoid phenomenon similar to the epileptoid psychotic reactions we have already considered in Chapter 5. In that chapter we differentiated the nonproductive group of episodic psychotic reactions characterized by an extreme reduction in consciousness with general apathy and lack of initiative associated with centrencephalic epilepsy as an ictal phenomenon (petit mal status) or as a post-ictal phenomenon, associated with neuronal depression following an excessive discharge. Referring, again, to our schematic repre-

---

to the author's lack of competence to evaluate the literature in this area, but in part is due to the fact that research in the area is still so controversial and the results so contradictory that the clinical usefulness of the data as well as the scientific validity remains undetermined. The reader is referred to reviews on the subject by Heath (1962a) and Kety (1966).

sensation (Fig. 15), in this group the perceptions are severely limited, hence all integrative functions are attenuated and motor coordination (competence) is impaired. In this group only the cruder stimuli are responded to (such as physical restraint) and the result is a primitive seizure or instinct dyscontrol, a response of fight or flight on one hand, or reaching out for affection and closeness on the other. Without the crude stimulus, there is seldom a dyscontrol response. However, in Chapter 5 we were able to identify a second group referred to by Landolt (1958) as the "productive psychoses." In these instances the psychotic behavior was more florid. The level of consciousness was not so much "reduced," but either "distracted" or typically "primary process thinking" and accompanied by intense, usually dysphoric moods. Referring again to the scheme of Fig. 15 with the "distracted" consciousness the selection of unimportant from important stimuli is seriously impaired, accompanied by restlessness and attention to any and all stimuli, a function which we have already related to the temporal lobe-limbic system, particularly the hippocampus, and also to diffuse cortical damage (Laufer, 1957). However, the defect in consciousness that usually accompanies the "productive psychosis" is characterized by "primary process thinking," which in our scheme would be represented by marked disturbance in the affect-memory integration, that is, failure in logical cause-effect reasoning.

Clinically, the identification of the epileptoid episodic psychotic reaction is important for our therapeutic planning. The fact that excessive neuronal discharge in one way or another plays a part in many of the episodic reactions suggests greater reliance on somatic measures, with the relearning process (psychotherapy) an adjunctive therapy (Monroe, 1960c). There is also evidence that a differentiation of the episodic psychotic reaction in terms of those with (1) reduced or clouded consciousness, (2) distracted consciousness, and (3) primary-process thinking are probably important for selection of the appropriate pharmacologic agent. We will discuss this matter in Chapter 11 on the somatic therapies.

9.4.2 *Psychodynamic mechanisms.* An additional question

arises as to whether such episodic psychotic reactions can be a pre-dominantly motivated response rather than due to excessive neu-ronal discharge. Observations would strongly suggest that this is so. For example, there can be an attempt at adaptation through a psychotic withdrawal, a response most often seen in a situation of overwhelming stimuli; e.g., a catastrophe such as war, fire, flood, and the like. In such a situation, the most common behavioral pattern, and one that seems to have at least some adaptive value as a response to overwhelming stimuli, is limitation of the stimuli through what we might call "reduced" consciousness. Such a syn-drome is characterized by general torpor, slowness of thinking, lack of initiative, emotional blunting, and apathy; symptoms very similar to those accompanying petit mal status (American Psy-chiatric Association, 1956). Again, this syndrome is characterized by inhibition of action with little motor response except as a consequence of direct restraint. Because this is so common, in a situation of overwhelming environmental stress it might even be considered a normal adaptive response. On the other hand, in a similar situation of overwhelming environmental stress, the re-sponse may be characterized by a dissociated consciousness (e.g., hysterical fugues) or primary-process thinking (e.g., the ten-day schizophrenic reaction). All these behavioral changes are reac-tions to what the communication engineers would defer to as in-put overload. In this sense then the most common response of "reduced consciousness" would seem to be adaptive, while the other response would more likely be the precipitation of mal-adaptive behavior in predisposed individuals. Again, what is important to the clinician is whether he can distinguish between those episodic disturbances that are epileptoid and those which are motivated responses. Our analysis would suggest the following kind of reasoning. If the precipitating situation was such that it would have been overwhelming, and the behavior response char-acterized by reduced consciousness, the possibility is highly likely that it is a predominantly motivated adaptive withdrawal from reality into psychosis. If, on the other hand, no matter how overwhelming the situational stimuli, the response was one of a dissociated or distracted consciousness, or primary-process thinking, we would presume either epileptoid or motivational predisposition. If the precipitating event in the episodic psychotic reaction does not appear traumatic to the average individual, but can be established symbolically as a catastrophe, it is more likely a motivated response or, rarely, an emotionally precipitated epileptoid phenomenon, but in either instance a response that would only be elicited in a severely predisposed individual. If the precipitating situation, on the other hand, was both overtly and covertly neutral, the more likely would the episodic psychotic reaction be a strictly epileptoid response in an individual with a precarious neurophysiologic adaptive balance. Such a commonsense differentiation is not easily deciphered from the clinical data, nor will one likely achieve much consensus among several professional evaluators, despite comparable levels of training and sophistication.

Perhaps the patients themselves, in terms of their own retrospective evaluation of the episodic disorder, can give us valuable clues regarding the relative importance of epileptoid and motivational factors. Strangely, the more the reaction is epileptoid, the more likely the patient assumes responsibility for his actions. At the same time he experiences a feeling of "drivenness" beyond his volitional control, even referring to the experience as an "attack" or "spell." He asks for restraint or isolation and, if he has recognizable prodromal symptoms, begs for anticipatory restraint or help. After the episode itself, the patient may admit his sickness, readily talk about his symptoms, and seem more than willing to accept any concomitant punishment or hospitalization. The difference between these patients and the motivated group is the acceptance of their own behavior without the sense of guilt and shame which elicits denial in the motivated group. Self-esteem seems relatively maintained, no matter how atrocious their behavior. It is this group that we have designated as having an episodic brain syndrome.

On the other hand, the more motivated the behavior, the more responsibility for the behavior has to be renounced through some defensive mechanism. This is the group of patients with complete amnesia (other than those with grand mal seizures and simple automatisms). These are the patients who project, seeing themselves as passive victims of the manipulations of others or of harsh fate beyond their control. These are patients who, if they do accept responsibility for the act, say that the act was committed without premeditation. It is their unconscious realization of the unacceptable intentions of their acts that require subsequent defenses of repression, denial, undoing, projection, and rationalization in order to deny guilt and maintain some level of self-esteem. This group is designated as having episodic schizophrenia, or episodic dissociation.

These are probably our best (but far from infallible) data upon which to balance the episodic psychotic reactions in terms of the epileptoid or motivational mechanisms behind them. In fact, a similar evaluation is useful in differentiating the epileptoid and motivational aspects of episodic dyscontrol acts. The differentiation between motivated and epileptoid episodic behavioral disorders will be discussed in more detail in Chapter 10, and is illustrated by specific clinical material in the psychodynamic-neurophysiologic consideration of the clinical reports (Appendix).

9.5 WEAK CONSCIENCE MECHANISMS: EPISODIC SOCIOPATHIC REACTIONS

The epileptoid episodic sociopathic reactions have been discussed in some detail in Chapter 6, and here we will add only those comments which emphasize points not previously mentioned. We have already described a motivated episodic psychotic reaction resulting from an "input overload," such as might occur in any catastrophic environmental situation. Studies in sensory deprivation (Bexton, 1954; Lilly, 1956) lead us to consider the other possibility of an input deficiency—that is, whether a minimal level of sensory experience is necessary to maintain reality contact. This would seem to be the case, the question arises: how often would the natural environment be such as to fall below this minimal input? It must happen infrequently and only in very unusual circumstances. However, one must consider the possibilty that there are certain individuals who seem to need a heightened level of input or stimulation to maintain their sense of well-being. Such has been reported (Quay, 1965) particularly for sociopaths. These individuals seem to be so unresponsive to the usual environmental stimulation that they must elicit violent or dramatic reactions from the environment. Thus, an optimal level of environmental stimulation is insured, providing the excitement, pleasure, or concern necessary for their well-being. Such individuals at the phenomenological level would be characterized by episodic sociopathic behavior. Such behavior is often noted on hospital wards (MacDonald, 1965) and the event of hospitalization itself might be the stress, in terms of reducing external stimuli making it necessary for these individuals to "incite" trouble. These are precisely the individuals referred to in the psychoanalytic literature as extremely narcissistic. One possible way to look at this problem is that these individuals cannot see or respond to the finer nuances in their environment, the world appearing as dull and grey in comparison with their fluctuating internal urges and needs. The less one can perceive the ordinary needs of people around him, or the broad implications of a given situation for others as well as for oneself, the more one will have to incite crises to keep up this necessary minimal level of stimulation. Again, perhaps because we were studying predominantly hospitalized patients, we did not find a good clinical example of such among our episodic sociopathic reactions; only two of our 70 patients were given this primary diagnosis. Such patients would more likely be found incarcerated in penal institutions. Many of our patients, however, did complain about life being dull unless they were in trouble. The following patient is an example.

Much of the behavior of Patient S283 was psychopathic; that is, essentially acting out with psychopathic partners. The ordinary life of being a spouse, housewife, and mother was too "boring." She would leave her husband almost nightly to go carousing with her friends. This included visiting homosexual bars, wild and uninhibited dancing, frequent transitory affairs, and a psychotherapeutic dilettantism. At one time she was involved with individual therapy, group therapy, family therapy, and two to three Alcoholics Anonymous meetings per week. If she were forced to stay at home she would incite a quarrel, accompanied by a dramatic display of emotions and acting out, often "just to stir things up." Such behavior was also characteristic of Patients F287, S288, 0289, S219, and 0236. In therapy it was necessary to guide the patient into a socially acceptable sublimation of her need for excitement.

There are other possible explanations for the development of an episodic sociopathic reaction. Kaufman (1963) in his evaluation of impulse-ridden character disorders in juvenile delinquents points out the importance of differentiating between the schizophrenic and the true sociopath. In the first instance, the child often reacts with a senseless, bizarre and violent crime as a reaction to overwhelming fears of annihilation. The sociopath seems to be responding to separation anxiety, having experienced a significant and painful object loss in the past. His act is a reaction to fill the void of deprivation, or an angry retaliation against the deprivation, rather than the insufficient "input" that we suggested above.

Patient S282 is a clear example. Whenever he felt deserted by mother and stepfather, as when they refused to let him come home from boarding school during spring vacation, he responded with a series of antisocial acts. The result was that he was sent home by the authorities. Patient S290, described in detail in Appendix 3, is an example of pathological sexual acting out whenever separation anxiety became intense.

We must repeat that the primitive quality of the urges acted upon, the failure in inhibitory controls, and the inconsistency in world view present in all episodic behavioral disorders often means that action has an antisocial quality. However, we would diagnose episodic sociopathic reaction only if such behavior not only represented a true disruption in the life style of the individual, but also if this disruption was characterized by lack of restraining conscience mechanisms and an extreme narcissistic preoccupation with need gratification. Either this is accompanied by a noticeable lack in anticipatory anxiety, hence no reflective or choice delay, or the anxiety of separation or loss of a loved object is so intense that there is an angry striking out against society. If the behavior is truly episodic and not a way of life, the chances that it is epileptoid or a maturational lag are great. If it is predominantly motivational, yet periodic or occasional, the precipitating situation would have to have catastrophic significance, usually at a unique symbolic level. This behavior is typical of adolescence, but is seen in adulthood.

Patient S286, although representing an example of an episodic psychotic reaction, clarifies this point. Brooding over being compromised by men, and talking with her sister who had recently given birth to an illegitimate child, she mumbled, "Seventy-five percent of all men should be dead because of what they do to women." She then proceeded with a plan to kill her paramour bizarrely.

Patient 0289 (Appendix 7), for twenty-nine out of thirty days, was a somewhat prudish, typical upper-middle-class housewife and mother, the epitome of responsibility in her community. But on the thirtieth day she dissociated to become the prostitute street walker. In part, this was a rebellion against the "double standard," striking out at her husband, who was at the time having an affair.

9.6 INAPPROPRIATE CONSCIENCE MECHANISMS: EPISODIC NEUROTIC REACTIONS

The best discussion of episodic neurotic reactions is by Epstein (1960). He identifies episodic disorders per se, and describes the possible epileptoid mechanisms behind a case of fetishism. In his patient, who had a shoe fetish, there were a number of characteristic aspects of the psychopathology which suggested the type of symptom which we have seen with epileptoid mechanisms. These were: (1) sudden transitory fear and depression unrelated to specific thought content; (2) imperative urge to perform certain motor acts; (3) forced thinking; (4) marked ease and readiness for sexual arousal even by nonerotic affects, such as fear; and (5) repetitive catastrophic mutilation dreams. Most of these symptoms had an episodic, transitory quality and, as we have suggested, Epstein emphasizes the imbalance between "organismic excitability and attempts at control." Control mechanisms included obsessive-compulsive symptoms and a facade of emotional reserve. He points out that the fetishistic dreams and fantasies have a stereotyped quality and that there is a tendency to act out the fantasy. However, the acting out only momentarily relieves the tension because, as we have seen, the intention is so disguised and deflected that the true source of the tension is not alleviated, nor is there a true gratification of needs. In Epstein's patient the episodic disorder sometimes had a more primitive quality, sounding more like our instinct or impulse dyscontrol. It would be interesting to know, but the reported data do not offer an answer, whether these lower levels of episodic dyscontrol with more direct gratification led to a more pronounced or long-lasting discharge of tension. As we have observed in our patients, the lack of true gratification of the urges is manifest by the frequent repetition of the act. Epstein points out, as we have, that the failure in repression is probably due to the "increased excitatory state," or what we would call "excessively strong urges." It may also be significant that Epstein's patient had experienced abnormal stimulation during childhood by an overly seductive mother.

Throughout this book we have noted the similarity between epileptoid manifestations and episodic neurotic reactions, and we will not discuss them in detail here. The frequency of the episodic, short-lived depression is one example (3.3.3 and 6.3). The episodic hypochondriases and physiologic reactions were referred to in the context of visceral auras with or without seizures (6.4 and 7.5) and as a manifestation of truly epileptoid phenomena accompanying 14 and 6 cycle per second positive spike abnormalities (5.5.5). In Chapter 7 we discussed studies which suggest "central nervous system instability" as measured by activated paroxysmal slow waves in patients with episodic physiologic reactions.

The differentiation between motivated altered levels of awareness, that is, hypnoidal states, hysterical reactions, and epileptoid confusions, will be discussed in the next chapter. The differentiation which we proposed for determining whether the episodic psychotic reaction was epileptoid or motivated would also apply to the episodic neurotic reaction; that is, the patient's attitude towards his behavior. The more the behavior is motivated, the more responsibility is denied through repression and the less willing the individual is to accept any confrontation regarding his behavior. On the other hand, the epileptoid patient is more likely to see his behavior as "driven" and ego-alien, but at the same time more willing to assume responsibility for it.* Also, the motivated episodic neurotic reactions are more likely characterized during the interepisode period by inhibition of action. Failure of the integrative mechanism is due to an excessive but immature conscience mechanism. The dyscontrol acts, if they accompany the episodic neurotic reactions, are likely to be a rebellion against this overly strict conscience, hence most often acting out rather than the more direct expression of urges. As we have said, guilt is avoided and self-esteem maintained in these motivated reactions by denial and repression.

Why the episodic neurotic patients develop an episodic quality to their symptoms and do not remain typically chronic inhibited neurotics is not always clear, but is discussed in some detail in the clinical reports (see Appendix). It would appear that sometimes the episodic quality results from an episodic excessive neuronal discharge (Patient F250), while at other times it results from intermittent environmental stress with which the more chronic neurotic defenses are unable to cope (Patient F284).

---

* Although Hulfish (1969) points out that epileptics with frequent minor seizures since early childhood have "egosyntonic" attitudes towards their seizures. In fact they often don't even recognize the seizures as such, symptoms being reported only by astute observers in the patient's environment.

9.7 A REEVALUATION OF THE PSYCHOANALYTIC FORMULATIONS OF ACTING-OUT AND IMPULSE NEUROSES

A number of points have been stressed in the literature regarding the dynamics and the genetics (in a psychoanalytic sense) of the impulse neuroses and acting out that have not been specifically mentioned in our present dynamic synthesis (Abt, 1965; Kanzer, 1957; Bellak, 1963). Partly this is due to the fact that we have tried whenever possible to avoid the sometimes confusing psychoanalytic jargon and partly because much of what has been reported in the psychoanalytic literature, while representing a clinical "truth" for a given patient or patients, seems to lack clinical specificity for the episodic disorders in general. Nevertheless, many of these observations are of such importance that they cannot be dismissed without further discussion.

One of the most frequently mentioned characteristics of patients demonstrating impulsivity and acting out is that they are narcissistic and fixated at the oral level of development (Fenichel, 1945; Greenacre, 1950). These concepts have such a broad implication in psychoanalytic theory that it is not always clear how they apply to acting out and impulsivity. With regard to the first, the psychoanalysts generally refer to the characteristic preoccupation of impulsive patients with their own need gratification rather than the needs of those acted upon. Such behavior within our scheme results from two factors: the excessive strength or urgency of these needs or the reflective failure which limits, as Shapiro (1965) says, the associative connotation the object would have if reflection took place. In acting out, where we propose reflection does take place, the associations as we have seen are rich and varied, but through repression and substitute gratification inappropriate for the situation. Hence, there is lack of concern for the true needs of the objects acted upon. In libidinal terms this has been expressed by Blos (1963) as an autoerotic use of the outer world. Anna Freud (1949) expressed a similar idea when she said, "acting-out . . . is a derivative of phallic masterbation . . . its substitute and representative."

The oral fixation seems to refer to the demanding behavior of these impulsive patients as well as their hypersensitivity to separation anxiety and their rebellion against dependency needs (Segal, 1963). As we will see, these observations are valid, but again, probably not specific for the episodic behavioral disorders. They are just more obvious because of the dramatic quality of the act. What may be specific, however, is the need of the individual to assert his independence and rebel against strong dependent needs and passivity by action (Rubin, 1965). To these individuals the "alloplastic readiness to act" is also an "autoplastic need to act"; that is, they seem to be guided by the dictum "action speaks louder than words." In this instance the conflict resolution is sought through an interaction with objects rather than through introspection. This is what the analysts often refer to as externalization of the conflict (see Patient S282).

Most analysts, and Alexander (1930) in particular, emphasize the self-destructive quality of the act in impulsive behavior and acting out (Frosch, 1954). Two elements are involved in this self-destructive quality: the first and all pervading aspect is that any disordered act is, by its very definition, maladaptive; hence, in the long-term, self-destructive. In this sense then, to say that the disordered act is self-destructive is a redundancy. The other aspect is the more blatant self-destructiveness that comes in the form of self-mutilation, suicide, or so called "moral masochism." As the aggressive nature of many of the impulsive acts is resisted to varying degrees, particularly in our groups designated impulse dyscontrol and acting out, the partial control of this aggression by turning it on oneself is inevitable. In our dynamic formulation such reflected aggression because of overly strict conscience mechanisms should be more common in precisely these groups, while less obvious in the group we have designated instinct dyscontrol. The frequency of suicidal attempts and self-mutilation in those with instinct dyscontrol belies this point and suggests that primitive forms of self-destruction must have another but still unclear explanation. In this situation one is reminded of the largely rejected hypothesis of Freud concerning the "death instinct" (Freud, vol. XXI).

Almost all current reviews of acting out refer to the group of adolescent patients studied by Adalaide Johnson and co-workers (Johnson, 1949). A dynamic consideration within our framework suggests that this is a unique group that does not fit into any of our groups, whether designated seizure dyscontrol, instinct dyscontrol, impulse dyscontrol, or acting out; nor, strictly speaking, are they examples of episodic sociopathic reactions. Johnson makes two important observations that lead us to this conclusion. The first is that the pressure to change or modify behavior does not come from the individual patient himself (here the behavior is truly ego-syntonic, both during the act and in retrospect), nor does the pressure come from the family, inasmuch as the adolescents are acting out the forbidden wishes of the parents. The pressure comes from social institutions outside the families— neighbors, schools, courts. It is obvious that there is at least a covert approval within the family itself for the direct gratification of urges through action. If this were conscious and openly expresssed, the situation would be described as sociopathic behavior in an amoral environment. The fact that the communication is at an unconscious level gives the reaction its distinctive morbidity. Returning to our schema (Fig. 15) the perceptual, integrative-reflective, and intentional behavior is intact, so that within the family unit the external expectations and the individual expectations, though largely unconscious, are congruent with the behavior, even if conventional morality and controls are verbalized. The fact that outside disapproval of the behavior so often elicits surprise shows how feebly these conventional mores are maintained. This, then, is an example of a sick family more than of a sick individual and might be clearly differentiated from the group we are discussing as an "acting-out family." Johnson (1952) makes this distinction when she says there is "no obvious impairment in the reality testing of the child but it [reality testing] is oriented towards the unconscious wish of the elders."

We have to consider the proposal of Greenacre (1950) that those who act out are characterized by a "special emphasis on visual sensitization producing a bent for dramatization (derivatives of exhibitionism and scoptophilia)." Either I do not understand the full implications of this statement or the observation is only a selective one, appearing in some situations but not all or perhaps even many. The crux of the statement would be the tendency to dramatization and the magic of action, a subject we have already discussed earlier (9.2.3). The new element and perhaps the valid one is the imitative quality that the word "dramatization" implies. That the direct expression of primitive impulses as occurs in our seizure dyscontrol and instinct dyscontrol, and even impulse dyscontrol has a profound impact, therefore is dramatic, is obvious, but dramatization in the sense of imitation is certainly not characteristic, the behavior having an unusually frightening sense of realness. However, in acting out as we define it (and Greenacre seems to be referring to behavior we would label acting out), the act is disguised in terms of its affect and its intentions and in such a situation would undoubtedly have an imitative quality. In fact, it is pointed out that among professional actors, acting out is frequent (Ekstein, 1965). Occasionally we have had patients explain their scoptophilia as "finding out how I should act." However, in our present series, exhibitionism and scoptophilia did not seem to be particularly characteristic of the patients manifesting episodic dyscontrol.

As some have proposed, we have occasionally designated the group of disorders under discussion as a "neurosis of action." In the sense that neurosis implies inhibition, we see that such a term would be justified, in referring to acting out and to a lesser degree to impulse dyscontrol. The seizure and instinct dyscontrols, however, are neuroses of (inhibition of) reflection. This we have indicated in Fig. 2 on the episodic dyscontrols in the column on the right labeled "Dynamic Differentiation." Seizure and instinct dyscontrol, then, are uninhibited actions and at the same time an inhibition of reflection. Acting out at the bottom of our diagram is an inhibition of action and excessive reflection. What we have designated as impulse dyscontrol is a transitional disorder.

In Chapter 1, discussing the phenomenology of episodic dyscontrol, we also mentioned that these disorders seldom appear as the only or even the predominant disordered behavior, but most often are superimposed on the underlying neurotic, psychotic, sociopathic, epileptic, or otherwise organic patterns. As such then, episodic dyscontrol can be used secondarily in the service of the underlying disorder. Much of what has been written about the dynamics of acting out and impulsive behavior would seem to confuse the dynamics of episodic disorders with the dynamics of the persisting character traits, neuroses, or psychoses (Segal, 1963; Angel, 1965; Bird, 1957).

10   Motivation and Epilepsy

We noted earlier that episodic behavioral disorders could be superimposed on more basic or persistent psychopathology. Often, episodic behavior is utilized by the patient in the service of this underlying pathology to dramatize his illness, manipulate the environment, or otherwise attain secondary gains. The same can be said for epileptic or epileptoid behavioral disturbances where the motivational elements may so obscure the underlying neuropathology that the basic mechanism of "excessive neuronal discharge" is overlooked. Such obscuring of the fundamental mechanisms may lead to serious prognostic and therapeutic mistakes and so deserve special consideration here.

10.1   Epileptic Interruption of Life Flow

An important common denominator underlies both the epileptoid and the motivated episodic behavioral disorders: in each case there is a precipitous onset and remission, the disordered behavior representing an interruption in the life style and the life flow, so that the behavior appears out of character for the individual and out of context for the situation. Let us consider what effect such an interruption in the life style or life flow would have. If the episodic behavioral disorder is more than a momentary reaction, the behavior is accompanied by considerable perplexity: "What is happening to me?" "Am I losing control?" "Am I going mad?" and "Why can't I think straight," all reflect this perplexity.

Patient S288 (Appendix 4) clearly expressed this when she reported transitory, unexplained, indescribable, "ominous" feelings with accompanying tension, saying, "I'm mystified as why I should feel like I do. Sometimes the tension is so strong, a force inside of me so intense, that I just want to scream off the top of my head, yet there is no reason why I should have such feelings."

We have already mentioned that if the episodic behavior is motivated, the individual may be reluctant to look at this period of disturbed behavior and, in fact, even deny its existence. If the behavioral change is epileptoid, the individual is more likely to see this as something alien, a foreign body to be scrutinized, reflected upon and understood; hence, the patient's willingness to discuss the symptoms in much detail. Admittedly there are some exceptions to this distinguishing characteristic between the epileptoid and motivated episodic behavior disorder, particularly in patients who have had frequent seizures since early childhood.

Such episodes, whatever the basic mechanisms, make the future unpredictable, give an impermanence to the world, or make the world seem capricious. Anticipation then lacks the predictable quality it has for others; the future is clouded with doubt, the world fragmented and discontinuous. This unpredictability, we have already suggested, interferes not only with the development of "reflective" and "choice" delay, but also must interfere with more stable attitudes, those necessary for developing any persistent moral and ethical codes. Such interruptions, as Shapiro (1965) says, "interfere with the firm sense of the objective, the independent reality and permanance of time." It is likely that there will develop a sense of fatalistic passivity, insecurity, and helplessness. More than this, if there is also an altered sense of awareness or consciousness this interferes with self-identity, self-control, and relatedness or belongingness to the world.

Patient O289 (Appendix 7) expressed this futility about her behavior (dissociative reactions with double personality) as well as her resignation about the breakup of her marriage and loss of her children. However, once legal proceedings started, and she fully realized the danger to her children from their sadistic father, she "pulled herself together," and since then has manifested no further episodic disorder. The fact that the basic mechanisms in this instance were motivational, rather than epileptoid, was probably the reason that she could do this.

The anxiety that accompanies this lack of permanance and all its related consequences often elicits a defense reaction of excessive control, a fact we have previously discussed under the epileptic personality. The defense reaction to this impermanence and loss of control is the development of a cold, calculated, rigid, conventional, meticulous, and pedantic personality. We have already mentioned that such personality traits are a reaction formation against basic sado-masochistic urges. From our series we have found preoccupation with such urges particularly prominent in those patients with "specific" EEG abnormalities predominantly of the temporal lobe. A conceptualization proposed by Ostow (1957) helps us in understanding this phenomenon. He pointed out that the temporal lobe appears to be concerned with apperceptions, the interpretation of perceptions. Inasmuch as excessive neuronal discharge in the same area is almost always dysphoric, the apperceptive judgments may not only be impaired in other ways but because of this dysphoria, be usually negative. For instance, the ictal or postictal behavior of the temporal lobe patient seems to represent what we have called "separation response," that is, a fight or flight response, pleasurable responses seldom occurring. In contrast, often during the postictal stage of grand mal seizures, we see a reaching out for closeness and bodily contact. Thus we can presume that the patients with a temporal lobe, limbic system dysfunction will be deficient in their pleasurable apperceptions of reality. This must have a profound influence on their behavior, the world appearing as a hostile aggressive place with little neutralization by sympathetic, affectionate, caring attitudes (Rado, 1956, 1967).

As we will see later in the chapter, however, the actions based on these dysphoric attitudes in the typical epileptic are so diffuse and so poorly coordinated that they have little social effectiveness; in fact this very aspect of seizural dyscontrol can be used to protect one against the more effective dyscontrol acts at a higher hierarchial level.

10.2 EMOTIONAL PRECIPITATION OF EPILEPTIC SEIZURES

Reflex epilepsy is a well-observed phenomenon, frequently reported in the literature. In this form of epilepsy, a rather specific sensory experience, visual, auditory, or cutaneous, may elicit a seizure. The patient often identifies the precipitating phenomenon and can easily manipulate his illness. In a case reported by Goldie (1959) and well documented with careful EEG observation, seizures elicited by rubbing the face could also be precipitated even by thinking about rubbing the face or the hallucinatory experience of such under hypnosis. If the precipitating event of reflex epilepsy is a complex emotional situation such as orgasm, there may be a strong emotional component behind the seizure, or superficial medical evaluation might lead to the mistaken conclusion of a strong motivational aspect when it is in fact a simple reflex phenomenon. An example is the patient described by Hoenig (1960), in whom orgastic stimulation resulted in the seizure without any apparent significant emotional content. Somewhat analogous to reflex epilepsy are clinical seizures precipitated by emotions (Chafetz, 1959; London, 1956), and it is suggested that specific conflicts can lower the threshold of neuronal elements so that the seizures occur (Groethuysen, 1957). Stevens (1959) reported that stressful interviews precipitated epileptiform EEG abnormalities in ten epileptic patients even though they had normal baseline recordings. Previously observed seizural abnormalities could be reduplicated in another ten patients. Such emotional activation did not occur in a control group. It was

Stevens's impression that the psychomotor group were more likely to be activated by this procedure than those with centrencephalic epilepsy. Similar emotional activation of the EEG pattern has been reported by Barker (1950) and Small (1961).

Chafetz (1959) reports in some detail on four patients whose seizure histories were far overshadowed by emotional problems, and the EEG was often repeatedly negative before a positive one was recorded. In these same patients the response to antiepileptic medication alone was usually ineffective, effective treatment requiring a team approach combining anticonvulsant medication and psychotherapy. Chafetz reported that only by psychotherapy was it possible to reduce the psychological tensions sufficiently so that the seizures could be controlled by medication. These patients would undoubtedly have been considered "hystero-epileptic" without such thorough clinical evaluation. It is obvious then that emotional precipitation of the seizure cannot be used, as it often is, as evidence for a purely motivated or hysterical seizure. On the other hand, emotional precipitation does indicate that complex psychological factors have come to surround the seizural episodes.

A similar diagnosis of hysteria is often made if the seizure has more blatant purposeful intentions; that is, if the content of the seizure concerns current or recurrent psychological problems. Epstein (1956) reports in detail about two epileptic patients whose manifest dream content and experiences during seizures were similar to each other, at times even identical, expressing both current and lifelong conflicts. Most impressive was the fact that there was a change in the seizure and dream content during therapy with the therapist now becoming a significant figure in both the dreams and seizures. Again this emphasizes that such observations of the "meaningful" content of seizures cannot be used to differentiate between "hysterical seizures" and epileptoid ones, but they do indicate the importance that seizures have acquired for motivated behavior (Hendrick, 1940; Epstein, 1956, 1964; Weinstein, 1959; Forster, 1963). It would seem then that emotional factors in epilepsy can be important from two points of view. First, any emotional stress, regardless of whether it is symbolically related to epilepsy or not, can so reduce the central nervous system threshold that seizural activity occurs. However, more specifically, seizures can have a defensive role in protecting the individual against more effective and blatant dyscontrol acts at a higher hierarchial level; therefore they are either consciously or unconsciously induced or wished for to protect one against these more efficient dyscontrol acts (see below).

10.3 DRIVE-CONTROL CONFLICT

Epstein (1956) suggests that it is precisely when the drive-control conflict reaches its highest pitch that typical grand mal seizures or simple automatisms occur. Patients even express the desire or hope for a seizure, inasmuch as the massive motor discharge relieves the mounting tension, hence the drive-control turmoil. However, there are other reasons patients actually wish for seizure. For example, if the epileptoid response is at the highest hierarchial levels of acting out, impulse dyscontrol or even some instinct dyscontrols, the primitive urge whether disguised or blatantly overt, is carried through to an effective completion. The result of the dyscontrol act is usually a disaster for the individual committing the act as well as for the object of the act. On the other hand, the seizural act, while reducing the tension, is characterized by such diffuse affects and poorly coordinated motor behavior that the primitive urge remains disguised, or at least acting on the urge is socially ineffective. As we discussed in the last chapter, the overwhelming urges in the seizural act not only disrupt the perceptual apperception function and the reflective delay but also the coordinated motor act.

The use of seizural acts as a defense against unacceptable dyscontrol behavior, even though the defense is primitive, suggests that the integrative mechanisms of memory, reflection, reason, and conscience must have been relatively intact during the period immediately prior to the seizure itself. At other times, however, this integrative mechanism itself fails and it is precisely in such situations that overt psychotic behavior appears with a more open and direct, hence, potentially socially disastrous expression of the primitive unacceptable urges. The object of these urges becomes symbolically significant and the affect clearly demonstrated even though the action is based on delusional content. At this time, the patients, because of their loss of control, are recognized as psychotic and they need the restraint of hospitalization to protect both themselves and others. During such periods the balance has shifted from a disturbance at the apperceptive-perceptive or the intention-planning area, to a deficiency in the central integrative mechanisms (see Fig. 15). Perhaps it is this balance in defensive mechanisms which explains the fact that as patients become psychotic there is often a relative absence of seizural dyscontrol. In dynamic terms then we could predict the frequent clinical observation of the inverse relationship between the various hierarchical levels of dyscontrol on one hand, and those of seizural dyscontrol or psychosis on the other. Patient F287 (described in detail in Appendix 2), is an example of this shift from episodic behavioral disorder to overt psychosis.

A precise answer to whether this inverse relation between seizures and psychotic behavior is determined by the above-mentioned motivational factors or shifts in the location and extent of the excessive neuronal discharge would require extensive subcortical exploration. Even then, if we think of the brain in the model of the "psycho-physiologic organ," we would be hard put to decide which came first, the motivation or the shift in excessive discharges. For example, Barker (1950) presents some data regarding the appearance of bursts of abnormal waves in epileptics under stress; that is, when communicating significant life problems and conflictual thoughts. He shows that such bursts occur with stress-induced disruptions of integrative mechanisms such as problem solving. These are often preceded by arousal and alerting patterns which indicate sudden intensification of integrative effort. The bursts are correlated with momentary arrests in integrative functioning, and suggest a temporary relief in tension. Such reactions are also elicited by sudden stimulus events designed to startle the subject, and also appear as a rebound phenomenon after integrative effort. Barker's data are a remarkable demonstration of the brain as a psycho-physiologic organ.

Unfortunately for the clinician, it will seldom be clear which comes first in an individual patient, the motivational or the physiological changes. But, as we will discuss below, the less stereo-typed the seizural patterns and the more integrated this pattern is with current and past conflictual situations, the more impor-tant are the motivational elements in the disordered behavior. Hence the necessity for a reeducational program (psychotherapy) in treating the patient. If this psychotherapy is to be effective, however, it should focus not just on the content of the conflict, but also on the form of the defense; that is why on one occasion the patient will use more primitive responses like seizural acts, on another occasion psychotic behavior, and on a third the more direct expression of primitive urges in the form of a higher hier-archial levels of dyscontrol, namely impulse dyscontrol and act-ing out.

10.4 ACTION INHIBITED BY SEIZURES

Thus far we have been emphasizing defensive shifts in patterns of episodic behavior at the intention (motor) phase of behavior, but such defensive shifts have also been reported as predominantly limited to the perception-apperception phase (see Fig. 15), that is, control of urges accomplished through an impaired conscious-ness such as is characteristic of petit mal epilepsy. This was re-ported a number of years ago by Bartemeier (1943) and in a re-markably thorough case study by Barker (1948). In this situation control is achieved through an impaired consciousness which turns off or blocks mounting tension. However, there may be a significant difference between this type of control and the control in those cases in which it is achieved through a generalized motor discharge. However massive and excessive the neuronal discharge may be in petit mal, it is not accompanied by a motor act; there-fore it would not seem to be as effective in relieving the tension. For example, following a grand mal seizure the characteristic sub-jective response is relief of tension lasting for several days or weeks, but in Barker's patient, if the underlying tension was not relieved through some abreactive experience in therapy, the petit mal attacks continued with increasing frequency up to 75 per day. There did not seem to be what Ribble (1936) suggests, an acting out of the repressed wishes in a dreamlike fantasy accompanying the petit mal attack, hence a relief in tension. The fantasies and dreams that did occur in Barker's patient occurred during the intervals between attacks and did not relieve or discharge tension. On the other hand in his patient a convulsion would give an immense sense of relief. He also reported shifts in the epileptic manifestations as well as the appearance of other disordered behavior whenever the petit mal defense failed, much as we have suggested in the last section. At such times there was substitute narcoleptic sleep, psychomotor acting out, major convulsions and "other epileptic symptoms." In fact, he reported more complex behavioral defenses, such as psychosomatic disorders and hysterical reliving and abreacting of earlier childhood experiences. Only when an acceptable display of emotions and self-assertiveness occurred did the epileptoid phenomenon diminish. He summarizes his patient's behavior as follows: "thus the patient's petit mal attacks obscured real emotional responses to contemporary life experiences and concealed the repressed significant events of the past in which emotions and behavior originated, suppressing the past enabled her to avoid consideration of the future and to live in an apparently unemotional present."

If the momentary absence, unlike grand mal and simple automatisms, do not provide discharge of tension, is this because the excessive neuronal discharge has a distinctive localization or is it because the neuronal discharge is so brief? Petit mal status might give us a clue but neither the author's experience nor a review of the reported cases suggests a definite answer to this question. Landolt (1958) reports that in some patients the petit mal status is followed by sleep, which would suggest that there is a relief of tension. In others, the petit mal status ends in a grand mal seizure, and in some the petit mal status terminates with insomnia and restlessness. These last two observations would suggest that even prolonged petit mal discharge in itself does not relieve tension. It seems most likely then that the petit mal attack as a motivated defense for mounting tension; however effective it is in limiting awareness of situations which elicit danger-

ous impulses, does not either directly or indirectly provide a substitute discharge for these impulses as do grand mal seizures and
simple automatisms. As a defense then, it would be reasonable to
assume that petit mal epilepsy would fail in its defensive function, if the tension reaches a level where it is internally perpetuated or reinforced.

10.5 Motivational Use of Impaired Consciousness

Disturbance of this drive-control balance at both a perceptual-
apperceptual point and the intentional point in our schema (Fig.
15) can undoubtedly be purely motivational, with no evidence of
"excessive neuronal discharge." Dickes (1965) reports a series of
such observations of altered awareness which either reinforce inhibition or circumvent it. He points out that these hypnoidal
states are so fleeting and mild that they are often overlooked, but
suggests that there are excessively strong instinctual demands occurring in these patients which are probably related to unusually
intense or frustrating stimulation during the individual's early
development. This coincides with our impression that this frequently occurs in patients exhibiting what we have designated as
episodic dysinhibitions. A report by Smith (1959) also suggests
such a motivated interference with consciousness in narcolepsy.
The interplay of epileptoid and motivational factors in the episodic inhibitions will not be considered in this volume; it has
been discussed by others (akinetic mutism by Cravioto [1960],
cataplexy by Smith [1959] and Levin [1953]). The two patients
in our series who demonstrate some of these points are F223 and
S243. The motivated altered state of consciousness which circumvents inhibitory controls, that is, dissociated consciousness as
manifested by fugue states or dual personalities, has been designated as an episodic dissociative state. In our group of patients it
occurred surprisingly infrequently (see patient 0289, Appendix
7). The problems such motivated altered states of consciousness
present in a differential diagnosis with epileptoid altered consciousness have been reviewed by Revitch (1958) and Abrams
(1964) and will be discussed later in this chapter.

In contrast to the motivated or simulated epileptoid phenomena, we should mention the opposite possibility, which has important clinical implications: defensive denial of epilepsy by the epileptic patient. In our patients we found denial of epilepsy a more common defense than the simulated epilepsy. This denial may prevent the clinician from obtaining anamnestic data which would lead to proper diagnosis and treatment. Apparently, in such patients the connotation of having epilepsy is so horrifying to either the patient or his family or both that he insists that he is neurotic or psychotic instead. Such a group of patients has been reported by Tippett (1957).

Patient F287 (Appendix 2) is a case in point. The first of several EEG's showed no evidence of epilepsy, perhaps because it was obscured by barbiturate spindling. Both the patient and his family at first denied any history of seizures, a history which would not have been uncovered except that his wife, who was a physician, reported that she had heard the family discuss childhood seizures. When confronted with this information both the patient and the family sheepishly admitted that during early childhood the patient had had grand mal seizures on a number of occasions, although from adolescence onward, at least until the onset of his present illness, no seizures were noted. This information led to reevaluation of his present illness in which two grand mal seizures had been interpreted as solely due to withdrawal from barbiturates. As we persisted in our efforts to find an abnormal EEG, focal abnormalities were ultimately uncovered. It is important to note that the patient continued to deny epilepsy as a significant symptom (even though he, too, was a physician), apparently preferring to be considered neurotic or even, at times, psychotic.

10.6 PSYCHODYNAMIC SIMILARITIES BETWEEN THE EPILEPTIC AND THE IMPULSIVE PATIENT

Most psychoanalysts have followed Freud's early formulation in his essay on "Dostoevski and Parricide" (Freud, vol. XXI) in viewing epilepsy as a struggle between murderous aggressive criminal impulses on one hand and attempts to control these on the other, resulting in sado-masochistic behavior. The grand mal seizure then, represents to the analyst a fusion of murderous rage and guilt (Berg, 1941). At other times the seizure has been described as an extragenital orgasm or orgastic equivalent (Abraham, 1910). What may be important from our point of view is how often the dynamics proposed for the epileptics are similar to those proposed for the impulse disorders and acting out. Greenson (1944) in his article "on genuine epilepsy" mentions that Ferenczi thought that epileptics were fixated at the narcissistic level, a similar observation being made by Fenichel (1945) for acting out. Kardiner (1932) remarks upon the similarity between epilepsy and the traumatic neuroses. This has also been noted for acting out and the traumatic neuroses. Greenson (1944) emphasized the interweaving of scoptophilic and exhibitionistic tendencies in his epileptic patients, as Greenacre (1950) reported for acting out. Also, it has been suggested that the epileptic has a tendency to accumulate tension rather than discharge it in small quantities, a characteristic which has been noted for the impulse disorders. Other similarities are the characterization of both disorders as a regression to the pregenital phase of development accompanied by a masochistic or self-punishment quality in the behavior. Finally the seizure on one hand and the acting out on the other allow for the discharge of hitherto repressed fantasies (as illustrated by the homicidal acting out in a patient who was probably epileptic, [Rose, 1960], and a somewhat similar patient of Hendrick [1940]).

10.7 DIFFERENTIAL DIAGNOSIS BETWEEN MOTIVATED AND EPILEPTOID EPISODIC BEHAVIORAL DISORDERS

By now the reader should be significantly impressed with the difficulties in separating motivated behavior from behavior accompanying excessive neuronal discharges. Even patients with identical genes develop variable phenotypic expressions of their epilepsy (Inouye, 1960). Raher (1963) reports on monozygotic twins with almost identical abnormal EEG's and a very similar onset in their epilepsy. They subsequently became quite disparate in their symptoms when the more independent twin broke a symbiotic relationship.

> Twin F285 was included in our series. Subsequent to Raher's report I was supervising family therapy. When the "healthier" twin finally broke the symbiosis and married, the other twin committed suicide.

Most investigators suggest that the appraisal of neurotic behavior prior to the onset of seizures gives us some clues to the complication of epilepsy by motivational factors (Chafetz, 1959). But in view of our present knowledge, much of the preseizural behavioral disturbance might have been an unrecognized epileptoid phenomenon before this possibility became obvious with the appearance of classic seizures. For example, London (1956) points out that in one of his patients typical preictal responses of estrangement and depression were identical with such episodes the patient experienced a number of years before the onset of his grand mal seizures. Dominian (1963) found that 28 of 51 epileptics had obvious psychopathology before the onset of epilepsy per se, particularly depression. Thus the evaluation of pre-epileptic behavioral deviations as differentiating criteria between motivated and epileptoid seizures may be distorted by the rather arbitrary point in the course of the development of epilepsy at which the seizures are finally recognized by the clinician.

We have already mentioned the fallacy of rejecting epilepsy on the basis of the negative EEG, unless repeated studies have been made utilizing special activating techniques. What about the reverse, that is, an abnormal EEG being a spurious finding which may mask what is basically a motivational disturbance, particularly a conversion? Kessler (1952) reported on what he believes are just such patients. His clinical summary certainly emphasizes the importance of emotional factors in eliciting and perpetuating seizures. This was proven by the effectiveness of psychotherapy and environmental manipulations, while anticonvulsants alone

had failed. In some patients the EEG's were of questionable significance and the seizures convincingly hysteric or motivated.
But in light of our present knowledge, many of the patients must
have had true seizures, parhaps hysterically elaborated and all
utilizing their seizures to some degree for secondary gains (from
this point of view it may be important that the study was done
at a Veterans Hospital). Many of the criteria Kessler used for
determining hysteria we would now question as reliable guides
for making such a distinction. The guides he used were: the
minimal cortical EEG changes during an attack; the lack of postictal depression, either behaviorally or electroencephalographically; consciousness during seizures; seizures only when observers
were present; and the fact that patients did not hurt themselves
during the seizural act. The author also assumed hysteria if the
attacks were emotionally precipitated and atypical in pattern no
matter how characteristic the EEG was of seizural discharges (e.g.,
spike-wave patterns). The detailed study by Ajmone-Marsan
(1957) discussed in 7.2 and 7.5 reveals how cautious one must
be in making a differential diagnosis on such criteria.

Most neurologists and psychiatrists today, are differentiating
the motivational episodic reactions from the epileptoid episodic
reactions on criteria suggested by Gowers (1907). Despite the fact
that he was an astute observer, sixty years later we should have
better criteria. For Gowers, the diagnosis of hysteria was clear if
the episode was emotionally precipitated, lacking in a specific
sensory aura, characterized by a more gradual onset of symptoms
with perhaps rigidity of the body; if there were struggling or
flailing movements, quasi-volitional vocalizations, lack of in-
continence or no biting of the tongue; prolonged seizures with
display of violence, and episodes which usually occurred when
observed. It was also assumed that the seizure was hysterical if
consciousness was not completely impaired.

Until we have a more definite technique for proving the existence of excessive neuronal discharge somewhere in the brain, we
have to be cautious in criticizing these criteria. It is now obvious
however that any one of the supposed symptoms of hysteria, in
fact all of them together, can be characteristic manifestations of

the excessive neuronal discharge. As clinicians, we should now be much more humble and determine as best we can the possible motivational elements and the possible neurophysiologic ones, as guides for effective therapy with the episodic behavioral disorders.

Unfortunately, the most frequent and crudest differential test, often applied with disastrous consequences, is a slipshod trial on anticonvulsants. The trial with drugs is often not adequate in terms of either dosage or length of trial so that a poor response which may reflect only an inadequate regimen is used as a decisive indication that the episodes are motivated. On the other hand, therapy, whether drug or surgery, may be adequate in controlling the seizure, but the motivational aspect of the seizures and the importance of being sick to the individual in manipulating his environment may be overlooked, with possible suicidal-homicidal acting out following improvement in the epileptic symptoms.

In place of the above criteria we would like to suggest the following. Patients are more likely to come near the pole of "pure" excessive neuronal discharge if one makes the following observations:

1. Despite varied environmental situations, there is a stereotyped repetitive pattern of behavior during the episodic disorder. This statement has increasing validity the richer and more varied are the behavioral patterns between the episodic disturbances and the more spontaneous and intelligent and flexible the personality of the patient under consideration. For instance, a mental defective with obsessive compulsive personality traits might display a repetitive, stereotyped, purely motivated seizural act. The following patient is an example:

Patient S202 demonstrated a stereotyped instinctual act which nevertheless was to a significant degree motivated. The act itself was a fight-flight reaction, first running away from a situation, then an attack on whomever was closest at hand. She always misidentified this person as her father. Sometimes there was a tenuous association between the person attacked and the father, but more often it was the person within striking distance. However, except for the misidentification of the person, there was little evidence for altered consciousness or awareness. She remembered details of the act itself and was not confused during or immediately after the attack. The psychological examination revealed attempts to control impulses through rigid obsessive controls. The propensity for rigidity probably explained her stereotyped instinctual act. The fact that at other times she used episodic inhibitions, and even transitory psychotic behavior, is at least partially explained by the projective tests which revealed a hysterical propensity as well as some looseness of thought processes.

2. The more neutral the environmental situation in which the attack occurs, the more likely it is to be the result of excessive neuronal discharge. However, this statement needs considerable elaboration. Determining the "neutrality" of the eliciting situation is a difficult task, requiring more than simple questioning about the obvious external setting. As Barker (1948) has shown in evaluating his patient, what appears at first glance as a neutral environment was really quite an emotional one, his patient either consciously or unconsciously wanting to convey this neutrality, particularly if the attack was a defense against unacceptable impulses. At the other extreme, a setting which precipitates an attack may have a spurious emotionality. We have already noted that localized excessive neuronal discharges may precede a more typical seizure for days and even weeks with manifestations of mounting irritability and irascibility, which would only invite an emotionally laden external situation, leading to an explosion.

Patient F287, a physician, had a seizure while going downstairs at the hospital. He reported nothing unusual, saying that it was merely a routine errand; that is, taking a stool specimen to the laboratory for analysis. The therapist, feeling that it would be unusual for the physician to be making such a routine errand persisted in his questioning. Only after more prolonged interrogation did it come to light that this was his own stool specimen which he was taking to the lab, hoping to demonstrate that it was guaiac positive, thereby confirming his self-diagnosis of bleeding duodenal ulcer. He was desperate to prove that he was legitimately sick because he was in administrative difficulties in view of his irresponsible behavior, which included excessive self-medication. Later evidence suggested that he was probably inducing blood in the stool by anal manipulations. This patient was described previously as not only denying his epilepsy, but also as having long periods of mounting tension and irritability which seriously interferred with his interpersonal relationships and which probably were manifestations of "partial epilepsy."

The diagnosis of the condition of another patient, 019, is an example of a probably false impression that the seizures were precipitated by emotionally stressful situations. Although this might well have often been the case, this patient had subcortically implanted electrodes which allowed for monitoring in the rhinencephalic structures. She was usually a rather phlegmatic, emotionally dull person with underlying paranoid delusions. During several weeks prior to her seizure she manifested increasing irritability, hostility, and belligerence, particularly toward her mother and the hospital personnel. This of course elicited retaliatory responses from those involved. The day of her seizure she had been particularly upset because of a fight with her mother upon whom she was extremely dependent. However, monitoring throughout this period, one noted increasing hypersynchrony in the septal-hippocampal structures, so it was not clear which came first, the hostility or the hypersynchrony. However, in this case it was more clear than usual because the hypersynchrony had been induced through electrical stimulation of the hippocampal structures, the prolonged hypersynchrony representing an after-discharge, and, as already has been pointed out, such electrical stimulation does induce intense fearful or angry affects (4.1.1).

3. The lower the hierarchial level of response (e.g., seizure or instinct acts), the more likely would the behavior be the result of

excessive neuronal discharge. This should be qualified because such a low level motor response is accompanied by an equally impaired state of consciousness or level of awareness. The latter cannot be evaluated on the basis of subsequent amnesia alone, but only by actual testing of the patient during the attack itself. Also the behavior is more likely to be epileptoid if there is a marked disparity between the level of integration during the episodic behavior itself and the level of integration during the interval between episodic attacks.

> Patient F250 (Appendix 6) demonstrates this point. Although he was severely incapacitated by his emotional problems, psychological examination did not reveal any evidence of organic impairment nor schizophrenic thinking, but did indicate that he was a highly dependent individual utilizing both hysterical and obsessive-compulsive defenses. When, during the course of psychotherapy, he had a grand mal seizure, such a primitive defense seemed unlikely in this highly intelligent man with more sophisticated symptoms and defenses. The fact that this was a truly epileptoid seizure was reinforced by reports of his family that he was severely confused after the episode, his own claim for amnesia, and the fact that detailed questioning revealed the neutrality of the precipitating situation (riding in a car on his first day of vacation). However, his EEG was normal, so that he was not immediately placed on anticonvulsants. There were many secondary gains in his being ill, which together with the fact that in the past he had told people that he might have a brain tumor, raised the possibility of "hysterical" seizures. Subsequently he had a second grand mal seizure, again in a situation that seemed completely neutral, and now EEG's revealed a focus in the temporal lobes.

4. If the secondary gains from the episodic behavior are truly lacking, we would be more likely to suspect an excessive neuronal discharge. However, as we have pointed out, the reverse would not be true, because the epileptic often utilizes his illness to manipulate his environment.

Patient F222 illustrates this point. This was a girl whose hypersynchronous EEG was not only brought out by chloralose activation but also by simple hyperventilation. Four months before hospitalization she developed atypical "spells" precipitated by, or at least accompanied by, hyperventilation. The spells of this extremely emotionally deprived individual ceased upon hospitalization, where she established a close interpersonal relationship with her physician as well as a co-therapist nurse. However, for a short period, the spells were replaced by instinctual acts. Undoubtedly this girl found that she could induce seizures by hyperventilation, and the seizures were used to manipulate her environment, that is, convince her family that she needed psychiatric care.

As one approaches the opposite pole of motivated episodic behavioral disorder, the characteristics of the episodic attack would be the opposite of those described above: the attack itself is variable and complex, the conceptual distortions during the attack are interwoven with elements from the immediate situation and past experience, the intentions are clearer, the motor behavior more coordinated, and the objects more select or the behavior more purposeful and effective. There is also more compatibility between the level of integration of the episodic behavior itself and the behavior demonstrated between attacks. There is also a disparity between the subjective states of consciousness and the objectively determined level of awareness. That is, patients with motivated disorders will be responsive to the finer nuances of their environment, yet have lost their personal identity.

Patient O289 (Appendix 7) is a most extreme example of this. The best observed episodes were those in which the erotic tranference was acted upon in what otherwise was a rather straightlaced young matron. These occurred during dissociative states in which she adopted a new name and a new personality, that of a young, single, sexually seductive and promiscuous girl. These could easily be aborted by hypnosis. The dissociation between the altered state of consciousness (in which she lost her personal identity) and the level of awareness was dramatic. For example, she could always find her way back to her hotel, even in a strange city, and while playing the single, sexually promiscuous streetwalker, would take out her wallet and show her companions pictures of her children.

None of these are simple phenomena to evaluate, but a thorough consideration of these are better than a reliance on the seizure characteristics suggested by Gowers; the history of epilepsy in the family; neurological signs and symptoms; the EEG; or the response to medication. We have already mentioned how the patient's own appraisal gives us a clue as to the importance of excessive neuronal discharges versus motivated behavior; that is, the way he views his episodic behavior in retrospect. The more ego-alien it appears, and the more willing he is to discuss and understand it, the more likely is the episodic behavior due to an "excessive neuronal discharge." On the other hand if motivational determinants are dominant, there will be a need to deny responsibility or avoid retrospective scrutiny of the behavior.

Part Four   Therapy

11 Drug Therapy

It has been demonstrated repeatedly in the preceding chapters that many of the episodic behavioral disorders result from epileptoid phenomena. In these instances, however important psychotherapy may be, it often is an adjunct to drug therapy (Monroe, 1960c). The unique problems in combining psychotherapy and drug therapy will be discussed in the next chapter. We have also reported several instances in which typical grand mal with an unquestioned epileptic EEG made the diagnosis of epilepsy obvious, yet the ideal therapeutic regimen was psychotherapy without anticonvulsant medication, or psychotherapy with anticonvulsant medication merely as an adjunct. Two examples follow:

For Patient F206 (see Appendix 1) anticonvulsant medication had to be discontinued and reliance placed solely on psychotherapy. Diphenylhydantoin (Dilantin) pushed to toxic levels did not significantly control her seizures, and, in fact, some of the problems which led to hospitalization were actually toxic symptoms to the drug. The basic frequency of seizures was one per month, any increase above this level apparently being due to emotional problems, particularly sexual conflicts. These emotional problems, since resolved through psychotherapy, stabilized her seizures at the one per month level. Anticonvulsants do not reduce the seizure frequency further, even if pushed to the toxic levels; she is therefore better off without any anticonvulsants at all, despite the fact that her EEG reveals paroxysmal slow and hypersynchronous wave forms appearing diffusely but with a definite left posterior temporal predominance.

Patient F247 is one for whom the anticonvulsant therapy becomes definitely an adjunct to psychotherapy. Anticonvulsants were gradually withdrawn (this girl was part of a research project) so that a metabolic baseline could be obtained following withdrawal. At first there was an increase in seizures, which would have meant a return to anticonvulsants had she been on a regular clinical service. However, as we persisted because of the investigative nature of her hospitalization, it became obvious that what appeared to the patient (and to the observer alike) as an inverse relationship between her grand mal seizures and her psychomotor seizures (that is, as the anticonvulsants controlled the grand mal seizures, they were replaced by psychomotor attacks) was a fictitious observation. What did become apparent was the motivational elements in her seizures, particularly the psychomotor seizures and these were eventually replaced by obvious temper tantrums. This patient was using seizural and instinctual dyscontrol to escape adult responsibilities as well as to excuse her social and occupational failures. With this insight she ultimately gave up her temper tantrums, stabilizing at a level at which occasional grand mal seizures were at least partially controlled by Dilantin. She, too, had a definite epileptic EEG with bursts of high amplitude rhythmic 4- to 5-per-second wave forms, mixed with low amplitude spikes and sharp waves bilaterally and synchronously, but occasionally with a right mid-temporal focus.

Our simplest dynamic description of the episodic behavioral disorders is that the episode itself is precipitated by a sudden imbalance between urges, drives, or instinct on one hand and the ego controls or inhibitory mechanisms on the other. This imbalance can be one of overwhelming urges or at the other extreme one of impaired control, but in the more severe episodic disorders it is probably a combination of both. We have seen in Chapters 4, 5, and 6 that both overwhelming urges and impaired controls can result from ictal phenomena, particularly those involving rhinencephalic structures or their cortical projection areas, the frontal and temporal lobes. We have also noted that such ictal phenomena can occur without symptoms characteristic of epilepsy and may not be revealed by abnormalities on the routine EEG.

In Chapter 10 we described some of the clinical symptoms which give us clues as to the relative importance of epileptoid or motivational mechanisms behind the episodic disorders. However, we pointed out that such criteria are still vague or at other times difficult to establish reliably. Remembering the precautions we brought up in the last chapter, we are often forced to use a trial with drugs as part of the diagnostic evaluation. If the patient responds to drugs of known anticonvulsant activity, we assume that a substantial part of the mechanism behind the episodic disturbances was epileptoid, making allowance for possible placebo effects in a group that show a high degree of oral dependency (Lohrenz, 1962).

> Patient F287, described in detail in Appendix 2, demonstrated marked placebo effects to all drugs, particularly anticonvulsants. Both the clinical history and the psychological tests revealed "oral dependency" as well as "addictive traits." The EEG revealed a left temporal and left anterior temporal spike focus and the patient reported typical grand mal seizures as well as complex psychomotor attacks. Almost any drug, whether anticonvulsant or not, was taken with enthusiasm approaching euphoria and resulted in immediate clinical improvement. This was true of phenobarbital, diphenylhydantoin (Dilantin), primidone (Mysoline) and chlordiazepoxide (Librium) as well as dextroamphetamine (Dexedrine), and some of the phenothiazines. However, within a month or two on a given drug regimen, particularly when the patient was under psychological stress, the symptoms returned. To complicate the matter, the patient then began taking excessive amounts of whatever drug had been prescribed.

Aside from the anticonvulsants, which should influence neuronal excitability, thus reducing the ictal "excessive neuronal discharge," we might assume that the tranquilizers, by reducing the emotional responsivity in the individual and eliminating the frequent emotional precipitation of an ictal response, would also be helpful. However, as we will discuss later in the chapter, some of the tranquilizers increase the potentiality for "excessive neuronal discharges," so that their tranquilizing effect might be counteracted or rendered ineffective through this "epileptogenic" action. The ideal drug would be one that combines optimal tranquilizing qualities with anticonvulsant action. In this chapter we will first consider the anticonvulsants, then the tranquilizers, and finally drugs combining both these qualities.

Although we have seen that there is only a highly irregular correlation between the EEG and behavior, we will note whenever there are data suggesting a correlation between normalizing action on the EEG and normalization of behavior. For reviews of drug efficacy in the treatment of epilepsy per se, the effects of drugs in general on the EEG, or the general literature on the psychotrophic drugs and the EEG, the reader is referred to reviews by Towler (1962), Fink (1964), and Muller (1965). We will focus on studies reporting data pertinent to the treatment of the episodic behavioral disorders.

11.1 ANTICONVULSANTS

Although there are isolated reports in the literature on the use of anticonvulsants in behavioral disorders (Lohrenz, 1962), and the subject was reviewed at the Fifth Annual Meeting of the American College of Neuropsychopharmacology, Puerto Rico, December 1966 (Cole 1967; Symposium, 1967), anticonvulsants have not found general acceptance for this purpose. This is because the more complicated the behavioral abnormalities associated with epilepsy are, the more likely that the therapeutic results will be poor with anticonvulsants alone. In fact, in a number of instances, control of seizures with anticonvulsants has actually increased the behavioral problems. The most commonly used anticonvulsant in the treatment of grand mal and psychomotor epi-

31

lepsy is diphenylhydantoin (Dilantin) which has proven to be the safest, cheapest, and most effective agent (60 percent to 85 percent effective for grand mal seizures). It is surprising, then, that animal studies reveal that Dilantin, unlike phenobarbital and trimethadione (Tridione), does not elevate the seizural threshold to EST or pentylenetetrazol (Metrazol). However, it does modify seizures, eliminating the tonic phase of the tonic-clonic convulsion and apparently inhibiting the cortical spread of the "excessive neuronal discharge" (Goodman, 1966). This may explain why diffuse dysrhythmias are more likely to disappear under Dilantin, while the focal abnormalities remain (Tolman, 1949). The advantage of Dilantin in the treatment of epilepsy is that, although it is an effective anticonvulsant, it has few concomitant sedative effects, although a recent study does show that it might have minor tranquilizing properties (G. B. Fink, 1962). Its value in the treatment of episodic behavioral disorders is in combination with one of the psychotropic drugs, although there are occasional reports of its effectiveness alone (Lohrenz, 1962; Cole, 1967). Primidone (Mysoline) has also been mentioned as effective in treating the behavioral concomitants of epilepsy (Monroe, 1965b). Wider acceptance of the anticonvulsants for the treatment of behavioral disorders with or without epilepsy but with abnormal EEG's has been found in the behavioral disorders of children, although dextroamphetamine (Dexedrine) is usually as effective as, or more so than, the anticonvulsants (Gross, 1964).

Patient S218 (Appendix 8) is an excellent example of those who show a therapeutic response to Dilantin. She was not typically epileptic; in fact, for many years, she had been treated by innumerable doctors in several different hospitals for unexplained episodic physiologic disturbances. At times these would approach stuporlike states which were thought to have been suicidal attempts or toxic reactions to overdose of medication. However, both these episodic stupor states and psychophysiologic reactions responded well, as did her impulsive acts, when the administration of Dilantin, 0.1 gm. b.i.d. was handled by her mother.

Patient F283 is another in whom Dilantin had a surprising therapeutic effect. The decision to place her on anticonvulsants occurred when she reported symptoms suggesting a gustatory aura. Not only did the Dilantin control this aura; it also seemed to exert a salutary effect on her impulse dyscontrol.

11.2 PHENOTHIAZINES

Despite occasional reports that the phenothiazines are helpful in the treatment of the epileptic patient (David, 1953; Winkelman, 1954; Kinross-Wright, 1955; Head, 1955; Bonafede, 1957), and that they may antagonize experimentally induced convulsions (Longo, 1954), or at least not lower the seizure thresholds (Bradley, 1957), the consensus is that in humans the phenothiazines do lower seizure threshold and increase the frequency of seizures in epileptics (Merlis, 1955; Kinross-Wright, 1955a, b; Bradley, 1957b; Friedlander, 1959; Liberson, 1958) and increase EEG abnormalities (Bente, 1955; Turner, 1956; Fabish, 1955; Stewart, 1957; and Logothetis, 1967). This is true even though, at the usual clinical doses, the phenothiazines are not convulsants themselves, although patients who have taken huge doses in suicidal attempts will sometimes go into status epilepticus (Samuels, 1957). Stewart (1957) studied 50 hospitalized epileptics, 28 of whom showed increased abnormalities or new abnormalities compatible with their clinical diagnosis after the IM injection of 50 mg. of chlorpromazine. In four cases focal seizures occurred and one patient had a tonic-clonic convulsion. Fabish (1955) reported that seven of 20 epileptics with fairly regular baseline EEG recordings showed abnormalities and 18 of the 20 epileptics with irregularities or abnormal baseline EEG's showed an increase in abnormalities following administration of chlorpromazine. On the other hand, this reaction was found in only three of 20 control subjects. Of interest is their finding that, of the seven epileptics with stable baseline EEG's, six showed paroxysmal bilateral synchronous activity after receiving chlorpromazine. This is the type of pattern which we identified in Chaper 7 on activation procedures as possibly having a specific relationship to the episodic behavioral disorders. This seems compatible with the findings of Szatmari (1955) that chlorpromazine definitely lowered the (Metrazol) threshold to convulsions.

Other observers have noted that paroxysmal EEG disturbances are seen in nonepileptic patients with unstable resting EEG's (Bente, 1963 and Ulett, 1965). In fact, Bente made the observation, particularly pertinent for us, that patients who developed paroxysmal disturbances during treatment with the phenothiazines are neither clear-cut schizophrenics nor typical manic-depressive psychotics, but seem to present a syndrome which he labels "atypical psychosis." He considered that these disorders were related to, but not identical with, epilepsy. Unfortunately, he did not give the clinical information necessary to allow us to make an interpretation that these might be episodic psychotic reactions.

Bente also reported that, after the acute administration of chlorpromazine, there is an increase in voltage and synchronization and a decrease in frequency in the basic activity, and that a later stage is similar to early sleep, with a flattening of the record and low amplitude slow waves. Monroe (1955a), in a limited series of patients with cortical and subcortical electrodes, found the response to chlorpromazine characteristic of sleep, but different from barbiturate sleep in that there was a lack of fast activity or spindling. Animal studies reveal that the hippocampus is particularly sensitive to chlorpromazine and may (at least in cats) show seizural activity (Kaelber, 1958), although Monroe (1957) showed that chlorpromazine blocked the hypersynchrony induced in the hippocampal region of humans by both LSD and mescaline. Eidelberg (1963) found that the phenothiazines block seizural discharges in the hippocampus that were induced by cocaine. Hollister (1959), in investigating the type of seizural abnormalities induced in human EEG's, reported a number of abnormalities with chlorpromazine, but not particularly the bilateral paroxysmal slow activity, although he did find this type of reaction with thioridazine (Mellaril). His studies were done on schizophrenic rather than epileptic patients. Denber (1958) in a similar group also induced a number of seizural discharges, as did Swain (1960) in a group of elderly patients with chronic brain syndromes. (Monroe, 1965a, 1967b), using alpha-chloralose activation in psychiatric patients, found no increase in the incidence of activated abnormalities in schizophrenic patients while they were on phenothiazines, but he did note that the extent and amplitude of the activated abnormality was increased; while Ulett (1965), studying nine different tranquilizers noted that all induced EEG dysrhythmias, and that this was particularly true with chlorpromazine and hydroxyzine. (Vistaril, Atarax).

From these studies it is apparent that chlorpromazine as well as many other phenothiazines, even though they may block hypersynchronous activity in the EEG induced by some other drugs, will bring out seizure-type abnormalities or bilaterally synchronous paroxysmal slow activity in predisposed individuals (e.g. those with a history of epilepsy), as well as induce such patterns in some psychiatric disorders. As we suggested in Chapter 7 the bilaterally synchronous paroxysmal slow activity may correlate with the epileptoid episodic behavioral disorders. Reasoning along these lines, we think that phenothiazines should increase the frequency of dyscontrol acts, or perhaps precipitate episodic reactions in predisposed individuals. This author knows of no specific reports in the literature validating this, but some of our clinical observations suggest that such an interpretation of the data would be possible. We have already pointed out that three of 70 patients, all with episodic behavioral disorders, did poorly when treated with phenothiazines alone, and that in all the patients who responded well to the phenothiazines, it was the chronic persisting symptoms that improved, not the episodic ones. In rare instances it did seem that the episodic psychotic reactions responded to phenothiazine therapy, although this is hard to evaluate because of the tendency of this group to show spontaneous remissions. It is important to emphasize, however, that in this group maintenance doses of phenothiazines are not necessary, and may in fact even increase the possibility of the recurrence of episodic reactions. From what we know now, it would seem that if the phenothiazines are necessary as a temporary expedient, it would be best to combine them with either an anticonvulsant or a benzodiazepine (Librium, Valium).

In Chapter 3 on the episodic reactions we pointed out that the episodic psychotic reactions can occur either in a typical schizophrenic form, that is with clear sensorium, or in episodic psychotic reactions in which the schizophrenic symptomatology is accompanied by significant clouding of sensorium. We suggested these might better be considered an episodic brain syndrome. We also suggested that in patients with clouded sensorium, there is a significant epileptoid mechanism, while those with clear sensorium may be manifesting a more typically schizophrenic or a "hysterical psychosis." Our data on the response of these two groups of patients with episodic psychotic reactions to drugs are not easily interpreted, although one would expect that the two groups should respond differently to pharmacologic agents. For example Patients 0262 and 0274 both had episodic psychotic reactions of the "pure" schizophrenic type, that is, with no clouding of sensorium. In both the psychological tests suggested a "hysterical" psychosis. Both patients seemed to respond to phenothiazines. Neither showed EEG abnormalities nor evidence suggesting epileptoid elements behind the psychoses. One could seriously doubt whether medication was necessary, and consider whether these patients would have remitted spontaneously without drugs. Certainly discontinuing the phenothiazines as soon as the symptoms abated did not lead to a relapse. Probably any drug with a sedative action would have been effective. Patient S229 (Appendix 5), on the other hand, did show paroxysmal slow activation patterns, and during this patient's acute psychotic reaction there was a significant clouding of sensorium. This patient, too, seemed to respond to chlorpromazine, although one might have suspected that chlorpromazine could have made the patient worse. It may be that in these instances the lethargy and lack of motor spontaneity induced by the drug would mask or inhibit the potential for dyscontrol acts. Such acts then might be more easily seen under low doses of phenothiazines or particularly those phenothiazines which do not induce excessive lethargy and motor retardation, such as trifluoperazine (Stelazine). We have seen just such reactions in patients receiving 2 to 6 mgs. trifluoperazine per day, although Vasconcellos (1960) reports that high doses of this drug are effective in severe behavioral disorders characterized by frequent antisocial acts.

> Patient S202 gave such a response to trifluoperazine. On admission to the hospital, she was placed on 1 mg. t.i.d. because she was responding to vague auditory hallucinations, was restless and overactive, as well as manifesting frequent instinct dyscontrol, particularly in attacking people and running away from the hospital. Although the instinct dyscontrol lessened somewhat with hospitalization and this medical regimen, dramatic improvement occurred when the trifluoperazine was discontinued altogether. Other examples of a poor response to phenothiazines are Patient F221, in whom the dyscontrol acts were definitely increased when the patient was placed on chlorpromazine, and Patient S251, in whom the chlorpromazine regimen seemed to induce frequent episodic confusional states and depersonalizations. Such a reaction also seemed to be true in Patient S288. In this patient, pushing the phenothiazine medication to toxic level did not control the episodic reactions, whereas substituting one of the benzodiazepines (Librium) did.

11.3 BENZODIAZEPINES

This group of drugs (our experience is primarily with chlordiazepoxide [Librium]) are known for their antianxiety and taming properties particularly in neurotic disorders. It has also been reported that they have the capacity to normalize abnormal EEG's, and possess some anticonvulsant qualities. In a single dose, Winfield (1961) found chlordiazepoxide effective in promoting sleep activation, which is somewhat surprising in view of the fact that chronic medication rather consistently induces low voltage fast activity and lowers the mean output of the recording (Pfeiffer, 1964), with suppression of any seizural activity (Towler, 1962). There probably is a significant difference in the EEG effects of a single I.V. dose when compared to chronic medication over a period of weeks. For instance, Kerskiner (1962) reports that intravenous chlordiazepoxide induces changes similar to those resulting from chlorpromazine, that is, slowing of the alpha rhythms with a shift to the theta range (5–7 cycles per second), and an increase in amplitude and percent time of alpha rhythms, increased synchronization of background frequencies, and a decrease in response to outside stimuli. He also noted a decrease in electromyographic activity, drowsiness, or light sleep similar to physiologic sleep and a subjective sensation of relaxation. However, Bercel (1961) casually mentions that he did not notice such changes, nor do such changes appear in patients under chronic medication.

The EEG effects of chronic administration of chlordiazepoxide or diazepam in normal subjects are more similar to the effects of meprobamate (Miltown, Equanil) than to the effects of phenothiazines. There appear fast frequencies in the 20-to-30-cycle per second range of low to moderate voltage, first in the frontal areas and then with a general distribution. This develops six days after the start of the drug and persists for an average of seven days after the drug is discontinued (Towler, 1962), a response that is quite different from that seen with the phenothiazines. In fact, Ulett (1961) found that chlordiazepoxide counteracted the EEG effects of the phenothiazines by reducing alpha and theta activity while increasing the beta activity. He also noted that clinical improvement accompanied the combined use of chlordiazepoxide and phenothiazines and that this was correlated with a return of the phenothiazine-induced changes in the EEG towards a more normal baseline pattern. When we used alpha chloralose activation in a group of hospitalized schizophrenics or severe neurotics (Monroe, 1965a), we found an activation rate of 46 percent in patients on phenothiazines and those on no drugs, while the activation rate of those receiving chlordiazepoxide, even if they were also receiving phenothiazines, was only 6 percent (Table 16). In a more detailed study of 15 subjects, we used the same patients as their own controls by administering no drugs, an inert placebo, chlordiazepoxide, trifluoperazine, and chlorpromazine, with drug sequences determined by

Table 16. Effect of drugs on activation

Drugs	Number of studies	No activation	Activation
Chlordiazepoxide. (21 alone, 11 in combination with phenothiazines)	32	30 (93.8)[a]	2 (6.2)
Phenothiazines	28	15 (53.6)	13 (46.4)
No drugs	13	7 (53.9)	6 (46.1)
Dilantin	6	3 (50)	3 (50)
Total (nonchlordiazepoxide)	47	25 (53.2)	22 (46.8)

Source: R. R. Monroe, M. D. Kramer, R. Goulding, and S. Wise, "EEG activation of patients receiving phenothiazines and chlordiazepoxide," *J. Nerv. Ment. Dis.* 141:104, 1965.

[a] Figures in parentheses represent the percent of total.

latin square technique; thus each patient had five studies with both EEG and behavioral observations. The activation data in this study are summarized in Tables 17 and 18.

Table 19 summarizes the correlation between the clinical and activation data. There was a gross correlation between improvement in behavior and the subjective sense of well-being with normalization of the EEG. It was noted in that study that four of the seven patients manifested dyscontrol acts while they were on phenothiazines, two making suicidal attempts and the other two becoming agitated and aggressive.

A number of reports support these findings. Kaim (1960) found that chlordiazepoxide elevated pentylenetetrazol (Metrazol) thresholds, a finding similar to that of Bercel (1961), who noted that it also elevated the EST threshold. Rosenstein (1960) reported that in an epileptic patient not only was the Metrazol threshold elevated, but the patient was successfully treated with chlordiazepoxide (Librium) alone; whereas the same patient could not be controlled successfully by a combination of diphenylhydantoin (Dilantin) and phenobarbital. In another study Kaim (1961) was convinced that the beneficial effects of chlordiazepoxide were due to its anticonvulsant action, not its tranquil-

Table 17. Statistical analyses of drug effects on activation rates

EEG condition	Treatment				
	No drug	Placebo	Chlor-diazepoxide	Chlor-promazine	Trifluo-perazine
Baseline abnormality[a]	26.7%	26.7%	0.0%	13.3%	13.3%
Activation abnormality[b]	46.7%	53.3%	20.0%	60.0%	73.3%

Source: R. R. Monroe, M. D. Kramer, R. Goulding, and S. Wise, "EEG activation of patients receiving phenothiazines and chlordiazepoxide," *J. Nerv. Ment. Dis.* 141:105, 1965.

[a] Baseline—Cochran $Q = 5.89$ with 4 degrees of freedom; $p < .30$, not significant.

[b] Activation—Cochran $Q = 14.67$ with 4 degrees of freedom; $p < .01$, significant.

Table 18. Degree of activated abnormality under drugs

Change in EEG	Treatment			
	Placebo	Chlor-diazepoxide	Chlor-promazine	Trifluo-perazine
More severe	13.3%	6.7%	46.7%	60.0%
No change	80.0%	46.7%	46.7%	33.3%
Less severe	6.7%	46.7%	6.7%	6.7%

Source: R. R. Monroe, M. D. Kramer, R. Goulding, and S. Wise, "EEG activation of patients receiving phenothiazines and chlordiazepoxide," *J. Nerv. Ment. Dis.* 141:105, 1965.

izing qualities. He found that it alone controlled seizures in 12 and reduced the number of seizures in eight of 34 epileptics. Bercel (1961) reported seizure reduction of 50 percent in ten grand mal and/or petit mal epileptics, and in 75 percent of epileptics, if combined with diphenylhydantoin (Dilantin). In another group of subjects with psychomotor epilepsy, he found that the chlordiazepoxide-primidone (Librium-Mysoline) combination reduced seizures 50 percent when compared with a previous regimen of either primidone alone or primidone combined with

Table 19. Drug effects (controlled study)

Identification			Clinical Data						No Drug			Placebo			Chlordiazepoxide			Chlorpromazine			Trifluoperazine		
Age	Sex	Race	Diagnosis	Epilepsy	Depression	Episodic	No. of hospitalizations	Follow-up[a]	Baseline[b]	Activation	Behavior[c]	Baseline	Activation	Behavior	Baseline	Activation	Behavior	Baseline	Activation	Behavior	Baseline	Activation	Behavior
51	F	W	Neurotic depressed	No	Yes	Yes	4	Out	1	2	18	1	2	13	0	1	9	0	3-S	2[d]	0	4-S	10
32	F	N	Schiz	No	Yes	Yes	4	In / Out	0	2	36	1	2	4	0	0	4	3-S	4-S	22	2-S	3	5[d]
39	F	W	Schiz	Yes	Yes	No	3	Out / In	0	0	14	0	1	11-C	0	0	7[e]	1-S	3-S	13[d]	0	2	12
41	F	W	Schiz	No	No	No	3	Out	0	0	6	0	0	4	0	0	2[e]	0	0	2	1	1	8
27	F	W	Schiz	No	No	No	5	Out / In	0	0	23	0	0	4-out	0	0	13	0	0	4-out	0	0	4[d]
39	F	W	Schiz	No	Yes	Yes	3	Out	2-S	3-S	7	2-S	0	7	0	0	5	0	3	2	0	3	3
46	F	W	Anxiety	Yes	Yes	Yes	4	Out / In	2-SW	3-SW	9	0	1	5-out	0	1	9[d]	0	0	5-C(?)	0	1	9-C(?)
41	F	W	Schiz	No	No	No	4	Out	0	0	10	0	0	6	0	0	6	0	0	0	0	0	5
41	F	W	Schiz	Yes	No	Yes	2	Out	0	0	8	0	0	7	0	0	7[e]	0	0	9	0	0	9[d]-C(?)
53	F	W	Anxiety	No	No	No	4	Out / In	0	0	0	0	2	0	0	0	0	0	1	0[e]	0	1	0[d]
40	M	W	Schiz	No	No	Yes	3	Out	0	2	11	0	2	11	0	0	8[e]	0	3	9	0	3	9
47	M	W	Schiz	No	No	No	1	Out	1	2	14	0	2	14	0	0	8[e]	0	3	7	0	0	14[d]
45	F	W	Schiz	No	Unknown	Unknown	2	Out	0	0	14	0	0	3[e]	0	1	3	0	1	0	0	3	7
44	M	W	Anxiety	No	No	Yes	1	Out	0	1	13	1	2	10	0	0	10	0	1	10	0	2	10
44	F	N	Schiz	No	No	No	4	In	0	0	26	0	0	0	0	0	19	0	0	15	0	0	26[d]

Source: R. R. Monroe, M. D. Kramer, R. Goulding, and S. Wise, "EEG activation of patients receiving phenothiazines and chlordiazepoxide," *J. Nerv. Ment. Dis.* 141:103; 1965.

a In, in hospital; Out, out of hospital. b 0 = no abnormality; 1 = minimal abnormality; 2 = moderate abnormality; 3 = marked abnormality; and 4 = continuous abnormality. c M.S. rating scale (higher numbers indicate greater pathology). d Subjectively felt worse. e Subjectively felt better. S = Hypersynchrony; SW = spike wave; C = convulsion.

phenobarbital. In ten other subjects whose psychomotor epilepsy was complicated by interictal behavioral disturbances, six showed improvement when chlordiazepoxide (Librium) was added to their anticonvulsant regimen. Bercel's last group of subjects consisted of nine children under sixteen years of age without seizures or specific seizural records, but whose behavior was episodic and whose EEG's were characterized by occipital and posterior temporal, sharp wave dysrhythmia, chlordiazepoxide therapy alone induced decided improvement in behavior in six of these nine patients, particularly improvement in school performance in that they were less distractable, even through there were no marked changes in their explosive behavior. Kuniya (1964) noted remarkable control of seizures in 45 percent of epileptic children, pointing out that paroxysmal slow waves were particularly suppressed, although there was no absolute correlation between improvement in the EEG and clinical improvement. In 12 of 28 subjects this correlation was present while in six other cases the EEG remained abnormal even though there had been decided clinical improvement.

It is pertinent to mention several animal studies. Schallek (1962) found tht chlordiazepoxide had a taming effect on rats made vicious by septal lesions, and that both chlordiazepoxide and meprobamate apparently had a depressant action on the limbic system as measured by after discharges induced by electrical stimulation. Eidelberg (1965), using cocaine as an activating agent (because in cats it selectively induces convulsive discharges in the amygdala which might be a good pharmacologic model for temporal lobe epilepsy), noted that benzodiazepine derivatives were "highly effective in protecting the animals against these cocaine-induced amygdala seizures."

There is considerable evidence, therefore, that chlordiazepoxide has anticonvulsant effects. What evidence is there that it effects epileptoid behavioral disturbances or what we would call the episodic behavioral disorders? Pilkington (1961) noted both clinical improvement and improvement in the EEG of mentally retarded children with epilepsy and psychopathy. Contrary to many early reports, Kaim (1960) reported beneficial effects from chlordiazepoxide in chronically hospitalized psychotic patients. Kraft (1965) found that chlordiazepoxide was effective in reducing anxiety and emotional overload in children, so that symptoms of hyperactivity, fears, night terrors, enuresis, reading and speech problems, truancy, and bizarre behavior were reduced by 50 percent. However, he makes the important observation that, in several children, paradoxical responses occurred. One became hyperactive, one showed an increase in "hysterical seizures," one developed a rage reaction, and five "went wild." Of the latter five, three had 14 and 6 cycle per second EEG patterns. Inasmuch as Bercel (1961) also reported that two subjects "went wild," this paradoxical response must be kept in mind. The meaning of it is still unclear, but following Kraft's lead, we should try to discover whether it is related to 14 and 6 positive spike abnormalities. Dickel (1962), comparing meprobamate, chlordiazepoxide, and phenobarbital, found chlordiazepoxide less effective than meprobamate but more so than phenobarbital in controlling anxiety.

We made a detailed study of ten patients (Monroe, 1967b), all chronic, long-term schizophrenics with many previous hospitalizations. Most of these patients had abnormal EEG's, which were "normalized" by chlordiazepoxide. We found no straightforward, uncomplicated correlation between the EEG as modified by chlordiazepoxide and behavior; however, the patients who improved most on chlordiazepoxide were those whose EEG had been normalized. There were a number of startling clinical effects in utilizing chlordiazepoxide either alone or in combination with the phenothiazines in this particularly chronic group of patients. Table 20 summarizes these findings. Column E indicates that the best regimen was a combination of chlordiazepoxide and phenothiazines in three instances and chlordiazepoxide alone or with anticonvulsants in four. Section D summarizes the clinical impression of the response to chlordiazepoxide, listing behavioral changes such as verbalization, openness, initiative, socialization, overall activity, and impulsiveness as parameters that significantly changed under this drug. The dotted line in the middle of the squares indicates a hypothetical mean or norm of activity for the patient in question. The left side of the vector indicates the level of behavior before chlordiazepoxide

#	(A) Patient Age	Race	Sex	(B) EEG Activation		(C) Improv. Imps Motor	Retard	Concept.	(D) Clinical Response Verbal	Openness	Initiative	Activity	Impulse	Social	(E) Best Regime Chlor-diazepoxide	Pheno-thiazine	(F) Repeat Results	(G) Hospital Adjustment
1	39	W	F	+++	H										C	±anti-convul.	yes	out
2	46	W	M	++	H										C	P	yes	boarder
3	34	W	M	+	F										C	P	yes	unsupervised
4	47	W	M	+											??	?	yes	unsupervised
5	44	C	F	++											C		yes	supervised
6	39	C	M	0											C		yes	closed
7	31	W	F	++	H	?									??	?	yes	supervised
8	37	W	F	+++											C	P	no	closed
9	40	W	M	+++	H			?							??	?	yes	supervised
10	36	W	M	0				?							C		yes	closed

H= Hypersynchrony; F= Focal

Table 20. Summary of clinical response to chlordiazepoxide.

Source: R. R. Monroe and R. Dale, "Chlordiazepoxide in the treatment of patients with 'activated EEG's,'" *Dis. Nerv. Syst.* 28:394, 1967.

therapy and the right side or head of the arrow indicates the status of the patient at the time of evaluation while he was receiving chlordiazepoxide alone. The most consistent response was a reduction of the impulsivity occurring in eight of ten subjects. A second observation was a change in the patients' overall activity. If this was low initially, it approached normal; if it was high, it was reduced. Another frequent and often dramatic response was an increase in the verbalization occurring in six of ten patients and in all of the patients who showed significant verbal paucity during their baseline evaluation. In all patients except one there was an increase of openness during the interview, which was confirmed by observations of the ward personnel. By openness is meant that the patients discussed with considerably more frankness their deviant behavior or past traumatic experiences.

There was also a considerable increase in patient initiative, illustrated by one of the better integrated patients who made plans to leave the hospital while on chlordiazepoxide although she had been resisting this for many months prior to the experimental regimen. This is Patient 523, mentioned later in the chapter. This increase in initiative was particularly reported by work supervisors, who said that the patients were more efficient in performing their tasks and more interested in their job assignments. Before the chlordiazepoxide regimen was initiated, eight of the ten patients demonstrated dyscontrol acts to such a degree that they required confinement on the most disturbed ward, with close supervision and frequent isolation. This dyscontrol behavior was usually manifested by sudden physical attacks, without provocation or warning, on other patients or personnel: less frequently it was bizarre suicidal attempts or inappropriate sexual behavior. In all instances there was dramatic improvement, and usually a complete disappearance of this episodic dyscontrol. The overall impression of ward personnel was that five of the ten were much more sociable. They used such adjectives as "friendly," "nice" and even "lovable." Column C indicates improvements on the Inpatient Multidimensional Psychiatric Scale (Lorr 1963) for the categories "motor disturbance" (posturing, muscle tension, grimacing, repetitive movements, slovenly appearance); "retardation and apathy" (slow speech and movement, lack of goals, apathy, failure to answer questions, memory defect); and "conceptual disorganization" (irrelevant, incoherent, rambling speech, with neologisms and stereotypy). Improvement was determined by adding the scales when patients were on the placebo and baseline phenothiazine regimen then subtracting from that the combined IMPS score while the patients were receiving chlordiazepoxide alone plus the chlordiazepoxide-phenothiazine combination. Again improvement occurred in all categories in four of the ten, and was significant in seven of the ten subjects. This clinical improvement was not such that the patients could leave the hospital (only one accomplished this), but this is not surprising if one considers how markedly regressed this chronic group of patients were. Most of the patients, however, were much more active in the hospital, were shifted to open wards, and were able to visit relatives, all behavioral patterns that they had not attained for a number of years previously. The severity of their regression was useful in dramatizing the clinical changes obtainable. In another study (Monroe, 1965b) of 55 severely disturbed psychotic patients, we found that although 80 percent had been relegated for most of their hospital stay to an acutely disturbed ward because of uncontrolled impulsivity, if one added chlordiazepoxide and/or primidone (Mysoline) to their previous phenothiazine regimen, the behavior could be considerably modified. Table 21 summarizes these patients in terms of those who definitely improved, those in whom the im-

Table 21. Clinical response to chlordiazepoxide and/or primidone

	Definitely improved	Equivocal	No Response	Total
Patients				
N	23	17	15	55
Median age	28	32	25	28
Median years hospitalization	2.0	2.5	2.9	2.5
Diagnoses				
Schizophrenia	17	11	9	37
Brain syndrome	4	3	1	8
Other	2	3	5	10
Seizures[a]	5	5	2	12
Present status				
Home	6	3	3	12
Open ward	10	5	3	18
Closed ward	6	1	5	12
Disturbed ward	1	8	4	13
Drugs				
Chlordiazepoxide	8	6	8	22
Chlordiazepoxide and primidone	10	7	5	22
Primidone	5	4	2	11
Average improvement[b]	7.8	4.7	1.9	

Source: R. R. Monroe and S. Wise, "Combined phenothiazine, chlordiazepoxide and primidone therapy for uncontrolled psychotic patients," Amer. J. Psychiat. 122:694, 1965.

[a] See text.

[b] Average improvement in score on rating scale (see text).

provement was equivocal, and those who showed no response. These patients were rated on the following scale for the evaluation in Table 22:

Acting out

0 No acting out during hospital stay.

1 Emotional instability expressed verbally but never physically. This includes inappropriate anxiety, rage, depression, sexual feelings, etc.

2 Emotional instability occasionally expressed in physical behavior; however, so rare or so mild that it did not require isolation or close supervision.

3 Acting out severe enough or frequent enough to require close supervision and occasionally temporary isolation.

4 Acting out behavior severe enough to require five days or more of isolation per month.

5 Actual attempts of homicidal, suicidal or sexually assaultive behavior, or aggressive elopements.

Thinking disorder

0 No evidence of psychotic thinking.

1 Looseness of association (primary-process thinking) so that there was some difficulty in following or understanding the patient's productions, but no obvious impairment in judgment and insight.

2 No obvious delusional symptoms but insight was impaired and judgment in planning for the future limited.

3 Systematized delusions either openly expressed or acted upon.

4 Disorganized delusional systems and/or hallucinations; negativistic but, nevertheless, communicative.

5 Productions completely unintelligible or patient mute.

Work assignment

0 Proven capacity to assume enough responsibility to be discharged from the hospital or actually working outside hospital.

1 Off-ward assignment in the hospital with minimal supervision.
2 Off-ward assignment requiring close supervision.
3 Incapable of off-ward assignment but did cooperate with ward chores.
4 Only capable of self-care.
5 Unable to care for self.

It is obvious that in the definitely improved and equivocal groups (Table 22), acting out of sufficient severity to require close supervision and at least occasional temporary isolation was the rule rather than the exception. It was precisely in this area that the most dramatic improvement occurred. In fact, the dyscontrol acts almost completely disappeared in the definitely improved group. Before the study was begun, the isolation rooms, of which there were four for a ward of 40 patients, were usually filled. After the chlordiazepoxide and/or primidone regimen was initiated, it was unusual for any of the rooms to be in use. For this reason there was an equally dramatic improvement in their work assignment, but again it was the clinical impression that this improvement in work assignment was not due merely to the inhibition of dyscontrol acts, but to increased initiative and ambition. Improvement of thinking disorders as defined above was much less dramatic.

Among the 70 patients reported in Chapter 8 a number demon-

Table 22. Specific pattern of improvement with chlordiazepoxide and/or primidone

Group	Acting Out Before	Acting Out After	Thinking Before	Thinking After	Work Assignment Before	Work Assignment After
Definitely improved (N = 23)	3.4	0	3.1	1.5	4.0	1.2
Equivocal (N = 17)	2.9	0.7	2.7	2.2	3.8	1.9
No response (N = 15)	2.4	1.7	2.6	2.1	3.3	2.7

Source: R. R. Monroe and S. Wise, "Combined phenothiazine, chlordiazepoxide and primidone therapy for uncontrolled psychotic patients," Amer. J. Psychiat. 122:697, 1965.

strate the value of chlordiazepoxide either alone or in combination with other drugs, particularly in controlling the episodic behavioral disorders. Table 15 indicates that this was true in seven of 11 patients taking this drug. In the other four there were not enough data to evaluate drug effect. It must be remembered that in our series of 70 patients there was no systematic attempt to evaluate drug therapy, the cooperating physicians being free to place their patients on whatever regimen they chose. If our activation studies induced paroxysmal high amplitude slow waves, we recommended that chlordiazepoxide at least be tried as an adjunct to the current therapeutic regimen. We also recommended chlordiazepoxide if the patient had seizures and showed a specific abnormality on the EEG, if seizure control was not obtained with an anticonvulsant alone. However, for only one third of the patients was this recommendation followed.

Patient S278 is one who showed both improvement in seizural dyscontrol as well as improvement in episodic conversion reactions when chlordiazepoxide was added to her anticonvulsant medication. Patients F250 (Appendix 6) and S251 showed episodic depressive reactions and were either not helped or made worse by antidepressants, but they responded rapidly to chlordiazepoxide. Patient F267, with a history of two episodic psychotic reactions (acute brain reactions), responded much more quickly to therapy when chlordiazepoxide was added to the medical regimen (four days versus two weeks for the first hospitalization). Patients F222 and F221 are examples of patients with a specific EEG abnormality who responded rapidly to chlordiazepoxide medication.

11.4 A PHARMACOLOGIC REGIMEN FOR THE EPISODIC BEHAVIORAL DISORDERS

It is obvious from the discussion thus far that there is no specific drug or simple therapeutic regimen for the episodic behavioral disorders, but certainly the same can be said for classical epilepsy. It is apparent, however, that there is a more effective pharmacologic regimen than is generally recognized by the psychiatric profession. If the disordered behavior is judged episodic and if there is even the slightest indication that epileptoid mechanisms may play a part, pharmacologic therapy should be considered despite the problems this may bring up when combined with psychotherapy (discussed in Chapter 12). A tentative proposal for an effective drug combination, necessary for the proper treatment of the episodic disorders with a significant epileptoid component follows.

Good medical practice suggests that, even though a combination of drugs might ultimately be necessary, each drug should be initiated separately so that the regimen can be as simple as possible to obtain the desired results. However, because of the episodic quality of the disorder, it often takes considerable time to establish an effective regimen and many times patients with episodic disorders arrive at the psychiatrist's office having taken some pharmacologic agents for extended periods. Unless there are other contraindications, it may be desirable first to add one of the proposed drugs to the current regimen, and then, if the results are satisfactory, gradually withdraw the old medication, to see if the new drug alone will maintain the noted improvement.

If there is a history of typical epilepsy, either grand mal or simple automatisms, we start with an anticonvulsant, pushing the dose to toxic levels before assuming that it is ineffective. Diphenylhydantoin (Dilantin) and primidone (Mysoline) are the drugs that we have effectively used most often. No matter what other episodic disorders are present, if the patient has a history of grand mal seizures we are most likely to use diphenylhydantoin. On the other hand, if the epileptic seizures are more typically simple automatisms, we first start with primidone. It must be remembered, however, that with these drugs there is very little difference between the effective therapeutic dose and toxic levels. With diphenylhydantoin we start with 0.1 gm. three to four times a day, working up to double that dose in the large male patients if they can tolerate it; while with primidone we start with 250 mgs. once a day, increasing it until such a dose is given four times a day. In our experience, females can seldom tolerate the highest dose levels. As soon as such symptoms as nystagmus, double vision, tremor, unsteadiness, giddiness, weakness, drowsiness, or nausea develop, the does level is reduced until the patient is unaware of any side effects. If at this level the clinical effect leaves much to be desired, then one would add chlordiazepoxide at the level of 10 mgs. three or four times a day to the regimen, again increasing the dose until side effects develop. This can be anywhere from 30 to 180 mgs. per day. In treating outpatients, the dangers of ataxia, dizziness, and lack of coordination become a problem. Patients should be warned about these side effects and particularly admonished not to drive during the initiation of such a regimen. They also should be alerted to the possible synergistic effects of such a regimen and alcohol.

Patient 195 is an example of this. A woman in her early sixties, she was coerced into therapy by her spouse, who described his wife's behavior succinctly as follows: "when she's had a few drinks she gets mean." At such a time she would berate and nag her husband unmercifully, having no memory of this the next day but accepting his word as to what happened. At the same time she was quite contrite regarding her behavior although not contrite enough to give up her drinking. She had been a heavy drinker for a number of years but could not as yet be considered a chronic alcoholic. The alcoholic bouts were preceded by periods of mounting tension, restlessness, and insomnia. Chlordiazepoxide 10 mgs. q.i.d. was prescribed, and although she was warned that she would be more sensitive to alcohol, she was not specifically forewarned about driving a car. Two weeks after the start of this regimen, she was jailed for having sideswiped another car and having left the scene of the accident. She was not aware that she had even hit the other car although there was considerable damage to both cars. It was established that she had had only two cocktails at a friend's house before driving, an amount of alcoholic intake which in the past had not led to difficulty. It seemed likely that the combination of chlordiazepoxide and alcohol led to a disturbance in judging distance, which was, in part responsible for the accident. However, the judge was unmoved by such a plea.

If the anticonvulsant-chlordiazepoxide combination is successful, we would first withdraw any other medication that the patient had been receiving at the time of consultation, and then, if the patient is still satisfactorily controlled on the anticonvulsant-chlordiazepozide combination alone, we would begin reducing the anticonvulsant to establish the lowest possible dose necessary to maintain clinical improvement. This type of program has the advantage of most often assuring a quick therapeutic result which is dramatic enough to be recognized despite the episodic nature of the patient's disordered behavior. At the same time it ultimately results in the simplest, yet most effective drug regimen.

When the episodic behavioral disorders are not characterized by typical seizural activity, we arbitrarily start the regimen with chlordiazepoxide rather than one of the anticonvulsants, only adding the latter if the former does not induce the desired improvement. If the patient also demonstrates psychotic disorganization, which we have called the episodic psychotic reaction, it may be necessary to combine the regimen described above with phenothiazine as an antipsychotic agent. Such complex drug combinations are usually considered medically unsound or unjustified, but in this instance all the drugs have specific and different actions, in some ways antagonistic (e.g., the phenothiazines versus the anticonvulsants), but in other ways complementary or supplementary (Monroe, 1965b).

In the last chapter we pointed out that the episodic psychotic reactions with a significant epileptoid component seemed to be classifiable into three types, on the basis of alteration in the state of consciousness. One of these types occurs in patients with reduced consciousness, occurring particularly in children and often related to petit mal status. In such states, trimethadione (Tridione) might be the drug of choice, although we have had no personal experience in treating this type of disorder. In another reaction, the consciousness is distractible, again seen often in children and often labeled "hyperkinetic" syndrome. In these instances dextroamphetamine seems to exert a paradoxical effect, calming the patient and reducing the distractibility as well as other symptoms. The third group, characterized by what has been called "primary-process thinking," seems to respond best to the anticonvulsants or anticonvulsant-chlordiazepoxide combination. Such a differential drug effect based on characteristic altered states of consciousness in an adult is not as obvious. It is hoped, however, that as a result of refining clinical differentiation of the episodic behavioral disorders which we have proposed in this volume, more specific and effective pharmacologic agents will be discovered. The need to find new and better pharmacologic agents for these disorders is obvious. Some drugs now available may be quite useful, but as yet we have not personally had adequate clinical experience with them. For instance diazepam (Valium) is reported as an even more effective anticonvulsant than chlordiazepoxide, and it might be more effective in the episodic behavioral disorders (Galambos, 1965). Other new pharmacologic agents have been successfully used by others (Livingston, 1967 and Peterson, 1967).

One observation that we have repeatedly made is that episodic depressive reactions respond poorly to antidepressant medication. However, they can respond dramatically to either benzodiazepines or anticonvulsants or a combination of the two. Patient F250 (Appendix 6) is an example of such a response. In fact in many of these patients the usual antidepressant only makes matters worse (Patient S251).

The precipitous withdrawal of any benzodiazepines as well as phenothiazines and barbiturates have been noted to increase EEG abnormalities and they may induce typical convulsions or a temporary increase in the episodic behavioral disturbances (Bokojic, 1960).

Patient 523 is an example of this. She was a research subject under study to compare the effects of chlordiazepoxide with the phenothiazines (Monroe, 1965a, 1967b). In these studies all drugs plus placebos were being administered in a double-blind procedure. During the month in which she was receiving chlordiazepoxide (of course, unknown to the ward physician and ward personnel), she showed marked improvement, and for the first time expressed some initiative in wanting to leave the hospital. Her psychiatrist, who had been urging discharge for many months, jumped at this opportunity, ignoring the fact that she was on a research project. In the meantime the research staff had shifted her medication rather abruptly to placebo medication. Within 24 hours after discharge she had several seizures. Following the seizures she ran out on the street in a nightgown screaming that she was going to die. She was picked up by a taxi and taken to the emergency room of the local hospital. She complained of heart trouble and not being able to breathe. At times she was incoherent and apparently delusional and hallucinating. She was confused, thinking she was back at the mental hospital, and suddenly began "tearing up the emergency room." Under heavy sedation she was returned to the mental hospital where dyscontrol acts continued until the chlordiazepoxide regimen was re-established.

Finally, we will only mention here that in extreme instances of episodic behavioral disorders, just as in extreme uncontrolled epilepsy, unilateral temporal lobectomy has been resorted to. In fact, attempts are being made to find an innocuous bilateral procedure, despite the risk of inducing intellectual or personality defects. Such investigations were previously discussed (4.3).

12 Psychotherapy of the Episodic Behavioral Disorders

Most of the episodic behavioral disorders manifest an interplay between "faulty equipment" (instability of the central nervous system due to delayed maturation, excessive neuronal discharges, or diffuse brain damage), and "faulty learning." A therapeutic regimen will usually be a combination of pharmacologic (and perhaps even surgical) and reeducational or psychotherapeutic techniques. In providing this regimen, a decision will have to be made whether to utilize a team approach combining the skills of the neurologist and the psychiatrist or to delegate the primary responsibility to a single physician representing one or the other discipline. The advantages and disadvantages of each will be discussed at the end of this chapter, as well as the special problem in combining somatic therapy with psychotherapy. In the treatment of the episodic behavioral disorders, a single form of treatment will rarely be sufficient. However, for expository reasons we will first discuss "pure" psychotherapy and then later in the chapter discuss combining psychotherapy with the somatic therapies.

A problem that always confronts the psychiatrist is how much to expect of therapy and how much to expect of the patient. Put another way, how much of the "faulty equipment" can be reversed or restored, and how much will relearning modify the effects of years of "faulty learning"? With our present state of

354

knowledge, this becomes a clinical opinion rather than sound judgment based on clinical facts. Certainly in the long run, patients are going to accomplish no more than their physicians expect of them. Therapy is much like the self-fulfilling prophecy. If the physician feels that his patient can never emancipate himself from a morbid heredity ("tarred with the genetic brush"), the patient will fulfill this expectation. The good therapist is probably one who errs on the side of optimism (see Patient O289).

On the other hand, if the therapist's expectations are completely unrealistic he will in the long run only compound the patient's difficulties because of the frustrations and disappointments when the therapeutic goal is not obtained. This result is further exaggerated by the unrealistic and magical expectations all patients have of psychotherapy, hoping that in the process they will somewhere find untold capacities for intellectual and creative skills that heretofore have been dormant. The patient desires more than to be a realistically healthy, effective human being, yearning instead to become a genius or superhuman. Sometimes in the early years of applying new psychotherapeutic techniques such enthusiasm is shared by the therapist himself. An example of this is the cure of acting out reported by Emerson after a three week "psychoanalysis" (1915).

From both our motivational and neurophysiologic considerations, we have seen that for many patients with the episodic behavioral disorders our expectations realistically can be high, particularly the more normal the individual during the interepisodic period. In other instances we have noted that many of these disorders represent maturational lags, disappearing in time even without specific therapeutic intervention or observable environmental change (Symposium, 1963). In still other instances we have seen that the neurologic dysfunction may be severe and irreversible, or the "faulty learning" may have occurred at an extremely early age, resulting in a pervasive disturbance in subsequent development. In such instances our expectations must be limited, and in the most severe, the only solution may be institutional control to protect the patient or society.

To a considerable extent psychotherapy still remains more an art than a science; consequently there is a legitimate question whether one can write about psychotherapy in general terms or whether one is limited to a discussion of a particular individual in his unique situation. If the therapy is a planned interaction between patient and therapist (and to be designated psychotherapy it should be a planned interaction), it must be based on psychodynamic considerations. The value of a psychodynamic formulation lies in the fact that it is unique for the patient under consideration in his specific environment with his specific problems. It should be applicable to this one patient and only to this one. On the other hand, if our motivational analysis of the episodic behavioral disorders is to have any pragmatic value, it is precisely because it suggests generalizations regarding the appropriate reeducational techniques to be used in treating these patients. In a discussion of therapy we will carefully avoid at one extreme vague and meaningless generalizations which could apply equally to the psychotherapy of any patient, and at the other extreme a picayune "cookbook" prescription which might have value for an individual patient, but be of limited applicability as a generalization.

12.1 PSYCHOTHERAPY OF EPISODIC DYSCONTROL

12.1.1 *Establishing therapeutic motivation.* We have defined episodic dyscontrol as an abrupt, precipitous act or short series of acts with a single intention carried through to completion, resulting in relief of tension or gratification of a need. While the internal tension has been reduced, the consequences of the act may lead to an increase in tension between the individual and his environment. The act itself is conspicuous or morbid because it interrupts the life style of the individual, appearing both out of character for the individual and out of context for the situation. We have already emphasized that during the course of action itself the behavior is egosyntonic, that is nonconflictual. However, we have further emphasized that contrary to the usual psychiatric opinion, this act is often quite readily seen in retrospect as ego-alien. The act is a "surprise" to the actor in terms of its quality or consequences. In other individuals, even though the ego-alien quality of the act is not immediately admitted, it must be seen as such at the unconscious level, because the act is defensively justified through repression, projection, or rationalization. If the ego-alienness is consciously expressed, we have designated the behavior as a *dyscontrol act,* whereas if it is only unconsciously accepted as ego-alien, and hence defensively denied or otherwise justified, we designate it as a *dyscontrol neurosis.* In both cases, there is an internal discomfort and a sense of being sick or needing help. In these instances it is usually easy to develop a therapeutic motivation, even though it may be some time before the dyscontrol neurotic is willing to see the specific episodic acts as ego-alien. However, as the pathology approaches what we have designated as a *dyscontrol disorder,* that is, those episodic dyscontrols in which the act is egosyntonic at both the conscious and unconscious level, and in which, no matter how uncomfortable the behavior of the patient makes those in his environment, he himself remains at ease or indifferent to the effects of his behavior on either himself or others, the more immediate becomes the problem of developing an effective therapeutic motivation. These are the patients we have previously mentioned who show very little evidence of anxiety, even on psychometric examination, and, in fact, we have wondered whether or not the EEG is actually useful in identifying them, in view of the lack of low amplitude fast beta activity usually taken as an indication for tension or anxiety. Because the episodic acts are often antisocial and because, if they are egosyntonic, they are likely to be recurrent, these individuals often are found in prisons or in contact with the parole officer rather than in the hospital or the psychiatrist's office. Psychotherapeutic interventions are most often ineffectual in this group, yet incarceration only temporarily limits the disastrous consequences of their acts. Drastically new techniques are needed. The psychiatrist is occasionally called upon to handle such problems when patients, particularly children and adolescents, are coerced into therapy by the court or their families. Obviously this type of episodic dyscontrol has to be converted from the dyscontrol disorder to the dyscontrol neurosis and finally to the dyscontrol act if treatment is to be effective. At some level the actor must see his behavior as ego-alien and yet his responsibility. If the patient does not, therapy requires some form of strict, unambiguous, and impartial external control. These patients need a reward-punishment discipline which will develop the inhibitory anxiety which is the precursor of a conscience mechanism. In the literature on the treatment of impulse disorders and acting out, there is much debate about the use of prohibition in treatment (Frank, 1959; Greenacre, 1963). In the patient with dyscontrol disorder, it would seem that prohibitions are a crucial prerequisite for developing an effective therapeutic motivation, but whether this external prohibition or reward-punishment system should be the responsibility of the therapist who is ultimately striving for "insight" is a complex matter (Frank, 1959).

For such patients it is obvious that verbal prohibitions during the therapeutic hour alone are totally ineffective; inasmuch as any restrictions on dyscontrol acts require 24-hour surveillance, which cannot be provided by the therapist in his office, but only by some form of institutionalization, or, for children, new, effectively authoritative, parental surrogates. In such instances, it is often proposed that the hospital administration provide the disciplinary restrictions, while a therapist unassociated with this restrictive environment provide individual insight psychotherapy. Other solutions, particularly with adolescents, have been to send them to military school or let them be drafted (these sometimes work), or, with younger children, to find a foster home that provides consistent discipline. In such instances there can be a distinct separation between the disciplinary environment and the therapeutic setting.

There are exciting possibilities for innovations in the field of treating adult dyscontrol disorders, which up to now have been handled in a conventional manner with negligible results. A unique experience in dealing with such individuals is the Maryland Patuxent Institute for Defective Delinquents (Boslow,

1966). Here, there is use of the indeterminant sentence, and freedom can be attained only after the inmate demonstrates his capacity for controlled behavior. Another unique aspect of this program is that freedom is a slowly progressive step by step process, which again is dependent on the demonstrated ability to exert increasing self-control. These steps first occur within the walls of the institution; the subject moves from tier to tier, each with an increasing range of freedom as well as responsibility; then he moves to part-time life outside the institution under intensive supervision; and finally complete freedom from the institution, but still under intensive outpatient care. Unlike the modern psychiatric hospital, this institution is not a permissive environment, but in fact a very restrictive one, far different from Aichhorn's Cottage for delinquent boys (1936). It remains to be seen whether this technique will be effective in the long run. Certainly our hopes are tempered with doubt because of past failures.

A more common clinical example of how such discipline can be established in the usual psychiatric outpatient setting follows:

The wife of Patient 103 is an actor-outer, controlling and manipulating him until he, the healthier one, is miserable enough to seek therapy. His treatment included working with the passivity that led him to tolerate this manipulating behavior, until he was forceful enough to insist on controls and on her seeking psychiatric help. He accomplished this first by proposing marital counseling for the pair, but only when his behavior became forceful enough to resist her manipulations to the point of suggesting separation was sufficient anxiety mobilized in the spouse (manifesting a dyscontrol disorder) so that an effective therapeutic motivation could be developed in her. In counseling sessions, the main goal was to arouse this anxiety and some inner awareness of her own responsibility for her spouse's discomfort until, ultimately, she too sought individual therapy. Here the significant controls had been established by an important peer in the actor-outer's environment. Of course, if the patient, because of her own narcissism, totally lacks the capacity to empathize with her spouse, this is ineffective.

There are several essentials in the development of an effective therapeutic motivation in those patients whose behavior is so egosyntonic and narcissistic that anxiety at either the overt or covert level is lacking: the restrictions must be pervasive and complete, requiring constant surveillance; there must be a concrete measure of performance; there must be painful deprivations which cannot be escaped if performance is not forthcoming; and finally there must be immediate direct rewards if the performance is satisfactory. Objectivity in administering discipline, free from angry retaliation or recrimination, is required. The patient with dyscontrol neurosis might welcome such external controls because they alleviate the underlying guilty discomfort of mature decision making, but such controls would be deleterious because they would only enhance his dependency gratifications. We suggest that such strict environmental controls should be provided only for those patients with too little anxiety, the intent being to develop enough inhibitory anxiety so that insight psychotherapy or reeducation is feasible. However, it is highly unlikely that anyone identified with a punishing, prohibitive institution can effectively elicit the spontaneous introspection necessary for the ultimate development of insight. In most instances, in order for such a prohibitive restrictive program to be ultimately effective it must be accompanied by some form of insight therapy. Some nonrestrictive figure therefore must be available to deal with the developing anxiety and guilt when it occurs. A possibility to be investigated is whether changes in the psychometric tests or even the EEG could indicate when the individual has developed the prerequisite anxiety for such psychotherapy.

For Patient S282, controls were not maintained long enough. This boy, who committed a number of antisocial acts in his adolescent identity struggle, was allowed the freedom of living in the hospital, yet working at an outside job. He immediately abused this responsibility by leaving the job without telling anybody, yet maintaining his passes which offered freedom from the hospital routine. When this was discovered, he was tried on a somewhat more restrictive environment, that is, he was allowed to attend school. Again he was a truant from his responsibilities, and finally it was insisted that he remain in the hospital and attend school in that restrictive setting. After this backtracking the patient, having tasted freedom, refused to continue with hospitalization, and in collusion with his mother signed out against medical advice.

On the other hand, another patient, who had been given the primary diagnosis of an episodic sociopathic reaction (Patient S212), finally controlled her promiscuous sexual behavior when her second husband insisted on accompanying or supervising her whenever she left the house. This restraint on her sexual impulsivity, accompanied by the meeting of her dependency needs, provided a security she was looking for so that she could tolerate her previous frustrations and accept the restrictive control.

One might ask whether exposure to such an environment in itself would be sufficient to resolve the episodic dyscontrol. Clinical intuition would suggest that this might be the case during early maturation when the restricting, but at the same time rewarding, environment could be incorporated in the individual's developing internalized super-ego or conscience. Among our 70 adults and 16 children we found none for whom a restrictive environment alone was sufficient; on the contrary, unless such an environment was accompanied by meaningful individual psychotherapy, it failed. However the way we selected our subjects for study may have eliminated those individuals who could have responded to such an environment alone. Of the various classifications in our diagnostic schema (Fig. 2) restriction alone would be predicted to be successful in the motivated primary episodic dyscontrols (seizure and instinct dyscontrol), which if learned disorders are due to a disciplinary deficiency in the early dependency period; that is, those patients who were reared by mothers so preoccupied with the gratifications of their own frustrated need that they could not tolerate frustrating their offspring. In these individuals the result is a complete lack of the inhibitory anxiety that is necessary for what we have called "choice" delay; hence there is little need for developing "reflective" delay. On the other hand, in those disorders in which the reflective delay is not so much absent but distorted by excessive neurotic inhibitions (excessive inhibitory anxiety), as we have seen for those designated as manifesting impulse dyscontrol or acting out, such a prohibitory program would be merely the first step in therapy, and then useful only if the dyscontrol acts were truly egosyntonic.

There is one kind of patient with episodic disorder who might show little anxiety and probably demonstrate behavior we have categorized as instinct dyscontrol, for whom the technique of establishing a restrictive environment would be contraindicated. This is the individual who handles even the slightest tension and urges in a traumato-phobic manner. If, as we have previously described, this results in a pouting withdrawal, the patient would manifest an episodic inhibition; if, on the other hand, the patient handles the tension in terms of immediate gratification through motor acts, he would represent, in all likelihood, an example of instinct dyscontrol, appearing as a shallow, unstable, unpredictable individual with little or no anxiety. But lack of anxiety would merely be a facade. Even the slightest prohibitions inherent in entering any serious psychotherapy would be sufficient to arouse the anxiety necessary for a sustained therapeutic relationship and, in fact, might arouse so much anxiety that the patient would panic and run away from therapy. An example follows:

> Patient 187 was a nineteen-year-old who in childhood was the "good, mama's boy," but who, since age 16, had been a hellion, with most of his impulsive acting out of an extremely self-defeating nature, often self-destructive. It was obvious that such acts were thinly disguised suicidal attempts. On the surface, however, he gave the picture of a blasé, unstable, superficial adolescent who didn't "give a damn." He repeatedly broke off treatment and because he was in late adolescence without overt or covert signs of psychosis, he was allowed to do this, although informed that he would be accepted back as a patient any time he so desired. Twice he resumed psychotherapy, but the third attempt to do so was not fortunate. A crisis with his girlfriend occurred

at the time his therapist was on vacation. Unable to find any other confidant, and taunted by his peers for being jilted, he shot and killed himself.

In this boy the phobic avoidance of any anxiety-producing situation, his intense guilt, and overwhelming self-destructiveness were well hidden by the more overt adolescent bravado. His interruptions in therapy were due, not to lack of motivation because of the egosyntonic character of his symptoms, but to phobic withdrawal from an anxiety-producing confrontation. It is this type of individual who responds to therapy which is forced as a condition for parole, or when some other counteracting reward for the pain of psychotherapy is provided.

For Patient 111, the reward of being able to get away from boarding school for the day while she visited the therapist's office in a nearby city was sufficient to overcome the anxiety that therapy aroused. The school environment, which restricted her acting out at the price of considerable anxiety could be counteracted by a day's shopping, lunch, and movies in conjunction with the therapeutic session.

It becomes extremely important to recognize this group because of the superficial appearance of shallowness or indifference which suggests that some severe prohibitions might be necessary, but in reality only means that a frantic flight reaction may occur.

12.1.2 *Selective restraint of dyscontrol acts.* Even when there is sufficient therapeutic motivation, the intensity of this motivation will fluctuate during the course of treatment. The one dyscontrol act that can definitely defeat therapy is, of course, sudden, unannounced termination. It was precisely this behavior of Freud's patient, Dora (Freud, vol. VII), that led to the first recognition and labeling of acting out. A more subtle, but at times equally defeating act, is the missed appointment. In the long run, of course, the patient's own recognition of this impulse as an ego-alien act, and his desire to understand why the urge to interrupt or terminate is current, are the best methods for handling the problem. However, there will be a preliminary period before such recognition is possible and long before any solution through interpretation is appropriate. Early in therapy we must rely on external but meaningful pressures to force the individual to continue his therapy even though he has the impulse to quit. This type of acting out must be anticipated and worked out during periods of good motivation, preferably at the start of therapy. The therapist can discuss this possibility with the patient, pointing out that charges will be made for missed appointments, no matter how good the patient's rationalization; if somebody else is paying the bill, the missed appointments will be listed, or in some way the referring or authoritative figure will be informed whenever therapy is avoided. Such procedure, established at the time of the patient's sincere motivation, may not prevent subsequent acting out, but at least gives the therapist a lever when the problem arises.

For Patient S290 (Appendix 3), this technique was necessary. He was afraid to miss appointments because his stepfather, who was financing therapy, would "raise hell," and he was dependent on his stepfather for other financial help. Although he agreed to the arrangement of indicating missed sessions on the bill at the onset of therapy, he later objected and was resentful that his therapist had proposed it. The therapist pointed out that there was one way to circumvent that situation; the patient might pay for therapy himself by selling a small amount of stock he was tenaciously holding onto, stock that he had inherited from a distant relative, but that proposal was even more unacceptable. For a while he expressed his obsequious dependency and simultaneous hostile rebellion by coming to sessions promptly, staying for the full hour, but not saying a word. The therapist remained silent also. After 11 sessions with no communication, the patient was ultimately forced to talk about the transference situation, that is, his ambivalent fear-rage response to authoritative figures, in a way that was quite meaningful to him. (For a detailed discussion of this patient, see Monroe, 1968).

In the adult nonpsychotic patient who has contracted for his own treatment, such outside pressures may not be easy to develop. In such instances, a commitment should be secured from the patient, again at a time when the therapeutic motivation is strong, not to discontinue therapy without several sessions to discuss the matter before the decision is final. In cases of brief episodic dyscontrol maintaining contact in this way is usually sufficient to bridge the gap between the impulse to terminate and the more stable motivation for therapy. If it is not, the only way the therapist can maintain his relative neutrality (this is discussed below) is to express his reluctance at the patient's departure and tell him that he will hold time available for a specified period, should the patient change his mind. Another alternative is to suggest that the patient accept consultation regarding the matter or even referral to another physician for treatment. Only in the case of the decompensated psychotic, early adolescent, or young child, should the therapist combat termination with hospital commitment or forced institutionalization, although sometimes an effective motivation can be developed in this way if the referring physician uses such a "club" (see Patient S219).

Generally there is considerable pressure on the therapist to maintain treatment, particularly when there is concern regarding possible homicidal, suicidal, or other aggressive dyscontrol acts. However, the therapist has to be able to tolerate taking chances and calculated risks, even though this occasionally fails with spectacular and catastrophic results. Such failures arouse in the therapist appropriate guilt feelings, not to mention the impact such acting out by one of his patients might have on the psychiatrist's reputation in the community. On the other hand, if the therapist is forced by his own anxieties to play it safe, it is almost impossible to treat the episodic dyscontrol patients. As soon as the patient feels that the therapist is assuming responsibility for the patient's behavior, the dyscontrol acts will increase and be used to manipulate and particularly to punish, the therapist. It is this factor (at least in part) that the analysts refer to when they make statements that the therapist must maintain his neutrality (Greenacre, 1963). This neutrality means placing the responsibility for behavior on the patient himself, even though this becomes particularly complicated when the therapeutic regimen combines psychotherapy with drug therapy.

If, when the patient has finally reached the point at which the dyscontrol acts are truly ego-alien (and if the acts are really distressing), should hospitalization with external controls become necessary it is readily accepted by the patient. In fact, there are a number of ways the dyscontrol acts can be controlled when they are at least retrospectively recognized by the patient as ego-alien and long before insight into the origins and meanings of these acts has been attained. Therapist and patient can work together in identifying and thereby avoiding precipitating events, particularly in what we have defined as impulse dyscontrol characterized by a prodromal period of mounting tension. Through simple exhortation, the patient can be asked to control action until the situation and mounting tension are discussed in treatment, thus introducing an artificial reflective delay. During such periods there may be an indication for frequent, even daily, sessions, even though the technique is not conventional psychoanalysis. Should this be impossible, a substitute is to allow for emergency phone calls wherein a brief contact with the therapist may be sufficient to abort or prevent the act. This privilege at times will be used to manipulate therapy, but most often it is effective in preventing serious acting out.

Patient O289 (Appendix 7) responded to this technique. Because she lived in a distant city, psychotherapy was limited to two or three sessions held over a two-day period each week. The therapist arranged to have the patient call by long-distance if she felt she was losing control and was alerted to this by the prodromal mounting tension. Unfortunately, by the time these calls were completed, the patient was already in such a state of altered consciousness that it was virtually impossible to establish contact with her. However, during previous hypnotic sessions, cues had been established which were sufficient to place the patient in a rather deep hypnotic trance even with the altered awareness. Through this technique, tranquilization and sleep were suggested before the dyscontrol acts could be carried out.

As long as there is some warning between the stimulus or urge to act and the act itself, such as seen in impulse dyscontrol and sometimes even in acting out, there is a possibility of using drugs to delay or postpone the act. Drug postponement induces other complications, which are discussed later in this chapter. It is important to remind the reader, however, that these measures are only temporary and not a definitive technique for permanently alleviating the impulse dyscontrol or the acting out.

12.1.3 *Making the act ego-alien.* A generalization which should be explicit by now is that we are changing the dyscontrol disorders into dyscontrol neurosis and then finally into the dyscontrol acts. Put in another way, we are trying to shift from a behavioral pattern in which the dyscontrol acts are completely egosyntonic into one in which the behavior, even though sitll consciously seen as egosyntonic, at least makes the patient uncomfortable; and, finally, to a situation in which the specific dyscontrol acts are seen as truly ego-alien (Frank, 1959). What techniques do we have at our disposal, when the patient is only aware of this discomforting anxiety that accompanies his behavior, but still does not see the individual acts as resulting from an inappropriate loss of control? We must guide the patient into some retrospective reflection on his behavior in the hope that he will gradually develop an awareness of how ineffectual his behavior is. Of course, the long-term goals are not only that he will see this behavior retrospectively as ineffectual, but also prospectively that he will be able to identify the ego-alien intentions through reflective delay.

Before the patient is willing to accept his actions as inappropriate, we can at least focus on what needs he was hoping to gratify through these acts. This task is generally made easier because the acts have generally failed to truly gratify needs, or if they do, the interpersonal tension due to the narcissistic quality of the act arouses sufficient anxiety to provide a motivating therapeutic force. By focusing on the patient's needs and implying that these needs are not abnormal or unjustified, or at least that their more sublimated or socialized equivalents are not abnormal (e.g., self-assertion for hostility, concern for anxiety, love for dependency, etc.), we can avoid the immediate confrontation with the patient's narcissism. This circumvents the resistance that a more direct confrontation would elicit. At first we do not even focus on the intensity of the needs as being pathological, but instead suggest exploring alternatives (do not use such words as "better" or "preferred") in meeting these needs. Thus, by not questioning his intentions or needs, only the methods by which he is trying to meet these needs, we are in the position of being an ally of the patient and not a critical observer denying or frustrating these needs. Thus we do not immediately have to struggle with the patient's narcissism. At some point the patient will arrive at a level of reflection where he can say, "why did not I think of this or that alternative myself." This is the breakthrough, as it means the dyscontrol acts are becoming ego-alien. This approach is somewhat at odds with Greenacre's suggestion that the primary emphasis should be interpreting the patient's narcissism (Greenacre, 1963). On the contrary we would utilize this narcissism in our first attempt in the resolution of the acting out. However, as we will discuss later, the narcissism has to be worked through at some point.

A frequently mentioned problem in the psychoanalytic literature (because it is a particular consequence of the psychoanalytic technique) is that the dyscontrol acts do not even come up for consideration in therapy, and therefore there is little opportunity to work them through. If they are presented at all it is in such a disguised way that they are misconstrued even by the astute therapist as an external stress inflicted on the patient by neurotic relatives or significant peers. In the classic psychoanalytic procedure, there is too little flexibility to allow for much acting out within treatment; that is, the constraints placed on such acting out by the formal use of the couch, the stereotyped entrance and exit, and the rigidity of the treatment rules. If the dyscontrol patient flouts the rules in psychoanalytic therapy, he usually terminates treatment. On the other hand, if the treatment setting is less formal, there will arise many opportunities for dyscontrol acts within the therapeutic setting.

There are two ways whereby this hiding of acting out can be exposed. The first is to look for and work with any dyscontrol acts that occur within the treatment setting. Minor ones at first should be ignored because early confrontation before the acts become flagrantly inappropriate will be rationalized by the patient, and subsequent, more obvious dyscontrol inhibited.

Patient 123 had taught her therapist through previous experience that even dramatic acting out within the treatment setting could be stubbornly rationalized. Then she began a new series of actions which her therapist determined to let pass until they became so dramatic and bizarre that rationalization would be impossible. It all began with her wearing increasingly shorter skirts and more deeply cut blouses in the days before miniskirts. Without comment her therapist let this pass until a number of sessions later she arrived for her appointment accompanied by her Great Dane, who spent the hour lying on the floor between the therapist and patient, looking at the therapist with most suspicious eyes. This was even more bizarre when one considers that she had to bring the dog through a hospital entrance and ride the elevator to the sixth floor. It must have taken some doing to get the dog past both the doorman and the elevator operator. Her therapist cautiously questioned her about bringing her dog to therapy, but her immediate rationalization was that she had no one to leave him with.

Predicting that more dramatic acting out was destined in the near future, the therapist let the matter ride. The very next session she again arrived with the dog, sat down in her chair and after a few minutes of preliminary small talk, proceeded to unbutton and take off her blouse, sitting in the chair clad in a skirt and fancy semi-transparent brassiere. It would have been hard not to have made a comment at this point. He first asked her why she had taken off her blouse, and was countered by the immediate rationalization that it was very hot in the office. Opening the window might have relieved the tension but would not have resolved the situation; instead, he questioned whether this was her usual behavior when visiting friends. Her immediate rebuttal was "of course." The therapist expressed doubt, but she stubbornly persisted. He asked for examples, and she gave several which were obviously fabricated. Finally the therapist said that he thought she had other reasons for taking her blouse off. Her reply to that was, "Yes, of course, I know. You interpret everything as sexual. You think that I am trying to seduce you, don't you?" He replied that he did not think that she was really trying to seduce him but did believe that she was trying to stir him up sexually and at the same time had brought her dog for protection. At this point she laughed at her therapist's naïveté. However, when he pointed out to her that, whether or not this was what she intended to do, her behavior was stirring him up sexually, she apparently found this a sobering thought, for she put her blouse back on. After remaining silent for several minutes, the therapist again intervened and pointed out that he thought she had been trying to stir him up sexually for some time now without perhaps even realizing it herself. By being allowed to carry through the acting out to such extreme proportions before being confronted with her intentions, the patient was finally able to accept not only this interpretation, but also a generalization that her sexual aggressiveness without even being aware of it might be one of the reasons for her view that all men are beasts, interested in her just for her body. Previous attempts to interpret minor acting out in the same context had failed.

The second possibility for bringing dyscontrol acts out into the therapeutic session is an occasional joint session with another significant person in the patient's environment, most often the spouse. Again, it is better to anticipate such possibilities early in therapy and suggest that this might be done in the future. The confrontation that occurs in such a setting usually exposes acting out even though it has not been mentioned in individual psycho-

therapy, or at least it provides clues as to what subsequent prob-
ing will bring such material into subsequent psychotherapeutic
sessions.

Patient S219 was informed in the first session that it would
probably be desirable to bring her husband into therapy
conjointly with her during the course of her therapy. She
accepted this with alacrity because at this point she projected
many of her difficulties on him ("he's even sicker than I
am"). At one point in therapy she was preoccupied with
what she described as "pathological jealousy on the part of
my husband," just because other men "find me interesting."
She further elaborated, "this is because I am intelligent and
an interesting conversationalist and has nothing to do with
sex." Although she gave no evidence for such during the
therapeutic session on the basis of her behavior in the treatment setting, the therapist could only assume she was being
sexually provocative. However, interpretation of this behavior in the transference context had so far been unsuccessful. A conjoint session with the husband was arranged the
next time she reported one of her husband's "fits of jealousy." In this session he pointed out that at a dance several
nights previously she had been throwing herself at one of
their male acquaintances, dancing with him continuously,
then sending her husband home early to relieve the baby-
sitter while she spent the rest of the night with her dancing
companion. This story was quite different from one she
had presented in her session, she having failed to mention
that the "several hours of serious conversation" had taken
place at four in the morning, with the two of them parked
in his car on a lonely lane. When thus confronted, she admitted the facts as presented by her husband but pleaded
innocence "because nothing happened." At the next session,
with the patient alone, she wanted to "forget the whole
matter because it isn't important." Insisting on a confrontation, the therapist approached the issue not on the basis
of any discrepancy between what she and the husband reported, but why so many pertinent facts were left out of

her story, emphasizing that because of this the therapist was really in the dark as to what had gone on. She finally accepted that she must have felt guilty because of her behavior, hence hid pertinent information. With this initial step she was able to see how her behavior was really intended to elicit the jealousy on the part of her husband which she had previously rationalized as his neurosis. This was the start of a long series of interpretations, readily accepted by the patient, that she projected "fault" onto others whenever she felt guilty herself.

Flexibility, then, in the treatment of episodic dyscontrol is not just a pious pronouncement, but, in the sense we have been discussing it, it is a necessity for exposing defensive rationalizations or denials of the distorted intentions in the episodic dyscontrols. Later in the chapter we will discuss those aspects of therapy that should be rigidly controlled; that is, when flexibility is contraindicated.

12.1.4 *Restoring drive-control balance.* Another generalization we have made concerning episodic dyscontrol is that it represents an imbalance between drives and urges on one hand and controls on the other, with either normal or excessive urges overwhelming unusually weak or normal controls respectively. We have already discussed the problem of substituting external controls for internally weak ones, and we will discuss later the development of appropriate internal control (conscience mechanisms). Here we will consider ways in which we might influence the drives or urges. From our psychodynamic and neurophysiologic considerations, it is obvious that our best technique may be pharmacologic, particularly for the seizural or instinctual dyscontrols; but perhaps pharmacology may not be so effective in treating the secondary dyscontrols, that is, the premeditated ones which we have labeled impulse dyscontrol and acting out.

A fortuitous example of this is Patient F283. Despite many dyscontrol acts, this patient's behavior seemed primarily motivated, that is, the giving in to primitive, aggressive, sexual impulses as a rebellion against an overtstrict infantile conscience, rather than an overwhelming of conscience by excessive urges. In an offhand manner she reported that for many months she had had a strange, if transitory, experience. This was the sudden sensation of an all-pervasive smell that was decidedly unpleasant but lasting for only a few minutes and accompanied by a peculiar metallic taste. Because this sounded as though it might be an epileptic prodrome or aura, EEG studies were initiated and revealed a left temporal focus. She was given diphenylhydantoin (Dilantin) 0.1 gram t.i.d. and within a week the olfactory and gustatory sensations disappeared. There was also considerable amelioration in her impulsivity and less imperativeness to the underlying urges. It must be pointed out that she was simultaneously receiving psychotherapy, which undoubtedly played a part in her improvement, but the fact that there had been little improvement during the preceding months in therapy, and that there was rather sudden improvement on Dilantin, strongly suggests that the drug played a part in reducing her urges.

Generally, however, in patients showing impulse dyscontrol and acting out in which motivational factors are increasingly important, reducing the intensity or force of these motivations depends upon insight and working through (discussed below). Only in this way can the infantile needs be renounced and more realistic adult ones substituted in their place.

12.1.5 *Interpreting the act.* In impulse dyscontrol and acting out the overwhelming urges build up to a large extent because normal sublimated expression of such urges is seriously inhibited by neurotic anxiety. Reducing the urges requires developing a healthy everyday self-assertiveness, which is lacking because such assertiveness symbolically represents unacceptable intentions. It is particularly in these disorders that the old psychoanalytic dictum that the unconscious must be made conscious is appropriate. In impulse dyscontrol, the intention may be so thinly disguised that it needs little effort to bring it from the preconscious to the conscious level, but in acting out, repression is strong, and considerable skill in working through is necessary. One approach is to unmask the unacceptable intention, behind what should be just a mundane decision making or a spontaneous expression of feeling. When one discovers the unacceptable intentions leading to this neurotic inhibition in ordinary decision making, one also discovers the unacceptable intentions behind the acting out. This, of course, can be accomplished by searching for the meaning behind the disordered acts with all of its unconscious derivatives. The best way to discover these unconscious derivatives, however, is not to approach directly the content of the act itself, but to understand why the act in this particular situation was carried to completion, whereas usually actions are inhibited. Again, this is an effective way to circumvent resistances by revealing unique unconscious associations between the current situation and the repressed conflict, before the repressed conflict can be specifically identified either in the mind of the therapist or through interpretation in the mind of the patient.

Patient 102, for example, acted out through a sexual encounter which risked pregnancy. She was asked to consider the fact that she was usually sexually restrained; that she had had many such opportunities for extramarital affairs in the past, but that only in the current situation did she carry this through to completion. Why then at that moment was she able to act whereas in the past she had not? This brought up the question of anger toward her husband, who had recently been judged sterile and then rendered impotent by the discovery. But, as she realized, she had turned down other opportunities since this medical discovery. She considered the fact that as her therapist had been out of town at the time, she did not have to discuss the episode with him immediately, but again she remembered other encounters at times when he had been out of town, yet she had restrained herself. It suddenly occurred to her that the paramour was an older man who at one time had been her boss and mentor. These thoughts revived a series of associations first that a similar situation had formerly existed between her and her husband, and that she now maintained a similar attitude towards her therapist. The pieces of the puzzle then fell into place. She had been rejected by one father figure (her husband) who would not let her become mother, she had been deserted by a second, the therapist, who left on a trip as her own father often did (to travel with a paramour). The combined anxieties of these two desertions threw her into the arms of the third "father," the one who was available at the moment. Thus, the acting out represented a recapitulation of the adolescent experience of rejection by her father and further associations led to memories of a particularly sudden rejection by her father during the oedipal period when he precipitously discontinued his cuddling and physical fondling, probably because he recognized the sensuous intentions of his behavior.

In this situation important associational links were uncovered by first focusing on why the act was carried to completion in this situation and not in many other supposedly similar ones in the past. However, resolution of the potential for acting out does not occur with insight. It was only when the patient developed the capacity for normal sublimated expression of these urges, in this instance, a normal sexual assertiveness with her husband, seen not as a father but as a spouse after he had overcome his own impotency, that her potential for acting out was resolved.

Because it is so important to counteract the inhibitions in actions characteristic of the actor-outer and to a lesser extent those patients with impulse dyscontrol, prohibitions against acting out and impulsivity should be used sparingly. Otherwise therapy will only compound the problem. What one is trying to encourage is normal adult decisiveness carried through to an appropriate action. A period of disordered decisiveness or acting out may be inevitable as a prelude to this mature self-assertiveness (Levitt, 1959; Rosen, 1965). As Ekstein (1965) says, "acting out is an attempt to resolve the conflict." We might say that there is a need in psychotherapy not only for "working through" but for "acting through."

12.1.6 *Resisting manipulation.* Sooner or later, acting out is used by the patient in an attempt to manipulate the therapist. To minimize this, it is necessary that the therapist maintain his neutrality (Study Group on Acting Out, 1965). This does not mean the neutrality as often conceived by the analyst; that is, being merely a reflecting mirror, or an ambiguous nonentity, or even consistently opinionated. It does mean that the therapist must neither assume responsibility for the patient's behavior nor take a moral stand regarding the consequences. The profession of such neutrality is seen by the patient as a lack of concern on the part of the therapist, and the patient rightly does not really believe that the therapist can be so unfeeling about his patient's behavior. True unconcern would require a callousness and an indifference that would be disastrous for any effective therapy. However, the patient must realize that the concern of a therapist for the well-being of his patient, however strong it may be, is infinitesimally small compared with what should be the patient's own concern for his own behavior. It is part of the patient's narcissism to have difficulty in comprehending this relativity of involvement. As he is so preoccupied with his own inner needs, he assumes that everybody in his environment should be equally preoccupied with his (the patient's) needs.

> Patient S290 (Appendix 3) would withhold information about taking drugs for several sessions, then guiltily confess his transgression. At the onset of therapy he had been told that the therapist could not help if he continued to take drugs, and that it would defeat therapy if the therapist was responsible for policing him. Several times previously the patient had come to therapy obviously "high" on dexedrine. Neither the patient nor the therapist made any mention of this fact. In later sessions he would allude to the therapist's imperceptiveness and lack of competence for not recognizing his drug intoxication, which was countered by the therapist's: "You mean last Thursday you were on drugs and just because I didn't mention it, you thought that I was not aware of it." He was surprised and chagrined that it had been noticed and even more surprised that it had not been mentioned, but was reminded of the original statement regarding the matter. A further comment by the therapist was "if you want to take drugs, that is your decision. It does not matter to me. However, as I have already pointed out, you

are wasting your time much more than you are wasting mine. After all, I am still getting paid." This, of course, was designed to make him indignant and was successful in doing just that, the patient replying (with some truth) that he could not believe his therapist didn't care whether he got well or not. This opened the subject of who was responsible for what, and the relative importance of the therapist's obtaining a "cure" and the patient being "cured." It was in this way that the therapist was finally able to penetrate the patient's narcissism.

A related issue is that the therapist must convince the patient that the former's confidence and self-esteem as a therapist does not depend upon curing the patient. Almost invariably with the dyscontrol patient it eventually must be pointed out that between 20 and 30 percent of his patients do not improve. The therapist can add that he does not think the present treatment will be a failure, but if the patient wants to, he can bring about a treatment failure and all the therapist can do to prevent this is to point out what is happening. Such a forceful interpretation of areas of responsibility is the only way to counteract the narcissistic attitudes of the patient manifesting episodic dyscontrol. Insisting that the patient take responsibility for his dyscontrol acts is one of the most important ways to reduce manipulation. However, the control of manipulation is much more difficult in those episodic behavioral disorders that are more sustained, that is, characterized by disordered behavior which we have labeled episodic reactions. This, of course, is particularly true if the episodic reaction is an episodic psychotic reaction.

12.2 PSYCHOTHERAPY OF THE EPISODIC REACTIONS

12.2.1 *The question of hospitalization.* Much of what has been said previously about the treatment of episodic dyscontrol applies to the treatment of episodic reactions, inasmuch as the episodic reactions are usually characterized by a series of dyscontrol acts. If these acts are accompanied by a central integrative disorganization of psychotic proportions, the patient presents a particularly different problem. It is obvious that the therapist must be ready and able to hospitalize the patient immediately. However, these patients are notoriously afraid that this is what will happen. The therapist must develop a conviction in the patient that no matter what comes up during the therapeutic sessions nor how crazy it sounds, he will not hospitalize the patient just because he is "crazy." The therapist must demonstrate a sincere preference for outpatient treatment, as well as a willingness to take chances on individual dyscontrol acts which are at least potentially dangerous for the individual or society. When such potentially dangerous acts are repetitive and accompanied by marked delusional distortions or a severely altered level of awareness, a firm insistence on hospitalization becomes necessary even to the point of using legal commitment. No matter how irate the patient becomes at being treated this way, if hospitalization is not truly a rejection the firmness and rationality in handling the situation will be appreciated by the patient as he views it in retrospect; that is, if the therapist can maintain the therapeutic contact in the same manner as in the past, following remission of the episodic psychotic reaction. If at all possible, during the period of hospitalization the therapist should try to keep regular appointments in his own office, leaving hospital care and restrictions to hospital personnel.

> Patient S254, a thirty-year-old housewife, was, during the course of psychotherapy lasting over a period of four years at two sessions per week, separated and divorced from her husband. Her most characteristic symptoms were impulsive acts, accompanied by long periods of wavering and doubt as to whether she should give in to the impulse, usually of a sexual or masochistic nature. Often the resistance to the impulses took the form of bizarre symbolic acts. The acts were sometimes thinly disguised but highly symbolic oral, sexual, or masturbatory substitutes, or, at other times, masochistic self-mutilations or suicidal attempts. Periodically she became habituated to drugs, particularly dexedrine and she would take prodigious amounts (allegedly 1,000 5 mg.

tablets in a one month period). At these times she would develop a florid psychosis with hallucinations and illusions reflecting oral masochistic preoccupation (Monroe, 1947). For example, she developed the idea that her therapist would hospitalize her to experiment with brain surgery or electric shock; or, again, developed a fantasy and then a delusion, that she was a "basket case," hidden in her therapist's attic, into which he surreptitiously would sneak to feed and care for her. Of course, in such a situation, hospitalization was imperative. If the therapist interceded early enough, she would accept the necessity for hospitalization, but she would be considerably upset when the therapist turned over her care to the hospital personnel. Fortunately, the hospital was on the floor above the therapist's office, so that his regular scheduled appointments with her could be kept; that is, she was brought to his office for the usual session. In this way it was possible to demonstrate to her that she was not deserted, and that therapy would continue as before, but the hospitalization emphasized that she could not manipulate extra care and attention by inducing a toxic psychosis. No matter how irate she became during the height of her psychosis, when this remitted she would accept the manipulative aspects of her self-induced psychosis.

It is possible then for psychotic episodes, whether self-induced toxic states or others, to be used by the patient to manipulate therapy, but with proper anticipatory moves this can be minimized. For example, a late call from one's patient, who is obviously toxic or psychotic and threatening suicide, should not bring the therapist running (though if this were an endogenous depression, it might). If possible it should be handled by a phone call to the spouse, friend, or patient's local physician who has been properly warned about just such a situation, asking him to evaluate the patient and, if it became necessary, to call the ambulance and transfer the patient to the hospital.

The patient just referred to (S254) would also misuse barbiturates in an attempt to manipulate her therapy. During the periods of separation from her husband, she would take excessive amounts of drugs and then call her therapist in an acute toxic state as a thinly disguised mechanism to get him to her house hoping thereby to seduce him. Fortunately, her estranged husband, who had considerable psychological understanding and still retained a certain amount of good will toward his wife, had been alerted to this possibility and had agreed to rush to her side and take her to the hospital if necessary. In this way she was unable to manipulate her therapist. The situation, however, became complicated when they were divorced and the husband remarried. In anticipation of further toxic states, her local doctor, who lived in the neighborhood, was asked to take over this role (with the patient's permission during one of her more rational periods). However, unless such anticipatory consultations are arranged, calling the local physician late at night and asking him to see and care for your patient may convey to him that you are just shirking your medical responsibility for a few hours of untroubled sleep.

If the patient seems destined to require recurrent hospitalization, the hospital staff should be alerted and encouraged to take over complete control from the time of admission. Again it is important, if possible, to continue seeing the patient at the regularly scheduled appointment in the regular setting. The first statement the patient may make upon arriving at the therapist's office after such a hospitalization will be, "Have you talked with Dr. So-and-So about what is going on?" It is desirable to be able to say, "No, he offered to discuss it with me, but I told him I would prefer to hear it from you." In other words, your relation with the patient should be rigidly established and maintained. The flexibility suggested above regarding the treatment technique then does not apply to appointment schedules and therapeutic setting. Here rigidity is the word if manipulation is to be controlled. As the manipulations fail, the patient becomes more and more enraged, hence there is a temporary increase in dyscontrol acts. At some point this anger inevitably reaches such a pitch of derogation directed towards the therapist and his attitudes that one can only suggest a consultation, pointing out to the patient that, as the therapist, you are convinced that your program is the best and that you are going to stick with it, but if in the opinion of a consultant it is felt to be undesirable, you, with the consultant, will arrange for another therapist. The point is to do this so that the patient neither feels deserted nor that he must save face by deserting you. If the situation is handled properly, the worst that happens is that he does seek consultation with a colleague who reassures the patient that he should continue his present therapy. After the rage has subsided the patient will try to let the matter drop, a behavior pattern which we have already noted is more common when motivational factors play a part in the episodic disorders. It is precisely in these patients, however, that the need for reflection on what has happened is imperative. It is only through this confrontation during periods of remission that insight is developed regarding the manipulative aspects of dyscontrol acts.

Patient S219 is one for whom this maneuver was repeatedly necessary. As her family was supporting therapy, she would incite them by describing in many vivid and distorted ways the therapist's incompetence. In anticipation of such maneuvers, the family had already been alerted to such a possibility, but even so the family had to be called in (with the patient present) so that the matter could be worked out. Twice, referral to consultants was necessary (if possible one of the patient's own choosing). Each time adroit handling by the consultant led to the patient's return to her therapist. Another favorite trick of this patient during such periods was to telephone the resident on call at the hospital where her therapist was director of the residency training program, a situation the patient was well aware of. She would vividly and in a distorted way describe what an imbecile her therapist was (much to the delight of the residents). This required detailed discussion with the residents on call regarding the therapeutic problems involved. Thus alerted, they handled the situation with tact and understanding as they knew that they were being intimately involved in the therapeutic program of one of their mentors.

12.2.2 *Episodic disorders in the hospital setting.* **Within the** hospital the handling of episodic disorders is particularly difficult because the dyscontrol acts irritate the personnel, so many people being involved that at least some will react with retaliatory counteraction. Whenever possible, controls should come through the group pressure of peers. Many of the proposals suggested by MacDonald (1965) for controlling the acting out of hospitalized sociopaths are equally applicable to the hospitalized patients with episodic psychotic reactions. In summary these proposals are: (1) set as few limits as possible, and certainly set no limits that cannot be rigorously enforced; (2) clearly define limits, avoiding any possible ambiguity which would be exploited in the manipulation; (3) punish limit-breaking promptly; (4) give sound reasons for the limits set; (5) the therapist should back all rules. I would also add that if mistakes in enforcing such a regimen have been made and the patient has been mishandled or treated unfairly, admit the mistake immediately without apology, focusing on the fact that the patient's acting out behavior invites such mistakes.

However adroitly acting out is handled in both the episodic psychotic and sociopathic reactions, such a regimen will arouse chronic resentment, eliciting all the defensive maneuvers of projection and rationalization. The best way to counteract such defenses is through group pressures, the group itself consisting of other patients subjected to the same regulations. Only when the patient realizes that his behavior elicits counteraction among his peers will his dyscontrol acts become ego-alien.

Patient O264, described in more detail elsewhere, is an example of this. A fifteen-year-old adolescent in a hospital with an open door policy, he would repeatedly run away until the doors had to be locked to keep him in. This meant that the other patients who wished to leave the ward had to find a nurse or an attendant to open the door for them. During the daily ward meetings they expressed their resentment over this inconvenience precipitated by the patient, yet agreed that as long as he acted as he did it was necessary. Because of this he was promptly ostracized by the group. Finally through these pressures his impulsive behavior was restrained.

The episodic hypochondriacal reaction and physiological reaction present particular problems of medical management concurent with psychotherapy. For these patients the services of an internist may be absolutely essential, but this raises all the problems of medical responsibility divided between two different specialists. As this type of reaction is sometimes also associated with abnormal EEG's, particularly 14 and 6 per second positive spikes, the treatment team may be complicated by the troika of internist, neurologist, and psychiatrist. If at all possible, after a preliminary medical and neurological investigation at the begining of treatment, it is best to leave the decisions regarding future consultations up to the primary therapist (usually the psychiatrist), who will then ask any cooperating internist or neurologist to leave the interpretation of the consultation finding as well as control of medication to the psychiatrist. Only in this way can the manipulative elements on the part of the patient be kept to a minimum.

12.3 Psychological Problems in Combined Somatic Therapy and Psychotherapy

12.3.1 *Interpersonal model for therapy.* An outstanding problem in psychotherapy is convincing the patient that he must assume personal responsibility for his actions and, for that matter, for the outcome of therapy itself. The usual doctor-patient model then is not particularly appropriate for the psychiatrist-patient relationship in insight psychotherapy (Monroe, 1951, 1960b, 1967c). In the conventional doctor-patient relationship the patient's expectation is that, if he follows a few simple directions (e.g. takes an antibiotic four times a day), the miracles of modern medicine will lead to a cure without further effort on his part. A similar expectation of magic is at least implicit in all patients seeking psychotherapy; in fact, sometimes it is even explicitly verbalized. The fact that during the course of treatment the patient is not yet well indicates that the doctor is still withholding the largess of health, until the patient in some fashion discovers and obediently meets the doctor's needs. The patient's goals become the discovery of what the therapist expects and the attempt to adhere to these expectations as the price for effortless health and happiness.

To circumvent this, the therapist can suggest to the patient that a more appropriate psychotherapeutic analogy would be the pupil-teacher model, particularly the piano pupil-piano teacher relationship: the therapist, like the piano teacher, can show the way, but only through hard work and practice will the patient be able to lead a more productive life. The difficulties of relying on such a model become obvious if the treatment regimen includes simultaneously both reeducational insight psychotherapy and drugs (Monroe, 1960c).

12.3.2 *Team approach or consultants.* The most common solution proposed for this dilemma has been a team approach, utilizing the skills of both the neurologist and psychiatrist (Chafetz, 1959). As has been pointed out, such a dual therapeutic responsibility is complicated by manipulative tendencies of patients with episodic dyscontrol. This is a problem even when both therapists are oriented toward a motivational, reeducational program, such as a team approach to family therapy (Weiss, 1959). It is difficult, not only because the patient can manipulate his various therapists, but also because even the more mature therapists become competitive with each other regarding their respective patients or techniques. This is more obvious (and therefore in some ways less malignant) when the neurologist or internist and the psychiatrist are simultaneously treating the patient as each is covertly or even overtly disparaging the therapeutic techniques of the other.

For this reason one or the other specialist should assume primary responsibility for therapy. This means that if the psychiatrist is to do this, he must be well informed regarding the somatic therapy of epilepsy; or if a neurologist is to assume primary responsibility, he must be equally adept at insight psychotherapy. In the present age of specialization, it is hard to find individuals who have competence in both fields, and adequate therapy may have to be augmented by consultation between specialists. The ideal situation is for the consultation to involve the treating physician and his complementary specialist without even the knowledge or involvement of the patient. At times this may be impossible. If the psychiatrist is pushing medication to the point of toxicity, it may require the skills of the neurologist to determine whether new symptoms are the result of pharmacologic toxicity or are an epileptoid reaction. When the patient becomes directly involved in a consultation, it is imperative that the therapist, not the consultant, translate the consultant's findings. With this emphasis on the single therapist, the patient is not subjected to dual, often incompatible messages, nor will he have the chance to play one therapist against the other. There may be exceptionally compatible "teams" where such dual responsibility can be carried out without contradictory communication but these are rare (Chafetz, 1959). Patient S218 (Appendix 8) affords an extreme example of the complications that arise with multiple therapists.

12.3.3 *Drugs or insight.* There is an inherent dual message whenever insight therapy and drug therapy are combined. The polarities and possible attitudes of patients under such a combined regimen are, on one hand, that the pill will solve all the problems, so why bother with the tedious long-term reeducational process; and, at the other extreme, that the therapist is not really interested in the patient's problems and therefore is trying to find an easy shortcut by administering pills. If a therapist rather consistently finds his patients adopting one or the other attitude, he should suspect that he himself is reinforcing this attitude and take steps to correct this within himself (Monroe, 1960c).

A useful way to present this "double barrel" approach, and one that should have meaning within the schematic framework utilized in this volume, is to suggest to the patient that the therapy will mainly rely on relearning and reeducation, but that that learning is impossible if affects such as fear, anger, rage, or depression are so intense as to overwhelm reason. We then utilize the drugs to reduce these tensions to a degree compatible with a rational understanding of why these episodically recurring, intense affects occur. The query the patient will usually make is: "but if these intense affects are the result of something misfiring in my brain, why will not medication be sufficient?" The only answer one can give to this is that our present state of knowledge is such that we do not know which comes first, whether it is the learned pattern of intense affective arousal which causes the abnormal firing or the abnormal firing that initiates the intense affect. We can only reassure the patient that, should one or the other prove sufficient, this double barrel approach will be dropped. The therapist must be convincing in clearly indicating to the patient that he is not an exclusive devotee of either the somatic or psychic form of therapy. Unfortunately, this is a position that not many psychiatrists maintain, most finding it more comfortable to be extremists, relying either on drugs or psychotherapy alone, but seldom on both together.

In terms of the phenomenological characteristics of the episodic dyscontrol, as the patients approach one pole (epileptoid) or the other (motivational), it may be worthwhile, rather than using the double barrel approach, to start out with a commitment to one or the other regimen, that is, either somatic or insight psychotherapy respectively. However, the possibility that the combined approaches might become necessary should be kept in mind, and the patient informed of this at the start of treatment so that he will be prepared for a broadening of the therapeutic regimen if this ultimately proves desirable. Such an anticipatory orientation for the patient is important because innovations during the course of therapy may well be disconcerting, the usual implication being that therapy is not proceeding well, or even failing, so that the physician is now desperately trying another regimen.

Patient F283 is a case in point. When suddenly epileptoid symptoms were discovered as well as an abnormal EEG, she wondered whether all her problems might magically disappear with medication. She soon realized that, even with better control of her impulses, a healthy adjustment depended upon continuing insight psychotherapy, as it could now be seen that she incited acute emotional upsets which then precipitated the epileptoid symptoms. What was crucial for her ultimate rehabilitation was an understanding of why she incited the "riots." Later, as her behavior improved, anticonvulsant medication proved unnecessary.

If one initiates therapy with this 'double barrel' approach, it is not always easy to ascertain whether both therapeutic regimens are truly necessary. A consideration of the episodic character of the disorder under discussion should make it obvious that only with an extended period of observation can one be reasonably certain. The very intermittent quality of the disordered behavior means that it is impossible to evaluate the progress of therapy, except by long-term effects. If with the start of medication there is dramatic improvement in behavior, this is not the time to discontinue psychotherapy or reduce the frequency of contact, even more intense scrutiny, and particularly contact with other significant individuals in the patient's environment, may be required. Any improvement, of course, means a change in the adaptive patterns not only in the patient but in the family with whom he lives. Even though such improvement can be viewed as health by the physician, it may increase conflicts for the patient or put a strain on the family who have adapted to, or even secondarily exploited the patient's illness as a solution to other problems. Patient F287 and the patient described below, are examples of this.

> Patient F285, the identical twin already reported in the literature by Raher (1963) and mentioned previously, is illustrative of this point. His illness held the family together; that is, kept mother and father from separating, and his sister and twin brother from marrying. Some improvement in his symptoms and discharge from the hospital made possible an estrangement between parents as well as his sister's and brother's marriages. Despite heroic efforts to compensate for these "desertions" the patient became more and more depressed, and ultimately committed suicide.

The possibility that the response to medication is a placebo effect is almost impossible to rule out, except by statistical studies of large groups of subjects, and even such studies of episodic behavioral disorders are difficult to document. In the individual patient, a regimen to try to establish possible placebo effects may be unwarranted, and lack of realistically appearing placebos usually makes it impossible, even when otherwise it might be practicable. To the patient it is probably sufficient to say, "who cares as long as the medication has helped you?" (and as long as the drugs are relatively benign and inexpensive).

12.3.4 *Habituation to drugs.* We have included examples where even drugs with a proven pharmacological value had to be spurned for specific psychological or environmental reasons (e.g., Patient F287). Eight of our 70 adult patients abused drugs by either becoming habituated or at least periodically taking them in excessive amounts. There are two considerations then which usually lead to a decision to withhold drug therapy. In the episodic disorders there is usually some altered awareness. If the patient is on a regimen of self-medication, such periods of confusion may be periods when the patient either stops medication (Patient 523) or takes excessive medication (Patient S218). Sometimes this complication can be circumvented by having another person dispense the medication, but this in itself introduces further psychological problems. To further confuse the issue, we have noted that the altered consciousness which occurs during the episodic reactions has many of the characteristics of an exogenous toxic psychosis, so that if the patient is examined during an acute episode, unless specific biochemical tests are made, it may be impossible to determine whether he had had too much or too little medication (Patient S218).

Closely related to the above is the additional problem that the basic orality which, as we pointed out in Chapter 8, seems to be particularly intense in precisely those patients with "specific" EEG abnormalities; hence those for whom anticonvulsants might be used are the very patients who are likely to become habituated to pills. The episodic quality of the illness, with frequent dysphoric prodromals which can be reduced by drugs, add to the problem. There develops an attitude that, if one pill helps, ten will have miraculous effects (Patient F287). In this way patients may become addicted to alcohol (Patient F250), amphetamine (Patients S254 and S290), and barbiturates (Patient F287). In many instances the point is reached at which all pill-taking has to be discontinued, ideally at a time when the patient himself is convinced that his behavior cannot be controlled otherwise (Patients S254 and F287). When such a decision is reached, it is still not easy to carry it out; usually hospitalization with an externally enforced control over medication is required. This is necessary because, by the time the patients seek help from the psychiatrist, they have usually developed sources for drugs which are beyond prescription control. Once therapy has returned to an outpatient regimen, the therapist is immediately defeated if he becomes the policeman, or if taking or not taking the drug becomes the focus of the psychotherapeutic session. Early in therapy, an anticipatory intervention must be made wherein the therapist convinces the patient that whatever he can contribute to the patient's improvement will be negated by the illicit use of drugs. When the patient guiltily confesses to such a transgression, the therapist must again emphasize that he is not going to prohibit drug-taking, but only reiterate the position that the patient is defeating therapy by taking medication outside of medical control. Whether the patient takes drugs or not is up to him. The therapist must however, focus on the childish rebelliousness and the guilty, obsequious behavior in reporting the transgression. In fact, as has already been pointed out, it is best not even to mention the use of drugs even when the patient appears for a therapeutic session obviously toxic. Again, in an anticipatory way it should have been arranged early in therapy that when the patient is in a toxic condition, a reliable and significant person in his environment can be called to take control and arrange for hospitalization, if necessary. The usual response of the patient is to insist angrily that his behavior is not due to drug toxicity. The therapist should refuse to become involved in this issue, not even trying to find out whether toxicity was established by laboratory studies. This is another example of trying to maintain therapeutic neutrality and placing responsibility on the patient alone for his behavior (Levitt, 1959).

Some of the unique therapeutic problems of treating episodic behavioral disorders have been discussed in the individual histories (see Appendixes). It should be obvious from the discussion that this is a particularly difficult group of patients, requiring the therapist, if he is to be successful, to take hair-raising chances. What further complicates the issue is that the therapist not only forces the patient to take responsibility for his own behavior, but also, during the period before controls are established, he must rely on outside controls supplied by a spouse, medical physician, or other psychiatrists. These individuals must assume responsibilities which on the surface would seem to belong to the treating psychiatrist. This means that one must anticipate the difficulties and make a special effort to clarify for these "adjunct" therapists why you have delegated these responsibilities. Otherwise it will appear to family and colleagues alike that you, as the patient's therapist, are shirking your medical responsibility. In these arrangements, as well as the technique within the therapeutic setting itself, the essence of treating the episodic disorders is anticipation of future difficulties, which are discussed during the rational periods between episodes. A corollary of this is to discuss retrospectively the dyscontrol acts when the patient has regained his equilibrium after the dyscontrol period has terminated, even though many patients will try to avoid such confrontation.

What makes these patients most worrisome to the psychiatrist is that dyscontrol acts may involve criticism of the therapist in the community at large, because the patient so misrepresents therapy that it sounds unethical to the point of malpractice. To withstand this requires an unusual degree of equanimity and self-confidence on the part of the therapist, as well as an impeccable reputation. The rewards are that this group of patients, no matter how unendearing, desperately need help and in the long run are most grateful for the results (as are friends and relatives). Seeing the problem through to the end usually leads to an excellent result. The fact that the disorders are episodic means that there are intervals when the patient can objectively reflect on his disordered behavior, a "split in the ego" which is necessary for all insight psychotherapy.

13 Summary

During the course of human development, the interaction of the human organism with the external environment elicits an increasingly complex repertoire of behavioral responses, some successful, others not. Through this trial and error, aided by parental guidance and social attitudes, the child learns that certain behavior patterns are more successful than others, that is, more likely to be rewarded or reinforced or are effective in avoiding pain or punishment. Such patterns tend to be repetitively utilized in similar or related situations until for most individuals a repeated response pattern becomes established. Rado (1956) has designated this as "established mechanisms of psychological adaptation." This gives an individual his unique "personality" or "character," and provides coherency and predictability to his "life style." Thus, close associates can usually predict how an individual will respond in a given situation. These established mechanisms of psychological adaptation are coherent and consistent whether adaptive (healthy or normal) or maladaptive (disordered behavior, e.g., neurosis, psychosis).

Some acts or behavior patterns, however, are unexpected; they abruptly interrupt or deviate from the individual's "life style" and therefore appear out of character. Certain "spontaneous" acts can be highly adaptive, such as the unique contributions of a genius or of the "man of action." More often, however, abrupt, precipitous acts that interrupt the individual's life style and life flow are either self or socially destructive. These are actions based on primitive emotions of fear, rage, or sensuous feelings, without concern for the effect on the immediate environment or the long-term consequences to the actor or to society. At the other extreme, the abrupt maladaptive responses may be sudden inhibitions of action when action is necessary. We have designated both such responses as episodic behavioral disorders, defined as precipitously appearing, maladaptive behavior that interrupts the life style and life flow of the individual. It is out of character for the individual and out of context for the situation.

The raison d'être for the book is that, although such behavior is widely recognized by psychiatrists, there has been no systematic classification of this behavior and no recognition of it in the official psychiatric nomenclature. This is even more surprising considering that the intermittent, abrupt, and precipitous quality of the disordered behavior must have specific etiologic, dynamic, and therapeutic implications. That such behavior is often antisocial, leading to sadistic and bizarre crimes, and at the same time is unpredictable underlines its unusually important social implications. A notorious failure has been our inability to identify and intercept the Oswalds, Rubys, Specks, Whitmans, Rays, Sirhans in our society. This monograph, I hope, is a step towards making such predictions possible.

We proceeded to classify these episodic behavioral disorders at the phenomenological (descriptive) level, hoping that such a classification would also have meaning at the dynamic, developmental, and neurophysiologic levels. We have already mentioned that there are two large subgroups of episodic behavioral disorders. One, inhibitory (in the sense of inhibition of motor response to an environmental stimulus) and the other disinhibitory, or an uninhibited response in the same sense. The former, which is represented by what we clinically label as narcolepsy, catalepsy, akinetic mutism, periodic catatonia, or petit mal status, was not systematically investigated in this monograph, but was discussed only to contrast it with the episodic disinhibitions.

Our attention focused on two subclassifications of the episodic disinhibitions which we designated as (1) episodic dyscontrol and

(2) episodic reactions (summarized in Fig. 1). In episodic dyscontrol, the interruption in life style and life flow was represented by an abrupt single act or short series of acts with a common intention, carried through to completion with either relief of tension or gratification of a specific need. Such terms as *acting on impulse, impulsivity, impulse neurosis, irresistible impulse,* and *acting out* have been applied to such behavior. The other subgroup, the episodic reactions, are more sustained interruptions in the life style and life flow, often characterized by multiple dyscontrol acts with varied intentions as well as other symptoms of a neurotic, psychotic, sociopathic, or physiologic nature. Episodic reactions and episodic dyscontrol have in common the precipitous onset and the equally abrupt disappearance of the disordered behavior which is qualitatively different from the established mechanisms of psychological adaptation. Most frequently the episodic reactions have been identified among schizophrenics, and variously, but inconsistently, referred to as "remitting" or "reactive" schizophrenia or oneirophrenia if the clouding of sensorium is a significant symptom.

We clearly distinguished between the episodic behavioral disorders and those disordered behavioral reactions that represent a waxing or waning of the established patterns of psychological adaptation. The latter would not be an episodic behavioral disorder because there is no true interruption in the life style or life flow. We pointed out, however, that even during the intervals of remission or quiescence of episodic behavioral disorders, the more persisting behavior patterns may be so severely disordered that the diagnosis of episodic dyscontrol or episodic reaction, though clinically important (and perhaps responsible for psychiatric hospitalization), should be a secondary diagnosis.

Much of our attention was focused on the episodic dyscontrol group of disorders. It seemed valuable to distinguish four hierarchial levels of dyscontrol acts ranging from the simplest and most primitive to the highest organized response: seizure, instinct, impulse dyscontrol, and, at the highest level, acting out. These hierarchial levels were determined by: (1) the level of differentiation in the instinctual drives or urges expressed; (2)

the co-ordination and complexity of the motor response; (3) and the specificity of the motivation or goals of the act (summarized in Fig. 2).

At the dynamic level, three considerations seemed to have the most heuristic value. The simplest statement that can be made regarding the dyscontrol acts is that "urges overwhelm controls," but this statement has little operational value unless we have some way of determining where an individual falls between the extremes of excessively strong urges overwhelming normal control mechanisms, and normal urges uncontrolled by weak or deficient inhibiting mechanisms.

The second dynamic consideration is whether the act was ego-alien or ego-syntonic. By our very definition of episodic dyscontrol it is obvious that during the act itself the behavior is ego-syntonic in that it is abrupt—often an explosively quick act carried through to completion, with relief of tension or need gratification, without any wavering or doubt. However, we pointed out that often even the actor himself retrospectively sees the act as ego-alien. When this is the case, we designate the behavior as seizural acts, instinctual acts, impulsive acts, or acting out at our four hierarchial levels. In other instances, responsibility for the dyscontrol act is defensively denied (e.g., amnesias), projected, or rationalized so that one can only assume the behavior is recognized as ego-alien at some level (usually unconscious). In such instances, the dyscontrol acts were designated at the four hierarchial levels as seizure, instinct, impulse, and acting out neurosis. Lastly, there are a few patients who are completely unconcerned by the dyscontrol acts, no matter how much anguish such acts cause in others. In these instances, the acts are truly ego-syntonic, both at the time and in retrospect. If such acts are also episodic (and not just a way of life), we designate them at the four hierarchial levels as seizure, instinct, impulse, and acting-out disorders. The "dyscontrol way of life" would not be categorized as episodic, because the dyscontrol acts are persisting patterns and not an abrupt interruption in the life style and life flow of the individual. It is this last group of individuals, with a dyscontrol way of life, who truly demonstrate "an alloplastic readiness to act." Sometimes such a dyscontrol way of life may have the appearance of episodic dyscontrol, but closer scrutiny reveals it as a waxing and waning of a persisting pattern, the intermittent quality representing need arousal alternating with satiation.

A third dynamic consideration was an attempt to identify more clearly and describe what has been called the "short circuit" between the stimulus and response. It is this short circuit, or action without premeditation, that supposedly results in the maladaptive quality of the impulsive act. But this is not necessarily so. First, there are spontaneous acts with little or no delay between the stimulus and the response, in which the behavior is adaptive. These are situations where snap judgments are required, a characterization of the man of action, often the leader in our society. Second, we noted precipitous maladaptive acts which, however abrupt they appear on the surface are revealed by dynamic considerations to have occurred only after considerable premeditation. Sometimes this premeditation is conscious, with much wavering and doubt during a period of mounting tension, as well as conscious attempts, often bizarre, to resist the impulse. This has usually been called "irresistible impulse," but we have designated such behavior as impulse dyscontrol. We also presume that such premeditation occurs in acting out, but at the unconscious level. We define acting out as a dyscontrol act so patently inappropriate to the situation, so out of character for the actor, and so inadequately explained by the actor, one can only conclude that the act is largely determined by unconscious motives to solve repressed conflicts, rather than a response to a realistic evaluation of the eliciting situation. In both these instances, rather than an "alloplastic readiness to act," we find that such patients demonstrate what could be characterized as a neurotic inhibition of action. The dyscontrol acts, when we can identify this conscious premeditation (impulse dyscontrol) or unconscious premeditation (acting out), are as a group designated *secondary dyscontrol*.

In the two lower hierarchial levels of episodic dyscontrol (seizure and instinct dyscontrol) we find a true "short circuit" between the impulse and the act. These we have designated *primary dyscontrol* (see Fig. 2). In analyzing the "act as a unit" (Fig. 15), we identified two types of, or perhaps two facets to, this delay between the impulse and the act. The first we designated *reflective* delay (often referred to in the psychoanalytic literature as "thought as trial action"); that is, the time necessary for establishing the uniqueness or familiarity of the external reality by associative connections with past experience; the time necessary to contemplate a series of alternative courses of action; the time necessary to project into the future and predict the outcome of these alternative actions. This we differentiated from *choice* delay, which would follow reflective delay and be a decision to postpone immediate gratification for long-term rewards, "biding one's time." There are groups of disorders in which, even though reflective delay takes place, choice delay is inappropriately used. The extractive individual who gives in to his urges for immediate gratification, consequences be damned (even though there may have been careful appraisal of the situation and a realization of the long-term consequences), has often been labeled an acter-outer, but by our definition he would not exemplify episodic dyscontrol. To fit our definition, the reflective delay either must be absent (with the associated absence of choice delay) as occurs in the primary dyscontrols (seizure and instinct dyscontrol), or the reflective delay must be severely distorted, as in the secondary dyscontrols (impulse dyscontrol and acting out). The calculating narcissistic psychopath, then, would not exemplify episodic dyscontrol.

Reflective delay (hence also choice delay) depends upon a complex interaction between affects, hindsight and foresight, reason, discrimination, and appropriate generalization, as well as conscience mechanisms. To reiterate, if any one of these is significantly deficient or inappropriately intense or dominant, the whole process fails and there is an absence of reflective delay (primary dyscontrol). On the other hand, if the reflective delay is not absent but distorted by an inappropriately harsh conscience mechanism the acts may occur equally abruptly but only after a period of premeditation. These premeditated but precipitous acts we have called secondary dyscontrol.

Of the primary dyscontrols the two hierarchial levels were differentiated as follows: in seizure dyscontrol, the act is characterized by intense indiscriminate affects; chaotic and uncoordinated motor patterns; the object acted upon indiscriminately selected, often the person closest at hand. There seems to be little specific need gratification although there is usually tension reduction. We also suggested that the intention is completely lost and the effectiveness of the act so limited that seizure dyscontrol at times is used defensively to abort the higher level responses where the intentions are obvious but at the same time unacceptable.

In the higher level of primary dyscontrol (instinct dyscontrol) the affects are more clearly differentiated and expressed (e.g., fear, rage, sexuality); the motor pattern, although lacking in subtleness, is nevertheless efficient and coordinated; the object acted upon has at least a simple associative link with past experiences and therefore is selected somewhat appropriately. The completion of the act more likely results in specific need gratification rather than just diffuse tension discharge. What is common to seizure dyscontrol and instinct dyscontrol, but differentiates the two primary dyscontrol acts from secondary dyscontrol, is the true lack of reflective delay; thus primary dyscontrol is characterized by inhibited reflection and disinhibited action, whereas in secondary dyscontrol the reverse is true: there is excessive reflection and generally inhibited action (except during the dyscontrol act itself). This is summarized in Fig. 2.

The capacity of the human organism to respond appropriately to the demands of the environment depends upon two factors—the individual's endowment or the functional integrity of the "equipment" he possesses, and the appropriateness and extent of his learned behavior. If he responds maladaptively, we would like to be able to assess how much of such behavior is due to "faulty equipment," and how much is due to "faulty learning." A significant portion of this book was devoted to the criteria by which we can make such an evaluation, since this is necessary if we are to make an accurate prognosis and effective therapeutic plans. We presented clinical material, suggesting that many of the primary dyscontrol patients had clinical histories of typical epilepsy, such as grand mal, petit mal, or simple automatisms. Similarly, we presented data demonstrating that some of the episodic dyscontrols at all hierarchic levels were associated with EEG abnormalities presumed to reflect (or be associated with) excessive neuronal discharges even though typical epileptic seizures were not prominent symptoms. Finally, although occasionally we see an inverse relationship between episodic behavior disorders and typical epileptic seizures, equally often, if the seizures are controlled by anticonvulsant medication or surgery, so are the other dyscontrol acts. Nevertheless we have no reliable clinical measure of this neurophysiologic deficit although certain EEG activation procedures may increase the validity of our tests for this deficit.

We suggested that certain phenomenological characteristics would give us clues regarding the contribution of "faulty equipment" and "faulty learning" to the etiologic mechanisms of episodic dyscontrol. We suggested that epileptoid mechanisms played an increasingly significant role if the dyscontrol acts were primitive and diffuse (primary dyscontrol), the eliciting situation neutral or ambiguous, and the secondary gains slight or absent. The complexities of coming to such conclusions on the basis of clinical data were discussed in detail. Another distinguishing factor is that the disparity between the hierarchic level of dyscontrol behavior and the behavior between episodes is greatest in the epileptoid patient. But the most important single criterion we discovered for determining the importance of epileptoid versus motivational factors is a careful evaluation of the perceptive-apperceptive capacity of the organism at the time of the act itself. Such capacity must be impaired in all disordered behavior, but we suggested that there is a difference in impairment in the epileptoid and motivated episodic dyscontrol that is far more subtle than the usual differential symptoms between the "brain syndrome" and "functional psychiatric disorder"; that is, the presence or absence of clouded sensorium. The epileptoid patient is more likely to have partial recall during the episodic behavior (except for the precise duration of the grand mal seizure or simple automatism) than is the motivated (so-called hysterical) patient. The epileptoid patient is more likely to accept responsibility for his behavior than the motivated patient, perhaps because in the latter the unconscious intentions of the act need to be denied. The result is that the epileptoid patient is likely to feel the behavior as "driven"; he is perplexed by both the quality and intensity of the act; and he is more willing to be confronted with his behavior in the hope of excising the "foreign body." In other words, he is more willing to accept the act as ego-alien.

We reviewed the kind of neurophysiologic and psychologic data, either reported in the literature or culled from the patients we studied, which would increase our understanding of the episodic behavioral disorders. The following generalizations seemed reasonable inferences.

1. Excessive neuronal discharges can occur in subcortical areas without any reflection in the routine scalp recordings. Also, typical epileptic behavior can occur in proven epileptics with known neuropathophysiologic dysfunction, without abnormalities occurring in the scalp recordings during either the aura, ictal response itself, or postictal period. Thus, the routine scalp EEG is no absolute measure of whether epileptoid phenomena play a significant role in episodic dyscontrol or episodic reactions.

2. Excessive neuronal discharges in subcortical structures may be sustained for considerable periods without spread to the cortex and without typical epileptic behavior. Often such limited excessive neuronal discharges are accompanied by marked behavioral changes, not usually identified as epilepsy, such as dysphoria, depression, mounting irritability, slight altered levels of awareness or consciousness, impulsivity, depersonalizations, and overt hallucinations or delusions. A common characteristic of the behavior concomitant with the excessive neuronal discharge (what has been called "partial epilepsy") and that of the typical epileptic seizures of a centrencephalic or temporal lobe epilepsy, is the precipitous onset and equally precipitous remission of the symptoms.

3. Activation procedures seem to offer a reasonable technique for reducing the number of false negative findings on the EEG without excessively increasing the incidence of false positives. Although this is probably true of many activating techniques, we

used alpha chloralose which, despite some disadvantages, has the one outstanding advantage of being almost universally accepted by the patient. Most activating drugs elicit some characteristic nonspecific toxic effect on the EEG which is easily recognized and differentiated from "positive activation." The positive activation is limited to two types of responses. The first pattern is "specific," that is, the focal appearance of hypersynchrony and/or slow waves, or a typical generalized pattern of centrencephalic epilepsy. If such a pattern occurs in the resting baseline record, it is augmented by the activation procedure. If the patient has a history of typical epileptic seizures but has a normal resting EEG, activation is likely to elicit a pattern compatible with the diagnosis. We found in this study that if the patient has primary dyscontrol episodes; that is the lower hierarchial levels of episodic dyscontrol, this "specific" activation pattern is more likely to appear.

The second type of EEG pattern, labeled an "aspecific" response, is characterized by high amplitude, paroxysmal slow waves (3–7/sec.) that are bilaterally synchronous and may or may not be intermixed with hypersynchronous wave forms in the same distribution. According to the literature, the prevalence of such patterns is high in uncomplicated epilepsy; and according to our findings, it is almost equally high in patients showing episodic behavioral disorders if there is other evidence suggesting the possibility of significant epileptoid mechanisms at the phenomenological level. This pattern occurs in 20 percent of contrast groups without psychopathology and most of the patients who show this pattern as well as episodic dyscontrol or episodic reactions have a clear-cut history of a psychologically traumatic past. This underlines the fact that the pattern itself, whether reflecting a true propensity for excessive neuronal discharge, or alternatively what might be called a maturational lag, is not a sufficient cause of the episodic behavioral disorder. In other words, if an individual is destined to become neurotic, psychopathic, or psychotic, for whatever reason, the behavior is more likely to be episodic if there is accompanying central nervous system instability as revealed by this activated "aspecific" pattern. The fact that a group of patients who demonstrate acting out (which by our definition would suggest a predominance of motivational mechanisms), also show this "aspecific" response to activation, suggests that even in this group, central nervous system instability may play an important role in the mechanism behind the pathological acts.

4. EEG recordings during episodic psychotic reactions in patients with a history of epilepsy suggests that there are two types of epileptoid psychoses. One correlates with centrencephalic epilepsy, either petit mal status (children) or what appears to be a prolonged postictal response (adults) characterized by torpor, apathy, and confusion, with minimal hallucinations and delusions. A second type of psychotic reaction, more likely correlated with focal, particularly temporal lobe abnormalities, is characterized by more florid psychotic behavior with manic-depressive or schizophrenic symptoms and varying degrees of episodic dyscontrol with clouding of sensorium.

5. Many psychiatrists have separated schizophrenia into two groups—a chronic, insidiously developing, progressive disorder, and an acute, remitting psychosis with florid symptoms and intense affects. There is some indication that at least many of the latter are related to an epileptoid phenomenon; at least there is a high incidence of baseline EEG abnormalities and a low convulsive threshold reported for this group. It is also true that the activated "aspecific" pattern is a frequent finding. In this remitting group, there again seem to be two subgroups, the first in which clouding of sensorium is absent or minimal, psychological test data suggesting an "hysterical psychosis." In this group, EEG abnormalities, activated or otherwise, are rare. In the second group, although schizophrenic symptoms dominate, there is also significant clouding of sensorium and confusion, which would otherwise suggest an acute brain syndrome. This group in the past has been labeled oneirophrenia, but the importance of the so-called "organic" symptoms is underestimated, perhaps because no identifiable toxic agent could be found. It is this group of episodic psychotic reactions that appear to be predominantly epileptoid. We have chosen, therefore, to divide the episodic psychotic

reactions into three subgroups: episodic schizophrenic reactions, most often motivated; episodic acute brain syndromes, predominantly epileptoid; and finally, episodic depressive psychoses.

6. One finding suggests that in some patients epilepsy may be a precursor to schizophrenia, appearing, on the average, 14 years before overt signs of psychosis. Thus it is suggested that schizophrenia, particularly the paranoid type, may be a late sequela of some epilepsies. Our data suggest an alternative, but not entirely incompatible, hypothesis. We found a high incidence of covert schizophrenic thinking and paranoid projective mechanisms in epileptic patients who had shown no overt clinical symptoms of schizophrenia (a finding which was even more frequent than evidence of "organicity"). This suggests that the two disorders may occur simultaneously or concurrently, with the psychotic symptoms, not becoming clinically important until sometime after the epileptic symptoms.

7. Although, for dynamic reasons, we saw that there was sometimes an inverse relationship between seizures and episodic psychotic reactions, there is contradictory evidence of such an inverse relationship at the neurophysiologic level. What we can state unequivocally is that there is now overwhelming evidence that psychosis and epilepsy occur together far more often than pure chance would predict.

We also considered in some detail what genetic (in the psychoanalytic sense of developmental) factors seem to play a part in the subsequent appearance of episodic behavioral disorders.

1. In our own series of patients and in the literature, one of the most consistent findings has been the presence of excessive stimulation of the patient during early infancy and childhood; that is, the families of these patients were particularly unstable, showed explosive outbursts of rage and fear, or excessive, even bizarre, sexual stimulation of their child. Psychoanalysts have suggested that such overstimulation is particularly traumatic if it occurs at an age before the child is able to discharge the resulting tension through coordinated motor acts or substitute an indirect path of discharge through thought as trial action or other forms of sublimation.

2. We noticed an inverse relation between the dyscontrol acts and speech and fantasy, the patients prone to episodic dyscontrol having limited capacity for fantasy and meaningful introspection.

3. The "alloplastic readiness to act," which is supposedly characteristic of some form of episodic behavioral disorders, seems to be associated with a physically well-developed individual with an athletic habitus.

4. In children, the episodic dyscontrol occurs much more frequently in males than in females, but in adult patients the reverse appears to be true, at least for the episodic behavioral disorders with activated "aspecific" EEG abnormalities. Some data suggest that this is an artifact in that males manifesting episodic dyscontrol are more likely to end up in jail while females are hospitalized.

5. Excessive anxiety, depression, and sexual disturbances were a universal finding in the episodic behavioral disorders, but equally prevalent in the nonepisodic group. However, there are subtle qualitative differences in these affects, in that they are sudden in onset and disappearance, relatively short yet extremely intense, and without the conceptual elaboration or associational richness seen in the nonepisodic group. The psychoanalytic literature emphasizes the narcissism, oral dependency, and sado-masochism of the impulsive patient. These factors, at least as measured by projective tests, do not seem to be specific enough to distinguish the episodic from the nonepisodic patient, although we found that oral dependency and sado-masochism were much more frequent in those patients with specific EEG abnormalities and typical epilepsy.

6. There is a wide disparity between the clinical evaluation of hysterical character and evidence of it on projective tests, and a similar disparity between conversion as an issue for the clinician and conversion as a mechanism uncovered on the projective test. Our evaluation of this disparity is that the hysterical character is underestimated by the clinician in patients with baseline EEG abnormalities or other signs of epilepsy or organicity. On the other hand, conversion reactions as a diagnostic issue are overemphasized in the patients with seizures, psychiatrists seeing

atypical seizures as a conversion. It must be added, however, that conversions and epilepsy did exist simultaneously in a surprisingly large number of our patients.

7. Children with evidence of diffuse brain damage seemed more likely to manifest serious aggressive behavior. In our adult patients, however, it was not the organic or the epileptic patients who were more seriously aggressive, but those patients showing the "aspecific" response after activation; that is the paroxysmal, high amplitude, slow waves. There was clinical evidence that seizural dyscontrol protects against effective homicidal and suicidal dyscontrol acts, allowing for a discharge of tension through a disorganized, chaotic, socially ineffective motor response.

8. A number of other defenses were utilized to protect against the destructiveness toward self and others through dyscontrol acts. Some patients developed both obsessive-compulsive symptoms as well as obsessive character traits. Others seemed to handle any stimulating situation in a traumato-phobic manner, avoiding exposure to such situations. A group usually described as "shallow," "emotionally unstable," or "intolerant of frustration" handled their mounting urges by immediate discharge before they built up to a dangerous level. Another defense could be described as counterphobic; that is, inciting the environment or seeking excessive stimulation in order to have an excuse for a dyscontrol act. Episodic inhibitory reactions were another possible defense, immobilizing the patient but seeming to have the disadvantage of not allowing even a deflected discharge of tension. A surprisingly rare defense among our patients was a dissociative state, allowing for expression of urges with denial of responsibility. A much more common technique seemed to be retreat into the hospital with the inevitable externally imposed controls.

9. The "phase-specific" episodic dyscontrol of adolescents was dealt with only briefly, the literature emphasizing the importance of rebellion against passivity, renunciation of previous object choices, and the identity crises as important explanations for this type of dyscontrol behavior. We proposed one additional factor. This was the importance of the anticipation of the distant future in the development of both reflective and choice delay, so neces-

sary for the calculated volitional act. Just as this distant anticipation appears late phylogenetically, so it seems to appear late ontogenetically, probably not until late adolescence or early adulthood. We suggested that there might be great individual difference in this maturation and in turn the maturation might be reflected in the EEG by the immature irregular slow patterns.

10. The opinion was expressed that we psychiatrists often overemphasize the possibility of weak controls, at the same time overlooking the possibility that control mechanisms may be relatively intact, but the affects powerful and uncomfortable, leading to an imperative need for discharge. If such is the case, then therapy means reducing the intense affects. The considerable evidence that such intense affects are often the result of "excessive neuronal discharge" emphasizes the importance of combined pharmacologic and psychologic therapy.

The heuristic value of these considerations depends upon whether such a framework aids in planning an effective therapeutic regimen in a group of patients who have presented particularly difficult therapeutic problems. What are some of these difficulties? The primary one is that, although these patients episodically may be seriously dangerous to both themselves and society, there are relatively long periods of quiescence or normalcy. This makes the recourse of hospitalization to protect the patient and others unacceptable. The symptoms of these patients may, and often do, abate within a few days after hospitalization, and yet they may recur only a few days after discharge, even after months of intensive milieu therapy within the hospital. Outpatient therapy is further complicated by the tendency of this group to precipitously terminate therapy as a dyscontrol act, or to otherwise manipulate the therapist with their impulsive behavior. Another complication is that, with episodic physiologic reactions or an abnormal EEG, such patients frequently have multiple therapists, hence mutiple, often conflicting, therapeutic regimens. The corollary is that an adequate therapeutic program often requires combined pharmacologic and reeducational techniques; this complicates the delegation of responsibility for "change" between the various physicians on one hand, and the physician and the patient on the other. A striking problem is the patient's frequent misuse of drugs, frantically trying to control the dysphoric affects by popping pills into his mouth. This is further complicated by the basic oral dependency of many of these patients; habituation to drugs or alcohol, therefore, becomes a primary problem. At the same time episodic confusions, wherein the patient does not remember whether he took the drug, or does not remember to take it, complicate the medical regimen, particularly as toxic symptoms of drug overdose and the episodic symptoms themselves are often similar, and a differential diagnosis can be established firmly only by biochemical tests when this is possible.

It is an asset to therapy that such patients are usually intelligent and have long periods of relative rationality during which they can examine the episodic disturbances with realistic concern. Thus there is the "split in the ego" which is so necessary for any reeducational insight psychotherapy.

To treat such patients effectively, the therapist has to be willing to take chances. If he becomes overly concerned about his patient's behavior it can be used unmercifully to manipulate or sadistically punish the therapist. The second general prerequisite for effective therapy is to anticipate the type of dyscontrol acts and make preparatory plans (discussed with the patient) for handling such behavior when it occurs. This may require the aid of responsible peers or cooperating physicians. A third generalization is that, as soon as there is a quiescent period after an episodic act, the therapist should relentlessly confront the patient with his behavior, particularly those patients who are most reluctant to reconsider it. The fourth generalization is that the therapist must be willing to combine drug and reeducational techniques, but to withhold all medication, even though it might otherwise appear indicated, if the patient abuses it or threatens to become habituated. The fifth aspect of an effective therapeutic regimen requires the physician to be flexible within the therapeutic setting itself, so that dyscontrol acts will occur in the office and can be miscroscopically scrutinized by the patient and therapist together. This flexibility also includes conjoint sessions with the patient and significant peers, but the flexibility does not apply to the frequency, time, or setting of the therapeutic sessions. A schedule must be rigidly adhered to in a consistent manner if the therapist is to resist manipulation. Last, it is desirable, whenever possible, to have the total medical management the responsibility of one clinician, who may utilize consultants but who interprets the consultants' findings and dispenses the recommended medications himself.

There are other therapeutic recommendations, but being more specific, they have more exceptions. It is particularly important to develop a therapeutic motivation in those patients who lack it (dyscontrol disorders) by external 24-hour control of environment with immediate, inescapable punishment for failures and an equally immediate and appropriate reward for successes, with the hope that the frustration and anxieties caused by such treatment will instill an appropriate motivation for change. This can rarely be provided by the same individual who is responsible for the reeducational insight program.

One must establish some procedure for preventing acting out in the form of termination or avoidance of effective therapeutic sessions. To do this, one must insist that the sole responsibility for the patient's behavior lies with the patient himself, no matter what neurophysiologic deficits there may be, nor how capricious his environment.

One must develop insight by making the dyscontrol acts ego-alien and then understand the full implications of the act itself. Resistance can be minimized by first utilizing the patient's narcissism rather than confronting it head-on; this means not disparaging the patient's needs themselves, but focusing on alternative and more effective ways of meeting these needs. Understanding the act is more rapidly accomplished, not by first examining the behavior pattern and consequences of, or associational connections with, the act, but by examining why the patient committed himself to action at a specific time and place. This is particularly true for the secondary dyscontrol acts, which occur in patients whose lives are generally characterized by a neurotic inhibition of action rather than an "alloplastic readiness to act."

In such patients, dyscontrol acts may be the first and inevitable sign of improvement.

Medications as an adjunct to, and sometimes as a primary form of therapy can be recommended in the following manner: the more epileptoid the etiologic mechanisms are presumed to be, the more one should try anticonvulsants; keeping in mind their several limitations. Anticonvulsants are not universally effective, even in typical epilepsy, and sometimes one will work when another fails. There is little difference between effective therapeutic dose and toxic levels. The therapeutic index can often be increased by combining several synergistically acting drugs. In the episodic dyscontrols this is best obtained by utilizing, either alone or in combination with the anticonvulsants, the benzodiazepines, the latter also having a normalizing effect on both baseline and activated EEG abnormalities. If control of the dyscontrol acts leads to the appearance of other disordered behavior, close scrutiny usually reveals that inadequate attention has been given to the reeducational psychotherapeutic program; that is, the importance of the secondary gains of the dyscontrol behavior has been overlooked, or no opportunity has been provided for the realistic expression of affects or the gratification of needs. Finally, clinical evidence suggests that, if at all possible, phenothiazines should be avoided as they may aggravate the dyscontrol acts. If they are needed, they should be combined with anticonvulsants and/or benzodiazepines. The fact that such a complicated pharmacologic combination may be necessary suggests that the ideal pharmacologic agent is yet to be found.

Other important observations in drug therapies are the following: the episodic depressions may respond well to the benzodiazepines, sometimes even to the anticonvulsants, whereas they may be untouched or perhaps aggravated by the usual antidepressants. The phenothiazines, if used to control episodic psychotic reactions and not to treat the chronic, persistent psychotic symptoms underlying episodic disorders, need not be maintained beyond clinical improvement. Maintenance medication, in fact, may be contraindicated.

Long-term follow-up suggests that, contrary to the usually expressed pessimism regarding therapy of these patients, with an adequate therapeutic regimen, they respond well and contribute significantly to society. In fact, despite the turmoil of the treatment process itself, the most gratifying therapeutic results, both for the patient, and the psychiatrist, occur in this group. To mention a few examples, a top level executive who had been incapacitated for five years, drinking heavily, completely neglecting his family, and wimpering childishly for help, is now abstinent, authoritatively assuming his role as head of the household, and has resumed his executive position. A mother, whose fugue states were so prolonged and irresponsible that she lost her husband and control of her children, becoming utterly dependent on elderly parents, now has completed her higher education, is successful as a schoolteacher, and has resumed caring for her children. Another woman, whose life was so totally chaotic that she too gave up caring for her children and divorced her husband, is now working in a highly competent professional position and at the same time caring for her children and household. A man who could function only on a menial clerical level because of his impulsiveness and frequent habituation to drugs now successfully manages a large business of his own. These results are typical of most of the patients who have been treated intensively over a sustained period of time. At yearly intervals, patients are asked to return for a checkup. Their devotion to the therapist and appreciation for the help received is truly touching. The therapist's pride in their accomplishment no longer needs to be hidden behind his professional neutrality.

Appendixes of Clinical Reports

References

Index of Subjects

Index of Authors

Appendixes of Clinical Reports

Appendix 1   Seizure Dyscontrol

Patient: F206

Diagnosis: Seizure dyscontrol (seizural acts, one per month). Characterological diagnosis: cyclothymic personality.

Identification: Female, 32-year-old, white, married schoolteacher; hospitalized two months; outpatient psychotherapy two years; four-year follow-up, two years without therapy.

Presenting problem: This patient had a history of grand mal seizures starting ten years before admission, seizures were never completely controlled by anticonvulsants. At the time she was first seen she was receiving 100 mg. of diphenylhydantoin (Dilantin) q.i.d., but the frequency of seizures, even with this medication, had been increasing, and recently a new symptom appeared which the patient labeled "blackout spells," described as periods of unresponsiveness to the environment lasting from a few seconds to several minutes with complete amnesia for this period. Both phenomena occurred when she was under slight stress, such as socializing with strangers or following several drinks of whiskey. The patient attributes the increased frequencies of seizures to two significant recent events, the death of a favorite niece from leukemia and the death of one of her favorite students. The presumed etiology of the seizures was a coronal skull fracture suffered at age 10 when the patient fell from a bicycle. She was hospitalized at that time and allegedly unconscious for two and a half days. Auras preceding the seizures consisted of "yellow spots" before her eyes, a feeling of fatigue, or migraine headaches. Seizures were more likely to occur during the premenstrual period.

Mental status examination: The patient was dressed in a neat, but casual manner. Movements were quick and nervous and her expression was alert. There was something mannish about her carriage, although at times she developed a dreamy, seductive expression. She was generally pleasant, cheerful, and cooperative. Superficially, she appeared elated, but underneath this there seemed to be considerable anxiety and some depression. There were no distortions of perceptions, nor delusions. Her main preoccupations were with her convulsions and her unsatisfactory sex life. The latter she spoke about quite openly and in view of the severity of this problem, quite indifferently. There was no clouding of sensorium, nor intellectual defects.

EEG, physical, and neurological examinations: These examinations were entirely negative, as were extensive laboratory studies, particularly metabolic ones which were pursued because it had been reported in the past that she suffered from hypoglycemia. Past EEG's had been read as borderline without further description. The current recording revealed a baseline with well-developed 10 per second alpha activity posteriorly, intermixed with law amplitude fast frequencies. With chloralose activation, the record became mildly dysrhythmic with excessive variations in frequency and amplitude. On several occasions there was evidence of slow and hypersynchronous activity appearing diffusely, but more prominent in the left posterior temporal area.

Psychological evaluation: The patient was particularly "jittery" during the testing situation, and in the second session had a "fit." This was described as falling off the chair onto the floor without violence or hurting herself, followed by a few clonic movements, and then a period of unresponsiveness for ten minutes, after which she woke up and said, "why does this happen to me," at the same time reaching out to clutch the attendant who had accompanied her. Tests revealed an IQ of 112 with a borderline psychotic adjustment and a basically hysterical personality pattern. The psychotic potential was revealed in the looseness of her associations and disorganization in thinking, particularly when talking about sex. Anxiety regarding the loss of maternal love with associated depressive feelings were dealt with by denial and projection. Ambivalent feelings towards parental figures were particularly obvious, but any hostile expression of these feelings was repressed. Her sexual identification seemed to be that of the tomboy rather than that of the mature woman, with many doubts about her own sexual adequacy, which in turn were projected onto the males, in that she was preoccupied with their sexual prowess.

Underlying this was a phobic reaction to the male genitalia. In the counterphobic manner she was often seductive.

Family and developmental history: The patient was the second of two children, having a brother three years her senior. The father was a passive "Milquetoast" who lived off his own father's estate, while the mother, an aggressive, domineering person, particularly within the family, kept close tabs on her daughter even after the daughter's marriage. The patient was coerced and manipulated by her mother, as was her husband with his. The patient quite openly remembered resentment over being a girl, and having had many opportunities to observe an older brother, she recalled longing for his penis and trying to urinate as he did. However, there were no particular psychological problems until mid-adolescence, when sexual pressures began to mount. During college she roomed with two homosexual girls, often handling the stress of this situation by having "blackout spells," at which time she would either fall or sit down, temporarily lose consciousness, and have no memory for the events that occurred during this period.

Because of vaginismus and dyspareunia, she had been able to complete coitus only twice during her marriage. These occasions were usually facilitated by excessive alcoholic intake which makes her "relaxed and sexy." Despite her sexual fears, she indulged in much sexual fantasy and overt but restrained sexual play with other men. She particularly enjoyed oral-genital play, describing the feeling as "like a child at its mother's breast." She has two names for herself; one, her full name, which she uses to describe herself whenever her behavior is "bad"; the other, a nickname, she uses to refer to herself whenever she is "good." In revealing this, she sounds much as if she has experienced true dissociative dual personality.

Treatment: Upon her admission to the hospital, all anticonvulsant medicine was gradually withdrawn. Some of the patient's symptoms, including difficulty in vision, weakness, and dizzy spells, were obviously toxic effects of the anticonvulsants, and they cleared after the withdrawal. During the first several weeks of medication, she had two typical grand mal seizures, both precipitated by stressful interpersonal situations on the ward, with a covert homosexual content. During the next six weeks of hospitalization, even though she received no medication, the seizures did not recur.

Follow-up: Upon discharge from the hospital, she was seen in private psychotherapy, in the hope of working out her sexual confusions and identity. Although diphenylhydantoin (Dilantin) was retried several times, there seemed to be no change in the frequency of her seizures, which upon discharge again began recurring regularly one per month, during the premenstrual period. A short trial on primidone (Mysoline) made her feel "much worse." During the first several years after discharge, she was periodically depressed with alternating periods of mild elation. However, following a move into the center of town where she could be more sociable, these mood swings became less frequent. Although she is still unable to obtain orgasm with penetration, she is more accepting of orgastic relief through mutual manipulation. There have been a series of crises, such as the death of her father, but this stress did not precipitate an appearance of blackouts or an increase in the seizural acts.

Psychodynamic-neurophysiologic synthesis: There would be little question, in view of this woman's history of severe head trauma and laboratory findings of an abnormal EEG, as well as the classic grand mal seizures, that she has epilepsy. However, there is also no question but that during periods of emotional stress, the frequency of seizures is considerably increased. It is also apparent that anticonvulsants, even at toxic levels, will not decrease the frequency of seizures during these periods of stress, nor has any combination of anticonvulsants reduced the basic level of one seizure per month, which has been consistent (except for the period of hospitalization) for the past ten years. However, other types of episodic disorders of the inhibitory type, namely the "blackouts," are less clearly of an epileptoid nature, in fact often seem to be motivated by the patient's desire to escape phobically from a situation which would otherwise arouse intense and frightening sexual feelings. What is significant in this patient is that careful projective evaluation reveals intellectual disorders not of the type usually seen with a central nervous system impairment, but more typically that seen in schizophrenia. At the same time this patient, as well as most of the others, did not show overt manifestations of psychotic behavior, even after careful history-taking or prolonged psychiatric observation. This observation, repeated many times in the present series, is particularly important in view of Slater's (1955, 1965) finding that many epileptics develop overt schizophrenia some years after the onset of the epileptic symptomatology. One wonders what the long-term follow-up of patients in whom such potentiality is demonstrated on projective tests before any clinical symptoms develop, will reveal.

Appendix 2   Instinct Dyscontrol

Patient: F287

Diagnosis: Instinct dyscontrol (neurosis) (2 to 3 times per week with rare seizure dyscontrol). Characterological diagnosis: Obsessive-compulsive personality.

Identification: Male, 26-year-old, white, married, physician. Outpatient psychotherapy plus drug therapy for eight months. Hospitalized four times, 12 months' follow-up, hospitalized at the time of follow-up.

Presenting problem: The patient allegedly consulted a psychiatrist voluntarily but at the same time was under considerable pressure from his training director to mend his ways. The reason for the consultation was that periodically he ingested excessive amounts of secobarbital (Seconal), which led to ataxia and slurring of speech. Three weeks before consultation, he had fallen downstairs, fracturing his knee. At the time he was first seen, he had been off barbiturates since the fracture, but prior to the fall he was taking 0.2 to 0.6 grams secobarbital per day, sometimes administering barbiturates to himself intravenously. Frequently he used amphetamines to overcome the barbiturate hangover, but he denied using other drugs. He attributed his present difficulties to increasing conflict with his immediate supervisor which had been building up for the past four months. Three months prior to his consultation, he had had a series of EEG's. The first was read as normal, the second revealed barbiturate spindles, and the third showed diffuse high amplitude slow waves with questionable left temporal spikes. Because of this, diphenylhydantoin (Dilantin) and phenobarbital had been prescribed. A fourth EEG, after the patient had been on anticonvulsants for one month, revealed a definite left anterior and left midtemporal spike focus.

Mental status examination: The patient appeared eager for help, contrite regarding his past behavior, particularly ingratiating, and at times disarmingly charming. He immediately developed an intense dependency upon his therapist, but showed little capacity for constructive introspection and consciously withheld any material which he felt would lead to rejection by the therapist. There was pressure of speech and hyperactivity. He was extremely sensitive, completely egocentric, and preoccupied with maintaining his own self-esteem. He constantly asked the therapist to intervene in his behalf with authorities and furthermore requested him to manipulate his wife and parents. There was a childish extravagance in both his verbalizations and living. For example, he called his parents by long distance almost daily "just to talk with them," but at the same time begged for more money. There was no evidence of any thought disorder, delusions, or hallucinations (except as referred to below). Emotions seemed extremely labile, but equally superficial.

EEG, physical, and neurological examination: Examinations were negative, except for stool examinations which were guiaiac positive. Hematocrit was slightly elevated and bleeding and clotting time abnormal. Proctoscopic examination revealed a 5 cm. mass with ulceration, but biopsy showed no malignancy. In view of possible self-mutilative behavior, there was some question whether or not the lesion might have been self-induced. EEG revealed that alpha rhythms were poorly organized and poorly stabilized, the frequency varying from 9 to 13 per second, with the wave forms often quite sharp. Frontal region showed runs of 18 to 20 per second spindling activity, resembling barbiturate effect. Random spike discharges appeared in the left temporal and left anterior temporal region. A subsequent EEG taken during the height of one of his episodic psychotic reactions showed not only the left temporal spikes, but generalized high amplitude slow waves.

Psychological evaluation: The outstanding finding on projective tests was extreme constriction of affect, in terms of response to his own inner life and most definitely in his response to the world about him. He appeared controlled and rigid, his thinking was stereotyped, and there was considerable indication of uneven mental functioning, although no evidence of psychotic disorganization. He appeared isolated from people and preoccupied with sex. Sexual stimuli usually eliciting an inaccurate perceptual response. Oral dependency and traits of the "addictive" personality were noted.

Family and developmental history: The patient was the only child of older parents, both of whom worked during his childhood. His mother was a nurse and his father a passive, dependent, somewhat withdrawn individual with a minor administrative job. What is striking about the history is the intense competitive relationship between father and son for mother's affection. During the patient's early school years, he did most of the household chores while his mother was at work. He struggled incessantly to please mother, bringing her gifts and taking her out in the evenings, whenever possible excluding father. Otherwise, he was isolated and withdrawn from peers, and the few friends he did have seemed eccentric or schizoid.

At soon as he left home for college, he became emotionally dependent upon a female student whom he married within the year. Both dreams and associations indicated confusion between wife and mother, and he idealized both, while derogating father or father figures. His wife, also a professional person and away from home much of the time, was willing to give to the patient many of the usual housewife chores, such as cooking, buying groceries, and decorating, and he was eager to accept. The patient even selected his wife's clothing, and one of his extravagances was to purchase dresses for his mother. Husband and wife lived in virtual social isolation, except for their professional contacts. The ambivalence of the patient in his marital relationship was obvious in that he vacillated between threatening divorce and contrite obsequiousness when his wife showed any independence. The patient's self-esteem and masculine image seemed to be maintained by the fantasy of becoming the omnipotent physician.

His wife first reported, and the patient and parents ultimately confirmed, that there had been two isolated seizures, at ages three and seven. Both were typical grand mal seizures not known to be related to any precipitating event. The patient also reluctantly admits having had temporary blackouts during childhood which sound as though they were petit mal attacks, but he expressed the opinion, that these seizures or "spells" were hysterical and not epileptic.

Treatment: The patient was seen in psychotherapy twice a week for an eight-month period, at the end of which his therapy was terminated because he insisted upon hospitalization in a distant city. With the patient's permission, his parents and wife were seen on several occasions. Twice during this eight-month period he had to be hospitalized because of acute psychotic episodes. Throughout this period he was taking both sedatives and stimulants, but not reporting this to the physician until confronted with evidence of it on the basis of EEG findings. During this period there were many episodes of confusion marked by acting out of primitive instinctual drives, particularly aggression, which would be directed towards anybody in his immediate surroundings: choking his wife, or inappropriately getting into fights with strangers or friends. Sometimes the aggression was directed towards himself, such as driving his car into a ditch, or stabbing himself with a knife. It never could be established precisely whether these episodes were precipitated by a continuing excessive use of drugs or whether the patient took excessive doses of drugs just during the dysphoric periods of mounting tension which preceded the dyscontrol acts. It seemed that sometimes it was the first and other times the second pattern. The episodic dyscontrol usually lasted for a few hours, and was followed by spotty amnesia for the events. However, on several occasions episodes lasted for several weeks or a month, requiring hospitalization because the patient was so belligerent, delusional, and at times potentially homicidal. During these episodes he developed full-blown paranoid ideas, expressing the belief that his wife and therapist were hospitalizing him so that the two of them could have an affair. Within a day or two after hospitalization, he usually became contrite, cooperative, and realized the delusional nature of his ideas. During the episodic psychotic reactions, episodic dyscontrol would be less obvious.

Because of the problem with drugs, it was initially agreed by both the patient and therapist that he should discontinue all medications including his prescribed phenobarbital and diphenylhydantoin (Dilantin). For two months after this, there was no further evidence of instinct dyscontrol or seizures. However, during the third month there were a series of dyscontrol acts, generally of an aggressive nature, directed towards his wife or himself. He again fell down stairs; whether this occurred as the result of a seizure, or was an instinctual act of a self-mutilative or suicidal nature could never be definitely established. Repeated EEG's during his treatment would reveal barbiturate intoxication, but also showed the temporal abnormalities reported above. Finally it was decided to reinstitute anticonvulsant therapy in the form of primidone (Mysoline) 250 mgs. q.i.d. Typically he responded to any new medication with euphoric enthusiasm for the drug. Over a period of six weeks there were no confusional episodes; soon, however, there followed a series of dyscontrol acts which made hospitalization necessary to protect him and his wife. He improved rapidly during a week's hospitalization, showed no further instinct dyscontrol, and admitted that for the two weeks preceding hospitalization he had been taking phenothiazines. Upon discharge without medication, the patient again developed dyscontrol acts which seemed to be precipitated by increasing difficulties with his wife, who was asserting her independence, saying that unless he functioned adequately she was going to leave him. At the same time, in psychotherapy he was preoccupied with the similarities in his relationships to his wife and his mother, surprised at how he often confused the two and realized the lack of really close feeling for either. He was forced to face his sexual inadequacy. All of these developments, of course, were severe blows to his self-esteem. In a desperate attempt to control him on an outpatient basis so that he would not lose his training appointment, chlordiazepoxide (Librium) 10 mgs. q.i.d. and primidone (Mysoline) were given. As had been true in the past, he again responded with a sense of well-being to the new drug combination, but this lasted only four weeks. Then, rehospitalization was necessary when, during another of his instinctual acts, he stabbed himself several times. He was committed at this time and at his family's insistence transferred to a private hospital out of state.

Follow-up: At the time of follow-up he was still hospitalized, and, as had been true in the past, making a satisfactory adjustment in the protective hospital environment, without medication, but even on short visits outside the hospital he tended to revert to his dyscontrol acts.

Psychodynamic-neurophysiologic synthesis: This patient is a classic example of instinct dyscontrol, although he rarely had typical grand mal seizures. Although there was constant underlying tension and periods when this tension would mount, the mounting tension would not focus on the expression of forbidden impulses or attempts to control these impulses, which is typical of the impulse dyscontrol patients. In this man the mounting tension was diffuse and without a specific object. The acts themselves were unmistakenly expressions of rage, but the object of this rage, when it was directed outwards, was usually the person closest at hand. Most often this happened to be his wife and undoubtedly had some motivational significance in that he was so ambivalently dependent upon her. But often it would be directed towards a complete stranger who happened to be standing next to him on a street or in a bar. There was marked confusion and disorientation during the instinctual acts and considerable but not complete amnesia for these periods. He blandly attributed his dyscontrol acts to "hysteria," thus beyond his control, but was most anxious regarding the consequences, and had enough underlying dysphoria that he recognized the need for psychotherapy.

The periods between the acts were characterized by obsessional controls, particularly reflected on his Rorschach examination. During remissions there was no evidence of bizarre psychotic material, but much did come out during the more prolonged episodic confusional states, particularly bizarre sexual fantasies in which his confusion regarding the mechanics of the sexual act and his own sexual identity was even more striking in view of his professional training as a physician. It is apparent at this time that this man's condition might have been classified as an episodic psychotic reaction, or, what we have preferred to call an episodic acute brain syndrome. This patient also presents another dilemma: the combination of drug habituation with episodic dyscontrol. In some instances the sequence of events seemed to be a period of mounting tension, a desperate attempt to control this dysphoria through the use of either alcohol or drugs, and then during the drug-induced toxic state, the expression of instinct dyscontrol or episodic psychotic behavior. At other times the chain of events seemed to be mounting tension, then a period of confusion, with the drug-ingestion not a precipitating event, but, as one of the instinctual acts, itself, a confused attempt at self-medication, the drug toxicity following rather than precipitating instinctual behavior.

Appendix 3   Impulse Dyscontrol

Patient: S290

Diagnosis: Impulse dyscontrol (impulse neuroses, intermittent, with drug habituation). Characterological diagnosis: obsessive-compulsive personality.

Presenting problem: This 28-year-old patient was admitted to the hospital because of habituation to amphetamine, 15 mgs. x 7, seco-barbital (Seconal), 0.2 grams x 2, per day. Three months before hospitalization he had been admitted to the medical service for a bleeding gastric ulcer, treated by gastrectomy. Because of this and the drug habituation, he had been unable to work for the preceding four months.

Mental status examination: Despite his recent medical problems this was a healthy-looking young man. Although somewhat tense, restless, and slightly overactive, the patient showed no outstanding deviant behavior patterns during the interview. He was meticulously dressed, and spoke in a rather flippant manner, giving the appearance of a "con" man. At times he appeared somewhat depressed, at other times euphoric, while still again frightened and slightly suspicious. However, his moods fluctuated appropriately with the content of thought. He alternately spoke about his failures and his successes, seeming to exaggerate both. He was obsequious in his relationship with the doctor and obviously quite concerned about creating a good impression. There was an attempt to be overfriendly and familiar as if he were hoping to establish a peer relationship rather than a doctor-patient one.

EEG, physical, and neurological examination: Physical and laboratory examination were negative. Neurological examination was negative except for hyperactive reflexes. EEG revealed a normal resting record, but after activation with alpha-chloralose there appeared bilateral paroxysmal bursts of 3 to 5 per second activity predominantly in the anterior quadrants.

Psychological evaluation: This revealed a passive, dependent individual with strong unsatisfied dependent needs, with insensitivity to the needs of others. He manifested a "cold affect" and an inability to make emotional investments. He turned his aggressiveness inward and his self-concept was one of unworthiness with no clearly distinguished pattern of values or objectives. There was poor sexual identification and perverse sexual preoccupations. He showed a reluctance to confront his major problems, instead choosing to lose himself in minutia and obsessive concerns. He also revealed a number of oral sadistic fantasies, and a likelihood to act out his sexual tensions impulsively.

Family and developmental history: The patient was the oldest of three children born to a well-to-do family, having two sisters three and five years his junior. His father, who divorced his mother when the patient was seven, was described as extremely cold and emotionally unstable, but at the same time a very energetic and effective senior officer of a large corporation. Since the divorce the patient has had rare contact with his father. The mother was described by the patient as a sweet, nervous, ineffectual person who had two "nervous breakdowns" during her first marriage until she finally had the gumption to divorce the patient's father. However, the way the mother was viewed by the patient and the way she was seen by the therapist were quite disparate. Although in her fifties, she was rather strikingly handsome, with peroxided hair and clothes which made her look at least 20 years younger than she really was. She acted quite seductive, yet subtly hostile and controlling. It is undoubtedly significant that the patient had such a distorted view of his mother at the conscious level, particularly when psychological examination revealed that he really saw mother as an inaccessible, depriving, and overbearing person who dominated both the patient and the rest of the family.

As a youngster, this patient had numerous phobias, occasional tics, as well as other evidence of tension, such as nail biting and hyperactivity. He remembers his constant attempts to please father, who apparently was intolerant unless the boy performed as a mature adult, even in his preschool years. For example, he has one memory of proudly showing his father a pinhole camera he made, which father "pooh-poohed" because of its crudeness and simplicity.

Shortly after the divorce, his mother remarried and almost immediately the patient was sent to boarding school, obviously to get him out of the way. His adjustment there, not surprisingly, was quite poor. He was chronically depressed, tried to return home, and tried in vain to establish a filial relationship with his stepfather, but again was rejected by a man who was very similar to his real father. He graduated, however, after several transfers from both preparatory school and college, largely because he had the verbal facility to "con" his teachers. After graduation he entered the military service, but six weeks later was discharged because of a bleeding gastric ulcer.

Following this, he left his home town, and, after a great struggle, managed to get himself employed in the entertainment industry as a producer of promotional films. He was successful at this and within two years was earning a good salary. However, he had to play the role of the big shot, buy sports cars, live in a fancy apartment, become involved with a number of "expensive" women. At the same time he began using stimulants to keep up the fast pace of his life, which in turn necessitated nightly sedation. Soon his behavior was so disorganized that he lost his job. Depressed and toxic, he was hospitalized and began outpatient psychotherapy three years before his present treatment. Periodically throughout his life, and again at this time, he found it necessary to make financial demands on his family (who could well afford it) to pay for either his medical bills or other heavy debts he had incurred. These seemed to be attempts to prove that his family did care, and in fact about the only way they were capable of showing they cared was through this financial support, even though it was given reluctantly and only to avoid disgracing the family.

After a period of dependency on the family, the patient secured a job as a door-to-door salesman. He was an immediate success at this, rapidly attaining a relatively high income from commissions. He hated the job, however, finding the tension of knocking on the door and trying to gain entry almost unbearable. His solution to this was the use of stimulants. At this time he married a girl he described as a sweet, passive, and devoted person. However, the wife, who was interviewed on a number of occasions, revealed herself as a rigid, obsessive-compulsive, manipulating woman. It is interesting that again he had such a distorted evaluation of the woman in his life. At the time of treatment he had a five-month-old son.

Treatment: The patient started psychoanalytic therapy four times a week. As might be expected of a person with such obsessive traits, despite repeated confrontations by the therapist, he talked rapidly and meaninglessly about minutiae in his life, without focusing on any pertinent conflicts, nor confronting any of his characterological difficulties. Shortly after starting therapy he again procured a job at a rather menial level in the entertainment business. His idea of a therapeutic session was to regale the therapist with the exploits and idiosyncrasies of the performing artist. Details of the therapy will not be reviewed here, but a number of examples of impulse dyscontrol will be described. Most of these were precipitated by what might be called separation anxieties or depressions, or were attempts to prove that he was loved.

The first involves drugs. Throughout the four years of therapy he did not again become habituated to drugs, but for many months whenever he visited his mother's or sisters' homes, he would note mounting restlessness and agitation. This would lead to an increased need to micturate and frequent trips to the bathroom. When in the bathroom he would look in the drug cabinet for pills, with an irresistible urge to take some. At first he would resist, only to return to the bathroom several times during the evening until finally he would abruptly open the drug cabinet and pop several pills into his mouth, regardless of what they were. It is also interesting, and undoubtedly related to this act, that he had recurring dreams, wherein, sitting on the toilet, constipated, he looked up to find hanging on the bathroom door his mother's purse, which he excitedly began to explore, only to find there was nothing important in it; instead it was "filled with trash."

A second type of impulse dyscontrol would occur on the job. He was working for several different bosses and there was much conflict between various factions within the organization. Whenever there was a meeting to which he had not been invited, he would sit morosely in his office, worrying about what was going on in the meeting, trying to resist listening through the transom or the wall, or perhaps even looking through the keyhole. He usually gave in to these impulses although he recognized his behavior as childish as well as potentially self-defeating.

The third type of impulse dyscontrol was sexual. This only occurred when his wife left town to visit her family. Over a period of several nights after her departure he would note mounting tension and a need to find a woman. He would resist this strongly until finally he was pacing the floor, taking frequent cold showers to calm himself, and then precipitously he would dash out of the house, trembling and perspiring, looking for a prostitute. When one was found, he was almost instantaneously orgastic, but the temporary relief would last only a matter of minutes or hours, and then the tension would mount again. This activity never occurred when his wife was at home, but he would have episodic autistic reveries involving the picture of girls in black stockings and garters. Again there would be mounting tension until he would go to the bathroom to masturbate. He claimed that all that was required to attain ejaculation was to touch the top of his erect penis with two fingers.

Slowly and grudgingly this man was forced to confront his problems, but resistance was fierce. He used every available excuse to miss appointments, but each rationalization, no matter how convincing, was rejected by the therapist. He went through one period when he came to eleven successive sessions without uttering a word. Again the therapist patiently outwaited him. (Such behavior has been discussed in detail in a previously published paper [Monroe, 1968].) He manipulated his family, hoping that they would allow him to discontinue therapy, inasmuch as they were subsidizing it. However, this had been anticipated, and the family had been forewarned and confronted with the prospect of five years of treatment with no promise of a cure. To reinforce this, the therapist had referred the family to a consultant. His pleas to the family, therefore, could be negated by again referring the family to this consultant.

The patient repeatedly would find a job on his own initiative, do exceptionally fine work until he was promoted, and then through a series of manipulations or acting out would get fired. The acting out consisted of trying to establish himself as the "favorite son" of one of the chief executives. However, this overt obsequiousness alienated him from his peers and often even from his supervisors. As his interpersonal relationships deteriorated, he became frantic, playing off one faction against the other, "knifing" people behind their backs, until everybody was fed up and he was summarily fired. He did begin to obtain some retrospective insight and then anticipatory insight into his behavior, but for a long time this was insufficient to control it. Towards the end of his fourth year of treatment it appeared as though he was manipulating his employment status so that he would be transferred out of town. There was really no need for this, and it was pointed out that he was probably acting in such a way to escape therapy. However, he successfully managed this final acting out and convinced his family that he would continue therapy elsewhere.

Follow-up: Following his transfer to another city, he made several abortive attempts to reestablish treatment, but finally gave up and for the past 12 months has not been in psychoanalysis. However, he has been performing exceptionally well in an executive capacity in a small operation, apparently better suited to be the large fish in the small pond. His wife reports that he is much more affectionate and considerate at home and relates better to his child. He seems to be utilizing the insight he gained in therapy and it is hoped that he will be able to continue to do this in the future.

Psychodynamic-neurophysiologic synthesis: Certainly motivational factors far outweighed any possible epileptoid ones as to the mechanisms behind his impulse dyscontrol. However, at times, apparently for no overt or covert reasons, he seemed to be more susceptible to mounting tension than at others, as for example when his wife would leave town for periods of one month to six weeks. It is obvious that one of the basic mechanisms behind the sexual impulsive acts that followed was the desertion by the imagined loving, motherly person, but the impulses themselves would mount at unpredictable periods during his wife's absence. Perhaps these were the times when the intermittent central nervous system instability made him more susceptible to the constant underlying depression and agitation. If one chooses to emphasize the conscious awareness of the mounting tension and the rather frantic attempts this patient made to control the impulses, the diagnosis would be impulse dyscontrol. On the other hand, if one chose to emphasize the unconscious mechanisms, particularly the past experiences that dominate his present perceptions, and the fact that the action is a primitive form of memory, dominated by emotional rather than rational connections, this would be classified as acting out, the act itself mistakenly perceived as the solution to the old oedipal conflict. This became particularly obvious during the analytic situation, when his preoccupation with stockings and garters approached fetishistic proportions, which was ultimately related to childhood memories of seductive stimulation by mother when she was in various stages of undress. How much these memories were retrospective falsification or childhood fantasies was impossible to establish, but inasmuch as the mother had two psychotic episodes during this period, there might have been overt sexual stimulation, as a real, not fantasied, act. This patient was considered an example of impulse neurosis because at the beginning of treatment he did not identify the impulse dyscontrol itself as an ego-alien act, either denying or rationalizing the inappropriateness of his behavior, but at the same time he did recognize his own discomfort and social failure.

Appendix 4   Acting Out

Patient: S288

Diagnosis: Acting-out dyscontrol (acting out, repeated, and unpredictable, with occasional episodic depressive reaction). Characterological diagnosis: passive dependent personality.

Identification: Married, 21-year-old housewife, hospitalized for three days. Outpatient psychoanalytic therapy two-and-a-half years; follow-up 36 months. (Patient committed suicide.)

Presenting problem: Three months prior to the start of therapy the patient had married a lifelong acquaintance who at the time was in postgraduate professional training. The marriage followed a long and stormy courtship. A two-week honeymoon was supposedly "great" with both partners making a rapid sexual adjustment. However, shortly after taking up routine housekeeping and wifely duties, the patient developed episodes of depression characterized by crying spells, disinterest in everything, and a "lack of close feelings towards my husband." During such periods she had thoughts of wanting to die, a feeling of being alone, and "a certain indescribable, strange, omnious feeling." The patient herself admitted that there was no reasonable cause for such feelings, except possibly her husband's long hours of work. On the other hand, he was affectionate and endearing, in fact, idealized his wife. As they were being partially subsidized by their respective families, there were no financial problems. The patient reported "I am mystified as to why I should feel like I do. Sometimes the tension is so strong a force inside of me that I just want to scream at the top of my voice." Although she admitted having such feelings rarely before marriage, they were now so frequent that she sought psychiatric help on her own initiative.

However, before arrangements could be made, she was found by her husband in a confused state, standing on the fire escape of their apartment as if contemplating suicide. An emergency consultation was then arranged.

Mental status examination: By the time the patient was seen by the psychiatrist she was no longer confused, although allegedly amnesic for the episode. She was, however, agitated, depressed, and tearful. She admitted that she might have been contemplating suicide because she had in the past, but denied any memory of such ideas immediately preceding her present behavior. Her thoughts were spontaneous and coherent, and her mannerisms not unusual except for considerable restraint, in that she sat almost motionless in the chair, while repeating her story in a dull, monotonous voice. There was no evidence of hallucinations or delusions. She did show enough insight to accept hospitalization voluntarily to protect herself from her own impulses. At that time no other dyscontrol acts were reported.

EEG, physical, and neurological examination: Physical examination revealed an attractive, tall, thin girl with no physical or neurological abnormalities. Laboratory studies were also negative. A routine EEG revealed no specific abnormalities, although there was a moderate build-up with hyperventilation and a slightly delayed return to the normal baseline. After chloralose activation, she showed definite paroxysmal bursts of high amplitude three to four per second activity, which by the end of the record were almost continuous.

Psychological evaluation: These studies, completed a few days after her initial contact with the psychiatrist, revealed an individual who was constricted in her emotional life with respect to both the outside world and her own inner needs. She defended herself against strong affects by narrowing her scope of activities and maintaining rigid control over her emotional responsiveness. There was evidence that she was subject to phobic fears, and found it necessary to maintain a distance from others; hence it was predicted that she would have difficulty in her interpersonal relationships. There appeared to be much anxiety specifically connected with her attitude towards her father, and it seemed that perhaps this relationship had seriously distorted her sexual perceptions, probably interfering with her mature sexual adjustment. She handled these anxieties by seeing herself as a little girl. There was evidence of much magical thinking in that all the TAT stories ended happily without any logical resolution of the plot. There was also evidence of depression and suicidal ruminations.

Family and developmental history: The patient was the oldest of three children born to a well-to-do, educated, urban family. She had a brother 6 years younger and a sister 10 years her junior. Despite the evidence in the psychological examination that there might have been a disturbed relationship between the patient and the parents, particularly her father, none could be elicited in the interviews with the patient, nor was such information obtained from the family. The father was an energetic, successful businessman, frequently away from home, but one who doted on his family, particularly his oldest daughter. The mother was an active housewife, involved in many community activities, but did not let this interfere with her rather indulgent, protective, giving attitude towards her children.

Behavioral problems were obvious almost from birth, which was normal. During the first year of life the patient had severe gastrointestinal upsets and for several years thereafter was considered a "sickly" child. For this reason, she was overprotected and indulged. During the preschool years she had many phobias (darkness, insects, animals), and such severe separation anxieties that she would not let her family leave her either with relatives or babysitters. From this early age onward she was able to coerce extravagant demands from her parents through her temper tantrums. After the birth of her younger brother, there was more difficulty; the patient was overtly hostile toward him, at the same time increasing her excessive demands on her parents. During the period when her father was in the military service, the family was able to stick together, traveling from one army camp to another, but the patient made life miserable for her parents by insisting that wherever they went, she be allowed to accompany them. During early adolescence, the patient was sexually aggressive, enjoying the kissing games and restricted petting characteristic of the age, but this was followed in later adolescence by a prudish reaction in which she became cold and aloof in heterosexual contacts, maintaining a certain pride in her "virginity." Because she was socially prominent and attractive, however, she had a wide circle of friends and participated actively in social life, although one gets the feeling there was no closeness with either male or female peers. She showed little intellectual interests, being preoccupied during her college years with becoming "the belle of the ball." She married not because of any passionate interest in her husband, but because it was the thing to do, as most of her girlfriends were getting married at the same time. It is significant that her husband insisted on some real, affectionate, dependent, and sexual closeness and it was precisely then that her symptoms developed.

Treatment: Within 24 hours after her hospitalization she began agitating for release, indicating that she was neither psychotic nor depressed as were the other people on the ward. She now recalled the events of the day which preceded hospitalization, stating that she had been depressed and lonely because her husband had been away from home for an extended period, but insisted she was sitting on the fire escape merely to get some sun and fresh air. She coerced everybody into allowing her to leave, and plans were made to involve her in a number of activities that would keep her busy while her husband worked. Over the first few months in therapy she showed a series of impulsive acts, characterized by mounting tension during the day and dramatic, aggressive outbursts upon her husband's return in the evening. These were either physical attacks upon her spouse or bizarre self-mutilative behavior. Some control could be maintained by allowing her to use meprobamate (Miltown, Equanil) 400 mgs. p.r.n. for the mounting tension, but on two occasions it was necessary to give the patient intravenous sodium amobarbital to calm down her aggressive, destructive behavior. Several times she broke up the furniture or tore up the drapes in her newly decorated apartment. Many times she attempted to control mounting tension by being sexually solicitous, hoping that orgastic relief would facilitate control over her emotions. However, during such periods she was seldom orgastic, and in fact, at the height of her sexual excitement, would often become physically and verbally abusive toward her husband. During these periods of what would be called impulse dyscontrol, the impulsive acts occurred almost daily, and at the same time her verbalizations in psychotherapy were almost worthless. She could only reiterate her boredom regarding her present life, the frustrations of now belonging to only one man and not being able to date or to go out on parties almost nightly as she had during the past several years. She was resentful of her husband's work and professional interest, sometimes even implying that he might have an outside liaison with another girl.

At the time this patient was being treated, reserpine (Serpasil) was at the height of its popularity, and it was tried at the level of 1 mg. per day. It had rather dramatic effects in controlling the impulsive acts, and increasing the patient's capacity to introspect. At the same time the patient began reporting a number of very frightening dreams, centered around sexual attacks, which revealed her concern that sex was an aggressive, destructive act. There were overt oedipal dreams, being in bed with her naked father. At the same time she realized with considerable amazement the intense hostility she harbored toward her mother and younger brother. The solution to her problem as she saw it during periods of free association or daydreaming was for her to be the indulged small girl, whose whims were met as soon as they arose, but upon whom no demands were placed. Despite the fact that reserpine facilitated introspection and limited the impulsive acts, it had to be discontinued because of mounting depression and episodes of depersonalizations, the latter being particularly frightening.

Although her dreams, as well as her overtly seductive behavior during the therapeutic sessions revealed developing erotic transference to the therapist, this never attained conscious awareness, and any tentative interpretations of it were steadfastly denied by the patient. However, she began acting out, revealing that she was trying to work through this transference through action rather than reflection, with displacement on figures in her external environment who had transference significance to her. For example, she rather energetically initiated and maintained an affair with an older man who was her bridge teacher. Her attitude towards the paramour reflected the unconscious conflict that she was trying to work out. On one hand, she played the role of the helpless little girl at the mercy of a strong father who would repay her for her sexual favors by love, gifts, and protection; on the other hand, she strove to be the teacher's pet, the one who learned the fastest and the best, thereby gaining love and admiration, a behavior pattern that was similar to her behavior within the therapeutic setting. This ambivalence, together with dreams, left no doubt that the paramour was a combination of father and therapist. At the same time during coital play she would invite aggressive, sadistic behavior which was not provided by her lover. Each coital experience with her paramour, then, alternated with a fugue state, during which she would travel to the tougher parts of town, drink in bars, seeking some kind of traumatic, aggressive sexual experience, but totally amnesic for her behavior except that she "came to" just at the time real aggression was imminent. Again dreams revealed that her picture of father's sexuality was one of aggressive, sadistic activity, during which time his female partner would be mutilated and destroyed. This aggressiveness during sexual play was exciting to her, facilitating orgasm and relieving guilt.

As she worked through, or as we might say, acted through, her sado-masochistic ideas of sexuality and her inhibited or deflective self-assertiveness, the acting out gradually subsided. Although at first she tended feebly to rationalize and justify these acts, she soon saw her behavior as definitely ego-alien, out of character for herself, and out of context for the situation. For this reason her acting out was considered as acting out, rather than as "acting-out neuroses."

Follow-up: Termination of the therapy became imminent when, because of her husband's completion of training, they were forced to leave the city. She made a precipitous commitment to maturity at this time, by actively and successfully trying to get pregnant. The birth of her first child occurred shortly after moving, hence shortly after the termination of her therapy. The expectation was that she would establish a competitive relationship with her child and that this would lead to anxiety and depression. She was confronted with this before she left, and encouraged to seek further therapy during her child's first year of life, in her new locality. However, she resisted this until it became obvious that the prediction was all too true. Reestablishing a treatment relationship, she reverted to many of her primitive defenses, particularly impulse dyscontrol and acting out. There were also periodic depressions, and several temporary hospitalizations were necessary because of suicidal attempts. Unfortunately, three years after the termination of the therapy with her first therapist, but while she was still under treatment with the second, one of these suicidal attempts was successful.

Psychodynamic-neurophysiologic synthesis: In retrospect one can speculate that her rush into maturity was too soon and too much. Although the motivational elements in her behavior are obvious, the fact that mounting tensions occurred at times when there were no discernible realistic or symbolic precipitating events, and the fact that this was particularly likely to happen during premenstrual periods, suggest again some epileptoid or hormonal elements to this girl's emotional instability and dyscontrol acts.

Although the patient had definite episodic depressive reactions, and in the final analysis might have been placed in this diagnostic category, during the time in which she was under study much of her episodic behavior was characterized by impulsive acts. The predominant problem in therapy was the acting out of a fantasied sado-masochistic sexual relationship with the father, under the impact of the transference neurosis that she refused to accept. She did partially resolve this but by acting through rather than working through the transference. This resulted in a temporary disappearance of her acting out and impulsive acts until the further demands of motherhood overwhelmed her. Nevertheless, the unhappy ending to the story indicates the importance of the episodic depression.

Appendix 5   Episodic Psychotic Reactions

Patient: O262

Diagnosis: Episodic psychotic reaction (schizophrenic reaction, single episode with frequent impulse dyscontrol). Characterological diagnosis: hysterical personality.

Identification: Female, 34-year-old, married nurse hospitalized for a period of one month. Previous marriage counseling and individual psychotherapy. Group therapy following hospitalization. Follow-up 18 months after discontinuing all therapy.

Presenting problem: Two weeks before admission and two weeks after the birth of her third child, this patient showed a sudden change in personality. Though previously devoted to her children, she now wanted to place them in a foster home. At the same time she became argumentative and violent, physically abusing her husband and occasionally even her children. The day of admission she became so abusive towards her family that it was dangerous to leave her at home.

Mental status examination: On admission she appeared restless, overactive, distracted, and excessively talkative, her speech rambling and at times incoherent. She expressed a number of delusional ideas, namely that she was under the control of some outside force, and some vaguely defined enemies were going to destroy her and her family. Emotional responses were either bland or markedly inappropriate. Sensorium was clear and there was some insight inasmuch as she recognized the need for hospitalization.

EEG, physical and neurological examination: Physical and laboratory studies were all within the normal range, and EEG performed the day before discharge, after the patient had remitted, revealed a resting record of low voltage fast activity which at times was mixed with a small amount of 9-per-second frequencies. With chloralose activation, patient showed normal drowsy and sleep patterns.

Psychological evaluation: This patient had three psychological evaluations, one at the time of hospitalization, a second two years before present admission and a third three years earlier. The current evaluation was performed one week after her admission at a time when she had already shown considerable improvement. However, testing did reveal a good deal of looseness in associations with childish imagery of a regressive quality and considerable paranoid fearfulness. There was a substantial undercurrent of depressive feelings and anxiety with developing insight that she was now entering the "quiet after the storm." All evaluations had indicated conflicts with regard to her feminine role and a sense of inadequacy regarding her ability to be a mature woman. The patient tended to identify with children, in fact with her own children. There were many masochistic features in her personality. It was thought that her present psychosis was only coincidentally related to the birth of her child, and that the current dissociative behavior was probably related to marital conflicts.

Family and developmental history: The patient was the oldest of six children in a family with an alcoholic father who had never worked, and a manic-depressive mother who had innumerable hospitalizations since the birth of her second child. One of the patient's younger siblings was described as a homosexual and another has transitory depressions, although he has never been hospitalized. There was no history of neurotic or developmental abnormalities during the patient's early years. She was forced into the role of mother at age nine because of her own mother's hospitalization. She is a smart, ambitious girl, who completed nursing school under the most adverse conditions, marrying shortly thereafter following a whirlwind courtship, as she says, "to get away from home." She had a child by this marriage. Because of constant bickering with her husband, she was divorced a year and a half later, marrying her present husband five years after her first marriage. This marriage too has been stormy. The husband is a violent, abusive man who physically attacks both his wife and his children, and is destructive of their personal belongings. At times the patient is equally violent, particularly following periods of mounting tension related to money matters or problems in running the house. Periodically the patient revolts against housework and caring for the children, forcing her oldest daughter into the role she once played as a surrogate mother.

Treatment: During the first three days of hospitalization, the patient required seclusion because of her destructive behavior. She was uncooperative for physical and laboratory studies and required intramuscular medication because she refused to take it orally. Throughout this period she hallucinated and was delusional, but not disoriented. By the fourth day, hallucinations had disappeared and delusions were lessening. At the same time emotional responses became more labile but also more appropriate, with the patient manifesting either extreme anxiety or depression. Her speech was now relevant and coherent. She began asking for her family and cooperating with the medical regime. She identified, probably correctly, the precipitating factors as increasing conflicts with her husband, as well as the added responsibility of the newborn baby, saying "I was exhausted and angry because I was getting no help." Her medications were discontinued before discharge, the patient being followed for six months in group therapy, as well as receiving family counseling from a social agency.

Follow-up: She was faced with considerable external stress upon discharge and survived this surprisingly well. Her husband refused to let her return home, and filed legal action for separation and custody of the children. She filed a countersuit, and after a considerable period of wrangling, obtained custody of the children and regained her home. Her husband, in a rather paranoid way, persisted in bedeviling her with legal actions which, though petty, caused considerable family anxiety: the middle child developing stuttering and tics; the oldest girl becoming a delinquent (e.g., drinking, sexual promiscuity, and running away). Eight months after discharge the situation finally resolved itself when the husband was transferred out of the country and the courts placed the 13-year-old daughter in a training school. The patient obtained work as a nurse, leaving the care of her two younger children with babysitters. She lives alone, but is active in the PTA, church, and civic organizations. She does not date, and because of her unhappy marital experiences, is reluctant to get involved with another man.

When seen for follow-up 18 months after discharge from the hospital, she was pleasantly, but plainly dressed, looking somewhat older than her 36 years, very much the prim and proper schoolmarm. She was animated, talked rapidly, and demonstrated the hysterical features suggested by the psychological evaluation. There was a certain degree of euphoria and pompous grandiosity with a tendency to project all of her problems onto her husband. This, and some slight suspiciousness of the reason for follow-up, were the only suggestive abnormalities in behavior noted. She was rightly pleased with what she had accomplished since her hospitalization.

Psychodynamic-neurophysiologic synthesis: In this patient the evidence would seem to indicate a truly "hysterical" or motivated psychotic reaction. The reaction was precipitated by realistic and intense environmental stress; that is, a severely disturbed marital relationship further complicated by the birth of an unwanted child. This stress was not the result of symbolic reinterpretation of the immediate reality, but was realistic stress in the sense that this woman had a spouse who was not only emotionally unstable and physically abusive, but also cold and ungiving in both emotional and materialistic senses. The stresses were beyond the wife's control, except that she was masochistically oriented in selecting such a spouse originally. This is an instance of motivated psychosis with little or no epileptoid elements, although the data would be more convincing in this respect if the EEG activation procedure had been conducted during the height of the psychosis. It is important to remember that she was not disoriented during the psychotic episode itself.

Patient: S229

Diagnosis: Episodic psychotic reaction (acute brain syndrome, two episodes). Characterological diagnosis: paranoid personality.

Identification: This patient is a 33-year-old, white, married housewife hospitalized one month with no further therapy, follow-up period of 36 months.

Presenting problem: One month before admission the patient had undergone a hysterectomy. Two weeks later she was brought to the hospital in an acute confusional state, expressing delusional ideas and apparently hallucinating. Actually, about one year before hospitalization some changes in behavior had been noted. She became depressed, fearful, and complained of insomnia. At the same time she developed an "enormous appetite" associated with excessive smoking and coffee drinking. At times during the preceding year, she says, "my thoughts were all mixed up and racing through my mind." She also had mild referential and persecutory ideas which developed into florid delusions during the acute episode.

Mental status examination: The patient was agitated, overtalkative, and overactive as well as confused about time and place. She spoke in a rambling, disconnected fashion about mental telepathy, an apprehension her husband was going to take her children away from her, and that he was Eichmann and she a spy in a concentration camp. She also expressed the idea that she was a mulatto being forced into a change of life. She described her own children as looking ugly and not wanting her, while at other times she insisted that she was raising the neighbor's children and not her own. She felt that the world was changing and was perplexed in not being able to find out the reason for this. She did not know the name of the hospital or the date, nor could she differentiate between doctors, attendants, and patients.

EEG, physical and neurological examinations: The findings of physical examination and laboratory studies were all within normal limits. The EEG taken three weeks after admission and one week after the symptoms had begun to remit, showed no abnormalities in the resting record, but after chloralose activation there was a considerable amount of high amplitude paroxysmal three to five per second activity which was bilateral and symmetrical.

Psychological evaluation: No projective studies were administered; however, the WAIS revealed that she was of average intelligence. There was no indication of central nervous system impairment at the time of the testing.

Family and developmental history: The patient was the third of six siblings born to a lower-middle-class family, which, according to all available evidence, was remarkably free of tension. Mother and father made a satisfactory, if somewhat aloof, marital adjustment, and the patient was more attached to her father than to her mother, remembering, however, that he was so proud of her that he used to embarrass her by showing her off in front of friends and relatives. There were no serious deviations in her developmental history, nor was there any evidence of childhood neurosis, but during adolescence she was active in sexual play with siblings and neighbors and used to put "meat on my genitals so my dog could lick me there." She remembers being sexually stimulated by close physical contact with several girlfriends, but denies overt homosexual play. She was married at age 19 to a man who, she said, was "just like father." She had three children from this marriage. Even with this family, for the past five years she has managed to work at some skilled position in an assembly plant and has received regular promotions. At the onset of her present symptoms, she had been under such pressure to learn a new job under the tutelage of a very domineering instructor that she found it necessary to quit her job. Another pressure was the increasing demand by her husband for oral-genital contact, to which she strenuously objected.

Treatment: Upon hospitalization, isolation was necessary because of her aggressive, destructive behavior. She was untidy and incontinent, and thought that her own urine was acid with which the staff was trying to poison her. She tried to swallow a cross necklace she was wearing, because of the delusional idea that this would protect her from this poisoning. She misidentified the nursing personnel as "Satan" or the "devil," and attendants as "jailers." She decided one of the female patients was really a man, wondering whether she, herself, was changing into a man, and frequently looking into the mirror to see if she had a penis. She was placed on heavy doses of phenothiazines and within a week began to quiet down, as well as give up many of her delusional ideas. Two weeks after her admission she was able to say "I haven't imagined anything in the past four days. I have always been impulsive and unstable. I guess I just didn't want to face reality." As the delusions cleared, she could talk in a realistic manner about her guilty feelings regarding sex and the demands that her husband was making on her. She worked through the idea she was inadequate and lacking in feminine charm since her hysterectomy but expressed some fears of losing her husband because of her sexual inhibitions. Ventilating these feelings, she was able to reintegrate fast enough to be discharged one month after hospitalization without medication. For the following year she attended group therapy sessions as an outpatient.

Follow-up: It is worth noting that this patient did not resume her job upon discharge. Two and one-half years after her discharge, her daughter was hit on the head by a neighboring child. The patient became excited, ran hysterically around the house, called the fire department, and when approached by a consoling neighbor, had another acute paranoid break, screaming in a most vituperative way at this neighbor to keep away from her child and expressing a number of referential persecutory ideas. Unfortunately we have no data on her sensorium during this episode. Within a few hours she had recovered from this acute episode and felt badly that she had acted in such an "unexplained fashion." For the past six months she has noted increasing lethargy. She stays in bed most of the morning, does her housework late in the afternoon and early evening, going to bed at twelve or one each night. She seems now to have withdrawn from her husband, describing their relationship as one of cold indifference. She denied any hallucinations or delusions, but one had the feeling that she was both suspicious and evasive. When confronted directly with the fact that she might need help, she agreed, but said "I'm too lazy to get it." It is ominous that the preceding evening she had visited her local medical doctor, complaining about hearing her pulse in her head. She thought that this might be a symptom of a brain tumor. When asked whether she was hearing other things, she laughed in a somewhat silly, inappropriate manner. At other times, even though expressing depressive ideas, her affect was bland. One had the feeling that she might be entering an acute episode at the time of follow-up.

Psychodynamic-neurophysiologic synthesis: In contrast to the previous patient, this one was definitely disoriented and confused during the original episodic psychosis. It is significant that the activation study with alpha chloralose revealed the bilateral hypersynchronous activity. This was also true of Patients S243, S229, and S269, all given the diagnosis of episodic psychotic reaction, and in each of these instances the sensorium was also clouded; thus, they showed evidence of the acute brain syndrome in contrast to the patient described above, who had acute psychotic reactions typical of schizophrenia without clouding of consciousness, and who showed no abnormalities with EEG activation.

Appendix 6   Episodic Neurotic Reaction: Anxiety and Depression

Patient: F250

Diagnosis: Episodic depressive reaction unpredictable, occurring every two to five months. Also episodic hypochondriacal and physiologic reactions. Characterological diagnosis: passive-dependent personality.

Identification: Forty-four-year-old, white, married, male executive. Outpatient supportive psychotherapy two times a week with eight hospitalizations over a period of four years; 12-month follow-up and 12 months without therapy.

Presenting problem: This man was referred with acute anxiety and depression of several weeks' duration following termination with his previous psychiatrist, who had moved out of town after having treated the patient over a period of two years for a "cardiac neurosis." To all external appearance this man had been living successfully; that is, he was respected in the community, was a junior executive in a large corporation, and lived in an upper-middle-class neighborhood with his wife and three children. Difficulties began four years before his present treatment, following hospitalization for a broken leg. This was a compound fracture with numerous complications which delayed his convalescence and rehabilitation, and allegedly led him into conflicts with his superiors, who accused him of "goofing off." During the next several years these conflicts mounted with increasing tension until two years before admission, while watching an exciting football game, the patient suffered a mild coronary occlusion. Since that event he has been frequently absent from work, has sought constant medical reassurance because of his hypochondriacal preoccupations, and was episodically so depressed that he voluntarily sought psychiatric care. His medical and psychiatric incapacities finally led to a demotion which, in turn, precipitated more depression and anxiety. Whereas previously he had been an independent decisive executive, he now became childish and dependent: for example, calling his wife frequently during the day for emotional support, and often crying over the telephone. At the time of admission he was so anxious that he was tremulous, perspiring, and agitated. He complained of insomnia, which he attempted to counteract by excessive alcoholic intake just prior to bedtime.

Mental status examination: This was a somewhat wan and debilitated individual who looks older than his stated age. He was obviously tense and restless but obsequious in his relationship with the psychiatrist, whiningly begging for sympathy, although he did not seem obviously depressed. There was no evidence of motor retardation. He was of superior intelligence and showed no particular suicidal preoccupations, but was obsessed with the idea that he was becoming an alcoholic. Over the years he has imbibed one or two martinis at lunch, one or two cocktails before dinner, and, recently, a nightcap, a program that is not atypical for his peers and one that he had been maintaining for many years. The only recent change in his drinking habits had been that sometimes during the night when unable to sleep, he would "take a slug of whiskey." He was discouraged because a rather meteoric rise in the business world during his early years has not only slowed but ground to a halt. He tended to blame this on his physical disabilities and, although protesting how great his company was, at the same time he cautiously expressed resentment over what he felt were their unfair demands during a period when he was physically ill for reasons beyond his control. He showed no capacity for meaningful introspection, and was content to sit back and wait for a magic word that would solve his problems without effort on his own part. Within a week after his initial visit, probably because an immediate cure was not forthcoming, his depression increased rapidly, with the appearance of suicidal preoccupations, which made hospitalization necessary.

EEG, neurological and medical examinations: Blood pressure was 146/96; pulse was 110; and respiration 16. The laboratory studies were all negative except for the electrocardiogram, which did indicate residual myocardial damage. At the time of his first admission there was no indication of a need for an EEG.

Psychological evaluation: The patient's full-scale IQ was 137 even though the performance tests indicated an IQ of only 105. This discrepancy suggested the possibility of some organic brain damage, but this was not confirmed by subsequent studies. Tests revealed that he was preoccupied with impulses of a hostile and sexual nature and that there was a "narcissistic preoccupation with his own body." The outstanding defenses were denial and repression, particularly aimed at controlling his feelings of anger and his sense of inadequacy as a male. He was seen as a highly dependent person with a truly infantile need for almost constant support and comfort, as well as structure, from authoritative figures. Depression was not outstanding, but the depression that did occur had an hysterical, narcissistic quality. He handled anxiety-provoking situations with obsessive controls and was described by both the psychiatrist and the psychologist as "pollyannish."

Family and developmental history: This man is an only child, born to an upper-middle-class family, but, though he was undoubtedly spoiled, until sophomore year in college there seemed to be no significant behavior deviations. At that time his mother died, and he was sufficiently depressed by this event to drop out of school for the year. It is significant that shortly after his mother's death, he began courting his present wife, and married her within the year. In fact, what seemed to be characteristic of this man was that he had to have a strong maternal figure to lean on. He also remained extremely close to his father, who died only a year before his present therapy began. The type of relationship is best reflected in his statement "Daddy and I were real pals. He was best man at my wedding and I was best man at his second marriage." He completed his college education by attending night school while working during the day. Except for two years in the service during World War II, he has worked with the same company all his life, rising from a menial laborer to the position of a junior executive. It became obvious during the course of treatment that his "happy" married life with his wife and children was fraught with many difficulties which he would not face. His wife was an extremely obese, dishevelled woman who appeared to be in poor health. Subsequently, she was found to have cirrhosis of the liver as a result of her chronic alcoholism.

Treatment: Within 24 hours after admission, the patient had what, in retrospect, might have been a seizural episode, although the tentative diagnosis at the time was that he had suffered a second coronary attack. When a ping-pong table on which he was leaning collapsed, he lost consciousness, becoming cold, clammy, and cyanotic. His pulse was rapid and weak, while his blood pressure was slightly elevated. Although he was studied carefully for the possibility of a recurrent coronary occlusion, laboratory tests did not corroborate this diagnosis, so it was assumed that he had had an acute anxiety attack. Although the therapist felt that his primary problems were with his wife, the patient focused on job difficulties.

Within one month he was discharged from the hospital, to be followed on an outpatient basis. Periodically the family was seen as a group in the hope of improving the family relationships. It was revealed during these sessions that his wife was extremely hostile and controlling, the patient obsequiously dependent except for intermittent episodes of explosive anger, which were directed most often towards his children, but on rare occasions towards his wife. Family life was constantly disrupted by his wife who, despite the fact she had been told she would die within the year if she continued to drink, did so to an even greater extent than before, saying that she would rather die than give up alcohol.

Six months after hospitalization, the patient was rehospitalized with a second coronary insufficiency and one year later he developed a new symptom. When on vacation, he had his first grand mal attack. EEG at that time was normal but repeat studies revealed on several occasions random sharp waves appearing in the anterior temporal region bilaterally with a shifting lateral predominance. Because of the patient's hypochondriasis and a tendency to exploit any physical illness in avoiding professional and family responsibilities, the seizure and EEG abnormalities were played down until later in the fall when the patient had a second seizure. At that time a neurological consultation was requested but no other abnormalities were discovered. The patient was started on diphenylhydantoin (Dilantin) 0.1 gm. q.i.d.

Two years after first seen, the patient was again hospitalized because he was functioning at a marginal level with periodic depressions. The day of hospitalization he had been sitting on a bridge contemplating suicide. Another reason for hospitalization was that he had been functioning so poorly that his job was in jeopardy, his company being more tolerant of his behavior if he was sick enough to need hospitalization. The patient at this time was depressively ruminating about his wife's poor health, his own "alcoholism," and the fact that he always had to be the "nice guy," but that his job demanded that he be a "tough egg." Again, the family was gathered together in one of the most pathetic sessions his therapist has ever witnessed. Three children, seventeen, fifteen, and eleven, were confronted with two depressed parents who had given up all hope and were both slowly committing suicide, oblivious to the needs of their children. Confronted with the anguish that this was causing the children, the parents both accepted hospitalization, and arrangements were made for other family members to look after the children.

Within the first week, the patient had three grand mal seizures, and it was subsequently discovered that he was not taking his prescribed anticonvulsants, apparently inviting the convulsions to elicit sympathy and care. He had even told friends that he was being hospitalized for a brain tumor. Within a month it was necessary to discharge both parents so that they could return to take care of their children, but within two months the patient was back in the hospital, supposedly with a coronary attack, which this time, was not confirmed by laboratory studies. Outside pressures again forced an immediate discharge, but within a month he was back for his fifth psychiatric admission, this time with a new symptom. On several occasions, late in the evening the patient would abruptly become confused and violent; he would beat his wife and children, but have no memory of the events. Originally, it was assumed that this occurred because he was drunk, but subsequent observations revealed that these spells occurred at times when he had not been drinking excessively. It was assumed that alcohol then, while not the cause of his aggressive behavior, might precipitate or "activate" what appeared to be a complex psychomotor seizure. Sometimes this seizure would be simply falling out of bed and thrashing about; other times it would be more directed, but still diffuse and poorly coordinated— kicking his wife out of bed, beating on her or anything else that was close at hand, such as the pillow, the wall, the bedstead. At this time prolonged hospitalization was insisted upon, and primidone (Mysoline), 250 mgms., was added to his regime of diphenylhydantoin (Dilantin). At the same time he was treated as an "alcoholic" in that the goal of therapy was for him to give up drinking altogether because it precipitated the epileptoid response. Activation studies during this hospitalization did not reveal the previous bilateral temporal focus, but did induce a paroxysmal bilateral and symmetrical high amplitude 3 to 6 per second response. He was subsequently committed to a state hospital for prolonged care, but four months after this he was released from the alcoholic ward, this being exactly three years after he had started therapy with his present therapist and five years after he had initiated psychiatric care. Two weeks after his discharge, his wife died from ruptured esophageal varices. His immediate response was to drink continuously for a day and a night, being brought into the hospital in a drunken, debilitated, semistuporous state. Despite this, he had to be discharged within a day to make arrangements for the funeral and to take care of family affairs.

The patient's life was further complicated by his daughter becoming pregnant shortly before her mother's death. She was married six weeks afterwards, and she and her new husband moved into the patient's house, the daughter functioning in essence as his housekeeper. Despite his extreme guilt over his wife's death and a long period of dependency on his wife, the depression lifted remarkably quickly. In part this may have been because of the pressing family needs, not only his daughter's marriage, but his oldest son's academic troubles, which meant that he too returned home from college. The youngest child, too, was chronically depressed and a behavior problem. Within two weeks after this family consolidation, the patient returned to work, gave up drinking, and as might have been predicted, several months later established a nonsexual, very dependent relationship with a spinster of his age who fortunately abstained from alcohol, and thus reinforced his control in this area. At this time

he was receiving diphenylhydantoin (Dilantin), o.1 gm. t.i.d., primidone (Mysoline) 250 mgs., each night, and occasional chlordiazepoxide (Librium) to control periods of anxiety. In a burst of independence he wanted to discontinue psychiatric care and try to make
it on his own and he was encouraged to do so.

Follow-up: He was seen 24 months after his last hospitalization, 12
months after his last formal psychotherapeutic session. He has functioned well enough on the job to be given added responsibilities and
a month previously married his girlfriend. During this period there
had been no drinking, no depression, and no subsequent grand mal
attacks, although he continues with his anticonvulsant medication.
This is an example of a happy outcome in what appeared for
several years to be a hopeless problem. The good therapeutic result
was undoubtedly due as much to fortuitous environmental changes
as to psychotherapy.

Psychodynamic-neurophysiologic considerations: In retrospect it
appears that the series of events preceding the overt psychiatric disability may have represented episodic physiologic reactions. Even the
initial event of breaking a leg was a fall under circumstances that
suggest a seizure. A series of hospitalizations for myocardial infarc-
tions, two revealing some evidence of actual coronary disease while
three others failed to do so, suggests the episodic physiologic reactions.
There were a number of other transitory physical complaints which
could have been again either episodic physiologic reactions or episodic hypochondriasis. Ultimately, this was replaced by episodic
depressive and anxiety reactions of increasing severity, complicated
by the appearance of more typical epileptoid seizures of a grand mal
and psychomoter type. One cannot be certain as to why this occurred
at age 40, except that data subsequently uncovered indicated that
this man's difficulties on the job did not follow his medical disabilities but preceded them by several years. For example, he had been
passed over several times for promotions, had been working for a particularly difficult person, and finally was working for superiors who at
one time had been his juniors and protegés. The narcissistic wounds
of failing to please the authoritative figures and maintain his favorite
son status were made specific by the appearance of actual physical disabilities, which were both proofs of his inadequacy and an excuse for
it. He might have survived the rejection of parental figures on the job
if the "wife-mother" at home had remained the supportive and nur-
turing figure she once had been. With her increasing alcoholism,

however, she failed more and more in this role. Apparently her death was not seen as the result of his unconscious death wishes but rather as the disappearance of the bad mother and an opportunity to find a good one. It is interesting that in the first psychological evaluation there were indications that, at least in fantasy, he set up a replacement for this neglectful wife. No data came up at that time to support the fact that he was either having an extramarital affair or a close emotional attachment with anybody outside the family, but the woman he ultimately married had been his secretary at that time, and may have been this idealized mother suspected in the studies done several years before his wife's death.

Patient: F284

Diagnosis: Episodic anxiety reaction occurring for the first time. A questionable episodic psychotic reaction some years in the past. Characterological diagnosis: paranoid personality.

Identification: Thirty-four-year-old, white, single, male executive; hospitalized for diagnostic evaluation; rehospitalized for definitive care; 12 month follow-up.

Presenting problem: This man was seen after he had been hospitalized for two weeks because of an acute episode of anxiety manifested by tachycardia, palmar sweating, shortness of breath, and associated depressive episodes, the latter lasting for only a few hours during which he would express serious suicidal thoughts. The current reaction had been precipitated by an engagement to a rather sensuous girl who was pressing for premarital relations. This aroused so much anxiety that the patient became impotent. There had been recurrent sexual dreams involving this girl as well as others, almost always accompanied by severe anxiety, so that the patient awakened in panic before being orgastic.

Mental status examination: The patient was in no obvious discomfort except that he was tense, guarded, and seemed particularly cautious. He was suspicious of the consultant and consciously withheld information. In a second interview, however, he began talking with a rather false bravado about his sexual problems and difficulties in relating to women. He preferred to keep his life simple by not marrying, but realized (particularly when physically ill the preceding winter at which time he was alone in his apartment) how important it was to have a wife and a family. There is some evidence of sublimated homosexuality, in that he emphasized his pleasures in sailing with the boys and revealed a marked attachment towards his business partner, from whom he recently has become estranged. During the initial interviews, his mother was constantly fluttering in and out of the room, quite overprotective and restrictive, a concern that the patient seemed to enjoy.

EEG, neurological and medical examination: Neurological examination revealed a suggestive weakness of the right side of the body and a mild aphasia. EEG indicated random sharp waves appearing in the left anterior and mid-temporal region and less frequently on the right independently, both during wakefulness and sleep. In addition, during the waking state there were bursts of high amplitude slow activity mixed with sharp forms appearing bilaterally and symmetrically.

Psychological evaluation: This revealed an extremely high level of anxiety as well as evidence of central nervous system impairment and mild aphasic disturbances. A careful and deliberate performance compensated in part for the organic intellectual defect. Tests also indicated phobias of a sexual nature; namely, that women were terribly predatory and devouring creatures, so that he had an obvious preference for the safer camaraderie of the male friend. Depressive features were noted with a tendency to see his illness as a morbidly inherited and malignant disease.

Family and developmental history: This is an only child, born to a wealthy, upper-class family, with no significant medical or psychiatric problems reported during infancy and early childhood. He attended all of the right schools, and did all of the right things, although one had a feeling that he was an "overachiever," striving hard to live up to his family's social and intellectual expectations.

There was a significant neurological history with hospitalization fifteen years before the present illness, at which time the patient fell off a motorbike, receiving a concussion and demonstrating a transitory right hemiparesis with dyplopia. Some years before this, he had also suffered a cervical spine fracture followed by persistent headaches. Nine years before his current admission, he sustained another head injury while wrestling, and eight years before admission he had a febrile episode followed by double vision, headache, and vomiting, and at the same time having what was described as a "seizure." Following this seizure the patient was described as restless, disoriented, and delusional. Extensive neurological investigations, including air encephalograms, and carotid arteriograms, were normal. Following the neurological procedures, he developed a transitory aphasis and hemiplegia. EEG at that time revealed bursts of high voltage three-per-second waves in the frontal areas, which were again seen on a second EEG performed ten days later.

After a struggle he graduated from college and immediately began a small business with his inheritance. He became quite independent and aggressive, and despite his personality problems, a financial success at an early age. He lived a very regular life, seldom varying his routine: nine-to-five on the job, evening at home with his friends, and every weekend sailing with friends.

Treatment: During his one month hospitalization he was encouraged to ventilate his sexual anxieties as well as to work out in a definitive way his relationships with his fiancee. He was encouraged when he made the decision to break off with this girl, but she thwarted his rather meek efforts to do this. Although anticonvulsants and chlordiazepoxide (Librium) had considerably reduced his anxiety and acute panic, the persistence of the more chronic depression and anxiety caused the patient to insist on hospitalization "in a distant city," undoubtedly as an excuse to get away from his girl friend. At the time of follow-up he was still hospitalized at that institution.

Psychodynamic-neurophysiologic synthesis: This patient is a dramatic example of an individual who has both temporal lobe (perhaps deep rhinencephalic) abnormalities, as well as paroxysmal synchronous frontal slow waves both in the resting record and on chloralose activation. By our prediction he should then be one of those individuals who would show an extreme degree of impulsivity and acting out. It is obvious that although this man does fear losing control of his impulses, his behavior is best characterized by overcontrol with impulses kept in check by isolation from any emotional stimuli and withdrawal from conflictual situations. Instead of impulsivity and antisocial behavior, he develops inhibited obsessional controls and sublimates many of his frustrations through his excessive striving for achievement. He does have a history, however, of a number of episodic reactions of a physiologic type; namely, aphasias and hemiplegias, as well as occasional seizural dyscontrol, one episodic psychotic episode, and his rather precipitous episodic anxiety and depressive reaction. Is this the price he pays for control of his impulses, and if so, which is the smaller price: physical and psychological disability or possible social censure and retribution if he gives in to his impulses?

Appendix 7 Episodic Neurotic Reaction: Conversion and Dissociative Reaction

Patient: O289

Diagnosis: Episodic neurotic reaction (dissociative reactions which are unpredictable but occur two to three times per month; also episodic depressive reactions, usually occurring premenstrually). Characterological diagnosis: passive-aggresisve personality.

Identification: Thirty-three-year-old, white, married housewife. Treatment consisted of outpatient insight psychotherapy and hypnosis for 284 hours over a 24-month period. Also hospitalization, EST and drug therapy. Forty-eight month follow-up.

Presenting problem: This woman, the mother of four children and the wife of a lawyer, living in a small rural community, was referred by her local physician because of confusional episodes during which she was disoriented, did not recognize her home, and assumed another name (significantly the initials of this name were the same as her maiden name). During these episodes she acted in an irresponsible, aggressive manner, throwing boiling water on her husband, drinking in strange bars, running away from home, and driving her car at inordinately fast speeds. She also appeared unsteady on her feet and her speech was slurred, giving the impression of intoxication. She actually did drink heavily during some but not all of these periods. However, the drinking usually followed the onset of an episode, rather than preceded it. For 24 hours after such an episodic reaction she was lethargic and drowsy. Although she had amnesia for most of the behavior during the periods of episodic dyscontrol, this could be penetrated easily with hypnosis. During the episode she showed a peculiar double orientation, inasmuch as while playing the role of the wild, promiscuous, single girl, she would take pictures of her children and family out of her purse, showing them to her companions without realizing the inconsistency in her behavior. Conscience mechanisms still operated during these dissociative periods because she never carried through to completion her irresponsible actions, and whenever she deserted her family, did so only at a time when her children were well cared for. On several occasions when "coming to" she was convinced that she had had coitus, reporting to her doctor panic-stricken. However, his examination revealed that this was highly unlikely. Other episodic symptoms included periods of extreme anxiety with tachycardia and tremulousness followed by depression. At other times there were episodes of hyperactivity and euphoria, the latter occurring in the late afternoon or evening, and often making it impossible for her to sleep without heavy sedation.

The referring physician thought that these episodes followed a "measles encephalitis" two years before her present examination; at that time the patient required hospitalization with seven days of temperatures over 104 degrees. However, detailed physical and laboratory studies, including extensive neurological examinations and routine EEG's, had all been normal.

Her own reports suggested a second possible explanation. Her relationship with her spouse had always been stormy. He was authoritative and dogmatic, and she was equally stubborn. After early resistance to his behavior the patient became obsequious and compliant until two years before the present examination, when she discovered that he was having an affair. Becoming enraged, she thereafter tried to be assertive, but his response was only increased belligerence; in fact, on several occasions he beat her so severely that she required hospitalization, once he broke her arm and another time he kicked her in the abdomen, inducing an abortion. Finally the episodic dissociative reactions and the marital physical abuse became so frequent and intense that the patient's mother moved into the household to protect both the patient and her children.

Mental status examination: There was a lack of depth in her emotional responsivity, which was judged a sign of restraint and inhibition rather than a symptom of more malignant pathology. The most striking fact noticed was an inability to report introspective material, with the impression that she was consciously withholding pertinent data. Subsequent hypnotic sessions confirmed this, and during these sessions she revealed the previously hidden malignant marital adjustment, as well as her morbid preoccupation with death because of her identification with an older sister who committed suicide. Certain paranoid traits were manifest in her inordinate pride and ambition, intense hostility, and fear of physical damage (the latter, however, having some basis in reality), as well as her intense rage and jealousy regarding her husband's infidelity. She revealed that she spends many hours daydreaming, particularly indulging in vivid and perverse sexual fantasies. She admitted to a number of recurrent nightmares, particularly one involving running down a tunnel that is tumbling in on her. The opening could be seen in the far distance, but her feelings are mixed about reaching this exit, because the exit does not mean escape but death. There were other stereotyped repetitive dreams of sinking ships, houses on fire, all with the same theme of impending disaster.

EEG, neurological and medical examination: Medical, neurological, and laboratory studies were all negative. She had a series of EEG's, all with similar baselines. Alpha activity was somewhat irregular, 11-per-second in the occipital and parietal areas, mixed irregular alpha and low voltage fast activity in other regions. All records were marred by frequent bursts of muscle potential. Relaxation was obtained through light hypnosis which reduced the muscle tension, but sleep was not obtained. Rarely were there small temporal amplitude and frequency asymmetries with a suggestion of small sharp waves in the left temporal area, but this was not considered definitive evidence of a temporal focus. Attempts to clarify this with activation studies were undertaken. Photic activation revealed driving at flicker rates of 7-to-9-per-second, but no abnormalities. Metrazol activation revealed possible random spike discharges in the left temporal area, but the validity of this finding was obscured by movement and muscle artifact. Chloralose activation revealed mild generalized slowing considered to be a nonspecific toxic effect of the drug, but no true activation. Sleep, even after heavy doses of barbiturates, was unsatisfactory, the patient either not being affected by the drug, or, if the barbiturate level was high enough, precipitously going into deep sleep, in which considerable barbiturate spindling masked any possible abnormalities. A fourth EEG study done two months after she had received electric shock therapy (see below) again showed slight but inconclusive evidence suggestive of random spikes in the left temporal area.

Psychological evaluation: The patient is of superior intelligence, and projective tests revealed that she maintained adequate reality contact, showing no marked distortions in thought processes, nor any evidence of organic impairment. There were phobic fears regarding sexuality but at the same time many sexual preoccupations. Her responses ranged from controlled mature decisiveness to undisciplined diffuse reactions. The primary defenses were repression, denial, and avoidance.

Family and developmental history: The patient is the middle of three siblings with a sister seven years older and a brother seven years younger. She describes her father as indulgent and loving, and her mother as permissive and understanding. A paternal grandmother also lived in the home until the patient was ten. This grandmother was considered to have a personality similar to that of the patient; that is, both were emotionally labile, easily angered, and argumentative. The patient and the grandmother frequently argued "just for the fun of it." Birth and early development were allegedly normal and, despite the fact that throughout childhood and adolescence the patient was considered irritable, demanding, and bossy, she had a wide circle of friends, being both scholastically and socially successful. Coming from an upper-class family, she attended exclusive girls' schools, marrying her husband after two years of college, while he was a law student. The husband appeared to the community as a loving and altruistic individual, uncompromisingly devoted to his clients, but in the home he showed considerable evidence of extreme paranoid attitudes, particularly by his need to derogate all women, insistence on control of his wife, compulsive use of severe punishment for his children, and sometimes almost delusional interpretation of family interactions.

Treatment: The patient was first seen six times a week on an outpatient basis, while living in a hotel with her mother. Despite the danger of further complicating the dissociative state, hypnosis was used because, as already mentioned, it was impossible by other methods to get pertinent clinical material. With hypnosis she relaxed, establishing a positive attitude toward her therapy and trust in her therapist, now being able to reveal information which she had at first consciously withheld. By the end of three weeks, hypnosis was used less and less until all sessions were carried out in the waking state. She was tried on 400 mgs. meprobamate (Miltown, Equanil) and o.2 gms. secobarbital (Seconal) each night. During the first month she had two dissociative episodes, one in the psychiatrist's office where she played out the role of her alter ego, insisting that she was not a patient, but a friend who had come to take the psychiatrist on a picnic. Cues used to elicit hypnotic trances were given and under hypnosis the dissociative state was terminated. Medication was shifted to promazine (Sparine) because of her restlessness, and methylphenidate (Ritalin) because of her depression, and finally diphenylhydantoin (Dilantin) because of her questionably abnormal EEG. None of these medications seemed to have a noticeable effect on her hyperactivity, depression or episodic dissociative reactions.

It became increasingly obvious that marital discord was a primary contributing factor in her difficulties, so that family therapy was attempted. However, the husband, after a brief trial, rejected this, picturing his wife as "crazy" or "a lush." During this period, both of the spouses were alternatingly threatening divorce and obsequiously making up.

As the patient had to return home to take care of her children, and this home was some distance from her psychiatrist, treatment was cut to two sessions per week on consecutive days, which meant a plane flight or long drive to get to the therapist's office. The dangers of this situation are obvious in that she had to spend one evening unsupervised and almost invariably during this evening there was a dissociative episode, with all kinds of self-destructive potential. Acting on sexual fantasies involving her therapist, she appeared at his house as her alter ego, but this state was terminated again by the use of hypnotic cues. The therapist and his wife insisted on returning the patient to her hotel room. Later that evening she made a serious suicidal attempt, requiring hospitalization. The depression rapidly lifted and insight quickly returned, so that discharge was arranged within several days. Over the next month, however, three other episodic suicidal attempts were made, the last one with one gram of phenobarbital, which led to such a deep coma that treatment with bemigride (Megimide) was required. At this time hospitalization for a prolonged period was insisted upon. During the entire four months of hospitalization she was chronically depressed and episodically dissociated. The depressive episodes waxed and waned but were particularly prominent during the premenstrual period. During the dissociative episodes she would be destructive of her clothes or the hospital furniture, but, interestingly, no matter how disturbed she was, she never destroyed the crucifix which hung on the wall of her room in the Catholic hospital. Repeat neurological evaluation at that time again revealed a questionably abnormal EEG. The spinal pandy was 2 plus, and there was a first zone colloidal gold curve, with total proteins at the upper limits of normal. Because of the equivocal significance of these tests they were repeated six months later, at which time all were normal. She received eight EST treatments with considerable improvement in her depression and was discharged shoftly thereafter.

Following this hospitalization, she realized that the only solution to her problem was separation from her husband. To accomplish this, however, meant deserting and perhaps losing forever her children. She was sincerely concerned about her children because she was realistically fearful her husband would inadvertently or delusionally harm them. She procrastinated for one year, in the meantime seeing her therapist intermittently for brief consultations. Her dissociative states and other symptoms continued, but there were no further suicidal attempts. She finally deserted her husband and children, returning to her family's home in a different city. She became acutely disturbed and distraught following this decision, requiring intensive psychiatric care from a new therapist for the next nine months. At that point her husband sued for divorce and, as she reports, "when I knew I had to get well if I was to see my children again, then I did, almost overnight." A year and a half after the separation she faced the first court hearing with confidence and, without further psychiatric help or medication, and no return of her symptoms, she then followed through a lengthy court battle which stretched over three years. At the same time she returned to college, obtaining her teacher's certificate. Three years after the original separation, the courts restored her children to her. Her comment at the last follow-up was, "Thank you very much for the confidence you had in me." This illustrates the point in Chapter 12 on the psychotherapy of the episodic behavioral disorders that, despite what may appear to be an overwhelmingly bad prognosis, long-term treatment in this group of patients may be successful and it is imperative for the therapist to maintain at least a reasonable optimism regarding the outcome.

Psychodynamic-neurophysiologic synthesis: The original working hypothesis in the treatment of this patient was that the dissociative states represented a complex epileptoid phenomenon. Support for such a diagnosis was indicated by the mild, if questionable abnormalities on the first EEG, the definite history of measles with possible encephalitis two years before and at the time of onset of her symptoms; and the relatively successful adjustment before the precipitous onset of her present illness. However, as the investigation progressed, it became increasingly obvious that motivational factors were of prime importance. First, as we have previously discussed there were some striking disparities between her state of consciousness and level of awareness. During the dissociative episodes she lost her identity, in fact, assumed that of another person, and despite some ataxia and slurred speech (often induced by heavy drinking during the amnesic episode), she carried out skilled acts, drove long distances in her car, found her way back to her hotel in strange towns, and controlled her behavior when the "chips were down." At times, even when she had assumed the identity of the single, flighty, promiscuous girl, she would take out her wallet and show bystanders pictures of her children, with no awareness of the inconsistency in this behavior. More data, however, revealed the dissociative episodes to be escapes from a frightening and intolerable marital situation from which there was no other easy escape. The dissociative periods not only relieved tensions and frustrations in the patient, but also were attempts to coerce changes within her husband. When she finally accepted the fact that her behavior was futile and her only hope was to be healthy and independent, she "got well overnight." Further evidence that the motivational mechanisms were predominant was the failure of pharmacologic therapy, even though this was pursued intensively and relentlessly during the early stages of treatment. Her response to the extreme environmental stress was undoubtedly predetermined by her character structure in that she developed defenses of isolation, repression, and denial to control "acting on impulses," the latter having been expressed during childhood and early adolescence; with late adolescence and adulthood, she had had the intelligence and reality contact to develop "hysterical" defenses against these impulses, at least until the defenses were devastated by the marital conflict.

Appendix 8   Episodic Physiologic Reaction

Patient: S218

Diagnosis: Episodic physiologic reaction (recurrent at monthly intervals with seizural dyscontrol and episodic psychotic reactions). Characterological diagnosis: passive-aggressive personality.

Identification: 33-year-old, white, single female, jewelry maker, hospitalized many times. Follow-up, 42 months; 36 months without treatment.

Presenting problem: The patient was hospitalized for five days following a suicidal attempt in which she slashed her wrists and superficially cut her throat. Just prior to the suicidal attempt, hospitalization was being considered because of episodic confusional "stuporlike states" during which time she was confused, her speech was slow and slurred, and there was a loss of equilibrium. There was an amnesia for these episodes.

The current complaints went back three years before admission. During this period, the patient had been hospitalized on the medical wards at least five times, the first two for urinary retention, double vision, puffiness of the face, recurrent fever and headaches. Three

months later she was again admitted to the hospital in an unresponsive state, supposedly because of an overdose of barbiturates; however,
barbiturate blood levels were not significant. This coma was never
adequately explained. Two months later she was admitted with extreme abdominal pain and bladder distention, treated by dilatation
and pudendal block. Two months after that she was again admitted
for an alleged suicidal attempt, having taken an overdose of barbiturates which required treatment with a respirator.

Mental status examination: Although at the time of admission the
patient was languid, confused, and disoriented; by the time a formal
examination was undertaken she was alert and oriented. She tended
to be belligerent and sarcastically hostile, superficially cooperative
one moment, but completely uncooperative the next. She constantly
complained either about the poor physical care within the hospital or
about numerous symptoms for which no objective evidence can be
found. Despite her hostile aggressiveness, there was also fear and depression. She was frightened of the other patients. She said that it was
stupid that she attempted to commit suicide, insisting there was no
longer any need for her hospitalization because she would not "think
of it" again.

EEG, physical and neurological examination: A general physical
examination was never significant except for evidence of bladder retention, when this was the predominant complaint. The neurologist
noted nystagmoid jerks on both right and left lateral gaze. The patient walked with a short step and a wide base. She was unable to
perform tandem walking, and although she swayed from the ankle on
the Romberg test she did not fall to either side. The reflexes of the
upper extremities were noted to be more brisk than those of the
lower. Laboratory studies, including LE preparations were negative.
The patient had extensive biochemical and endocrinologic studies,
all of which were negative. Radioactive scans were negative. X-rays of
the spine, chest, and skull showed no abnormalities. Right brachial
arteriograms revealed no intracranial disease. Pneumoencephalogram
showed no definite abnormalities; there was, however, an irregular
outline on the tomograms between the vallecula and the right cerebellar hemisphere. Because of the episodic and so-called seizural characteristics of some of her disorders, she had an extensive series of
EEG's. At one time in the past, 6-per-second positive spikes had been
reported, but none were seen in the current studies. Seven of the
studies were done with methyprylon (Nodular) sedation; five of the

seven were perfectly normal; two, however, showed moderate amounts of paroxysmal high amplitude slow waves with some hypersynchronous forms following hyperventilation. Chloralose activation revealed frequent bursts of high amplitude 2-to-4-per-second activity with a considerable build-up on hyperventilation.

Family and developmental history: This patient was the only child of a well-to-do family, apparently indulged and very much overprotected in a restrictive way by a rather hostile and aggressive mother. The father remained in the background, dying sometime during the patient's teens. From an early age the patient had been recurrently ill; that is, at the age of four she had what was diagnosed as peritonitis with a recurrence again at age six, followed by an appendectomy. Throughout early childhood she had recurrent febrile illnesses, so many, in fact, that her schooling was constantly disrupted and she seldom completed any one grade. Because of this she did not graduate from high school, despite her superior intelligence. Although she dated occasionally, she tended to live a rather isolated social existence, usually having only one or two girl friends. During recent years, she lived in an apartment with a live-in maid upon whom she was quite dependent. She did develop a skill in, and showed considerable creative capacity for, designing jewelry. Although partially subsidized by her inheritance, she earned a living by manufacturing and selling the jewelry. She has had four or five doctors attending her at any one time, and if she cannot get one, she calls another. She has had many different kinds of medications which she takes ad lib so indiscriminately that it is impossible to tell whether she is toxic or having one of her episodic confusional states. She often became confused late at night, and insisted that doctors come to her home. She was usually found in an acute, agitated, confused state. Because of her obstreperous and obnoxious behavior, she had alienated the medical profession so tended to patronize one hospital and one group of doctors for several years until they became fed up, at which time she moved on to the next group.

Descriptions of her behavior during the several weeks in which she was followed by the EEG recordings will give some understanding of this woman's symptoms.

October 2: The patient says she is feeling well, there is no evidence of slurred speech or unsteady gait, nor is she having diplopia. She says, however, she feels "whirly" which means that her mind is racing. Today she has insight into her personality and is contrite for her obstreperous behavior in the past. She says "I know right from wrong, but cannot always follow it. I get frantic." The day before she noted some neurological symptoms, that is, the slurred speech and staggering gait, but this disappeared later in the afternoon. She also complains of mounting bladder tension and says rather grandiosely, "I saved a marriage last night, talking to a friend over the telephone."

October 9: The patient is bright and alert this morning not complaining of any symptoms, although mild slurring of speech is noted. She says that the day before at 4:30 in the afternoon her right leg was cold. She began to feel frantic, noticed that her speech was getting slurred, and also was aware of double vision. From this point on she has only a partial recollection of the events of the day, but remembers intense abdominal pain. In an attempt to relieve this, she put her hand up her vagina. She says she felt as though there was a hot poker in her bladder. The pain was so intense that she would have to clench her teeth or bite on objects. With meperidine (Demerol) and sedatives the pain was finally relieved. Her maid reports that at this time the patient wanted to be hugged and kissed and told that she was loved, although there apparently was no overt sexual acting out. However, the next morning the patient insisted on talking in great detail to her maid about the latter's love life and complained bitterly about being unloved by her own mother and how much she, the patient, wanted to get married. The maid also reports that on and off during this period the patient would talk of suicide.

November 26: The patient is gaining weight, but feels well and has had only one transitory episode in the past two weeks, at which time she noted slurred speech. She has had no trouble with her bladder during this period.

December 4: The patient telephoned and gave the following story. On December 1 she noticed that she was forgetful and felt that she was in a daze. On December 2 she was depressed, irritable, and several times burst into tears. On December 3, upon waking, she felt that she was retaining fluids (her weight was 121 pounds, whereas on the first of October it was 105 and one week before it was 117). Her bladder pains returned during the course of the day and she was also ataxic. She had the sensation that things appeared distant but jumped at her. December 4, in the morning she awoke and noticed a peculiar numbness in the right side of her face, and also that her right foot was cold. She also had a jumping sensation in the muscles of her hands.

Treatment: After discharge, on her own insistence, the patient went to a neurological institute for full evaluation, being convinced that her difficulties were caused by a brain tumor. When these studies failed to confirm her expectations, she shifted her point of view, saying that we had referred her for neurological evalution, hence we were not too skilled as clinicians because we made such a misdiagnosis. She was discharged from that hospital, and shortly thereafter, following a whirlwind courtship, married a young man, who turned out to be a "con" man. He married her so that he could, through her jewelry store, determine which homes and which women to rob. He ultimately was jailed and at the time of her subsequent divorce was incarcerated on a long-term sentence. Following the divorce, she decided to try living with her mother. Surprisingly, this was a turning point in her rehabilitation. She gave control of her medication, which was diphenylhydantoin (Dilantin), 0.1 gm. b.i.d., and phenobarbital, 0.03 gm. at night, to her mother. With her mother limiting her medication, she has had no prolonged confusional states, although she occasionally wakes up with what she calls "double reflexes." These she describes as follows: whenever she makes a movement there is a rebound and repetition of the movement. This lasts for a short time, clearing up by ten in the morning, after which she is able to work in her shop. She believes that these are seizures, but also believes that if she takes further medicine in an attempt to control them, she will become toxic. She finally decided that to have the early morning symptoms without prolonged toxicity is the solution to her problem. In view of how well she is doing she may be right.

Follow-up: At the time of the 30-month follow-up, she was strikingly different than she had been. Although somewhat hostile and reluctant to come in for the follow-up study, once there she was pleasant, and friendly, not nearly as sarcastic or as hostile as in times past. Another difference was that she was now neat and tidy in her appearance, although wearing somewhat bizarre, mannish clothes. Physically, she had lost the puffy edematous look. She had a limited social life, only occasionally seeing friends, but preferring it this way as she likes to spend most of her time designing and creating jewelry, which was recently displayed at a prominent museum. She says, "I still have trouble with my memory. I have to write down everything or I will forget it."

Psychodynamic-neurophysiologic synthesis: This is an exceedingly complex medical, neurological, and psychiatric problem that, because of the patient's belligerent uncooperativeness and suspiciousness, was seldom worked up properly. In fact, she never consented to a full psychological study. She strikes one as having the "periodic disease" discussed by Reiman (1963), but what is equally striking, seems to adjust best with small doses of diphenylhydantoin (Dilantin) and phenobarbital. This suggests that control of some kind of "excessive neuronal discharge" in the central nervous system has not only controlled the episodic confusional states but also the episodic urinary retention, general bodily water retention, and febrile reactions.

Appendix 9   Episodic Sociopathic Reaction

Patient: S212

Diagnosis: Episodic sociopathic reaction (sexual promiscuity), also seizure and instinctual dyscontrol. Characterological diagnosis: passive-aggressive personality.

Identification: A twenty-seven-year-old, white, married housewife hospitalized for one month. Outpatient care, then rehospitalized again for one month. Follow-up, 39 months later, 17 months after her last hospitalization.

Presenting problem: This woman was admitted with the chief complaint of extreme nervousness which she felt was due to an insatiable sexual appetite. She is the mother of seven children, the first being conceived out of wedlock, and two others not children of her husband. The last illegitimate child, born three months before her admission, was recently given up for adoption. Sexual promiscuity began six years before admission, several years after her marriage, when she discovered that her husband had been unfaithful. First she made a suicidal attempt by swallowing 100 aspirin and, when this failed to make him sufficiently contrite, she decided she would "get even" by becoming promiscuous herself. After several months of this behavior, she and her husband reconciled by promising mutual fidelity, which lasted for four years until her husband, a soldier, was sent overseas. She then resumed her promiscuous behavior, often having sexual relationships with several men during the same evening. Although she felt disgusted by such activity in retrospect, she was not able to control her sexual tensions at the time of her acts. Her present paramour is particularly satisfying to her because, although capable of an erection, he cannot ejaculate. This means that she can have innumerable orgasms in one evening.

She also complains of spells which are momentary blackouts in which her mind is blank. Recovery from these episodes is slow, with her first efforts at speech hesitant and slurred. The spells occur as frequently as five or six times a day. She reports other episodes during which she feels as though things are closing in upon her and she has the impulse to break up the furniture or destroy her belongings. Occasionally, she acts on these impulses. At other times, mounting tensions will require some kind of random activity, such as walking or dancing, but at the same time she notices, or at least subjectively feels, that she is uncoordinated.

Mental status examination: The patient is plainly and neatly dressed and only slightly seductive in her behavior. She is mildly depressed, obviously distracted and preoccupied. She is tense and restless, fidgets, wrings her hands, rubs her neck, bites her nails, or rubs her thighs, particularly when discussing emotionally charged material. There is no evidence of disorganization in her thinking, but she says about herself, "I just think differently from other people. I am irresponsible and undependable. I know I am not all there. I'm some kind of a nut." She spontaneously suggests that her spells represent getting away from reality, adding that "sometimes I don't want to come back, it's so peaceful there." She reports a number of recurrent nightmares, one that she is walking through a fog, struggling to get into a clear area, and another of trying to climb into a boat but constantly slipping back into the water. Other dreams include walking into a bedroom and stabbing her husband or chopping his head off with an axe; living as man and wife with a bushy-haired, whiskered man in the mountains, and quietly walking through a wooded path and then swimming naked in a mountain pool.

EEG, neurological, and medical examination: Except for slight obesity, there was no abnormal physical, neurological, or laboratory finding. The patient had four EEG studies during her hospitalization. The baseline recordings in all were similar, with well-developed but somewhat irregular 10-to-11-per-second alpha activity posteriorly and low amplitude fast activity over the frontal regions. The record was stable to hyperventilation. The first study with chloralose revealed no changes; the second study with pentylenetetrazol (Metrazol) activation (12 ccs of five percent solution injected at the rate of 1 cc every 30 seconds) also revealed no changes. A second Metrazol study revealed after 9 ccs of five percent Metrazol a single burst of high amplitude 4-to-5-per-second activity, bilaterally and symmetrically. After 10 ccs there were several bursts of slow and hypersynchronous activity, which again appeared bilaterally and symmetrically. A repeat alpha chloralose activation using a double dose revealed bursts of high amplitude rhythmic 6-to-7-per-second activity bilaterally and symmetrically with occasional high amplitude 3-to-4-per-second activity appearing with greatest prominence in the temporal region (see below for subsequent EEG studies).

Psychological evaluation: Intellectual functioning was average with no evidence of either central nervous system impairment or disorganized psychotic thinking. Projective tests reflected extreme anxiousness and a refusal to admit sexual preoccupations. There was a weakening of repressive defenses with impulses welling up and then, when acted upon, being denied or rationalized. At times during a tense situation, when anxiety reached an extremely high pitch, she would develop a degree of confusion and blunting of affect that approached a temporary state of dissociation. Defenses also showed paranoid elements with a tendency to be overly vigilant regarding self-exposure and to project blame onto others. There was not much evidence of guilt, little internalization of social standards, and only superficial depression. There appeared to be a feeling of "drivenness" in her sexual needs, and gratification was only partial and temporary. It would seem that an affect hunger and a primary need for dependency upon others, inhibited by extreme fearfulness over possible rejection and abandonment, were more important than sexual gratification. Feelings of rejection elicited murderous rage. She also had many of the characteristics of the so-called "addictive" personality.

Family and developmental history: The patient is the younger of two children, having a brother three years older than herself. The mother was the dominant member of the family, who handled the money, enforced discipline, and made decisions for the patient even after she was married. The father, on the other hand, was passive, calm, and mild-mannered, but apparently cold and not really part of the family. She described her older brother as the all-American type who has been quite successful, whereas she was the one who was always causing trouble. She remembers that in her preschool days she initiated sexual play with the neighborhood children, and recalls having had what were apparently hyperventilation spells during her early school years. At that time she developed the habit of severely scratching herself with the metal end of a pencil after removing the eraser. She delighted in telling tall stories to shock other people, talked out loud to herself, and sat for hours listening to music while daydreaming that she was living by herself in an isolated mountain cabin. Other daydreams were more bizarre, including scenes of sexual torture, such as women having their breasts burned and men having their penises cut off. She always liked science fiction, murder mysteries, and weird tales. She had her first coital experience at fifteen and became pregnant at sixteen, marrying the boy who was responsible but soon returning home to mother. At seventeen she married for the second time, a man whom she described in ambivalent terms as a very nice person, even though he has a violent temper and frequently beat the children. This was her spouse at the time of her first admission.

Treatment: During the patient's month of hospitalization, treatment centered on environmental manipulation and medical support. At her request, tubal ligation was performed and arrangements made for her husband to return from overseas. Because of the epileptoid possibility, she was discharged on diphenylhydantoin (Dilantin), 0.1 gm. q.i.d., to be followed in the outpatient clinic. With drug therapy and minimal support, things went well for one year. Then, her husband was again transferred overseas, and within two months she had established a sexual liaison with another man. Although she claimed that this extramarital relationship was a satisfactory one, two months later she again developed spells (she had stopped anticonvulsants on her own initiative) similar to those she had had previously, in that she felt that things were closing in on her and noticed that she was uncoordinated and dysarthic. There was also mounting tension with two aggressive, destructive outbursts, which frightened her so much that she voluntarily sought rehospitalization. However, an attempt was made to maintain her on an outpatient basis, while arrangements were in progress for her husband to return home. He asked for a divorce when he discovered the state of affairs. She packed up and left him and her children, and then, again because of mounting tension and suicidal ideas, was rehospitalized. A repeat chloralose activation revealed more abnormalities than before, with frequent bursts of high amplitude 4-to-6-per-second activity appearing diffusely but with greatest prominence over the anterior quadrants and accompanied by spike and slow wave. Because of extreme anxiety and hyperactivity, she was placed on chlorpromazine (Thorazine) and, again because of possible epileptoid elements, given primidone (Mysoline) 250 mgs. t.i.d. Anxiety rapidly decreased, and she was discharged one month later to be followed on an outpatient basis. A follow-up contact 39 months later and 17 months after she had discontinued all therapy revealed that, shortly after discontinuing her contact with the clinic, she also discontinued her medication with no return of the previous episodes of amnesia, unsteady gait, "black outs," or feelings of losing her mind. Rarely, she does have an episodic rage reaction, usually provoked by a conflict with her new (and third) spouse.

There has been a considerable change in her life. She was divorced from her second husband, who left the country for an overseas assignment, has married her previous boy friend, and has now regained custody of her children. There have been no subsequent periods of sexual promiscuity, but it is important that her new husband is intensely jealous and will not let her out of the house at night without accompanying her. She complains about his lack of sexual interest inasmuch as he has sexual relations with her only once a week, whereas she would prefer two or three times at least, but she does not experience intense sexual urges, apparently having willingly traded sexual gratification for a more consistent, loving, and dependent relationship. She does not at this time report any recurrent dreams, mounting tension, or periods of depression.

Psychodynamic-neurophysiologic synthesis: Even after extensive medical work-up and prolonged observation, the relative importance of epileptoid or motivational phenomena remains unclear. On projective tests we see in this woman evidence of a basically sociopathic character structure. However, sociopathic acts occur in clusters with long periods of a relatively normal adjustment, particularly when her dependent needs are being met and external controls applied. Associated with her impulse dyscontrol, generally of a sexual but occasionally of an aggressive nature, are episodes which sound very much like ictal phenomena, particularly psychomotor seizures. However, repeated EEG and activation studies have revealed on only one occasion even the slightest evidence of a temporal focus. On the other hand, three of the five recordings have indicated the paroxysmal high amplitude slow activity which we have discussed in detail in 7.5. An evaluation of the effectiveness of anticonvulsant medication suggests that it was probably effective with the following qualifications. If tensions in her environment were extremely high, it was no longer adequate to control her behavior. On the other hand, if the tensions were absent and a safe, dependent, restricted environment provided, anticonvulsants were unnecessary.

Appendix 10   List of Patients

Patient	Part of Book	Patient	Part of Book
019	4.1.2, 10.7	O264	12.2.2
021	4.1.2, 4.1.3, 9.2.1	F267	9.2.3, 11.3
102	Preface, 9.3.1, 12.1.5	F271	5.4
103	12.1.1	F272	5.5.5
111	12.1.1	F276	8.3.3
123	12.1.3	S278	3.3.3, 11.3
187	12.1.1	O281	3.4, 7.5
195	11.4	S282	2.2.3, 9.2.2, 9.5, 12.1.1
F201	5.5.3	F283	5.5.3, 9.5, 11.1, 12.1.4, 12.3.3
S202	5.5.1, 9.2, 10.7, 11.2	F284	3.3.3, Appendix 6
S204	2.4.1	F285	10.7, 12.3.3
S205	3.4	S286	9.3.2, 9.5
F206	11.0, Appendix 1	F287	10.5, 10.7, 11.0, Appendix 2
F211	5.5.5	S288	7.4, 9.2.3, 10.1, 11.2,
S212	3.3.2, 12.1.1, Appendix 9		Appendix 4
F213	5.5.1	O289	3.3.3, 9.5, 10.1, 10.7, 12.1.2,
S218	11.1, Appendix 8		Appendix 7
S219	2.2.2, 12.1.3, 12.2.1	S290	12.1.2, 12.1.6, Appendix 3
F221	11.3	321	7.4
F222	10.7, 11.3	326	7.4
F223	5.4	400	5.5.5
F227	5.5.1	402	5.5.5
S228	2.2.1, 5.5.1	403	6.1.1
S229	3.3.1, Appendix 5	404	6.1.1
S232	7.5	405	6.1.1, 9.2.1
O236	7.5	406	5.5.5
S243	2.5	407	5.5.1, 6.1.1
F246	2.4.2, 5.5.5	408	6.1.1
F247	5.4, 11.0	409	6.1.1
S248	3.3.3	410	6.1.1
F250	3.3.3, 9.4, 10.7, 11.3, Appendix 6	411	6.1.1
S251	11.2, 11.3	412	6.1.1
S254	12.2.1	413	6.1.1, 9.2.1
O260	7.5	414	6.1.1
O262	3.3.1, Appendix 5	415	6.1.1
O263	9.2.3	523	11.4

References

American Psychiatric Association, Committee on Civil Defense. 1956. *Disaster fatigue.* Washington, D.C.

Abraham, K. 1910. "Hysterical dream states," in *Selected papers on psychoanalysis.* New York: Basic Books, 1953.

Abraham, K., and Ajmone-Marsan, C. 1958. "Patterns of cortical discharges and their relation to routine scalp electroencephalography," *Electroenceph. clin. Neurophysiol.,* 10:447.

Abrams, A. L. 1964. "Shop-lifting in a fugue state in a somnambulist," *Amer. J. Psychiat.,* 121:273.

Abramson, H. A. 1950. *Problems of consciousness.* New York: Josiah Macy, Jr., Foundation.

Abt, L. E. and Weissman, S. 1965. *Acting out, theoretical and clinical aspects.* New York: Grune & Stratton.

Ades, H. W. 1962. "EEG findings in relation to episodes of altered consciousness in aviators," *Aerospace Medicine,* 33:263.

Adrian, E. D., Bremer, F. and Jasper, H. H., eds. 1954. *Brain mechanisms and consciousness,* a symposium organized by the Council for International Organizations of Medical Sciences. Springfield: Charles C Thomas.

Aichhorn, A. 1936. *Wayward youth.* London: Putnam.

Ajmone-Marsan, C. 1961. "Electrographic aspects of 'epileptic' neuronal aggregates," *Epilepsia,* 2:22.

Ajmone-Marsan, C., and Ralston, B. L. 1957. *The epileptic seizure: its functional morphology and diagnostic significance: a clinical electroencephalographic analysis of metrazol-induced attacks.* Springfield: Charles C Thomas.

Alexander, F. 1930. "The neurotic character," *Int. J. Psycho-Anal.,* 11:292.

Almansi, R. J. 1965. *Drive aspects in acting out, study group on acting out.* New York: New York Psychoanalytic Society.

Alstrom, C. H. 1950. *Study of epilepsy and its clinical, social, and genetic aspects.* Copenhagen: Monksgaard.

Altschule, M. D., and Brem, J. 1963. "Periodic psychosis of puberty," *Amer. J. Psychiat.,* 119:1176.

Ando, M., and Ito, K. 1959. "Clinical and EEG studies on catatonia," *Folia psychiat. neurol. jap.,* 13:133.

Andy, O. J., and Akert, K. 1955. "Seizure patterns induced by electrical stimulation of hippocampal formation in the cat," *J. Neuropath. exp. Neurol.,* 14:198.

Angel, K. 1965a. "Loss of identity and acting out," *J. Amer. psychoanal. Ass.,* 13:79.

――――. 1965b. *Some genetic considerations of acting out, study group on "acting out."* New York Psychoanalytic Society.

Arthurs, R. G. S., and Cahoon, E. B. 1964. "A clinical and electroencephalographic survey of psychopathic personality," *Amer. J. Psychiat.,* 120:875.

Asano, N. 1967. "Clinico-genetic study of manic-depressive psychoses," in H. Mitsuda, ed., *Clinical genetics in psychiatry.* Tokyo: Igaku Shoin.

Baldwin, M., and Bailey, P., eds. 1958. *Temporal lobe epilepsy.* Springfield: Charles C Thomas.

Baldwin, M. 1960. "Electrical stimulation of the mesial temporal region," in Estelle R. Ramey and Desmond S. O'Doherty, eds., *Electrical studies on the unanesthetized brain.* New York: Paul B. Hoeber.

Balis, G. U., and Monroe, R. R. 1964. "The pharmacology of choloralose," *Psychopharmacologia,* 6:1.

Bard, P. 1928. "A diencephalic mechanism for the expression of rage with special reference to the sympathetic nervous system," *Amer. J. Physiol.,* 84:490.

Barker, W. 1948. "Studies on epilepsy. The petit mal attack as response within the CNS to distress in organism-environment integration," *Psychosom. Med.,* 10:73.

Barker, W., and Barker, S. 1950. "Experimental production of human convulsive brain potentials by stress induced effects upon neural integrative functions: dynamics of the convulsive reaction to stress," *Ass. Res. nerv. Dis. Proc.,* 29:90.

Barndt, R. J., and Johnson, D. M. 1955. "Time orientation in delinquents," *J. abnorm. soc. Psychol.,* 51:343.

Bartemeier, L. H. 1943. "Concerning the psychogenesis of convulsive disorders," *Psychoanal. Quart.,* 12:336.

Baruk, H., Verdeaux, G., and Joubert, P. 1949. "Nouvelles recherches sur le scopochloralose, etude EEG," *4th International Neurological Congress*, 2:144. Paris: Masson.

Bellak, L. 1963. "Acting out: Some conceptual and therapeutic considerations," *Amer. J. Psychother.*, 17:375.

Bender, L. 1953. *Aggression, hostility, and anxiety in children.* Springfield: Charles C Thomas.

Benet, H. E. 1965. "Mental disorders associated with temporal lobe epilepsy," *Dis. nerv. Syst.*, 26:275.

Bente, D., and Itil, T. 1955. "Zur Wirkung des Phenothiazinkoerpers Megaphen auf das menschliche Hirnstrombild," *Arzneimittel-Forsch.*, 7:158.

Bente, D. 1963. *Anthropologische und naturwissenschftliche Grundlagen der Pharmakopsychiatrie*, edited by F. D. Achelis and H. V. Ditfurth. Stuttgart: Thieme.

Bercel, N. A. 1953. "Experience with a combination of scopolamine and alpha chloralose (S.A.C.) in activating normal EEG's of epileptics," *Electroenceph. clin. Neurophysiol.*, 5:297.

———. 1961. "Chlordiazepoxide (Librium) as an anticonvulsant," *Dis. nerv. Syst.*, 22:1.

Berg, C. 1941. "Clinical notes on a case diagnosed as epilepsy," *Brit. J. med. Psychol.*, 19:9.

Bessman, S. P., and Fishbein, W. N. 1963. "Gamma-hydroxybutyrate, a normal brain metabolite," *Nature*, 200:1207.

Bexton, W. H., Heron, W., and Scott, T. H. 1954. "Effects of decreased variation in the sensory environment," *Canadian Journal of Psychology*, 8:70.

Bickford, R. G., Petersen, M. C., Dodge, H. W., Jr., and Sem-Jacobsen, C.A. 1953. "Observations on depth stimulation of the human brain through implanted electrographic leads," *Proc. Mayo Clin.*, 28:181.

Bingley, Torsten. 1958. "Mental symptoms in temporal lobe epilepsy and temporal lobe gliomas," *Acta psychiat. scand.*, 33:1.

Bird, B. 1957. "A specific peculiarity of acting out," *J. Amer. psychoanal. Ass.*, 5:630.

Bishop, M. P., Elder, S. T., and Heath, R. G. 1963. "Intracranial self-stimulation in man," *Science*, 140:394.

Blatt, S. 1965. "The Wechsler scales and acting out," in L. E. Abt and S. L. Weissman, eds., *Acting out.* New York: Grune & Stratton.

Blos, P. 1963. "The concept of acting out in relation to the adolescent process," *J. Amer. Acad. Child Psychiat.*, 2:118.

Boelhouwer, C., Henry, E. C., and Glueck, B. C., Jr. 1968. "Positive spiking; double-blind control study on its significance in behavior disorders. Both diagnostically and therapeutically," *Amer. J. Psychiat.,* 125:473.

Bokojic, J. E. N., and Trojaborg, W. 1960. "The effect of meproba-mate on the EEG during treatment, intoxication and after abrupt withdrawal," *Electroenceph. clin. Neurophysiol.,* 12:177.

Bonafede, V. I. 1957. "Chlorpromazine (Thorazine) treatment of dis-turbed epileptic patients," *A.M.A. Arch. Neurol. Psychiat.,* 77:243.

Bond, D. D., Randt, C. T., Bidder, T. G., and Rowland, V. 1957. "Posterior, septal, fornical and anterior thalamic lesions in the cat," *A.M.A. Arch. Neurol. Psychiat.,* 78:143.

Boslow, H. M. 1966. "Administrative structure and therapeutic cli-mate," *Prison Journal,* 46.

Bradley, P. B., and Elkes, J. 1957a. "The effects of some drugs on the electrical activity of the brain," *Brain,* 80:77.

———, and Jeavons, P. M. 1957b. "The effect of chlorpromazine and reserpine on sedation and convulsive thresholds in schizophrenic patients," *Electroenceph. clin. Neurophysiol.,* 9:661.

Brady, J. P. 1964. "Epilepsy and disturbed behavior," *J. nerv. ment. Dis.,* 138:468.

Braude, M. C., and Monroe, R. R. 1965. "Dimethylsulfoxide: Inter-active effects with alpha chloralose," *Curr. Ther. Res.,* 7:502.

———, 1966. "Effects of alphaglucochloralose on positively reinforced behavior in rats," *Pharmacologist,* 8:2.

Bray, P. F. 1962. "Temporal lobe syndrome in children," *Pediatrics,* 29:617.

Brazier, M. A. B., *et al.* 1954. "Electroencephalographic recordings from depth electrodes implanted in the amygdaloid region in man," *Electroenceph. clin. Neurophysiol.,* 6:702.

Brockway, A. L., Gleser, G., Winokur, G., and Ulett, G. A. 1954. "The use of a control population in neuropsychiatric research (psychiatric, psychological and EEG evaluation of a heterogene-ous sample)," *Amer. J. Psychiat.,* 3:248.

Brody, E. B., Derbyshire, R. L., and Schleifer, C. 1967. "How the young adult Baltimore Negro male becomes a Maryland mental hospital statistic," chap. 7. R. R. Monroe, G. D. Klee, and E. B. Brody, eds., in *Psychiatric epidemiology and mental health plan-ning. Psychiat. Res. Rep. No. 22 Amer. psychiat. Ass.*

Brown, W. T., and Solomon, C. I. 1942. "Delinquency and the EEG," *Amer. J. Psychiat.,* 98:499.

Browne-Mayers, A. N., and Straub, L. R. 1953. "Metrazol activation of electroencephalograms in psychiatric patients," *J. nerv. ment. Dis.,* 117:151.

Bruens, J. H. 1963. "Over psycholische toestondero," *Epelepsie Asten NBR Schriks' Drukkery.* N.V.

Buchthal, F., and Lennox, M. 1953. "The EEG effect of metrazol and photic stimulation in 682 normal subjects," *Electroenceph. clin. Neurophysiol.,* 5:545.

Burns, M. 1961. "An evaluation of alpha chloralose in electroencephalographic activation," unpublished thesis, Tulane University, New Orleans.

Carroll, E. J. 1954. "Acting out and ego development," *Psychoanal. Quart.,* 23:521.

Cazzullo, C. L. 1959. "Psychiatric aspects of epilepsy," *Int. J. Neurol.,* 1:53.

Chafetz, M. E., and Schwab, R. S. 1959. "Psychological factors involved in bizarre seizures," *Psychosom. Med.,* 21:96.

Chao, D. H. C., and Plumb, R. L. 1961. "Diamox in epilepsy, a critical review of 178 cases," *J. Pediat.,* 58:2.

Chapman, W. P., Brazier, M. A. B., and Poppen, J. L. 1954. "Physiological evidence concerning the importance of amygdaloid nuclear region in the integration of circulatory function and emotion in man," *Science,* 120:949.

Chapman, W. P. 1960. "Depth electrode studies in patients with temporal lobe epilepsy" in Estelle R. Ramey and Desmond S. O'Doherty, eds., *Electrical studies on the unanesthetized brain.* New York: Paul Hoeber.

Cleckley, H. 1955. *The mask of sanity.* St. Louis: Mosley.

Cohn, R., and Nardini, J. E. 1958. "The correlation of bilateral occipital slow activity in the human EEG with certain disorders of behavior," *Amer. J. Psychiat.,* 115:44.

Cole, J. O. 1967. Report of American College of Neuropharmacology Fifth Annual Meeting. *Psychopharm. Bull.,* 4:28.

Colony, H. S., and Willis, S. E. 1956. "Electroencephalographic studies of 1,000 schizophrenic patients," *Amer. J. Psychiat.,* 113:163.

Conference on Role and Methodology of Classification in Psychiatry and Psychopathology, sponsored by Amer. Psychiat. Ass. and Psychopharm. Serv. Center, NIMH, Washington, D.C., November 19, 1965.

Cooper, J. E., Kendell, R. E., Gurland, B. J., Sartorius, N., and Tibor, F. 1969. Cross-national study of diagnoses of the mental disorders: Some results from the first comparative investigation, *Amer. J. Psychiat.,* 125:30 (supp.).

Cravioto, H., Silberman, J., and Feigin, I. 1960. "A clinical and pathologic study of akinetic mutism," *Neurology,* 10:10.

Cure, C., Rasmussen, T., and Jasper, H. 1948. "Activation of seizures and electroencephalographic disturbances in epileptic and in control subjects with metrazol." *A.M.A. Arch. Neurol. Psychiat.,* 59:691.

David, M., Benda, P., and Klein, F. 1953. "The treatment of status epilepticus by chlorpromazine," *Bull. Mem. Soc. Med. Hop.,* 69:691.

Davidoff, R. A., and Johnson, L. C. 1964. "Paroxysmal EEG activity and cognitive-motor performance," *Electroenceph. clin. Neurophysiol.,* 16:343.

Davids, A., Kidder, C., and Reich, M. 1962. "Time orientation in male and female juvenile delinquents," *J. abnorm. soc. Psychol.,* 64:239.

Davis, P. A. 1942. "Comparative study of the EEG's of schizophrenic and manic-depressive psychoses," *Amer. J. Psychiat.,* 99:210.

DeHaas, A. M. L. 1958. *Lectures on epilepsy.* Netherlands: Elsevier Publishing Company.

Delay, J., Pichot, P., Lemperiere, T., and Perse, J. 1958. *The rorschach and the epileptic personality,* trans. Rita and Arthur Benton. New York: Logos Press.

Delgado, J. M. R. 1954. "Learning motivated by electrical stimulation of the brain," *Amer. J. Physiol.,* 179:587.

————. 1959. "Modification of social behavior induced by remote-controlled electrical stimulation of the brain," *Abstracts 21st Inter. Physiol. Congress Aviation.*

Dell, P., Bonvallet, M., and Hugelin, A. 1960. "Mechanisms of reticular deactivation," in G. E. Wolstenholme, W. O'Connor, and M. O'Connor, eds., *The nature of sleep.* Boston: Little, Brown.

Denber, H. C. B. 1958. "EEG findings during chlorpromazine-diethazine treatment," *J. nerv. ment. Dis.,* 126:392.

Deutsch, F. 1957. "A footnote to Freud's 'fragment of an analysis of a case of hysteria,'" *Phychoanal. Quart.,* 26:159.

Dickel, H. A., Dixon, H. H., Shanklin, J. G., and Dixon, H. H., Jr. 1962. "A clinical, double-blind comparison of Librium, meprobamate and phenobarbital," *Psychosomatics,* 3:129.

Dickes, R. 1965. "The defensive function of an altered state of consciousness, a hypnoid state," *J. Amer. psychoanal. Ass.,* 13:356.

Dietze, H. J., and Voegele, G. E. 1963. "The 14 and 6 per second positive spikes in the EEG and their relation to behavioral disturbances in children and adolescents." *ACTA Paedopsychiat.,* 30:392.

Dominian, J., Serafetinides, E. A., and Dewhurst, M. 1963. "A follow-up study of late-onset epilepsy, II, Psychiatric and social findings," *Brit. med. J.,* 5328:431.

Dongier, S. 1959. "Statistical study of clinical and electroencephalographic manifestations of 536 psychotic episodes occurring in 516 epileptics between clinical seizures," *Epilepsia*, 1:117.

Driver, M. V. 1962. "A study of the photoconvulsive threshold," *Electroenceph. clin. Neurophysiol.*, 14:359.

Echlin, F. A. 1944. "The electroencephalogram associated with epilepsy," *A.M.A. Arch. Neurol. Psychiat.*, 52:270.

Eichler, M. 1966. "The application of verbal behavior analysis to the study of psychological defense mechanisms: speech patterns associated with socio-pathic behavior," *J. nerv. ment. Dis.*, 41:658.

Eidelberg, E., Lesse, H., and Gault, F. P. 1963. "An experimental model of temporal-lobe epilepsy: studies of the convulsant properties of cocaine," in G. H. Glaser, ed., *EEG and behavior*. New York: Basic Books.

Eidelberg, E., Neer, H. M., and Miller, M. K. 1965. "Anticonvulsant properties of some benzodiazepine derivatives," *Neurology*, 15: 223.

Ekstein, R. 1965. "General treatment philosophy of acting out," in L. E. Abt and S. L. Weissman, eds., *Acting out*. New York: Grune & Stratton.

Ellingson, R. J. 1954. "The incidence of EEG abnormality among patients with mental disorders of apparently nonorganic origin: a critical review, EEG abnormality in mental disorders," *Amer. J. Psychiat.*, 111:263.

——. 1956. "Brain waves and problems of psychology," *Psychol. Bull.*, 53:1.

Emerson, L. E. 1915. "The psychoanalytic treatment of hystero-epilepsy," *J. abnorm. soc. Psychol.*, 11:315.

Epstein, A. W., and Ervin, F. 1956. "Psychodynamic significance of seizure content in psychomotor epilepsy," *Psychosom. Med.*, 18:43.

Epstein, A. W. 1960. "Fetishisms: A study of its psychopathology with particular reference to a proposed disorder in brain mechanisms as an etiologic factor," *J. nerv. ment. Dis.*, 130:107.

——. 1964. "Recurrent dreams (their relationship to temporal lobe seizures), *A.M.A. Arch. gen. Psychiat.*, 10:25.

——. 1966. "Ictal phenomena during REM sleep of a temporal lobe epileptic," *A.M.A. Arch. Neurol.*, 15:367.

Ervin, F., Epstein, A. W., and King, H. E. 1955. "Behavior of epileptic and nonepileptic patients with 'temporal spikes,'" *A.M.A. Arch. Neurol. Psychiat.*, 74:488.

Fabish, W. 1955. "Chlorpromazine and epilepsy," *Lancet*, 268:1277.

Fedio, P., Mirsky, A. F., Smith, W. J., and Parry, D. 1961. "Reaction time and EEG activation in normal schizophrenic subjects," *Electroenceph. clin. Neurophysiol.,* 13:923.

Fenichel, O. 1945a. *The psychoanalytic theory of neurosis.* New York: W. W. Norton.

——. 1945b. "Neurotic acting out," *Psychoanal. Rev.,* 32:197.

Fenton, G. W., and Edwin E. L. 1965. "Homicide, temporal lobe epilepsy and depression: A case report," *Brit. J. Psychiat.,* 111:304.

Fink, G. B., and Swinyard, E. A. 1962. "Comparison of anticonvulsant and psychopharmacologic drugs," *J. Pharmaceut. Sci.,* 51:548.

Fink, M. 1963. Quantitative EEG in Human Psychopharmacology: Drug Patterns in G. H. Glaser, ed., *EEG and behavior.* New York: Basic Books.

——. 1964. "A selected bibliography of electroencephalography in human psychopharmacology," *Electroenceph. clin. Neurophysiol.* 23:68.

——. 1965. "Quantitative EEG and human psychopharmacology," in W. P. Wilson, ed., *Applications of electroencephalography in psychiatry.* Durham, N.C.: Duke University Press.

Fischer, C. 1965. "Psychoanalytic implications of recent research on sleep and dreaming," *J. Amer. psychoanal. Ass.,* 13:197.

Forster, F. M., and Liske, E. 1963. "Role of environmental clues in temporal lobe epilepsy," *Neurology,* 13:301.

Frank, J. 1959. "Treatment approach to acting out character disorders," *J. Hillside Hospital,* 8:42.

Freud, A. 1949. "Certain types and stages of social maladjustment," in E. R. Eissler, ed., *Searchlights on delinquency.* New York: International Universities Press.

Freud, S. 1900. *The interpretation of dreams.* Standard Edition, vol. V. London: Hogarth Press, 1953.

——. 1905. *A case of hysteria.* Standard Edition, vol. VII. London: Hogarth Press, 1953.

——. 1911. *Formulations on the two principles of mental functioning.* Standard Edition, vol. XII. London: Hogarth Press, 1958.

——. 1913. *Totem and tabu.* Standard Edition, vol. XIII. London: Hogarth Press, 1955.

——. 1914. *Further recommendations in the techniques of psychoanalysis, remembering, repeating, and working through.* Standard Edition, vol. XII. London: Hogarth Press, 1958.

——. 1920. *Beyond the pleasure principle.* Standard Edition, vol. XVIII. London: Hogarth Press, 1955.

——. 1925. *Inhibitions, symptoms, and anxiety.* Standard Edition, vol. XX. London: Hogarth Press, 1959.

──────. 1928. *Dostoevsky and parricide.* Standard Edition, vol. XXI. London: Hogarth Press, 1961.

──────. 1930. *Civilization and its discontents.* Standard Edition, vol. XXI. London: Hogarth Press, 1961.

Friedlander, W. J. 1959. "Chlorpromazine as EEG activating agent," *Electroenceph. clin. Neurophysiol.,* 11:799.

──────. 1964. "Sleep EEG's in a late teenage prison population," *Dis. nerv. Syst.,* 23:370.

Fries, M. E., and Wolff, P. 1953. *Some hypotheses on the role of the congenital activity type in personality development, psychoanalytic study of the child.* New York: International Universities Press.

Frosch, J., and Wortis, S. B. 1954. "A contribution to the nosology of the impulse disorders," *Amer. J. Psychiat.,* 111:132.

Fuster, B. 1953. "EEG activation under natural or induced sleep," *Electroenceph. clin. Neurophysiol.,* 4:108.

Galambos, M. 1965a. "The long-term use of Valium," *Amer. J. Psychiat.,* 121:811.

──────. 1965b. "Long-term trial with diazepam on adult mentally retarded persons," *Dis. nerv. Syst.,* 26:305.

Gardner, G. E. 1963. "Discussion of a developmental concept of the problem of acting out," *J. Amer. Acad. Child Psychiat.,* 2:17.

──────. 1965. In L. E. Abt and S. Weissman, eds., *Acting out, theoretical and clinical aspects.* New York: Grune & Stratton.

Garmezy, N. 1965. "Process and reactive schizophrenia, some conceptions and issues." Conference on the role and methodology of classification in psychiatry and psychopathology, the American Psychiatric Association and the Psychopharmacology Service Center, National Institutes of Mental Health, Washington, D.C., November 19–21.

Gastaut, H. 1950. "Combined photic and metrazol activation of the brain," *Electroenceph. clin. Neurophysiol.,* 2:249.

Gastaut, H., Naquet, R., Roger, A., and Badier, M. 1951. "Response irradiee derebelleuse a la stimulation lumineuse chez le chat soumis a l'action du cardiazol," *C. R. Soc. Biol.,* 145:916.

Gastaut, H. 1953a. "Technique, indications and results of metrazol activation," *Electroenceph. clin. Neurophysiol.,* 4:121.

──────. 1953b. "So-called psychomotor and temporal epilepsy," *Epilepsia,* 2:59.

──────. 1954. "The brain stem and cerebral electrogenesis in relation to consciousness," in *Brain mechanisms and consciousness.* Springfield: Charles C Thomas.

──────. 1956. "La maladie de Vincent Van Gogh envisagee a la lu-

miere des conceptions nouvelles sur l'epilepsie psychomotrice,"
Ann. med.-psychol., 1:43.

——. 1964. "Proposed international classification of epileptic seizures," *Epilepsia*, 5:297.

Gibbs, F. A., Gibbs, E. L., and Lennox, W. G. 1938. "The likeness of
the cortical dysrhythmia of schizophrenia and psychomotor epilepsy," *Amer. J. Psychiat.*, 95:255.

——. 1943. "Electroencephalographic classification of epileptic patients and control subjects," *A.M.A. Arch. Neurol. Psychiat.*,
50:111.

Gibbs, F. A., Bagchi, B. K., and Bloomberg, W. 1945. "Electroencephalographic study of criminals," *Amer. J. Psychiat.*, 102:294.

Gibbs, F. A., and Gibbs, E. L. 1947. "Diagnostic and localizing value
of electroencephalographic studies in sleep research," *J. nerv.
ment. Dis.*, 26:366.

Gibbs, F. A., Gibbs, E. L., and Fuster, B. 1948. "Types of paroxysmal
syndrome," *A.M.A. Arch. Neurol. Psychiat.*, 60:4.

Gibbs, F. A. 1951. "Ictal and non-ictal psychiatric disorder in temporal lobe epilepsy," *J. nerv. ment. Dis.*, 113:522.

Gibbs, F. A., and Gibbs, E. L. 1951b. "Electroencephalographic evidence of thalamic and hypothalamic epilepsy," *Neurology*, 1:136.

——. 1952. *Atlas of electroencephalography*, vol. II. Cambridge,
Mass.: Addison-Wesley Press.

——. 1963a. "Borderline of epilepsy," *J. Neuropsychiat.*, 4:287.

——. 1963b. "Fourteen and six per second positive spikes," *Electroenceph. clin. Neurophysiol.*, 15:4.

Ging, R. J., Jones, E., and Manis, M. 1964. "Correlation of electroencephalograms and multiple physical symptoms," *J. Amer. med.
Ass.*, 187:579.

Gjessing, R., and Gjessing, L. 1961. "Some main trends in the clinical
aspects of periodic catatonia," *Acta psychiat. scand.*, 37:1.

Glaser, G., and Golub, L. 1955. "The EEG of psychomotor seizures in
childhood," *Electroenceph. clin. Neurophysiol.*, 7:329.

Glaser, G., Newman, R., and Schafer, R. 1963. "Interictal psychosis
in psychomotor-temporal lobe epilepsy: an EEG psychological
study," in Gilbert H. Glaser, ed., *EEG and Behavior*. New York:
Basic Books.

Glaser, G. 1967. "Limbic epilepsy in childhood," *J. nerv. ment. Dis.*,
144:391.

Glaser, K. 1965. "Suicide in children and adolescents," in L. Abt, E.
Weissman, and S. Weissman, eds., *Acting Out: Theoretical and
Clinical Aspects*. New York: Grune & Stratton.

Gloor, P., Tasi, C., and Haddad, F. 1958. "An assessment of the value of sleep-electroencephalography for the diagnosis of temporal lobe epilepsy," *Electroenceph. clin. Neurophysiol.,* 10:633.

Goldensohn, E. S., and Gold, A. P. 1960. "Prolonged behavioral disturbances as ictal phenomena," *Neurology,* 10:1.

Goldensohn, E. S. 1963. "EEG and ictal and post-ictal behavior," in G. H. Glaser, ed., *EEG and behavior.* New York: Basic Books.

Goldie, L. 1959. Personal communication.

Goldie, L., and Green, J. M. 1961. "Spike and wave discharges and alterations of conscious awareness," *Nature,* 191:200.

Goldman, D. 1962. "Electroencephalographic changes brought to light under pentothal activation in psychotic (schizophrenic) patients, with particular reference to changes produced by pharmacologic agents," *Ann. N.Y. Acad. Sci.,* 96:356.

Goldman, D., and Rosenberg, B. 1962. "EEG observations in psychotic children," *Comp. Psychiat.,* 3:93.

Goldman, D. 1964. "Electroencephalographic manifestations associated with psychotic illness: pentothal activation technique and pharmocologic interrelationships," *Comp. Psychiat.,* 5:2.

Goodman, L. S., and Gilman, A. 1966. *The pharmacological basis of therapeutics.* 3rd ed. New York: Macmillan Co.

Gottesman, I. I. 1966. "Schizophrenia in twins: 16 years' consecutive admissions to a psychiatric clinic," *Brit. J. Psychiat.,* 112:809.

Gottschalk, L. 1953. "Effect of intensive psychotherapy on epileptic children," *A.M.A. Arch. Neurol. Psychiat.,* 70:361.

Gowers, W. 1907. *The borderlines of epilepsy.* Philadelphia: P. Blakiston & Son & Co.

Green, J. G. 1961. "Association of behavior disorder with an EEG focus in children without seizures," *Neurology,* 11:4.

Greenacre, P. 1950. "General problems of acting out," *Psychol. Quart.,* 19:455.

————. 1963. "Problems of acting out in the transference relationship," *J. Amer. Acad. Child Psychiat.,* 2:144.

Greenson, R. 1944. "On genuine epilepsy," *Psychoanal. Quart.,* 13:139.

————. 1957. As reported in Mark Kanzer, "Acting out and its relation to impulse disorders," *Amer. Psychoanal. Ass. J.,* 5:138.

Groethuysen, U. C., *et al.* 1957. "Depth electrographic recordings of a seizure during a structured interview (report of a case)," *Psychosom. Med.,* 29:5.

Gross, M. D., and Wilson, W. C. 1964. "Behavior disorders of children with cerebral dyrhythmias," *A.M.A. Arch. gen. Psychiat.,* 11:610.

Grossman, C. 1954. "Laminar cortical blocking and its relation to episodic aggressive outbursts," *A.M.A. Arch. Neurol. Psychiat.,* 71:576.

Guerrant, J., *et al.* 1962. *Personality in epilepsy.* Springfield: Charles C Thomas.

Guttmacher, M. S. 1960. *The mind of the murderer.* New York: Grove Press.

Hashi, N. 1967. "Symptom changes" during the course of the atypical psychoses, in H. Mitsuda, ed., *Clinical genetics in psychiatry.* Tokyo: Igaku Shoin.

Head, R. G. 1955. ("The use of chlorpromazine as an adjunct in the treatment of psychomotor epilepsy: a preliminary report," *Bull. Tulane med. Fac.,* 15:23.

Heath, R. G., ed. 1954. *Studies in schizophrenia.* Cambridge, Mass.: Harvard University Press.

Heath, R. G., Monroe, R. R., and Mickle, W. A. 1955a. "Stimulation of the amygdaloid nucleus in a schizophrenic patient," *Amer. J. Psychiat.,* 111:11.

Heath, R. G., Mickle, W. A., and Monroe, R. R. 1955b. "Characteristic recording from various specific subcortical nuclear masses in the brains of psychiatric and non-psychiatric patients," *Trans. Amer. neurol. Ass.,* 80:17.

Heath, R. G. 1957. "Correlations of electrical recordings from cortical and subcortical regions of the brain with abnormal behavior in human subjects," *Confir. a Neurol.,* 18:306.

Heath, R. G., and Mickle, W. A. 1960. "Evaluation of seven years' experience with depth electrodes in human patients," in E. R. Ramey and D. S. O'Doherty, eds., *Electrical studies of the unanesthetized brain.* New York: Paul B. Hoeber.

Heath, R. G., and Verster, F. de B. 1961. "Effects of chemical stimulation to discrete brain areas," *Amer. J. Psychiat.,* 117:980.

Heath, R. G., and Leach, B. E. 1962a. "Brain recordings with schizophrenia behavior: some metabolic factors responsible for physiological alterations," *Ann. N. Y. Acad. Sci.,* 96:425.

Heath, R. G. 1962b. "Common characteristics of epilepsy and schizophrenia: Clinical observation and depth electrode studies," *Amer. J. Psychiat.,* 118:11.

———. 1962c. "Common characteristics of epilepsy and schizophrenia: Clinical observation and depth electrode studies," *Amer. J. Psychiat.,* 118:11.

———. 1963a. "Closing remarks, with Commentary on Depth Electroencephalography in Epilepsy and Schizophrenia," in Gilbert H. Glaser, ed., *EEG and behavior.* New York: Basic Books.

———. 1963b. "Electric self-stimulation of the brain in man," *Amer. J. Psychiat.,* 120:571.

———. 1964. *"Pleasure integration and behavior,"* in Robert G.

Heath, ed., *The role of pleasure in behavior'*. New York: Hoeber Medical Division, Harper & Row.

Heath, R. G., and Guerrero-Figueroa, R. 1965. "Psychotic behavior with evoked septal dysrhythmia: effects of intracerebral acetylcholine and gamma aminobutyric acid," *Amer. J. Psychiat.*, 121:11.

Heath, R. G. 1966a. "Schizophrenia: biochemical and physiological aberrations," *Int. J. Neuropsychiat.*, 2:597.

Heath, R. G., Nesselhof, W., Jr., and Timmons, E. 1966b. "DL-methionine-d, l'sulfoximine effects in schizophrenic patients," *A.M.A. Arch. gen. Psychiat.*, 14:213.

Hebb, D. O. 1954. "The problem of consciousness and introspection," in *Brain mechanisms and consciousness*. Springfield: Charles C Thomas.

Heimburger, R. F. 1966. "Stereotaxic amygdalotomy for epilepsy with aggressive behavior," *J. Amer. med. Ass.*, 198:741.

Hendrick, I. 1940. "Psychoanalytic observations on the aura of two cases with convulsions," *Psychosom. Med.*, 2:43.

Henry, C. E. 1963. "Positive spike discharges in the EEG and behavior abnormality, in G. H. Glaser, ed., *EEG and behavior*. New York: Basic Books.

Higgins, J. W., *et al.* 1956. "Behavioral changes during intercerebral electrical stimulation," *A.M.A. Arch. Neurol. Psychiat.*, 76:399.

Hill, D. 1944. "Cerebral dysrhythmia: its significance in aggressive behavior," *Proc. roy. Soc. Med.*, 37:317.

———. 1952. "The EEG in episodic, psychotic, and psychopathic behavior," *Electroenceph. clin. Neurophysiol.*, 4:419.

———. 1956. "Clinical application of EEG in psychiatry," *J. ment. Sci.*, 102:264.

Hill, D., *et al.* 1957. "Personality changes following temporal lobectomy for epilepsy," *J. ment. Sci.*, 103:430.

Hill, D. 1963. "The EEG in Psychiatry," in D. Hill and G. Parr, eds., *Electroencephalography*. New York: Macmillan Co.

Hill, D., and Parr, G. 1963. *Electroencephalography*. New York: Macmillan Co.

Hill, D., and Watterson, D. 1942. "Electro-encephalographic studies of psychopathic personalities," *J. Neurol. Psychiat.*, 5:47.

Hoch, P., and Polatin, P. 1949. "Pseudo-neurotic forms of schizophrenia," *Psychiat. Quart.*, 23:248.

Hockett, C. F., and Ascher, R. 1964. "The human revolution," *Amer. Scien.*, 52.

Hoenig, J., and Hamilton, C. M. 1960. "Epilepsy and sexual orgasm," *Acta psychiat. scand.*, 35:488.

Hollister, L. E., and Barthel, C. A. 1959. "Changes in the electroencephalogram during chronic administration of tranquilizing drugs," *Electroenceph. clin. Neurophysiol.*, 11:792.

Hollister, L. E., et al. 1963. "Drug-induced EEG abnormalities as predictors of clinical response to thiopropazate and haloperidol," *Amer. J. Psychiat.*, 119:887.

Hughes, J. R. 1960. "A statistical analysis on the location of EEG abnormalities," *Electroenceph. clin. Neurophysiol.*, 12:4.

Hughes, J. R., Gianturco, D., and Stein, W. 1961. "Electro-clinical correlations in the positive spike phenomenon," *Electroenceph. clin. Neurophysiol.*, 13:4.

Hughes, J. R. 1965a. "A Review of the Positive Spike Phenomenon," in W. P. Wilson, ed., *Applications of electroencephalography in psychiatry.* Durham: Duke University Press.

Hughes, J. R., Schlagenhauff, R. E., and Magoss, M. 1965b. "Electroclinical correlations in the 6 per second spike and wave complex," *Electroenceph. clin. Neurophysiol.*, 18:71.

Hulfish, B. 1969. "Limbic epilepsy," paper presented at the Psychiatric Institute, University of Maryland School of Medicine, March 24.

Hullay, J. 1955. "Surgical treatment of temporal epilepsy," *Acta med.*, 7:295.

Inouye, E. 1960. "Observations on forty twin index cases with chronic epilepsy and the co-twin," *J. ment. Dis.*, 130:401.

Jasper, H. H., and Kirschman, J. 1941. "Electroencephalographic classification of epilepsies," *A.M.A. Arch. Neurol. Psychiat.*, 45:903.

Jaspers, K. 1963. *General Psychopathology.* Chicago: University of Chicago Press.

Jenkins, R. L., and Pacella, B. L. 1943. "Electroencephalographic studies of delinquent boys," *Amer. J. Orthopsychiat.*, 13:107.

Johnson, A. 1949. "Sanctions for superego lacunae of adolescents," in K. R. Eissler, ed., *Searchlights on delinquency.* New York: International Universities Press.

Johnson, A., and Szurek, S. A. 1952. "The genesis of antisocial acting out in children and adults," *Psychoanal. Quart.*, 21:323.

Johnson, L. C., et al. 1960. "Cortical activity and cognitive functioning," *Electroenceph. clin. Neurophysiol.*, 12:861.

Johnson, L. C., and Davidoff, R. A. 1962. "Brain activity, seizure discharges and behavior," *Proc. San Diego Sympos. Biomed. Eng.*

Jonas, A. D. 1965. *Ictal and subictal neurosis.* Springfield: Charles C Thomas.

Joubert, P. 1954. "Le scopochloralose," (thesis) Willefranche-de-R, ouer, gue (Aveyron), Imprimerie Salingardes, 1954.

Kaada, B. R. 1951. "Somoto-motor, autonomic and electrocardiographic responses to electrical stimulation of the 'rhinencephalic' and other structures in primates, cats and dogs," *Acta physiol. scand.*, 24:1.

Kaelber, W. W., and Correll, R. E. 1958. "Cortical and subcortical electrical effects of psychopharmacologic and tremor-producing compounds," *A.M.A. Arch. Neurol. Psychiat.*, 80:544.

Kahn, E., and Cohen, L. M. 1934. "'Organic drivenness,' a brain stem syndrome and an experience," *New Engl. J. Med.*, 210:748.

Kaim, S. C., and Rosenstein, I. N. 1960. "Anticonvulsant properties of a new psychotherapeutic drug," *Dis. nerv. Syst.*, 21:1.

———. 1961. "Experience with chlordiazepoxide in the management of epilepsy," *J. Neuropsychiat.*, 3:12.

Kanzer, M. 1957. "Report of a panel on acting out and its relation to impulse disorder," *J. Amer. psychoanal. Ass.*, 5:136.

Kardiner, A. 1932. "The bio-analysis of the epileptic reaction," *Psychosom. Quart.*, 1.

Kasanin, J. 1933. "The acute schizoaffective psychoses," *Amer. J. Psychiat.*, 90:97.

Kaufman, I. C., and Watson, C. W. 1949. "A brief review of the methods used to elicit or accentuate abnormalities in the EEG," *Electroenceph. clin. Neurophysiol.*, 1:237.

Kaufman, I., et al. 1963. "Delineations of two diagnostic groups among juvenile delinquents: The schizophrenic and the impulse ridden character," *J. Amer. Acad. Child Psychiat.*, 2:292.

Kawi, Ali A. 1960. "Electroencephalography and the sedation threshold," *Dis. nerv. Syst.*, 21:9.

Kellaway, P., Crawley, J. W., and Kagawa, N. 1960. "Paroxysmal pain and autonomic disturbances of cerebral origin: A specific electroclinical syndrome," *Epilepsia*, 1:466.

Kellaway, P., Crawley, J., and Maulsby, R. 1965. "The electroencephalogram in psychiatric disorders in childhood," in W. P. Wilson, ed., *Applications of electroencephalography in psychiatry*. Durham: Duke University Press.

Kemph, J. P., Zegans, L. S., Kooi, K. A., and Waggoner, R. W. 1963. "The emotionally disturbed child with a convulsive disorder," *Psychosom. Med.*, 25:441.

Kennard, M. A., Rabinovitch, M. S., and Fister, W. P. 1955. "The use of frequency analysis in the interpretation of the EEG in patients with psychological disorders," *Electroenceph. clin. Neurophysiol.*, 7:29.

Kennard, M. A. 1956. "The electroencephalogram and disorders of behavior," *J. nerv. ment. Dis.*, 124:2.

Kennard, M. A., and Schwartzman, A. E. 1957. "A longitudinal study of electroencephalographic frequency patterns in mental hospital patients and normal controls," *Electroenceph. clin. Neurophysiol.*, 9:263.

Kennard, M. A., Schwartzman, A. E., and Miller, T. P. 1958. "Sleep, consciousness, and the alpha electroencephalographic rhythm," *A.M.A. Arch. Neurol. Psychiat.*, 79:328.

Kershman, J. 1949. "The borderland of epilepsy," *Arch. Neurol. Psychiat.*, 62:551.

Kerskiner, A., and Lloyd-Smith, D. L. 1962. "Effect of intravenous chlordiazepoxide on the electroencephalogram with some clinical observations," *J. nerv. ment. Dis.*, 134:218.

Kessler, M. M., *et al.* 1952. "Psychogenic motor phenomena in the presence of an abnormal electroencephalogram," *J. nerv. ment. Dis.*, 116:1.

Kety, S. S. 1952. "Consciousness and the metabolism of the brain," in H. A. Abramson, ed., *Problems of consciousness*. New York: Corlies, Macy & Co.

———. 1966. "Recent biochemical theories of schizophrenia," in P. Hoch and J. Zubin, eds., *Psychopathology of schizophrenia*. New York: Grune & Stratton.

Killam, D. F., and Killam, E. K. 1956a. "The action of lysergic acid, diethylamide on the central afferent limbic pathways in the cat," *J. Pharmacol. exp. Ther.*, 116:35.

Killam, E. K., and Killam, D. F. 1956b. "A comparison of the effects of reserpine and chlorpromazine to those barbiturates on the central afferent system in the cat," *J. Pharmacol. exp. Ther.*, 116:35.

Kinross-Wright, V. 1955a. "Chlorpromazine and reserpine in the treatment of psychoses," *Ann. N. Y. Acad. Sci.*, 61:174.

———. 1955b. "Complications of chlorpromazine treatment," *Dis. nerv. Syst.*, 16:4.

Kizu, M. 1967. "The personalities of parents of schizophrenics with special reference to the rorschach test," in H. Mitsuda, ed., *Clinical genetics in psychiatry*. Tokyo: Igaku Shoin.

Kleitman, N. 1955. "The role of the cerebral cortex in the development and maintenance of consciousness," in Harold A. Abramson, ed., *Problems of consciousness*. New York: Corlies, Macy & Co.

Kluver, H., and Bucy, P. C. 1937. "Psychic blindness and other symptoms following bilateral temporal lobectomy in rhesus monkeys," *Amer. J. Physiol.*, 119:352.

————. 1939. "Preliminary analysis of functions of the temporal lobe in monkeys," *A.M.A. Arch. Neurol. Psychiat.*, 42:979.

Knott, J. R., and Gottlieb, J. S. 1943. "Electroencephalogram in psychopathic personality," *Psychosom. Med.*, 5:139.

Knott, J. R. 1956. "Electroencephalograms in psychopathic personality and in murderers," in William P. Wilson, ed., *Electroencephalography in psychiatry*. Durham: Duke University Press.

Kooi, K. A., and Hovey, B. H. 1957. "Alterations in mental function and paroxysmal cerebral activity," *A.M.A. Arch. Neurol. Psychiat.*, 78:264.

Kraft, I. A., *et al.* 1965. "A clinical study of chlordiazepoxide used in psychiatric disorders of children," *Int. J. Neuropsychiat.*, 1:433.

Kuniya, T., Aoyama, T., and Harada, S. 1964. "Experience with the use of chlordiazepoxide in epileptic children," *J. Pediat. Prac.*, 27:232.

Kubie, L. S. 1953. "Some implications for psychoanalysis of modern concepts of the organization of the brain," *Psychoanal. Quart.*, 22:21.

————. 1954. "Psychiatric and psychoanalytic considerations of the problem of consciousness," in E. D. Adrian, F. Bremer, and H. H. Jasper, eds., *Brain mechanisms and consciousness*. Springfield: Charles C Thomas.

Laborit, H., *et al.* 1960. "Generalities concernant l'etude experimentale et l'emploi clinique du hydroxybutyrate de Na," *Rev. Agress.*, 4:397.

Landolt, H. 1958. "Serial electroencephalographic investigations during psychotic episodes in epileptic patients and during schizophrenic attacks," in A. M. Lorentz De Has, ed., *Lectures on epilepsy*. Netherlands: Elsevier Publishing Co.

Laufer, M. W., and Denhoff, E. 1957. "Hyperkinetic impulse disorder in children," *Psychosom. Med.*, 119:38.

Lauter, H. 1967. "Periodic diencephalic disorders: their relationship to manic-depressive psychoses," *Int. J. Neuropsychiat.*, 3 (4):319.

Lennox, W. G., and Lennox, M. A. 1960. *Epilepsy and related disorders*. Boston: Little, Brown.

Lesny, I., and Vojta, V. 1960. "Eserine activations of the EEG in children," *Electroenceph. clin. Neurophysiol.*, 12:742.

Lesse, H. *et al.* 1955. "Rhinencephalic activity during thought," *J. nerv. ment. Dis.*, 122:433.

Lesse, H. 1960. "Rhinencephalic electrophysiological activity during 'emotional behavior' in cats," *Psychiat. Res. Rep. Amer. psychiat. Ass.*, 12:224.

Levin, M. 1953. "Aggression, guilt and cataplexy," *A.M.A. Arch. Neurol. Psychiat.,* 69:215.

Levin, M., *et al.* 1959. "Intelligence and measure of inhibition and time sense," *J. clin. Psychol.,* 15:224.

Levin, S. 1952. "Epileptic clouded states," *J. nerv. ment. Dis.,* 116:215.

Levitt, M., and Rubenstein, B. O. 1959. "Acting out in adolescence: a study in communication," *Amer. J. Orthopsychiat.,* 29:622.

Levy, D. M. 1947–1948. Lectures, "Psychoanalytic clinic for training and research," Columbia University: College of Physicians and Surgeons.

——. 1962. "The 'act' as an operational concept in psychodynamics," *Psychosom. Med.,* 24:49.

Levy, S., and Kennard, M. A. 1953. "The EEG pattern of patients with psychological disorders of various ages," *J. nerv. ment. Dis.,* 188:416.

Liberson, W. T. 1944. "Functional electroencephalography in mental disorders," *Dis. nerv. Syst.,* 5:357.

Liberson, W. T., Scoville, W. B., and Dunsmore, R. H. 1951. "Stimulation studies of the prefrontal lobe and uncus in man," *Electroenceph. clin. Neurophysiol.,* 3:1.

Liberson, W. T., Scherer, I. W., and Klett, C. J. 1958. "Further observations on the EEG effects of chlorpromazine," *Electroenceph. clin. Neurophysiol.,* 10:192.

Lidz, T. 1963. "Discussion of a developmental concept of the problems of acting out," *J. Amer. Acad. Child Psychiat.,* 2:19.

Lilly, J. 1956. "Mental effects of reduction of ordinary levels of physical stimuli on intact, healthy persons," *Psychiat. Res. Rep. Amer. psychiat. Ass.,* 5:1.

Livingston, S. 1964. "Epilepsy and murder," *J. Amer. med. Ass.,* 188:172.

Livingston, S., *et al.* 1967. "Use of carbamazepine in epilepsy," *J. Amer. med. Ass.,* 200:204.

Logothetis, J. 1967. "Spontaneous epileptic seizures and electroencephalographic changes in the course of phenothiazine therapy," *Neurology,* 17:869.

Lohrenz, J., Levy, L., and Davis, J. F. 1962. "Schizophrenia or epilepsy? A problem of differential diagnosis," *Comprehen. Psychiat.,* 3:54.

London, N., Richter, P., and Bliss, B. E. 1956. "Temporal lobe (psychomotor) epilepsy," *Psychosom. Med.,* 18:427.

Longo, V. G., Vonneberger, G. P., and Bovet, D. 1954. "Action of nicotine and of the 'ganglioplegiques centraux' on the electrical activity of the brain," *J. Pharmacol. exp. Ther.,* 3:349.

Lorr, M., Klett, C. J., and McNair, D. M. 1963. *Syndromes of psychosis.* New York: Macmillan Co.

McCleary, R. A., and Moore, R. Y. 1965. *Subcortical mechanisms of behavior.* New York: Basic Books.

MacDonald, J. M. 1961. *The murderer and his victim.* Springfield: Charles C Thomas.

———. 1965. "Acting out," *A.M.A. Arch. gen. Psychiat.,* 13:439.

MacLean, P. D., and Delgado, J. M. R. 1953. "Electrical and chemical stimulation of fronto-temporal portions of the limbic system," *Electroenceph. clin. Neurophysiol.,* 5:91.

MacLean, P. D. 1954. "The limbic system and its hippocampal formation," *J. Neurosurg.,* 11:29.

———. 1959. "The limbic system with respect to two basic life principles," in M. A. B. Brazier, ed., *Report of second conference on central nervous system and behavior.* New York: Josiah Macy, Jr. Foundation.

MacLean, P. D., and Ploog, D. W. 1962. "Cerebral representation of penile erection," *J. Neurophysiol.,* 25:29.

MacLean, P. D. 1962. "New findings relevant to the evolution of psychosexual functions of the brain." *J. nerv. ment. Dis.,* 135:4.

Macrae, D. 1954. "On the nature of fear with reference to its occurrence in epilepsy," *J. nerv. ment. Dis.,* 120:385.

Magoun, H. W., *et al.,* 1937. "Associated facial, vocal and respiratory components of emotional expression, experimental study," *J. Neurol. Psychopath.,* 71:241.

Mahler, M. S. 1952. "On child psychosis and schizophrenia, autistic and symbiotic infantile psychoses," in K. R. Eissler, *et al.,* eds., *Psychoanalytic study of the child,* vol. VII. New York: International Universities Press.

Malmo, R. B. 1959. "Activation: A neurophysiological dimension," *Psychol. Rev.,* 66:367.

Malone, C. A. 1963. "Some observations on children of disorganized families and problems of acting out," *J. Amer. Acad. Child Psychiat.,* 2:22.

Medlicott, R. W. 1966. "Brief psychotic episodes (temporary insanity)," *N. Z. med. J.,* 65:966.

Meissner, W. W. 1967. "Hippocampus and learning," *Int. J. Neuropsychiat.,* 3 (4):298.

Meduna, L. J. 1950. *Oneirophrenia, "the confused state."* Urbana: University of Illinois Press.

Menninger, K. 1954. "Regulatory devices of the ego under major stress," *Int. J. Psycho-Anal.,* 35:1.

Menninger, K., and Mayman, M. 1955. "Episodic dyscontrol: A third order of stress adaption," *Bull. Menninger Clin.*, 20:153.

Merlis, J. K., Henriksen, C. F., and Grossman, C. 1950. "Metrazol activation of seizure discharges in epileptics with normal routine electroencephalograms," *Electroenceph. clin. Neurophysiol.*, 2:17.

Merlis, S. 1955. *Chlorpromazine and mental health.* Philadelphia: Lea & Febiger.

———. 1960. "Cardrase: A new carbonic anhydrase inhibitor," *Neurology*, 10:210.

Metrick, S., and Rentz, L. 1965. "Mephenoxalone as a psychotherapeutic agent in children with cerebral dysrhythmias," *Dis. nerv. Syst.*, 26:116.

Michaels, J. J. 1955. *Disorders of character: persistent enuresis, juvenile delinquency and psychopathic personality.* Springfield: Charles C Thomas.

———. 1957. "Character disorders and acting upon impulse," *J. Amer. psychoanal. Ass.*, 5:136.

Milner, B. 1958. Discussion in B. Maitland and P. Bailey, eds., *Temporal lobe epilepsy.* Springfield: Charles C Thomas.

———. 1959. "The memory defect in bilateral hippocampal lesions," *Psychiat. Res. Rep. Amer. psychiat. Ass.*, 11:43.

Milstein, V., and Stevens, J. R. 1961. "Verbal and conditioned avoidance learning during abnormal EEG discharge," *J. nerv. ment. Dis.*, 132:50.

Mirsky, A. F., *et al.* 1960a. "A comparison of the psychological test performance of patients with focal and nonfocal epilepsy," *Exp. Neurol.*, 2:75.

Mirsky, A. F., and Rosvold, H. 1960b. "The use of psychoactive drugs as a neuropsychological tool in studies of attention in man in L. M. Uhr and J. G. Miller, eds., *Drugs and behavior.* New York: John Wiley & Sons.

Mirsky, A. F., and Van Buren, J. M. 1965. "On the nature of the 'absence' in centrencephalic epilepsy," *Electroenceph. clin. Neurophysiol.*, 18:334.

Mitsuda, H., ed. 1967. *Clinical genetics in psychiatry: problems in nosological classification.* Tokyo: Igaku Shoin.

Monnier, M. 1952. "Experimental work on sleep and other variations of consciousness," in H. A. Abramson, ed., *Problems of consciousness.* New York: Corlies, Macy & Co.

Monroe, R. R., and Drell, H. J. 1947. "Oral use of stimulants obtained from inhalers," *J. Amer. med. Ass.*, 135:909.

Monroe, R. R., and Heath, R. G. 1951. "Psychotherapy," *Bull. Tulane med. Fac.*, 11:38.

Monroe, R. R., *et al.* 1955a. "A comparison of cortical and subcortical brain waves in normal, barbiturate, reserpine and chlorpromazine sleep," *Ann. N. Y. Acad. Sci.*, 61:59.

———. 1955b. "Cortical and subcortical recordings correlated with behavior in patients and animals during the administration of Rauwolfia, Thorazine, and Meratran," *Psychiat. Res. Rep. Amer. psychiat. Ass.*, 1:25.

Monroe, R. R., Jacobson, G., and Ervin, F. 1956a. "Activation of psychosis by a combination of scopolamine and alpha chloralose," *A.M.A. Arch. Neurol. Psychiat.*, 76:536.

Monroe, R. R. 1956b. "Correlations of subcortical recordings and behavior," *Electroenceph. clin. Neurophysiol.*, 8:530.

Monroe, R. R., *et al.* 1956c. "EEG activation with chloralosane," *Electroenceph. clin. Neurophysiol.*, 8:279.

———. 1957. "Correlation of rhinencephalic electrograms with behavior," *Electroenceph. clin. Neurophysiol.*, 9:623.

Monroe, R. R. 1959. "Episodic behavioral disorders—schizophrenia or epilepsy," *A.M.A. Arch. gen. Psychiat.*, 1:205.

———. 1960a. "Discussion: an interpersonal approach to training in psychotherapy," in N. Dellis, ed., *The training of psychotherapists: a multi-disciplinary approach*. Baton Rouge: Louisiana State University Press.

———. 1960b. "Values in therapy," in J. Masserman, ed., *Psychoanalysis and human values*. New York: Grune & Stratton.

———. 1960c. "Psychotherapy as an adjunctive treatment for schizophrenia," in H. Stone, ed., *Psychotherapy with schizophrenics: a reappraisal*. Baton Rouge: Louisiana State University Press.

Monroe, R. R., and Heath, R. G. 1961. "Effects of lysergic acid and various derivatives on depth and cortical electrograms," *J. Neuropsychiat.*, 3:75.

Monroe, R. R., and Balis, G. U., and Ebersberger, E. 1963a. "The hypnotic effects of alpha and beta chloralose in rats," *Curr. Ther. Res.*, 5:141.

———. 1963b. "Anticonvulsant activity of alpha and beta chloralose in rats," *Curr. Ther. Res.*, 5:154.

Monroe, R. R. 1963c. "The daseinanalytic use of dreams," *Amer. J. Psychother.*, 23:1.

Monroe, R. R., *et al.*, 1965a. "EEG activation of patients receiving phenothiazines and chlordiazepoxide," *J. nerv. ment. Dis.*, 141:100.

Monroe, R. R., and Wise, S. 1965b. "Combined phenothiazine, chlordiazepoxide and primidone therapy for uncontrolled psychotic patients," *Amer. J. Psychiat.*, 122:694.

Monroe, R. R., and Mickle, W. A. 1967a. "Alpha chloralose-activated electroencephalograms in psychiatric patients," *J. nerv. ment. Dis.*, 144:59.

Monroe, R. R., and Dale, R. 1967b. "Chlordiazepoxide in the treatment of patients with 'activated EEG's'," *Dis. nerv. Syst.* 28:390.

Monroe, R. R. 1967c. Discussion of article by Dr. Searles in C. Harrison, ed., *Cross currents of psychiatry and psychoanalysis.* New York: Lippincott.

Monroe, R. R., Klee, G. D., and Brody, E. B., eds. 1967d. "Psychiatric epidemiology and mental health planning," in *Psychiat. Res. Rep. Amer. psychiat. Ass.* no. 22.

Monroe, R. R. 1968. "The Compulsive," in E. W. Strauss and R. M. Griffith, eds., *Phenomenology of will and action.* Pittsburgh: Duquesne University Press.

Moore, B. E. 1965. "Phenomenology and the problem of definition of acting out and neurotic behavior," *Study group on acting out.* N. Y. Psychoanalytic Society.

Moore, B. E., and Fine, B. D. 1967. *A glossary of psychoanalytic terms and concepts.* New York: American Psychoanalytic Association.

Morris, A. A. 1956. "Temporal lobectomy with removal of uncus, hippocampus, and amygdala," *A.M.A. Arch. Neurol. Psychiat.*, 76:479.

Moruzzi, G. 1950. *Problems in cerebellar physiology.* Springfield: Charles C Thomas.

Moyer, J. H., Kinross-Wright, V., and Finney, R. M. 1955. "Chlorpromazine as a therapeutic agent in clinical medicine," *A.M.A. Arch. int. Med.*, 95:202.

Mulder, D. W., and Daley, D. 1952. "Psychiatric symptoms associated with lesions of the temporal lobe," *J. Amer. med. Ass.*, 150:173.

Muller, H. F., and Muller, A. K. 1965. "Effects of some psychotropic drugs upon brain electrical activity," *Int. J. Neuropsychiat.*, 1:224.

Mundy-Castle, A. C. 1947. "The electroencephalogram and mental activity," *Electroenceph. clin. Neurophysiol.*, 9:643.

Muratorio, A., and Inghirami, L. 1956. "L'alfa cloralosio come attivante," *EEG Clinica*, 2:2.

Narabayashi, H., et al. 1963. "Sterotaxic amygdalotomy for behavior disorders," *A.M.A. Arch. Neurol.*, 9:1.

Neidermeyer, E., and Knott, J. R. 1962. "The incidence of 14 and 6 per second positive spikes in psychiatric material," *Electroenceph. clin. Neurophysiol.*, 14:285.

Nielsen, J. M. 1958. "Amnesia for life experiences," *Bull. Los. Angeles neurol. Soc.*, 23:143.

Notkin, J. 1930. "Affect epilepsy and hystero-epilepsy in psychopaths," *J. nerv. ment. Dis.*, 72:135.

Obrist, W. D., and Busse, E. W. 1965. "The electroencephalogram in old age," in W. P. Wilson, ed., *Applications of electroencephalography in psychiatry*. Durham: Duke University Press.

Olds, J., and Milner, P. 1954. "Positive reinforcement produced by electrical stimulation of septal area and other regions of the rat brain," *J. comp. physiol. Psychol.*, 47:419.

Olds, J. 1958. "Effects of hunger and male sex hormone on self-stimulation of the brain," *J. comp. physiol. Psychol.*, 51:320.

Olds., M. E., and Olds, J. 1963. "Approach-avoidance analysis of rat diencephalon," *J. comp. Neurol.*, 120:259.

Ostow, M., and Ostow, M. 1946. "Bilaterally synchronous paroxysmal slow activity in the electroencephalograms of non-epileptics," *J. nerv. ment. Dis.*, 103:346.

Ostow, M. 1957. "Psychic function of temporal lobe as inferred from seizure phenomena," *A.M.A. Arch. Neurol. Psychiat.*, 77:79.

Otsuka, F. 1967. "Rorschach study of schizophrenia, with special reference to the problems of the heterogeneity," in H. Mitsuda, ed., *Clinical genetics in psychiatry*. Tokyo: Igaku Shoin.

Pacella, B. L., Polatin, P., and Nagler, S. H. 1944. "Clinical and EEG studies in obsessive-compulsive states," *Amer. J. Psychiat.*, 100:830.

Papez, J. W. 1937. "A proposed mechanism of emotion," *A.M.A. Arch. Neurol. Psychiat.*, 38:725.

Parsons, T., and Shils, E. A., eds. 1951. *Toward A general Theory of Action*. Cambridge, Mass.: Harvard University Press.

Pearce, K. I. 1960. "Elipten: A clinical evaluation of a new anticonvulsant," *Canad. Med. Ass. J.*, 82:953.

Penfield, W., and Erickson, T. C. 1941. *Epilepsy and Cerebral Localization*. Springfield: Charles C Thomas.

Penfield, W., and Rasmussen, T. 1950. *The Cerebral Cortex of Man*. New York: Macmillan Co.

Penfield, W., and Kristiansen, K. 1951. *Epileptic Seizure Patterns*. Springfield: Charles C Thomas.

Penfield, W. 1952. "Memory mechanisms," *A.M.A. Arch. Neurol. Psychiat.*, 67:178.

Penfield, W., and Jasper, H. 1954a. *Epilepsy and the Functional Anatomy of the Human Brain*. Boston: Little, Brown & Co.

Penfield, W. 1954b. Studies of the Cerebral Cortex of Man in *Brain Mechanisms and Consciousness*. Springfield: Charles C Thomas.

Penfield, W., and Milner, B. 1955. "Memory deficit produced by bilateral lesions in the hippocampal zone," *A.M.A. Arch. Neurol. Psychiat.*, 79:475.

Perlin, S., Pollin, W., and Butler, R. N. 1958. "The experimental subject: I. The psychiatric evaluation and selection of a volunteer population," *A.M.A. Arch. Neurol. Psychiat.*, 80:65.

Peterson, W. G. 1967. "Clinical study of Mogadon—a new anticonvulsant," *Neurology*, 17:878.

Pfeiffer, C. C., *et al.* 1964. "Electroencephalographic assay of anti-anxiety drugs," *A.M.A. Arch. gen. Psychiat.*, 10:446.

Piaget, J. 1954. "The problem of consciousness in child psychology developmental changes in awareness in H. A. Abramson, ed., *Problems of Consciousness*. New York: Corlies, Macy & Co.

Pilkington, T. L. 1961. "Comparative effects of Librium and Taractan on behavior disorders of mentally retarded children," *Dis. nerv. Syst.*, 22:10.

Pilleri, G. 1966. "The Kluver-Bucy syndrome in man," *Psychiat. Neurol.*, 152:65.

Pollen, D. A., Perot, P. H., and Reid, K. H. 1963. "Experimental bilateral wave and spike from thalamic stimulation in relation to level of arousal," *Electroenceph. clin. Neurophysiol.*, 15:1017.

Pond, D. A. 1961. "Psychiatric aspects of epileptic and brain damaged children," *Brit. med. J.*, 2:1376.

———. 1963. "The development of normal rhythms," in D. Hill and G. Parr, eds., *Electroencephalography*. New York: Macmillan Co.

Pribram, K. H. 1961. "A further experimental analysis of the behavior deficit that follows injury to the primate frontal cortex," *Exp. Neurol.*, 3:432.

Preswick, G., Reivich, M., and Hill, I. D. 1965. "The EEG effects of combined hyperventilation and hypoxia in normal subjects," *Electroenceph. clin. Neurophysiol.*, 18:56.

Proler, M., and Kellaway, P. 1962. "The methionine sulfoximine syndrome in the cat," *Epilepsia*, 3:117.

Pupo, P. P., and Zukerman, E. 1956. "Some comparative results of activation methods," *Electroenceph. clin. Neurophysiol.*, 8:154.

Putnam, T. J., and Merritt, H. H. 1941. "Dullness as an epileptic equivalent," *A.M.A. Arch. Neurol. Psychiat.*, 45:797.

Quay, H. C. 1965. "Psychopathic personality as pathological stimulation-seeking," *Amer. J. Psychiat.*, 122:2.

Rado, S. 1956. "Hedonic control, action-self and depressive spell," in *Psychoanalyses of behavior*, vol. I. New York: Grune & Stratton.

———. 1967. "The theory of schizotypal organization and its application to the treatment of decompensated schizotypal organization," in *Psychoanalyses of behavior*, vol. II. New York: Grune & Stratton.

Raher, J. 1963. "Social and emotional problems in the treatment of epilepsy," *Psychosom.*, 4:27.

Ramey, E. R., and O'Doherty, D. S., eds. 1960. *Electrical studies of the unanesthetized brain.* New York: Paul Hoeber.

Rand, R. W., Crandall, P. H., and Walter, R. 1964. "Chronic stereotactic implantation of depth electrodes for psychomotor epilepsy," *Acta neurochir.*, 11:610.

Ranson, S. W. 1937. "Some functions of the hypothalamus," *Bull. N. Y. Acad. Med.*, 13:241.

Rapaport, D. 1951. "Consciousness: a psychopathological and psychodynamic view," in H. A. Abramson, ed., *Problems of Consciousness.* New York: Corlies, Macy & Co.

Rasmussen, T., and Jasper, H. H. 1958. *Temporal Lobe Epilepsy.* Springfield: Charles C Thomas.

Reardon, J. D. 1964. "Oneirophrenia—entity or enigma?" *Dis. nerv. Syst.*, 25:157.

Refsum, S., *et al.* 1960. "Clinical correlates of the 14 and 6 per second positive spikes," *Acta psychiat. scand.*, 35:330.

Reiman, H. H. 1963. *Periodic Disease.* Philadelphia: F. A. Davis Co.

Revitch, E. 1954. "Epileptic manifestations resembling psychiatric disorders," *J. med. Soc. N.J.*, 51:3.

———. 1958. "Psychomotor paroxysms of nonepileptic origin," *Dis. nerv. Syst.*, 29:1.

Rexford, E. N. 1963. "A developmental concept of the problems of acting out," *J. Amer. Acad. Child Psychiat.*, 2:6.

Rey, J. H., Pond, D. A., and Evans, C. C. 1949. "Clinical and electroencephalographic studies of temporal lobe function," *Proc. roy. Soc. Med.*, 42:891.

Ribble, M. 1936. "Ego dangers and epilepsy," *Psychoanal. Quart.*, 5:71.

Robinson, W. G., Guerrero-Figueroa, R., and Fronlance, C. 1966. "The clinical and electroencephalographic studies during wakefulness and natural sleep in patients with episodic behavioral disorders," Fourth World Congress of Psychiatry, Madrid.

Rochlin, G. 1963. Discussion of "Observations of Delinquent Behavior in Very Young Children," *J. Amer. Acad. Child Psychiat.*, 2:66.

Rodin, E. A. 1957a. "An electroencephalographic syndrome which correlates with severe disruption of the personality structure," *Neurology*, 7:10.

Rodin, E. A., *et al.* 1957b. "Relationship between certain forms of psychomotor epilepsy and schizophrenia," *A.M.A. Arch. Neurol. Psychiat.*, 77:449.

Rogina, V., and Serafetinides, E. A. 1962. "Epilepsy and behavior disorder in patients with generalized spike and wave complexes," *Electroenceph. clin. Neurophysiol.*, 14:3.

Romano, J., and Engel, G. L. 1944. "Delirium: I: EEG data," *A.M.A. Arch. Neurol. Psychiat.*, 51:356.

Rose, G. J. 1960. "Screen memories in homicidal acting out," *Psychoanal. Quart.*, 29:328.

Rosen, J. N. 1963. "Acting out and acting in," *Amer. J. Psychother.*, 17:390.

————. 1965. "The concept of 'acting-in'," in L. Abt and S. Weissman, eds., *Acting out—theoretical and clinical aspects*. New York: Grune & Stratton.

Rosenstein, I. N. 1960. "A new psychosedative (Librium) as an anticonvulsant in grand mal type convulsive seizures," *Dis. nerv. Syst.*, 21:1.

Rosvold, E. H., et al. 1956. "A continuous performance test on brain damage," *J. cons. Psychol.*, 20:5.

Roth, M., and Harper, M. 1962. "Temporal lobe epilepsy and the phobic anxiety-depersonalization syndrome," *Comp. Psychiat.*, 3 (4).

Rubin, I. 1965. "The defenses and other ego functions in acting out," *Study group on acting out*. New York Psychoanalytic Society.

Sacks, J. M., and Cohen, M. I. 1957. "Contributions of the Rorschach to the understanding of 'acting out' behavior," *J. nerv. ment. Dis.*, 125:1.

Salamon, I., and Post, J. 1965. "Alpha blocking and schizophrenia," *A.M.A. Arch. gen. Psychiat.*, 13:367.

Samuels, A. 1957. "Acute chlorpromazine poisoning," *Amer. J. Psychiat.*, 113:746.

Satten, J., et al. 1960. "Murder without apparent motive: A study in personality disorganization," *Amer. J. Psychiat.*, 117:48.

Saul, L. J., Davis, H., and Davis, P. A. 1949. "Psychologic correlations with the electroencephalogram," *Psychosom. Med.*, 11:361.

Sawa, M. 1957. "Epileptogenic factors in atypical endogenous psychoses," *Psychiat. Neurol. jap.*, 59:1.

Schachter, J. S. 1955. "Some considerations of the relationships of epilepsy to schizophrenia, the primary behavior disorders, and psychopathology: a family study," *J. nerv. ment. Dis.*, 121:117.

Schallek, W., Kuehn, A., and Jew, N. 1962. "Effects of chlordiazepoxide (Librium) and other psychotropic agents on the limbic system of the brain," *Ann. N. Y. Acad. Sci.*, 96:303.

Schilder, P. 1951. *Brain and personality*. New York: International Universities Press.

Schneider, J. 1954. "Etude electrographique et electrophysiologique des mecanismes d'actions des agents anesthesiques usuels," *Rev. neurol.*, 91:428.

Schorsch, G. 1960. *Epilepsy.* Berlin: H. W. Jruhle.

Schwab, R. S. 1947. "Epilepsy," *Ass. Res. nerv. Dis. Proc.*, 26:339.

Schwade, E. D., and Geiger, S. G. 1960. "Severe behavior disorders with abnormal electroencephalograms," *Dis. nerv. Syst.*, 21:616.

Schwarz, B. E., Sem-Jacobsen, C. W., and Petersen, M. C. 1956a. "Effects of mescaline, LSD-25 and adrenochrome on depth electrograms in man," *A.M.A. Arch. Neurol. Psychiat.*, 75:579.

Schwarz, B. E., et al. 1956b. "Behavioral and electroencephalographic effects of hallucinogenic drugs," *A.M.A. Arch. Neurol. Psychiat.*, 75:83.

Scoville, W. B., and Milner, B. 1957. "Loss of recent memory after bilateral hippocampal lesions," *J. Neurol. Neurosurg. Psychiat.*, 20:11.

Segal, M. M. 1963. "Impulsive sexuality: Some clinical and theoretical observations," *Int. J. Psycho-Anal.*, 44:407.

Sellden, U. 1964. "Electroencephalographic activation with megimide in normal subjects," *Acta neurol. scand.*, 40:1.

Sem-Jacobsen, C. W., et al. 1955. "Electroencephalographic rhythms from the depths of the frontal lobe in 60 psychotic patients," *Electroenceph. clin. Neurophysiol.*, 7:193.

Sem-Jacobsen, C. W., and Torkildsen, A. 1960. "Depth recording and electrical stimulation in the human brain," in E. R. Ramey and D. S. O'Doherty, eds., *Electrical studies on the unanesthetized brain.* New York: Paul B. Hoeber.

Sem-Jacobsen, C. W., and Sem-Jacobsen, I. E. 1963. "Selection and evaluation of pilots for high performance aircraft and spacecraft by inflight EEG study of stress tolerance," *Aerospace Med.*, 34:605.

Sem-Jacobsen, C. W. 1968. *Depth-electrographic stimulation of the human brain and behavior.* Springfield: Charles C Thomas.

Shagass, C., Naiman, J., and Mihalik, J. 1956. "An objective test which differentiated between neurotic and psychotic depression," *A.M.A. Arch. Neurol. Psychiat.*, 75:461.

Shagass, C., Muller, K., and Acosta, H. B. 1959. "The pentothal sleep threshold as an indicator of affective change," *J. psychosom. Res.* 3:253.

Shagass, C., and Schwartz, M. 1965. "Age, personality and somotosensory cerebral evoked responses," *Science,* 148:1359.

Shapiro, D. 1965. *Neurotic styles.* New York: Basic Books.

Shengold, L. 1967. "The effects of overstimulation: rat people," *Int. J. Psycho-Anal., 48*:403.

Sherwood, S. L. 1960. "Stereotaxic recordings from the frontal and temporal lobes of psychotics and epileptics," in E. R. Ramey and D. S. O'Doherty, eds., *Electrical studies on the unanesthetized brain.* New York: Paul B. Hoeber.

Shimoda, Y., *et al.* 1961a. "Statistical observation of six and fourteen per second positive spikes," *Yonago Acta Medica, 5*:102.

Shimoda, Y. 1961b. "The clinical and electroencephalographic study of the primary diencephalic epilepsy or epilepsy of the brain stem," *Acta neuroveg., 23*:181.

Shure, G. H., and Holtzer, M. N. 1958. "EEG patterns and behavioral vigilance," *Amer. Psychol., 13*:348.

Siegman, A. W. 1961. "The relationship between future-time perspective, time estimation, and impulse control in a group of young offenders and in a control group," *J. cons. Psychol., 25*:470.

———. 1962. "Future-time perspective and perception of duration," *Perceptual and motor skills, 15*:609.

Sila, B., *et al.* 1962. "The differentiation of psychiatric patients by EEG changes after sodium pentothal," *Recent Advances in Biol. Psychiat., 4*:191.

Silverman, D. 1943. "Clinical and electroencephalographic studies on criminal psychopaths," *A.M.A. Arch. Neurol. Psychiat., 50*:18.

Silverman, D., and Morisaki, A. 1958. "Re-evaluation of sleep electroencephalography," *Electroenceph. clin. Neurophysiol., 10*:425.

Simons, D. J., and Diethelm, O. 1946. "Electroencephalographic studies of psychopathic personalities," *A.M.A. Arch. Neurol. Psychiat., 55*:619.

Slater, E., Beard, A. W., and Glithero, E. 1955. "The schizophrenic-like psychoses of epilepsy," *Brit. J. Psychiat., 74*:488.

———. 1965. "The schizophrenic-like psychoses of epilepsy," *Int. J. Psychiat., 1*:6.

Slatter, K. H. 1960. "Alpha rhythms and mental imagery," *Electroenceph. clin. Neurophysiol., 12*:851.

Small, J. G., Stevens, J. R., and Milstein, V. 1961. "Electroclinical correlates of emotional activation," *J. nerv. ment. Dis., 138*:146.

Small, J. G., Milstein, V., and Stevens, J. R. 1962. "Are psychomotor epileptics different?" *A.M.A. Arch. Neurol. Psychiat., 7*:187.

Smith, C. M. 1959a. "Electroencephalogram in cataplexy," *Electroenceph. clin. Neurophysiol., 11*:344.

Smith, C. M., and Hamilton, J. 1959b. "Psychological factors in the narcolepsy-cataplexy syndrome," *Psychosom. Med., 21*:40.

Smith, S. 1965. "The adolescent murder," *A.M.A. Arch gen. Psychiat. 13*:310.

Smythies, J. R. 1966. *The neurological foundations of psychiatry*. Oxford: Blackwell Scientific Publications.

Sokolov, E. N. 1960. "Neuronal models and the orienting reflex in M. A. B. Brazier, ed., *Third conference on the central nervous system*. New Jersey: Madison Printing Co.

Spiegel, E. A., Miller, H. R., and Oppenheimer, M. J. 1940. "Forebrain and rage reactions," *J. Neurophysiol.*, 3:538.

Stafford-Clark, D., and Taylor, F. H. 1949. "Clinical and EEG studies of prisoners charged with murder," *J. Neurol. Neurosurg. Psychiat.*, 12:325.

Stevens, J. R., Glaser, G. H., and MacLean, P. D. 1954. "The influence of sodium amytal on the recollection of seizure states," *Trans. Amer. neurol. Ass.*, 79:40.

Stevens, J. R. 1957. "The 'march' of temporal lobe epilepsy," *A.M.A. Arch. Neurol. Psychiat.*, 77:227.

————. 1959. "Emotional activation of the electroencephalogram in patients with convulsive disorders," *J. nerv. ment. Dis.*, 128:339.

————. 1966. "Psychiatric implication of psychomotor epilepsy," *A.M.A. Arch. gen. Psychiat.*, 14:461.

Stevenson, H. G. 1963. "Psychomotor epilepsy associated with criminal behavior," *Med. J. Aust.*, 1:784.

Stewart, L. F. 1957. "Chlorpromazine: Use to activate electroencephalographic seizure patterns," *Electroenceph. clin. Neurophysiol.*, 9:427.

Stone, W. E., Tews, J. K., and Mitchell, E. N. 1960. "Chemical concomitants of convulsive activity in the cerebrum," *Neurology*, 10:241.

Strauss, E. W. 1966. *Phenomenological psychology*. New York: Basic Books.

Strauss, H. 1959. "Epileptic disorders," in S. Arieti, ed., *The handbook of psychiatry*. New York: Basic Books.

Study group on "acting out." 1965. New York Psychoanalytic Society.

Sugerman, A. A., et al., 1964. "EEG and behavioral changes in schizophrenia," *A.M.A. Arch. gen. Psychiat.*, 10:340.

Swain, J. M., and Litteral, E. B. 1960. "Prolonged effect of chlorpromazine: EEG findings in a senile group," *J. nerv. ment. Dis.*, 131:550.

Symonds, C., Hill, D., and Pond, D. 1962. "The schizophrenic-like psychoses of epilepsy (discussion)," *Proc. roy. Soc. Med.*, 5:311.

Symposium: brain mechanism and consciousness. 1954. Springfield: Charles C Thomas.

"Symposium: Acting Out," 1963. *J. Amer. Acad. Child Psychiat.*, 2:1.

"Symposium: Diphenylhydantoin," 1967. *Int. J. Neuropsych.* 3:2.

"Symposium: Acting Out," 1968. *Int. J. Psycho-Anal.* 49:165.

Szatmari, A. 1955a. *Clinical and electroencephalographic investigation on largactil in psychosis. Preliminary study.* Document 357, Poulenc Scientific Dept.

Szatmari, A., Schneider, R. A. 1955b. "Induction of sleep by autonomic drugs," *J. nerv. ment. Dis.*, 121:311.

Taylor, J., ed. 1958. *Selected writings of John Hughling Jackson.* Vol. I: *Epilepsy and epileptiform convulsions.* New York: Basic Books.

Temkin, O. 1965. *The history of classification in medical science.* Conference on the "Role and methodology of classification in psychiatry and psychopathology," sponsored by the American Psychiatric Association and the Psychopharmacology Service Center. Washington: National Institutes of Mental Health.

Terzian, H., and Ore, G. D. 1955. "Syndrome of Kluver and Bucy— reproduced in man by bilateral removal of the temporal lobes," *Neurology,* 5:373.

Terzian, H. 1958. "Observations on the clinical symptomatology of bilateral partial or total removal of the temporal lobes in man," in B. Maitland and P. Bailey, eds., *Temporal lobe epilepsy.* Springfield: Charles C Thomas.

Tien, H. C., and Williams, M. W. 1965. "Organic integrity test in children," *A.M.A. Arch. gen. Psychiat.*, 12:159.

Tippett, D. L., and Pine, I. 1957. "Denial mechanisms in masked epilepsy," *Psychosom. Med.*, 19:326.

Tizard, B., and Margerison, J. H. 1963. "Psychologic functions during wave-spike discharge," *Brit. J. soc. clin. Psychol.*, 3:6.

Tolman, J. E. P., and Davis, J. P. 1949. "The effects of drugs upon the electrical activity of the brain," *Pharm. Rev.*, 1:425.

Towler, M. L., Beall, B. D., and King, J. B. 1962. "Drug effects on the EEG pattern, with specific consideration of diazepam," *Sth. med. J.*, 55:832.

Treffert, D. A. 1964. "The psychiatric patient with an EEG temporal lobe focus," *Amer. J. Psychiat.*, 120:765.

Tsuda, K. 1967. "Clinico-genetic study of depersonalization neurosis," in H. Mitsuda, ed., *Clinical genetics in psychiatry.* Tokyo: Igaku Shoin.

Turner, E. 1963. "A new approach to unilateral and bilateral lobotomies for psychomotor epilepsy," *J. Neurol. Neurosurg. Psychiat.*, 26:285.

Turner, M., et al. 1956. "Modifications electroencephalographiques, electrodermagraphiques et electromyographiques provoquees par la chlorpromazine chez l'homme," *Electroenceph. clin. Neurophysiol.*, 8:25.

Turner, W. J., and Merlis, S. 1962. "Clincal correlations between EEG and antisocial behavior," *Med. Times.* (Lond.), 90:505.

Turner, W. J. 1967. "Therapeutic use of diphenylhydantoin in neuroses," *Int. J. Neuropsychiat.*, 3:94.

Ulett, G. A., and Gleser, G. 1952. "The effect of experimental stress upon photically activated EEG," *Science*, 115:678.

Ulett, G. A., et al. 1953. "The EEG and reaction to photic stimulation as an index of anxiety-proneness," *Electroenceph. clin. Neurophysiol.*, 5:23.

——. 1955. "Determination of convulsive threshold by photopharmacologic stimulation: A study of technique and reliability," *Electroenceph. clin. Neurophysiol.*, 7:597.

Ulett, G. A., Johnson, L. C., and Mills, W. B. 1959. "Pattern stability and relationship among electroencephalographic 'activation' techniques," *Electroenceph. clin. Neurophysiol.* 11:255.

Ulett, G. A., et al. 1961. "The influence of chlordiazepoxide on drug altered EEG patterns and behavior," *Med. exp.*, 5:386.

Ulett, G. A., Heusler, A., and Word, T. J. 1965. "The effect of psychotropic drugs on the EEG of the chronic psychotic patient" in W. P. Wilson, ed., *Applications of EEG in psychiatry*. Durham: Duke University Press.

Vaillant, G. E. 1963. "The natural history of the remitting schizophrenias," *Amer. J. Psychiat.*, 120:367.

——. 1965. "Schizophrenia in a woman with temporal lobe arteriovenous malformations," *Brit. J. Psychiat.*, 111:307.

Van Buren, J. M. 1963. "The abdominal aura: A study of abdominal sensations occurring in epilepsy and produced by depth stimulation," *Electroenceph. clin. Neurophysiol.*, 15:1.

Vasconcellos, J. 1960. "Clinical evaluation of trifluoperazine in maximum-security brain-damaged patients with severe behavioral disorders," *J. clin. exp. Psychopath.*, 21:25.

Verdeaux, G., Verdeaux, J., and Marty, R. 1954. "The activation of electroencephalograms with chloralose," *Electroenceph. clin. Neurophysiol.*, 6:19.

Vislie, H., and Henriksen, G. F. 1958. "Psychic disturbances in epileptics," in L. De Haas, ed., *Lectures on epilepsy, Folia Psychiat. Neerl.*, 2:29.

Von Scheyen, J. D. 1963. *Een Klinesch-Psychiatrische en Electroencefalografische Studie over Hypleria*. Utrecht: Byleold.

Walker, E. A. 1957. "Recent memory impairment in unilateral temporal lesions," *A.M.A. Arch. Neurol. Psychiat.*, 78:543.

Walter, R. D., et al. 1960. "A controlled study of the fourteen and six per second EEG pattern," *A.M.A. Arch. gen. Psychiat.*, 2:559.

Watson, J. B. 1920. "Is thinking merely the action of language mechanism?" *Brit. J. Psychol.*, 11:87.

Weil, A. A. 1959. "Ictal emotions occurring in temporal lobe dysfunction," *A.M.A. Arch. Neurol.*, 1:87.

Weinstein, E. 1959. "Relationship among seizures—psychoses and personality factors," *Amer. J. Psychiat.*, 116:124.

Weintraub, W., and Aronson, H. 1963. "The application of verbal behavior analysis to the study of psychological defense mechanisms. II. Speech pattern associated with impulsive behavior," *J. nerv. ment. Dis.*, 139:75.

Weiss, V. W., and Monroe, R. R. 1959. "A framework for understanding family dynamics: Part I and Part II," *Social Casework*, 40:380.

Werthem, F. 1941. *Dark legend.* New York: Duell Sloan & Pearce.

———. 1949. *The show of violence.* New York: Doubleday.

White, P. T., DeMyer, W., and DeMyer, M. 1964. "EEG abnormalities in early childhood schizophrenia: A double blind study of psychiatrically disturbed and normal children during promazine sedation," *Amer. J. Psychiat.*, 120:950.

Wiedeman, G. H. 1965. "Action and Acting Out," *Study Group on "Acting Out."* New York Psychoanalytic Society.

Wiener, J. M. 1966. "An EEG study of delinquent and nondelinquent adolescents," *A.M.A. Arch. gen. Psychiat.*, 15:144.

Williams, D. 1956. "Emotions reflected in epileptic experience," *Brain*, 79:29.

Williams, E., and Weekes, L., 1952. "Premenstrual tension associated with psychotic episodes," *J. nerv. ment. Dis.*, 116:321.

Wilson, W. P., 1965a. *Applications of Electroencephalography in Psychiatry.* Durham: Duke University Press.

——— 1965b. "The Electroencephalogram in Endocrine Disorders," in W. P. Wilson, ed., *Applications of Electroencephalography.* Durham: Duke University Press.

Winfield, D. L., 1961. "The use of chlordiazepoxide in clinical EEG," *J. Neuropsychiat.*, 2:191.

Winkelman, N. W., Jr., 1954. "Chlorpromazine in the treatment of neuropsychiatric disorders," *J. Amer. med. Ass.*, 155:18.

Winkler, E. G., and Train, G. J. 1959. "Acts of violence with electroencephalographic changes," *J. clin. exp. Psychopath.* 20:223.

Winters, W. D., and Spooner, C. E. 1965a. "A neurophysiological comparison of gamma-hydroxybutyrate with pentobarbital in cats," *Electroenceph. clin. Neurophysiol.*, 18:287.

———. 1965b. "Various seizure activities following gamma-hydroxybutyrate," *Int. J. Neuropharm.*, 4:197.

Wolff, P. H. 1960. *The developmental psychologies of Jean Piaget and psychoanalysis, psychological issues.* Monograph 5. New York: International Universities Press.

——. 1963. "Developmental and motivational concepts in Piaget's sensorimotor theory of intelligence," *J. Amer. Acad. Child Psychiat.,* 2:225.

Yamada, T. *et al.* 1960a. "A clinico-electroencephalographic study of ictal depression," *Bull. Osaka med. Sch.,* 6:117.

Yamada, T. 1960b. "Heterogeneity of schizophrenia as demonstrable in EEG," *Bull. Osaka med. Sch.,* 6:107.

—— 1967a. "Heterogeneity of schizophrenia as demonstrable in electroencephalography" in H. Mitsuda, ed., *Clinical genetics in psychiatry.* Tokyo: Igaku Shoin.

—— 1967b. "A clinico-electroencephalographic study of ictal depression," in H. Mitsuda, ed., *Clinical genetics in psychiatry.* Tokyo: Igaku Shoin.

Yeager, C. L. and Guerrant, J. S. 1957. "Subclinical epileptic seizures," *Calif. Med.,* 86:242.

Yoskii, N., Ishiwara, T., and Tani, K. 1963. "Juvenile delinquents and their abnormal EEG's: the 14 and 6 per second spike pattern," *Med. J. Osaka Univ.,* 14:61.

Zbroyzyna, A. W. 1963. "The anatomical basis of the patterns of autonomic and behavioral response effected via the amygdala, in the rhinencephalon and related structures," in W. Bargmann and J. P. Schade, eds., *Progress in brain research.* London: Elsevier Publishing Co.

Zeinan, W., and King, F. A. 1958. "Tumors of the septum pellucidum and adjacent structures with abnormal affective behavior: an anterior midline structure syndrome," *J. nerv. ment. Dis.,* 127:490.

Ziskind, E., and Bercel, N. A. 1947. "Preconvulsive paroxysmal electroencephalographic changes after metrazol injection," *Res. Publ. Ass. nerv. ment. Dis.,* 26:487.

Index of Subjects

Ablations. *See* Amygdalectomy; Lobectomy

Act: commitment to act, 279–282; definition, 254–256, 259; description, 12–16, 268, 269; morbid, 16, 26; neurotic, 16; pathological, 15–18; schematic, 254–256; spontaneous, 43, 44, 256; symbolic, 16, 22; symptomatic, 16, 22, 267; volitional, 15, 21, 44

Acting on impulse, 25

Acting out, v, 9–20; and neurotic action, 17, 18, 20, 41, 275n; psychoanalytic formulation, 9–12, 299–303

Acting-out dyscontrol: activation abnormalities, 228; and positive spikes, 137, 159; and reflective delay, 270; characteristics, 41, 42, 259, 273, 274, 428–434; definition, 20, 395; distribution in study, 240, 241; hierarchial level, 40–43; in epilepsy, 111, 147, 309; psychodynamic-neurophysiologic mechanisms, 275–282, 290; scale rating, 346; treatment, 357–363

Acting-through, 375, 433

Action: and anticipation, 234; and fantasy, 15, 279; and identity, 16, 58, 268; and intention, 265; and speech, 15, 265, 266; and thought, 14, 15, 254, 265, 279; for action's sake, 267; magic of, 265, 266, 302; practice, 15, 16; thought as trial, 258, 265, 266

Activation: abnormalities, 207–224, 227–249 passim; age differences, 228; alpha chloralose, *see* Alpha-chloralose activation; analeptics, 170, 171, 176–181, 208, 210, 331; aspecific, 191, 192, 224, 227–249, 400; children, 157–160; cocaine, 341; control group, *see* normal subjects; defined, 176–178; effects of drugs, 337–339; emotional, 307–309; episodic disorders, 238–246; false negatives, 220–224, 399, 400; false positives, 202, 204, 220–224, 248; hyperventilation, 213, 214; in psychosis, 168, 170; IQ differences, 229, 231; megimide, 170, 171, 209; metrazol, 170, 171, 176–181, 210, 214; nonspecific, *see* Aspecific; normal subjects, 181, 201, 202; patterns, ix, 228, 230, 232, 235, 240–246; photic stimulation, 177, 178, 210, 213, 214, 216; psychotic response, 186–188; sex differences, 203, 230; sleep, 177–179; specific, 227–249, 400; techniques, 178, 209, 226; with alcoholics, 203, 223

Activation, non-, 234–249, passim

Adolescence: EEG activity, 134, 264; impulsivity, 264, 281, 301, 362, 363, 404, 405; treatment, 357–359

Affect, 95, 254, 257, 260, 262, 392, 403; and electrograms, 68–70; and epilepsy, 171–173, 274; and episodic reactions, 47; and episodic schizophrenia, 168, 175; and impulse dyscontrol, 36, 273; and positive spike, 136, 137; and seizure dyscontrol, 35, 271; lack of, 272. *See also* Aggression; Depression; Dysphoria; Fear; Rage

501

Neurotic reaction, episodic: characteristics, 56–58, 450–456; classification,
3; neurophysiologic-psychodynamic
mechanisms, 296–298
Nonactivation, 234–249 passim
Nonepisodic disorders, 2, 235, 238, 239,
242–246
Normalization EEG. *See* EEG, normalized

Obsessive action, 22
Obsessive-compulsive, 245; behavior,
404
Olfactory sensations, and electrograms,
78
Oneirophrenia, 49, 52, 53
Oral dependency, 238, 299, 300

Panic reactions, 50
Paroxysmal abnormalities. *See* EEG
abnormalities; Electrogram activity
Paroxysmal disorders, 260–263
Patients: Numerical scheme, ix; **019**,
76, 77, 274, 320; **021**, 70–76, 80, 81,
261, 274; **102**, v, 276–278, 374, 375;
103, 359; **111**, 363; **123**, 369, 370; **187**,
263, 363; **195**, 350; **242**, 228; **275**, 228;
321, 184; **326**, 184, 400, 139; **402**, 140;
403, 55, 153, 157; **404**, 157, 158; **405**,
153, 154, 263; **406**, 138, 139; **407**, 116,
158; **408**, 158, 160; **409**, 158; **410**, 156,
158, 160; **411**, 153, 156; **412**, 153, 157;
413, 55, 153, 155, 156, 160, 263; **414**,
159; **415**, 153, 157; **523**, 344, 352;
F201, 129, 130, 228, 242; **F206**, 58,
146, 228, 327, 328, 413–416; **F211**, 142,
143, 146, 228; **F213**, 118, 119, 228;
F221, 228, 348; **F222**, 228, 322, 348,
352; **F223**, 109, 110, 164, 228, 313;
F227, 58, 120, 121, 228; **F239**, 146;
F246, 41, 42, 142, 228, 240; **F247**, 110,
146, 228, 240; **F250**, 57, 58, 224, 228,
242, 288, 298, 348, 352, 388, 440–447;
F267, 228, 242, 269, 348, 352; **F271**,
110, 228, 240; **F272**, 140–142, 228, 240;
F276, 228, 245; **F283**, 58, 127–129, 224,
240, 294, 295, 332, 372, 373, 386; **F284**,
57, 228, 242, 298, 447–449; **F285**, 146,
228, 240, 316, 387; **F287**, 58, 146, 228,
295, 310, 314, 319, 320, 388, 417–422;
O236, 221, 295; **O255**, 58; **O258**, 37;
O260, 58, 222; **O262**, 51, 52, 335, 434–

437; **O263**, 270; **O264**, 382; **O265**, 58;
O274, 335; **O281**, 59, 60, 223; **O289**,
57, 295, 296, 306, 313, 322, 323, 355,
366, 367, 450–456; **S202**, 119, 257, 258,
318, 319, 336; **S204**, 39, 40, 240; **S205**,
60, 61; **S212**, 55, 361, 461–465; **S217**,
224; **S218**, 242, 331, 385, 388, 456–461;
S219, 32, 33, 295, 365, 371, 372, 381;
S228, 30, 31, 114, 115, 131; **S229**, 52,
53, 335, 437–440; **S232**, 220, 221; **S239**,
58, 120, 146; **S243**, 45, 48, 53, 313;
S248, 57; **S251**, 348, 352; **S254**, 378–
380, 388, 389; **S278**, 57, 348, 352; **S282**,
33, 264, 295, 300, 360, 361; **S283**, 228,
294, 295; **S286**, 285–287, 296; **S288**,
187, 266, 269, 295, 305, 428–434; **S290**,
58, 364, 376, 377, 388, 422–428.
Pentylenetetrazol. *See* Activation, metrazol
Perception-aperception, 254
Periodic catatonia, 3, 49, 53
Personality. *See* Life Style
Personality description, epileptic, 103–
111
Perversion, 23
Petit mal epilepsy, 98, 101, 115–117,
147, 164, 179, 311, 312
Phase-specific dyscontrol, in adolescence, 264
Phenobarbital, 331, 342
Phenothiazines: chlorpromazine (Thorazine), 80, 333, 334; EEG activity,
332–335; trifluoperazine (Stelazine),
336; thioridazine (Mellaril), 333;
treatment, 332–336, 351, 352, 408
Physiologic reactions, episodic, 57, 127–
129, 174, 456–461; classification, 3;
defined, 56–58; psychotherapy, 383
Placebo effect, 329, 387, 388
Pleasure, 82–84
Positive spikes (14/6). *See* EEG abnormalities
Pregenital fixation, 26
Premeditation: acting-out, and impulse
dyscontrol, 20–22, 29, 38, 40, 43, 44,
273, 282, 285; and murder, 163; psychoanalytic theory, 14–15, 265, 266,
270; spontaneous act, 44. *See also*
Anticipation; Short circuit
Premenstrual periodicity, 54, 282
Primary dyscontrol: absent reflective
delay, 256–273; defined, 34–37, 396,
397; hierarchial levels, 34–37; psycho-

Index of Authors